LOUIS XIV AND EUROPE

LOUIS XIV
AND EUROPE

Edited by
RAGNHILD HATTON

Ohio State University Press

First published in the United Kingdom 1976 by
THE MACMILLAN PRESS LTD
London and Basingstoke

Published in the U.S.A. 1976 by
OHIO STATE UNIVERSITY PRESS
Columbus

Printed in Great Britain

Library of Congress Cataloging in Publication Data
Main entry under title :

Louis XIV and Europe

Includes index.
1. France—Foreign relations—1643–1715—Addresses, essays, lectures. 2. France—Politics and government—1643–
1715—Addresses, essays, lectures. I. Hatton, Ragnhild Marie.
DC127.3.L68   320.9'44'033   75–45334
ISBN 0–8142–0254–3

Contents

Preface

These essays are intended to put students in touch with important research in, or trends of thought on, the foreign policy and problems of Louis XIV's reign. Some of them will be familiar to academic teachers since they are either translations and/or amended versions of articles and contributions which have appeared in print; others have been commissioned for the volume.

The book is divided into two parts. The first is devoted to general views of various kinds. It opens with Tapié's analysis of Louis XIV's methods in foreign policy and with the editor's examination of Louis in a contemporary European perspective. Next follows Livet's discussion of Louis' relationship to the Germanies (the Holy Roman Empire as well as the Austrian Habsburg dominions), and Nordmann's resumé of Louis XIV's policy towards the Jacobites. In the second part, given up to specific case-studies, a chronological arrangement has been adopted. Pillorget's research into the relationship of the archbishop-electors of Trier to France, both before and after Louis XIV took over the government, is vital to an understanding of the eastern frontier problem. Bérenger's detailed study of the secret partition treaty of 1668 between the emperor Leopold and Louis XIV illuminates a significant stage in Austria's relations with Spain and France. Sonnino's interpretation of Louis' military memoirs for the Dutch War rests on minute detective work; and he clearly proves his point that Louis – though possibly less consciously than Sonnino assumes – tailored the finished memoirs to fit that picture of himself which he wished to bequeath to posterity. Symcox's examination of the outbreak of the Nine Years War explores new ground and is vital to our grasp of the situation in 1688–9. Janine Fayard's contribution is focused on North Germany and is especially important because she puts into perspective the sums spent on pensions and presents to further a given foreign-policy objective by a comparison with incoming sums in the same period. Handen examines a significant decision in Louis' foreign policy: the abandonment of France's traditional Italian objectives in the 1690s. Finally, Rule's analysis of the Torcy period, 1698–1715, throws light both on the relationship between Louis XIV and Torcy and on the developing bureaucratisation of the French foreign office.

The editor wishes to thank the contributors for their help and co-operation in making their work available for publication. The translations have been made by Dr Geoffrey Symcox of the University of California at Los Angeles and Dr Derek McKay of the London School of Economics, in collaboration with the editor. Hamish Scott of the University of Birmingham kindly helped with the proof-reading.

The editor is grateful to the Ohio State University Press for permission to reprint (with minor changes) her own contribution which originally appeared in _Louis XIV and the Craft of Kingship_, edited by John C. Rule; for permission to reprint other articles she must thank the _XVIIᵉ Siècle_, the _Revue d'Histoire Diplomatique_, and the _Revue des Travaux de l'Académie des Sciences Morales et Politiques_.

The editor has appended a glossary of French and German terms which may be unfamiliar, a list of persons mentioned where they are not sufficiently explained in the text or in the notes, and a chronology of significant dates for the foreign policy of the reign.

Notes on Contributors

JEAN BÉRENGER, Docteur ès Lettres, Professor at the University of Rennes II. Author of 'Charles Colbert, Marquis de Croissy', in R. Mousnier (ed.), *Le Conseil du roi de Louis XII à la Révolution* (1970); *Les Gravamina. Remonstrances des Diètes de Hongrie de 1655 à 1681* (1973); *Finances et absolutisme autrichien dans la seconde moitié du XVIIe siècle* (1975).

JANINE FAYARD, Maître-Assistant in Modern History at the University of Dijon, former member of Ecole des Hautes Etudes Hispaniques. Author of 'La tentative de réforme du Conseil de Castile sous la règne de Philippe V (1713–1715)', *Mélanges de la Casa de Velasques*, vol. II (1966).

RALPH D. HANDEN, Assistant Professor at the University of California (Riverside), has written a Ph.D. thesis at Ohio State University on France's relationship with Savoy during the Nine Years War. He is now working on the history of science, a subject for which both his earlier science degree and his undergraduate and postgraduate history degrees fit him well.

RAGNHILD HATTON, Professor of International History, University of London (L.S.E.). Author of *War and Peace 1680–1720* (1969), *Europe in the Age of Louis XIV* (1969), *Louis XIV and his World* (1972); co-editor of and contributor to *William III and Louis XIV. Essays by and for Mark A. Thomson* (with J. S. Bromley, 1968) and of *Studies in Diplomatic History. Essays in Memory of David Bayne Horn* (with M. S. Anderson, 1970).

GEORGES LIVET, Docteur ès Lettres, Professor of Modern History at the University of Strasbourg. Vice-President of the Comité Français des Sciences Historiques. Editor of three volumes in the *Recueil des Instructions aux Ambassadeurs et Ministres de France*, XXVII, *Etats Allemands*: vol. I, *Electorat de Mayence* (1962), vol. II, *Electorat de Cologne* (1963), vol. III, *Electorat de Trèves* (1966). Author of several books on Alsace, on the Wars of Religion and the Thirty Years War; and of a chapter in the *New Cambridge Modern History*,

A*

vol. IV (1970). His latest book is *Guerre et Paix de Machiavel à Hobbes* (1972).

CLAUDE NORDMANN, Docteur ès Lettres (Sorbonne), Professor of Modern History at the University of Lille III. Author of *Charles XII et l'Ukraine de Mazepa* (1966); *Grandeur et liberté de la Suède 1660–1792* (1971); *La montée de la puissance européenne*, Les Temps Modernes 1492–1661, in the series edited by Roland Mousnier (1972).

RENÉ PILLORGET, Docteur ès Lettres, Director of Studies at the Centre d'Etudes Supérieures de la Renaissance at the University of Tours. Author of numerous articles in *XVIIᵉ Siècle, Revue d'histoire moderne et contemporaine, Revue d'histoire diplomatique, Provence Historique, Les mouvements insurrectionnels de Provence entre 1596 et 1715* (1975); with Dr Suzanne Pillorget, *La France de la Renaissance* (1972).

JOHN C. RULE, Professor of History at the Ohio State University. Author of 'King and Minister : Louis XIV and Colbert de Torcy', in *William III and Louis XIV. Essays by and for Mark A. Thomson*, ed. Hatton and Bromley (1968); editor of *Louis XIV and the Craft of Kingship* (1969) and contributor of two chapters, 'Louis XIV, Roi-Bureaucrate' and 'Louis XIV : a Bibliographical Introduction'; author of 'France and the Preliminaries to the Gertruydenberg Conference : September 1709 to March 1710', in *Studies in Diplomatic History. Essays in Memory of David Bayne Horn*, ed. Hatton and Anderson (1970).

PAUL M. SONNINO, Associate Professor of History at the University of California, Santa Barbara. Author of 'The Dating and Authorship of Louis XIV's *Mémoires*', *French Historical Studies* (1964); *Louis XIV's View of the Papacy, 1661–1667* (1966); 'Louis XIV. Mémoires pour l'histoire de la guerre d'Hollande', *French Historical Studies* (1973).

GEOFFREY SYMCOX, Associate Professor of History at the University of California, Los Angeles. Author of *The Crisis of French Sea Power 1688–1697* (1974).

VICTOR-L. TAPIÉ, Docteur ès Lettres, Professor Emeritus of Modern History at the University of Paris (Sorbonne), member of the Institut de France and of the Académie des Sciences Morales et Politiques. Author of *La France de Louis XIII et de Richelieu* (1952; 2nd ed. 1967, translated and edited as *France in the Age of Louis XIII and Richelieu* by D. McN. Lockie, 1974); *Baroque et*

Classicisme (1957; 2nd ed. 1972; English translation entitled *The Age of Grandeur*, 1960); 'Das Zeitalter Ludwigs XIV', *Propyläen Weltgeschichte* VII (1964); and the entry on Louis XIV *in Encyclopaedis Universalis* (1971). He died in 1974 when this volume was in the press.

* Spanish; to Austria 1713/14   § Reconquered in its entirety for   The boundary of the Holy Roman Empire
† Spanish; to Savoy 1713/14   the Austrian Habsburgs by 1699   is indicated by a thick line
‡ Spanish; to Great Britain 1713   ¶ Venetian between 1699 and 1718

Europe in the age of Louis XIV

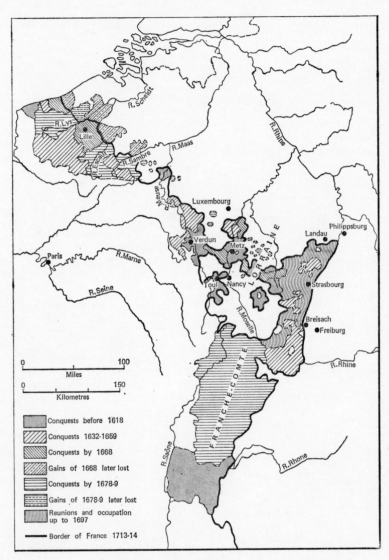

Legend:
- Conquests before 1618
- Conquests 1632–1659
- Conquests by 1668
- Gains of 1668 later lost
- Conquests by 1678–9
- Gains of 1678–9 later lost
- Reunions and occupation up to 1697
- Border of France 1713–14

French gains and losses on the north-eastern frontier, 1618–1714

Part I

GENERAL PROBLEMS

Part I

GENERAL PROBLEMS

1 Louis XIV's Methods in Foreign Policy*

VICTOR-L. TAPIÉ

Historians rarely agree, but there is general acceptance of the view that between 1661 and 1715 Louis XIV maintained personal control over foreign affairs and took full responsibility for their conduct. He regarded foreign policy as the essence of his function as king and acknowledged the deep attraction it held for him : it allowed him 'to watch the whole world, to be continuously informed of events in every province and nation, of the secrets of all the courts, and of the dispositions and weaknesses of every prince and foreign minister'. He believed that only a king apprised of this kind of information would be able to determine what was required by his 'glory and interests' – a phrase that recurs again and again in our texts – and to give the orders that would translate it into practical politics. For the rest, he held, 'the function of the king is mainly to allow the operation of common sense, which always acts naturally and without difficulty'.

This clear and forceful expression on the lines of Cartesian logic is not confined to Louis' early years as a king who ruled without a prime minister : on 20 November 1714 we find the same belief in the need for the king to exercise sound judgement.

If the affairs of state are to be conducted with success, it is wrong to make a decision one day and change it the next, merely on the report of one minister, whose information cannot be of great value. When I give [Philip V] my advice on a question of policy, it is not based solely on the information I

* First published in the *Revue des Travaux de l'Académie des Sciences Morales et Politiques,* IVᵉ série (1966) under the title 'Aspects de la Méthode de Louis XIV en Politique Etrangère'.

receive from one single source, but on all reports from other
places that may have some bearing on the affair. After careful
deliberation I give him my view, which I am ready to support
with strong arguments since I know that it is the best course
for him to follow.[1]

To explain Louis XIV's decisions and to understand how he
applied his methods, a variety of factors must be considered :
the king's mind and outlook, which altered with the passage of
time; his increasing fund of experience; the quality of the information at his disposal; the influences which must have been at
work on him (for each major decision a separate analysis is required); the effectiveness of the services on which he depended.
Important discussions took place in the *conseil d'en haut*, composed of a few members only, the ministers of state, one of whom
could be – and in fact usually was – the secretary of state for
foreign affairs. Nevertheless the king was not subject to any rules
or customary procedures when he came to make a decision of state.
For the execution of foreign policy he had a secretariat for foreign
affairs, organised as a proper ministry in the course of the reign.
Its head drafted the orders for ambassadors and other diplomats
and read their despatches. This office was held for long periods :
by Hugues de Lionne, Arnauld de Pomponne, Colbert de
Croissy, Pomponne once more, and, for the last sixteen years,
Torcy, son of Croissy and son-in-law of Pomponne, in whose
person the two ministerial dynasties met and merged. These men
were great officials, experienced diplomats and first-class administrators : but they always remained the king's servants. We know
that Turenne, Colbert and especially Louvois exercised as much, or
even more, influence on foreign policy; we know that Voysin and
Chamillart were consulted and that they sometimes corresponded
with French diplomats abroad. The diplomats did not yet receive
any special training: they were selected at random from the ranks
of government officials, the army, or the nobility; and the form of
their employment or the degree to which their advice was asked
depended on their personal effectiveness, or on the timeliness of
their services. In the closing years of the reign, Torcy did much
to organise the department on a regular footing. He organised
the archives properly and sought to lay down a ladder of regular
promotion. But these were matters of internal organisation. Torcy

was never in complete control of foreign policy, however jealously he guarded his status and its functions. We may assume that Louis XIV, equally jealous of his authority and regarding foreign policy as his most important activity, made sure that the minister did not become too important. Yet despite the incompleteness of their powers and the ambiguity of their position, the secretaries of state were the king's councillors, the loyal executants of his policy, experienced and highly competent.

The proper method in foreign policy was diplomatic negotiation. 'Negotiate unceasingly', Richelieu had said, 'openly or secretly, anywhere'. We are all familiar with that remarkable publication, the *Recueil des Instructions données aux Ambassadeurs et Ministres de France depuis les Traités de Westphalie jusqu'à la Révolution française.*[2]

If we analyse its preoccupations and the type of arguments employed, we are struck by two salient characteristics. In the first place, the arguments are always of a legal or juridical nature; negotiations are viewed as a defence of the king's interests, on the basis of rights acquired and legitimately enjoyed. These rights were rooted in ancient tradition, based on documents – feudal charters for instance – and on the interpretation of clauses in treaties concluded between sovereign states.

Force played its part here, for in the seventeenth century conquest created a presumptive right; though this could only be transformed into a legally binding right by being incorporated in a treaty. Military power was an essential instrument of foreign policy: it was necessary to defend what was already possessed and to make new acquisitions. French negotiators sought the implementation of the clauses of the Peace of Westphalia in respect of Alsace, and the Reunion policy took as its point of departure that the territories ceded to France by the Treaty of Nijmegen came with 'the rights and lands which belonged to them'.

Who was to be swayed by the arguments of the diplomats, and how was this to be done? The ambassadors' instructions concerned themselves mainly with foreign princes, their courts and ministers. The secret of success lay in finding a means of harnessing the personal and political interests of all these in the service of Louis XIV. This amounted to the creation, not of a solidly pro-French party abroad, but of a clientele dependent on

the French king. Like Richelieu, Louis XIV never shrank from
the enormous expense which these methods involved. From the
pensions paid to Charles II of England, to the pairs of gloves
presented to German princesses, the manna of 'sweetenings' was
scattered with amazing lavishness. This may seem normal to us in
the years of Louis' triumphs, when he seemed to dominate
Europe, but, surprisingly enough, such methods were used also
when Louis XIV seemed on the edge of disaster: during the
negotiations at The Hague in 1709 he still tried to bribe Marlborough, the general of the coalition opposing him, the favourite
of Queen Anne.

> I consent that you should give him a firm assurance that I will
> pay him two million livres, if through his good offices he can
> obtain one of the following conditions for me: the cession of
> Naples and Sicily for the king my grandson, or if the worst
> comes to the worst, of Naples alone . . . I will raise this grati-
> fication to three millions if apart from Naples, for my grandson,
> he can ensure that I retain Dunkirk with its harbour and
> fortifications. If I should be forced to give way over Dunkirk,
> I would give him the same sum for obtaining Naples for my
> grandson and the retention of Strasbourg by me . . . Finally,
> you may offer the duke of Marlborough four millions if he
> arranges that Naples and Sicily will go to the king my grand-
> son, while I keep Dunkirk with its harbour and fortifications,
> Strasbourg and Landau.[3]

Louis XIV did not invent 'gratifications' and they persisted
long after him. They do not conform to our ideas of political
morality. On the other hand, methods which were in daily use
during the Renaissance, and which are still found in Louis XIII's
reign, were no longer acceptable under Louis XIV: there is
no evidence that he ever tried to get rid of his enemies through
assassination, though we hear of poison being used elsewhere.

In his treatise *On the Manner of Negotiating with Princes*,
Callières (one of the negotiators at Ryswick) wrote: 'War in no
way destroys the rules of honour and generosity. In fact, it often
provides the opportunity for observing them with greater glory
for the minister who applies them, and for the prince who ap-
proves their application.' He tells of Grémonville, the French
envoy in Rome who at a time when France and Spain were at

war warned the Spanish ambassador, the marquis de la Fuente, of a plot against him; for this he was 'highly praised at the court of France and elsewhere, as his worthy action deserved.'

In the archives of the Department of Foreign Affairs I came across a letter from Chamillart[4] to the elector of Bavaria, dated 2 November 1704. An Austrian gentleman with a passport from Cologne had proposed kidnapping the emperor's elder son, the king of the Romans, to hand him over either to the Hungarian rebels or to the elector of Bavaria. This was no light matter and Chamillart immediately informed Louis XIV. He reported to the elector that 'His Majesty, who abhors all crimes' was so shocked by the offer that he had sent a military escort to remove the gentleman in question beyond the French frontier :

> His Majesty has ordered me to write to your Excellency to let you know what has occurred, and to request you to inform the King of the Romans. His Majesty feels sure that the King of the Romans will be grateful for this action and that the French officers and soldiers who are made prisoners will benefit from the clemency which is enjoined upon him by His Majesty's behaviour, as worthy of a great king as it is uncommon among the princes of the enemy.[5]

A sense of honour, even a certain spirit of chivalry, pervaded all negotiations. Honourable behaviour was important since it formed the basis of the king's reputation abroad. Louis XIV frequently stressed the need to observe promises and to honour agreements; though he argued, somewhat sophistically, that if both parties decide not to observe a treaty they are not really breaking it since they had clearly meant that its stipulations were not meant to be taken literally. These two attitudes seem to be in conflict, but for Louis they could be reconciled since 'in such questions fine distinctions have to be drawn, where judgement, equity and conscience can do much better than any words.' Indeed, one of the finer points of kingship was to know how to save the appearance, and even the essence, of honour; if treaties had to be circumvented, it must be done under the cloak of arguments which enabled one to shift the blame for the first breach on to the opposing party.

In any event the negotiators confined themselves to looking

after the interests of a very restricted social group. One of the
recent editors of the volumes of the *Instructions*, Georges Livet,
has perceptively pointed to the fact that economic questions are
not given the weight that one might expect. They loom large at
the time of the Dutch War, and in various instances connected
with Colbert's economic plans; but the limelight in general is
occupied by the great personages of this world – princes and
their idiosyncracies, ministers and the degree of favour they
enjoy. The fundamental interests of the people were never taken
into consideration, nor their collective mentality and those
emotional and ideological forces strong enough to move them.
These last were forces which were ignored in the formation of
Louis XIV's policy. This makes it easier for us to understand
why Louis made the mistake of underestimating the strength of
Dutch public opinion, and his having taken into account the
effect only of the terror which the ravaging of the Palatinate
in 1688 produced among the German princes without allowing
for the hatred and resentment that it aroused among their subjects.

Louis committed even graver errors. He appointed himself the
protector and defender of Catholicism abroad, and its restorer in
foreign lands – as instanced in Article 4 of the Treaty of Ryswick[6]
– but this never succeeded in mobilising spiritual and religious
sentiment on his behalf, as André Latreille has shown.[7] When
Innocent XI, the most devout pope of the seventeenth century,
enjoined Louis XIV to subordinate all else to the general welfare
of Christendom, denouncing the scandal of a war among fellow-
Christian princes, the legalistic minds of the king and his ministers
failed to discern any tangible reality in the papal demands : in
French diplomatic instructions they responded with arguments
of political profit and loss. Let me illustrate this by an example.
In 1682, at the height of his successes of the Reunion period, a
few months after the occupation of Strasbourg and Casale, Louis
XIV prepared to besiege Luxembourg in the hope of obtaining
a bargaining-counter to facilitate Spanish recognition of his annexations in Flanders. On 22 March he learned from Barillon,
his ambassador in England, that the Dutch Republic was planning
to send eight thousand troops to Luxembourg under the terms
of its alliance with Spain. Furthermore, the States General were
pressing England to join them. Charles II, Barillon reported,

could not postpone the calling of parliament as English public opinion was deeply alarmed. This was valuable information. Even in his hour of triumph, Louis XIV wished to proceed with caution. But how could he find an honourable pretext to cover his retreat? At about the same time despatches from Vienna and Constantinople had reported rumours – but no more than rumours – that the sultan was assembling troops in order to attack Hungary. On 23 March Louis XIV wrote to Barillon that there was no doubt that the sultan would invade Hungary that year with his whole army. He had therefore 'decided to place the common good of Christendom before all those considerations which could have led him to force the submission of Luxembourg and its dependent territories, as an equivalent for his claims in Flanders'. It was a clever point using a noble pretext; but it was not backed by any real concern for the welfare of Christendom. Fifteen months later – when a Turkish army of two hundred thousand men, the most formidable ever seen, was advancing on Vienna – Louis XIV, far from intervening, took advantage of the occasion to invade Flanders. The Turkish invasion sent a wave of terror through Germany and Italy (particularly in Venice and the papal states), through Poland and even Russia. The reputation of French arms and the prestige of France were still such that rulers and peoples turned to Louis XIV as their hope of succour, ready to forget the violence and injustices of which they had earlier complained.

The famous German preacher, Abraham of Sancta Clara, appealed: *Auf, auf, ihr Christen!* While he exorted all Christendom to a supreme effort, he reserved a special appeal for the king of France. But Louis XIV – and his ministers – saw in the Turkish attack no more than a diversion on the whole favourable to their interests, since is embarrassed the emperor and thus might facilitate recognition of the territories France claimed by the Reunions. This shows unwillingness to act outside the tenets of professional royal practice, and inability to realise that magnanimity could pay political dividends.

But even if magnanimity was lacking, prudency remained. After 1693, during the Nine Years War, Pomponne showed himself capable of drawing a distinction between the vital need to keep Strasbourg, and all the rest which were far less important. 'It is true enough that the Reunions were based upon the Treaty of Münster, but the way in which they were carried out was not always defensible. . . . It is not enough to overawe the princes of the Empire by a show of military might. We must persuade them of His Majesty's sincere desire to conclude a just and reasonable peace.'

However mistaken the Peace of Ryswick appeared to Vauban, who had a good enough case, the peace-treaty was in the spirit of moderation, as it sacrificed what was less important to preserve what was essential. It strengthened the position of Alsace and confirmed the annexation of Strasbourg. Though it restored the independence of Lorraine, this was done with all necessary guarantees of security for France. Dangeau was right in saying that even Louis XIV's enemies admired and praised his moderation. In the diplomatic correspondence of the time, the general peace of Europe is frequently mentioned : French hegemony had given way to a multi-state balance of power. Louis XIV proved quick to reach an understanding with England and the Dutch Republic to settle – by means of two partition treaties – the future problem of the Spanish succession, which could be activated at any time given the precarious health of Carlos II. The instructions for Tallard, the French ambassador to England, recently edited by Paul Vaucher, reveal a high degree of moderation in dealing with delicate questions such as the fate of James II, then in exile in France. Above all, the economic interests of England and the role of parliament are treated with an open-mindedness unknown before. Was this a real change in Louis XIV's ideas? We do not intend to examine here the reasons which led the king to accept Carlos II's will. But this acceptance completely reversed diplomatic relations with the Maritime Powers : Louis had given his word and then gone back on it. In English eyes, to have signed a treaty and then to refuse to carry it out was a breach of faith, and William III's attitude made this clear. Louis XIV's reputation, of which he was so jealous, was seriously compromised between November 1700 and May 1702.

In 1709, in still more dramatic circumstances, Louis XIV also broke his word, although by doing so he ensured the safety of France. In that year, when natural catastrophies added to the blow of military defeats, Louis resolved to sue for peace. Negotiations began at The Hague, at which Torcy appeared in person. This in itself was an innovation, for it was the first time that a royal minister had met representatives of the opposing powers. Louis XIV accepted a series of terrible demands : Lille, Tournai, Dunkirk and Strasbourg were to be surrendered, and Philip V was to renounce the Spanish throne in favour of his Austrian rival, the archduke Charles.[8]

Torcy sensed that he could divide France's enemies. The Dutch were mainly concerned with the question of their Barrier, and were less interested in the fate of Dunkirk or Strasbourg. They would, he thought, probably 'soften on the articles about the king of Spain' and perhaps grant him Naples and Sicily. Marlborough was unwilling to hear of any compensation for Philip V, and asked for Newfoundland for England, a condition which had not been foreseen. But it was Prince Eugène who proved intransigent; in the name of the emperor and the Empire he demanded the return of Alsace. Torcy concluded that it was best to break off negotiations and leave for home, but to avoid discouraging the Dutch he allowed the preliminaries of a treaty to be drawn up, which he took back with him to Versailles. The Allies were sure that their terms had been accepted, and appended their signatures to the preliminary text and settled down to wait for Torcy to return.

'Although my journey has been far from pleasant', Torcy wrote to Beauvilliers, 'I shall not regret it, if it is possible that the King may be satisfied with it. For I have learned a great many things on which our ideas were previously very vague or erroneous, and perhaps one day this information may be of use in His Majesty's service.'[9]

From Rotterdam Torcy wrote to Louis XIV, counselling him to reject Allied demands for the cession of places in Alsace 'rather than any of those demands which indirectly concern Spain, for . . . [the Dutch] . . . have taken it into their heads that Your Majesty has never intended to abandon that crown and the Indies, but merely to obtain peace for your own kingdom'.[10] Louis XIV thereupon broke off negotiations. In a letter addressed to all provincial governors he appealed to French public opinion. The king explained that impossible demands were being asked of him and expressed his certainty that his subjects would reject allied terms which were 'contrary both to justice and the honour of France'. He alluded to 'those insinuations they [the Allies] have made, that I should join my forces to those of the Alliance, to compel my grandson to give up his throne. The mere thought that I would be a party to such an alliance with them runs counter to any sentiment of humanity.' This suggestion had in fact been made, but only verbally; the preliminary text of the treaty (Article 4) contained nothing more than a vague agreement 'to take suitable measures together' if the places to be ceded in France and Spain were not handed over within two months. This phrase was repeated in Article 37. In the Vienna archives a commentary by Prince Eugène on the peace preliminaries has been preserved. The prince noted in connection with Article 37 that it would be impossible for the whole Spanish empire to be handed over in the space of two months. The remoteness of many of its possessions meant that orders from Europe would take a year to arrive; but he stressed that the article had been included in its entirety *because of Strasbourg*.[11] For the emperor the return of Strasbourg was crucial. By accepting a continuation of the war Louis XIV avoided the surrender of places vital to the security of French territory. He could only do this by refusing to sign the treaty, but in the eyes of the Allies he had once more reneged on a promise. The despatches from the German cities (e.g. Speyer) and princes received in Vienna during the summer of 1709 repay study. As soon as Louis resumed negotiations they all demanded that even more pitiless conditions be imposed on France. This explains the otherwise incomprehensible rigidity of the Allies at Gertruydenberg in 1710. France, however, survived this terrible test. English public opinion was the first to shift, less through any diminution of its hostility towards France than out of weariness at subsidising the Imperial army, and at allied losses in Spain. Public opinion in the Maritime Powers, combined with a return of good fortune to Louis XIV's armies once England had suspended hostilities,[12] accelerated the move towards peace. The result was the Peace of Utrecht of 1713.

This peace between France, the Maritime Powers and the lesser Allies had to be completed by a settlement with the emperor and the Empire. What happened between November 1713 and March 1714 illustrates the last stage in the development of Louis XIV's methods in foreign policy. The king was confronted by two diametrically opposite views, both focusing – oddly enough – on the person of Prince Eugène, the emperor's negotiator. Eugène offered a complete reversal of alliances. Torcy still bore him a grudge from the negotiations of 1709, while Villars felt a personal sympathy, and even friendship, towards his old antagonist and wished for a reconciliation between their two countries.

Torcy 'sabotaged' the negotiation between the two generals at Rastadt. He confided to Bolingbroke,[13] 'it is not surprising that a great general should adopt this method of negotiation. Ours, who is more used to plucking laurels than olive branches, believes that no soldier can conceal the truth and accords Prince Eugène the same trust that I give to Your Excellency. We shall soon see with what result.'[14] Villars wrote to Torcy, with delightful impudence : 'I know that ministers are not always to be believed, but Prince Eugène seems to me to be anything but dissimulating and he has sworn to me that he has taken upon himself more than any other man would have dared . . . I have no reason to believe he is lying.'[15]

This exchange may look like a dispute between a professional diplomat and a general in charge of a particular negotiation. There is an element of such rivalry, but the real issue was the choice between a policy of force and one of conciliation. To Villars it seemed that Torcy was succumbing to the temptation, now that the situation had altered in France's favour, to take revenge for the harsh and pitiless demands to which he had been subjected four years earlier. 'I beseech Your Majesty to forgive the liberty that I take', wrote Villars, 'when I state that this is very close to being a dictated and imposed settlement.'[16]

In the end a choice had to be made between sticking to the English alliance – which Torcy wanted – and an attempted alliance with the emperor in the hope of obtaining his renunciation of all claims on Spain and the Indies and the abandonment of his guarantees in favour of his erstwhile subjects, the Catalans. Villars was sure that the emperor no longer posed a threat to France. It was Louis XIV who made the final choice, adopting a policy in line with Villars' arguments. Some historians have doubted whether the old king, eighteen months before his death, was capable of as momentous a decision as this, involving a policy of friendship with Austria, his implacable enemy for so many years. But such doubt seems hyper-critical, though we are justified in searching for persons at Versailles working for the same ends as Villars. We should also take into account that Villars was aiming at the title of constable and that Louis XIV – although he was willing to load Villars with honours – set himself against revival of this office : 'He wanted to be Constable, and he knows that I am resolved not to make anyone Constable as long as I reign.' We are therefore entitled to conclude, in my opinion, that Louis XIV maintained his freedom of judgement to the very end of his life and chose the policy which appeared best to him. His choice between Villars and Torcy on this occasion seems dictated by his hope of restoring peace to Europe before his death.

His reign had begun auspiciously amid the general pacification secured by Mazarin. *Arbitriis pacans omnia regna suis* (By his arbitration bringing peace to all countries), so ran the inscription of a triumphal arch of 1660, to which I have had occasion to refer several times in my studies on the Baroque. And at the end of his reign, conscious of his age and growing weakness, and foreseeing the problems of the minority government that was to come, he laboured to stabilise Europe through peace. While maintaining good relations with the Maritime Powers, as Torcy recommended, he also sought a reconciliation with Germany. Bavaria was one of his client-states; he was ready to proffer the emperor his friendship, and even to make use of Prince Eugène, though he offered him nothing more than this compliment : 'For long now I have grown accustomed to regard Prince Eugène as the Emperor's subject, and as such he has done his duty. I am pleased with what you tell me of him, and you may inform him of this from me.' Eugène for his part had fostered a belief in Louis that the emperor would soon seek peace with Philip V and that he would use Louis' mediation for this purpose, a matter close to Louis' heart : *Arbitriis pacans omnia regna suis.*

There had been peace at the outset, and there would be peace at the close of the reign. Throughout the reign there was the king, with his average abilities, his attachment to methods which he had not the originality to transcend, his continual watchfulness, and his conception of kingship as something greater than himself; to historians these characteristics show Louis XIV at his best and his worst. The peace at the beginning had been one of triumph; that at the end was one of resignation and prudence. And between the two, how many wars and aggressions, how many deaths and burdens for subjects, his own and those of other monarchs.

Louis had not succeeded in dominating Europe, nor had he laid the foundations of European harmony. But he had enlarged and strengthened France; he left it still capable of playing a major role in a Europe that was now composed of more or less balanced forces.

NOTES

1 Archives des Affaires Etrangères (hereafter cited as A.A.E.), Correspondance Politique, Allemagne, vol. 56 (Le Dran collection) f. 95, Louis XIV to Brancas, French ambassador in Spain.

2 'Instructions for French ambassadors and ministers from the Peace of Westphalia till the French Revolution'.

3 A.A.E., C.P., Hollande, vol. 218, Louis XIV's letter to Torcy from Marly, dated 14 May 1709.

4 Minister for war; see alphabetical list of persons.

5 A.A.E., C.P., Autriche, Supplément, Chamillart's letter to Maximilian Emmanuel of Bavaria, 2 Nov 1704.

6 H. R. von Srbik has shown that Leopold I was the originator of this clause; but Louis – who acquiesced – had to bear the brunt of Protestant disapproval: see his *Wien und Versailles 1692–1697* (Munich, 1944) pp. 220, 286ff, and, briefly, R. M. Hatton, 'Louis XIV and his Fellow Monarchs', *Louis XIV and the Craft of Kingship*, ed. John C. Rule (Columbus, Ohio, 1969) p. 182, and below p. 43.

7 A. Latreille, 'Innocent XI pape Janséniste et directeur de conscience de Louis XIV', *Cahiers d'Histoire* (Grenoble, Lyon, 1956); V.-L. Tapié, 'Europe et Chrétienté', *Gregorianum* (Rome, 1961).

8 'Carlos III' of the Allies, between 1704 and 1713.

9 A.A.E., C.P., Hollande, vol. 218, f. 232, Torcy's letter to Louis XIV from Rotterdam, 22 May 1709.

10 Ibid., f. 244b.

11 Vienna: Staatsarchiv, Haagen-Friedenspräliminaren, f. 170 r. and v.

12 The victory of Denain was facilitated by England's suspension of arms in 1712. Dutch losses in this battle (decided before Eugène could arrive on the scene) predisposed the Republic towards peace (*ed.*).

13 See alphabetical list of persons.

14 A.A.E., C.P., Allemagne, vol. 56, f. 217.

15 Ibid., C.P., Autriche, vol. 185, letter of 21 Jan 1714.

16 Ibid., C.P., Autriche, vol. 97, letter of 2 Mar 1714.

2 Louis XIV and his Fellow Monarchs*

R. M. HATTON

Thanks to his exceptionally long personal reign,[1] Louis XIV had what might be termed – from the point of view of the space at our disposal in this chapter – a superfluity of fellow monarchs.[2] Moreover, their number increased between 1661 and 1715, since some of Louis' fellow sovereigns who were not monarchical heads of state (electors, dukes, landgraves, and lesser princes come into this category) attempted, and at times succeeded in achieving, the status of crowned head. In the European table of ranks it was relatively easy to cope with the few 'mixed cases': the elected kings of the Polish-Lithuanian Commonwealth, the *Rzeczpospolita Polska*, generally known in Western Europe as the Republic of Poland; the elected popes, who as temporal sovereigns of the small papal states counted little but carried great weight as the crowned spiritual heads of the Catholic church; the elected emperors of the Holy Roman Empire of the German nation, the office that carried the undisputed highest temporal honours, and on which the Austrian Habsburg family had so strong a hold that, in Louis' words, 'the imperial crown has become virtually hereditary in the house of Austria'.[3] It is more difficult to make a hard and fast distinction between fellow monarchical sovereigns and other categories of fellow sovereigns when surveying Louis' reign because of the several regencies during minorities or illnesses of rulers: in Spain after the death of Philip IV, and in Sweden after the death of Charles X; in Portugal when Alfonso VI was incapacitated by mental illness. At such times Louis' relationship with his fellow monarchs (whatever it might be in theory) was in practice transferred to influen-

* First published in *Louis XIV and the Craft of Kingship*, ed. John C. Rule (Columbus, Ohio, 1969), a paper read at a conference at Ohio State University in 1964.

tial individuals, as was the case with the oligarchic republics of Europe, those of the Dutch,[4] of Venice, and of Genoa. Even where the king was alive and of sound mind, there is evidence suggesting that unless he was a strong king his state tended to be looked upon, at least by Frenchmen, as a temporary republic.[5] Conversely, a strong republic could successfully battle to achieve equality with monarchies in diplomatic etiquette.

The division of Europe in Louis XIV's time into monarchies, or states that received monarchical honours, and 'the rest' can therefore be seen to be based in a rough and ready way on the estimation of the realities or – where a monarchy had become temporarily weak – potentialities of power. The very geopolitical situation of Louis XIV's France at the time when he took over personal responsibility was such that his attention had to be focused on his fellow sovereigns, whether these were fellow monarchs or not. In the first place, Louis was concerned with his immediate neighbours : with the kings of Spain, the rulers of Austria, the Stuarts of England, and that scion of the houses of Stuart and Orange, William, whom Louis hoped (for reasons of state as well as for the sake of monarchical solidarity) to make sovereign ruler of the Northern Netherlands long before 1672. After 1688, whatever the state of official recognition at any particular time, Louis regarded William as the reigning king of England and the *de facto* head of the Dutch state, although his title was that of a mere *stadholder*. The way in which Leopold (head of the Austrian Habsburg dominions since 1657 and emperor from 1658) tried to govern the Empire in foreign affairs, despite the terms of the capitulation imposed on him at the time of his election, rendered the German princes vitally important for Louis XIV's diplomacy. Further afield, the kings of Sweden, fellow guarantors of the Treaties of Westphalia, were of the greatest significance, the Swedish state comprising not only Sweden, Finland and the East Baltic provinces, but also the Swedish king's possessions in the Holy Roman Empire. The kings of Denmark–Norway had to be taken into account as well, since they shared control of the Sound with Sweden; but the tsars of Muscovy were just impinging on the European map of power politics toward the end of Louis' reign. It was also in the later years of his life that Louis was faced with a female fellow monarch : Anne, who succeeded William III in England in 1702.

Louis seems to have assumed (though not ranking Anne either with minors or lunatics) that with her accession England had more or less reverted to the republican form of government in which it had existed in Cromwell's time,[6] and his diplomatic contacts were with her ministers. In the War of the Spanish Succession Louis visualised recognition of Anne as queen and a guarantee of the Protestant succession as part of the price to be paid – and not a stiff one, in the circumstances – for the peace, along with the promotions of the elector of Brandenburg to king in Prussia and the duke of Savoy to king of Sicily. Shortly after the 1713–14 settlements, Louis granted 'Their High Mightinesses', the States General of the United Provinces, royal treatment in matters of precedence, ostensibly to compensate the Dutch for the implied loss of status suffered by William's death, but in reality to gain goodwill at a time of diplomatic rivalry.[7]

The hierarchical organisation of states was one that all Europe took for granted as the outward expression of power and prestige, and changes were not easily made: bitter enemies joined to resist innovations that might disturb the balance of the pyramid that had, haphazardly enough though on a realistic basis, been constructed. Before peace was concluded after the Nine Years War, Emperor Leopold, the electors of the Empire, and Louis XIV joined successfully to refute the claim of a mere prince, supported by Leibniz's pen, to send an ambassador to the peace congress on the plea that the Treaty of Münster had given all German princes sovereign rights and thus equality.[8] Louis himself jealously guarded his own rank and privileges lest concessions might become precedents working to the detriment of French prestige in the future. On the basis of incidents studied in isolation, it has become commonplace to assert that Louis regarded himself as the very apex of the hierarchical pyramid and demanded to be treated as above his fellow monarchs. One could cite Louis' insistence that Leopold of Austria must notify him of his election as emperor before his diplomats could be received at the French court;[9] the apology demanded from his father-in-law after the servants of Philip IV's ambassador to St James's had attacked those of Louis in a struggle for precedence;[10] the humiliation of the pope following a similar fracas in which members of the French suite were killed;[11] the forcing – by threats of reprisals – of the doge of Genoa, contrary to the laws of that city, to come to Versailles to transmit in person his promise to remain neutral during Franco-Spanish hostilities.[12] This view becomes less tenable once the cases used as illustrations are put into perspective[13] and compared with actions of other monarchs of the time in such disputes. The kings of England refused to grant reciprocity of salute in the Channel to Louis XIV and demanded in the most arrogant terms that the Dutch should salute their flag;[14] when the king of Denmark refused such salute, English diplomats worried whether the nation would stand for 'this affront' without recourse to war.[15] The Dutch denied the title of 'Your Holiness' to the pope at the Congress of Nijmegen;[16] rulers not infrequently had to ask satisfaction for the murder or wounding of servants of their envoys; there were constant squabbles about precedence at all courts with consequent demands for apologies and punishment of those guilty of transgressions. In reality Louis showed a remarkable flexibility and ease in matters of etiquette once his equality with all hereditary monarchs – under the Holy Roman Emperor, who by virtue of his elected office held the first rank – was accepted.[17] He was freer with the cherished *Frère* for aspiring fellow monarchs (prized above the *Cousin* for dukes and the *Sieur* or *Monsieur* for lesser princes) where it did not conflict with French interests;[18] he permitted his diplomats great freedom to find expedients in matters of precedence 'as long as the royal dignity is not impaired'.[19] He proved keen to agree to expedients suggested by other powers when he wanted negotiations to proceed : he accepted Temple's suggestion to get the traffic moving in the narrow streets of Nijmegen when rigid attention to rank threatened to paralyse the congress by the pile-up of carriages unwilling to yield on account of rank;[20] he co-operated meticulously in the mathematically contrived Dutch solution to ensure full equality between France and Spain at the signing of the peace treaty of 1678, when a table was so placed between doors that the two missions, entering simultaneously, reached the table at exactly the same time, to sign, with synchronised speed, respective copies on the coveted side of the document;[21] he worked with the English at the Congress of Utrecht 'to lay aside titles' in order to avoid trouble over rank.[22] Indeed, it is safe to assume that where Louis made any difficulty over a question of diplomatic etiquette, he had an underlying political motive

B

of some importance. This is true also of his fellow monarchs of
the first and second rank; it is possibly less easy to discern the
Realpolitik behind the refusal of the envoy of the elector of
Mainz to the Diet of Regensburg to deliver his credentials since
the particular staircase by which his predecessors had been admitted had been destroyed.[23]

The concern with political realities is also evident when we
go beyond etiquette to Louis' conception of royal behaviour in
international relations. He had, like most of his fellow monarchs,
a code of honour. He argued, as most of them did (exceptions
can be found, one of them Augustus of Saxony–Poland),[24] that
a ruler pledged his word. Treaty obligations must not be surrendered lest trust be dissipated and allies not forthcoming; the
promise and the threat must stand less the next ones be treated
lightly. But Louis, like other rulers of his time, would permit
mediators to release him from his pledge. In 1678–9 a scheme
was devised whereby Louis was persuaded to go back on his
promise not to make peace with Leopold before the prince of
Fürstenburg had been released from captivity by that prince's
brother petitioning Louis not to let his given word become the
obstacle to a peace so eagerly desired by all Europe; similar
ways were found to permit a minor concession to Brandenburg
in respect of land in Swedish Pomerania, once Louis' insistence
that the king of Sweden should have all his German possessions
restored, as promised, had been largely effective.[25] This loyalty
to the given word was part of the *gloire*, or reputation, of the
ruler, and of this every ruler was extremely jealous. Such and
such action would be against his *gloire*, Charles XII of Sweden
argued;[26] Leopold used very similar terms;[27] and so did William
II.[28] In twentieth-century historical writing there is too often
a tendency to equate *gloire* with military glory only, or at
most with military glory coupled with 'magnificence'. The military glory and the pomp and circumstance were obviously part of
gloire, but they were not all of it. It is significant that when an
Italian agent of Leopold's reported a conversation with Chamlay,
he translated *gloire* with *Reputation* or with *Ansehen*.[29] It is also
significant that crowned heads did not reserve the term only
for themselves as persons or representing the nation : Louis XIV
urged Turenne to act 'for the good of the state and the glory of
your arms'.[30] This concept, the *bienfait* of the nation, was in

Louis' case nearly always coupled with mention of his own *gloire*;[31] and indeed, the concern for *gloire* seen in its proper perspective sprang from a preoccupation, which is descernible in most of the monarchs of the period, with the verdict of history on the individual ruler.

The very task of an absolutist ruler in respect of foreign policy (and in foreign affairs, as we have been reminded, William III acted in England as independently as any absolutist king,[32] while in the Republic he had full control once he had learnt to manage the anti-Orangist regents)[33] tended to produce certain common characteristics. The work was hard, the responsibility weighed heavily, and the reward was often gross flattery to one's face[34] with criticism and unfavourable comment behind one's back: the latest story of favouritism, obstinacy and pride, or of stupidity, going the rounds of court and gossip. Neither William III, nor Louis XIV, nor young Charles XII drank much, fearing it might cloud brain and judgement ('I hope he does not expect good wine at my table', Louis drily commented on the arrival of an ambassador known to enjoy his glass). They read endless memoranda and dispatches, they listened to experts, and had, finally, to make up their own minds. They worried when things went wrong: Charles XII shut himself up and refused to see anyone while he got over private grief (the death of a beloved sister) and the public humiliation of the surrender of his army at Perevolochna;[35] William burst out in a moment of despair, 'There is nothing left for me here, I shall have to go to the Indies';[36] Louis wept over the miseries of the nation in the War of the Spanish Succession.[37] But all three (and other monarchs of their time in other, if less drastic, dilemmas) had to grit their teeth and fight back. The very weight of their responsibility and their concern for the *gloire*, for the verdict of history upon them, helped them to mobilise reserves of personal courage. They were all determined not to leave the state entrusted to them diminished and more defenceless than when they had received it: this would be the ultimate blot on their own *gloire*. 'Rather a forty years' war in the Empire', Charles XII commented on the eve of his 1718 offensive, 'than a bad peace'.[38] 'Shall I be the one', cried William in bitterness to Heinsius in 1701 when French troops poured into the Southern Netherlands, 'to lose without a battle what I have struggled for during more than twenty-eight years?'[39]

'Never', reported Chamlay, during the Nine Years War, 'have I, in the twenty years I have known the king, seen Louis XIV so angry as when it was suggested from Vienna he should give up the gains of the Treaty of Westphalia.' 'What!' Louis had exclaimed, 'am I to sacrifice the work of thirty years – I who have struggled so hard lest my enemies shall come into my house. . . . Rather war for ten years more.'[40]

If one is to make a distinction, and one ought to be made, between the three rulers whose attitudes have just been compared, it is between the two, William and Charles, who commanded armies in person, and Louis who, though passionately interested in the army,[41] was no commander in his own right. A difference in degree, therefore, between William, who said, 'I can always die in the last dike',[42] and Charles, who argued that it was up to him to risk his life encouraging the soldiers to be unafraid ('Better to die in battle than surrounded by doctors and weeping relatives', he once said),[43] and Louis, who, when he could not sleep because of bad news from the front, comforted himself that there was yet the grand army between the frontier and the capital.[44] And on the personal level, in any comparison between the three, the inclination to take risks characteristic of commanders in the field, once preparations are complete, is strongly marked in William and Charles ('We must take risks while we are in luck', was one of the Swedish king's standing phrases;[45] 'his almost reckless boldness', is a recent verdict on William by a Dutch historian),[46] and notably absent in the cautious Louis, who loved the craft of diplomacy and being at the centre of things, who planned ahead for all eventualities, but who sometimes missed opportunities by being too unwilling to take risks in the military sense. Typical of Louis was also a certain doctrinaire, legalistic outlook that is particularly noticeable in his attitude to the house of Stuart after the débâcle of 1688. Outward forms were insisted upon; the niceties of scrupulous use of the title 'Prince of Orange' for William III was maintained for years after Louis had decided that the restoration of James II was no longer feasible, partly as a lever in peace negotiations but also, as Louis' correspondence with Avaux between 1694 and 1698 makes clear, out of concern for the legal position of the Stuarts. It would be offensive to a fellow monarch who had been unlucky enough to lose his crown, and against Louis' *gloire*, to expose James publicly to shame and humiliation by a premature recognition of William : if peace did not result, such hurt had needlessly weakened James's position.[47] And it would seem, from evidence only recently brought to light, that it was the complaint of Mary of Modena that her son would, on James's death, be just an ordinary person (*un simple*) that helped to decide Louis in favour of granting royal title to James Edward in 1701 : William, it was argued, was king of England *de facto*; James II's son had the title by hereditary right, and to deny him the rank of king would be tantamount to a denial of his legitimate birth.[48] The dangers of recognition were clearly seen but accepted in the hope that no ill would come of it, since Louis was tied by the Peace of Ryswick not to foment trouble for William in the British Isles. To break the treaty would go against honour and *gloire*; but – it was held – if the British rose against William or, later, Anne, then armed assistance from France would be permissible. Similarly, support for a Stuart invasion in 1708 was held to be a 'legitimate' retort to the allied attempts to stir up trouble for Louis in the Cévennes[49] and to land troops in Toulon. Another field where Louis was forced into a more equivocal position than he might have preferred was the Habsburg struggle against the Turks. Louis was never the ally of the Ottomans,[50] and in the 1660s (when his relationship with the emperor Leopold was on the whole good)[51] he sent his contingent of six thousand men as a member of the League of the Rhine to fight bravely at St Gotthard, while a detachment of the French fleet joined that of Venice to do battle with the infidel at sea.[52] But Louis took no part in Europe's defence of Vienna in 1683. The years of *détente* with the Austrian Habsburgs had come to an end with the fall of Lobkowitz and Leopold's renunciation of the partition treaty of 1668, and Louis felt that the most he could do to live up to the title of 'His Most Christian Majesty' was to withdraw troops from his eastern frontier to make clear that he would not embarrass or hinder the fight against the Turks.[53] The Habsburg battle against the Ottomans in the 1680s enabled the House of Austria to rally the Empire to its side,[54] and the *gloire* that came to Leopold as the victor of 1683 was considerable. In Italy, French diplomats reported, it was Leopold's fame – not that of Louis – that rang through the land.[55] Yet, the tradition of French policy in the Near East[56] and Louis' own growing rivalry with Leopold over the Spanish succession prevented his playing an active role against the Turks, while his conception of his own *gloire* made it impossible for him to use the opportunity to attack Leopold.

Louis personally met very few of his fellow monarchs, and none while they were actually reigning, with the exception of his brief meeting with Philip IV on the Island of Pheasants in 1660. The Stuarts Louis knew as exiles, Charles II before the Restoration, James II after 1688; John Sobieski he met before his election as king of Poland.[57] His own grandson, Philip V of Spain, was in a special position. Louis' personal knowledge of the young man illuminates the post-1700 correspondence between them and makes it a particularly valuable (and underestimated for this purpose) source for Louis' concept of the duties of kingship.[58] Other monarchs he could only learn something about from diplomatic reports. The standard of the best French diplomats was very high indeed. Callières – himself an erstwhile diplomat and then *secrétaire du cabinet* – wrote on the duty of giving pen-portraits of the king and the chief ministers of the country where one resided:

> Thus the able diplomatist can place his master in command of all the material for a true judgement of the foreign country, and the more successfully he carries out this part of his duties, the more surely will he make his master feel as though he himself had lived abroad and watched the scenes which are described.[59]

But Louis was not only a passive receiver; he asked specific questions and ordered Callières, Harlay and Crécy (and was criticised for it by Vauban) to pay an extended call on William III after the French recognition of him in 1697. It is from a detailed report of this conference that we learn that William spoke excellent French, 'without any accent'; the word-for-word reportage and the description of behaviour and habits (the 'shy half-smile' reminding us of the more publicised half-smile of Charles XII – the protective device of rulers schooled to guard secrets) is extremely vivid.[60] From the time of the negotiations for the partition treaty, Tallard's dispatches from London are full of fascinating details of conversations with William, the king's every word and facial expression being recorded.[61] One particularly important conversation we can check against William's equally detailed report of the French ambassador's every word and facial expression to Heinsius at The Hague. The differences in interpretations are, however, noticeable : Tallard, pleased that he had skilfully manœuvred William into a position whereby he must move closer to France; William, delighted at the effect of his calculated statement that, were he to come to an agreement with Louis, he would separate himself from the House of Austria. ('I never saw a man in such joy, scarcely able to contain himself, and repeating it four or five times.')[62] But such temporary misinterpretations are inseparable from all diplomatic intercourse, and in the long run Louis' methods paid dividends. By carefully collecting and sifting information, by memorising the idiosyncracies of fellow monarchs and their ministers, useful guidance could be given to later diplomats. One striking example comes to mind. When Croissy (the brother of Colbert de Torcy) was sent to Charles XII at Stralsund early in 1715, he was told, 'Do not bother to penetrate this king's designs – he does not give anything away'.[63] There speaks the voice of experience. But the amount that could be found out, and the amount of pressure that could be put on ministers and officials abroad, was such that Louis himself was anxious to deny his fellow monarchs the advantages of negotiating important matters at the French court. Such negotiations offered too many opportunities for close observance and of influence with ministers; and Louis therefore preferred, if at all possible, to send his trusted men to other capitals to transact important business. For this reason few pen-portraits of Louis at work informally were sent home to his fellow monarchs : the one by Portland, who became as charmed as one of Louis' own diplomats (Pomponne) when he had the chance to see the king throw off the cloak of majesty and the proud haughty air he wore in public,[64] is worth noting : 'He did me the honour to speak to me as a private individual, with an obliging freedom and familiarity, often laughing, and quite throwing aside the gravity which is usual on such occasions.'[65]

The long reign and the constant diplomatic and military activity have made it difficult for historians to deal adequately with the theme of Louis and his fellow monarchs on a Europe-wide scale. The sheer bulk of the material to be handled, its relative inaccessibility when compared for instance to the published memoirs of the king himself, of courtiers, and of some of his

ministers, is not conducive to a balanced picture. It is very easy
to forget that his *Mémoires* were penned[66] when Louis was a
fairly young man and to let the views he expressed then remain
valid for the whole reign, thus denying him development. Even
so, clues in the *Mémoires* to regrets for past actions (as when
Louis, reviewing the Dutch War, suggests that ambition and a
desire to shine in combat might be forgiven 'in so young a ruler
as I was and one so favoured by fortune') have been ignored.[67]
Anti-Louis propaganda has also been easily available in the
many German and Dutch pamphlets of the reign, so that we
have become familiar with the warnings of Lisola and others
that Louis aspired to 'universal monarchy'.[68] The inevitably one-
sided arguments of propaganda warfare have tended to become
accepted as objective facts. Obviously, the circumstances sur-
rounding each discussion of Louis' candidature for the imperial
crown must be taken into account : in 1683 it was the elector of
Brandenburg who offered to work in the interests of Louis or
the dauphin, or any prince favoured by Louis, in the hope of
securing French co-operation against Sweden; in 1670, when
Louis suggested that the elector of Bavaria should vote for him,
it was with the proviso that the latter should be made king of
Rome – again, a diplomatic bargaining to gain support, this
time for France.[69] The very nature of the Grand Alliances forged
against France encouraged the two Maritime Powers (Protestant
in their religion) to give public utterance to their genuine horror
and fear at Louis' Catholic aggression against the Huguenots in
France after 1685; whereas the equally sincere protest of the
Dutch and the English against Leopold's treatment of the Protestants in Hungary, and the use of the Neapolitan galleys for those
who would not retract,[70] was delivered discreetly and privately.
Small wonder, therefore, that the treatment of Louis XIV in his
relationship to Europe is at times in the history books of those
nations who fought against him rather over simplified. The
twentieth century's experience of, and attitude to, war also helps
to brand Louis as the aggressor. Even the most objectively
intended non-French survey of the reign tends to superficiality :
'The period of undoubted great preponderance unfortunately
witnessed a series of aggressive wars, which Louis XIV undertook for purposes of international prestige, military glory, and
the extension of his frontiers.'[71]

Modern French survey works have been even harsher on Louis XIV, though the views of their authors are more varied.[72] He is often presented as a bully compelled by visions of personal glory, easy to mislead, and hardly ever taking the right advice. There is usually some sympathy for his moral courage during the War of the Spanish Succession;[73] and curiously little condemnation of the War of Devolution which is reckoned, with the Dutch War, among the 'defensive wars' of the reign[74] – the rest being 'aggressive wars' or 'unlimited wars'. It used to be fashionable to seek for one basic motivation in Louis XIV's foreign policy : for some the Spanish succession issue determined the king's attitude towards the rest of Europe throughout the reign; for others the dogma of the drive toward the 'natural frontiers' was paramount.[75] Today historians either deny any pattern,[76] interpreting Louis' policy as responses to incidents provoked by circumstances, or attempt a neat division into periods. One such division runs : the age of defensive warfare followed by the age of aggressive warfare. Yet another : Louis' foreign policy before and after the fistula (1686).[77] But all tend to assume that one underlying motive of the policy, however divided into periods, was the desire to control Europe, the search for hegemony and preponderance.

Material for a revision, or at least a modification, of this view does exist on the level of Louis XIV's diplomacy as such, on the place of Louis in France, and on the role of France in Europe and overseas. Historians who have worked on the foreign policy of their own countries have come to what seemed to them rather startling conclusions. Geyl found that 'Louis showed himself surprisingly moderate' in negotiations with the Dutch in the 1660s, and has stressed that it was the domestic struggles in the Northern Netherlands that prevented (in spite of De Witt's agreement) a Franco-Dutch solution of the problem of the Southern Netherlands.[78] Mark Thomson, while concluding that France's enemies had reason to distrust Louis during the peace negotiations that did not come to fruition in 1708–10, has in all his work stressed Louis' shrewdness and sense of responsibility.[79] Even monographic studies that are one-sided in their approach, such as that of Heinrich Ritter von Srbik on relations between Leopold and Louis in the Nine Years War (the intrigues of France are always 'Machiavellian' here),[80] have brought to light documents that are of the greatest importance for understanding the motives of the rulers and countries discussed. Srbik, just because he is so biased in interpretation, makes lively reading. The more objective studies of various aspects – or periods – of France's relations with Europe in Louis' reign are possibly duller but always valuable for the variety of material that is collected and studied, or for the microscopic examination of a particular topic. Mention must be made of Höynck's monograph on the Congress of Nijmegen; of the many studies connected with the Rhineland by Max Braubach and his pupils;[81] of the work by French and American historians on problems connected with the Alsace and Lorraine regions;[82] and of the fine analysis of Strasbourg's fate between 1648 and 1789 by Franklin Ford[83] to which we shall have occasion to return. Specialist work not directly connected with France, nor using French material, yet manages to throw indirect light on Louis' relations with Europe : Veenendaal's book on the Anglo-Dutch condominium of the Southern Netherlands;[84] Coombs's study of Anglo-Dutch relations during the War of the Spanish Succession;[85] Stork-Penning's examination of the Dutch attitude to peace with France between 1708 and 1711.[86] Any study of Jacobitism naturally enough touches on Louis XIV.[87] Swedish research into Franco-Swedish relations is also illuminating but less easily accessible, though happily a growing number of historians on both sides of the Atlantic read one (and thus all) of the Scandinavian languages : Andrew Lossky, whose main interest lies in the intellectual history of Louis' reign, has also made some significant contributions to the topic of French relations with the north of Europe.[88] Research even on the purely domestic history of France's neighbours helps the historians put Louis and his country into perspective : we must take into account that Spain's decline was (in the opinion of several scholars) arrested in the third quarter of the seventeenth century; and that a series of demographic and other studies have recently demonstrated that the Habsburg dominions were increasing in resources and power during Louis' reign.[89] In France diplomatic history as such has for some time been out of fashion (the only new work of importance for Louis, at the end of his reign, is by Claude Nordmann);[90] but the interest in officials and administrators – noticeable also among American historians working on French history[91] – is producing important bases from which to illuminate Louis' relations with those who worked with

him. The biographies published on Turenne[92] and on Vauban
(though written in the 1930s the latter has only just appeared)[93]
are of great value for an assessment of the role of military considerations, although Zeller's work on the frontier remains the
foundation on which all must build who want to study French
foreign policy. 'The natural frontier' as the guiding motive for
the reign was demolished by Zeller's book and articles, while his
lucid analysis of the part played by considerations of defence and
of the 'out-works' across the Rhine for defence as well as for
bargaining from strength stands unsurpassed.[94]

There are gaps. The chief one is that we do not know enough
about one of Louis' great adversaries, Leopold of Austria. We
possess a fine historiographical study of the older works on Leopold I, Joseph I and Charles VI;[95] we have brief but perceptive
character-sketches of these three emperors by Kann in his recent
work on Austrian intellectual history and by Wandruzska in his
history of the Habsburg dynasty.[96] There are monographs that
help to illuminate aspects of Habsburg policy in Louis XIV's
reign.[97] Braubach's massive biography of Prince Eugène[98] is of
special interest for us, but we still lack modern well-documented
studies of the Habsburg rulers between 1648 and 1740. From the
point of view we are here considering new light on Franco-
Habsburg relations may be thrown by work in progress in the
United States, for example, by Spielman's study of the relations
between the Maritime Powers and Austria during Joseph's reign
and by Snyder's work on Godolphin and the Marlboroughs.[99]
The interest of Canadian and American scholars in French
policy overseas during Louis' reign[100] is already yielding results
and may lead to reassessments of the impact of such policy on
Louis' European diplomacy.

My own interest in Louis XIV and Europe started, so to speak,
at the wrong end of the reign : I have moved backwards from
the post-Utrecht period all the time. My main preoccupation
is with diplomatic relationships during those two long wars, the
Great Northern War (1700–21) and the War of the Spanish
Succession (1702–13).[101] The study of Sweden, France and the
Maritime Powers – that convenient single name for the Dutch
and the English nations at a time when they were both allies and
rivals – has restricted me to the archives of London, The Hague,
Paris, and those of the Scandinavian countries. I have found,

however, that some of my hobby-horses, and in particular my curiosity about 'presents and pensions' and their role in foreign policy have pushed me back to 1688[102] and to considerations of even earlier years on a more Europe-wide scale. For the pre-1688 period there is fortunately a great deal of documentary material in print; the fine series of the French *Recueil des Instructions*,[103] and the magnificent edition now in progress in Germany of the Treaties of Westphalia.[104]

The year 1648 may seem to take us back a long way (since Louis XIV at that time was only ten years of age), but it is my contention that neither of the two big war periods that interest me can be understood without reference to the 1648 settlements : in the ambiguous terms imposed on each other by war-weary powers still reluctant to surrender cherished aims, in the elucidations and counter-elucidations that followed, we find the vital clue to the struggle between Louis XIV and the Habsburgs for the interpretation of the Treaty of Münster. The Treaty of Osnabrück – that between Sweden, the Empire, and the Habsburgs – was less ambiguous, but the struggle for interpretation still went on : for example, over the Swedish attempt, eventually unsuccessful, to include the town of Bremen[105] with the duchy of Bremen. The Great Northern War can be seen (as Hugo Hantsch noted as far back as 1929) as a late harvest sprung from the seed of the Thirty Years War.[106]

The connection between the settlement of 1648 and Louis XIV's foreign policy is obvious to Ford, who has had to cope with the knotty problem of the ten towns of Alsace (the *Décapole*) that were, in one paragraph, ceded by the House of Habsburg to France with all rights; then, in a later clause, had their sovereignty somehow kept for the Empire; yet with a final paragraph it was added that nothing previously stated should in any way diminish the sovereign rights accorded to Louis.[107] What becomes clear however, when all material at our disposal is studied, is that the struggle was not only about differing interpretations of French sovereignty in Alsace but of the virtual undoing of one of the main gains of 1648 for France : the transfer in that year of sovereignty over the bishoprics of Metz, Toul and Verdun (occupied by the French since 1552) to Louis XIV.

Both sides were aggressive. Leopold, Joseph and Charles insisted on the return of the three bishoprics, both before and after the French interpretation in respect of the Alsace towns had been confirmed at the Peace of Nijmegen. One of the aims of the Habsburgs in the Nine Years War, as well as in the War of the Spanish Succession, was the return of Metz, Toul and Verdun; after 1679 the reversal of the Nijmegen decision on Alsace, and of Spain's cession to Louis of Franche-Comté at that peace, loomed large among Austrian objectives.[108] There was a parallel move in the north of the Empire by Brandenburg to force Sweden out of her German possessions with the emperor's help – a German-wide movement, therefore, against the 'foreign' powers that influenced, and also was influenced by, Leibniz's scheme for a closer federation of Germany and by the so-called German mission of Leopold. For his part, Louis was determined to keep the gains of 1648 and tried to interpret all treaties and incidents in France's favour; first in relation to what had been gained in Alsace; then in the reunion clauses; and, finally, in the occupation of Strasbourg as a punishment for that city's help to Leopold. The French case was that the Habsburg side had been the initial aggressor, the emperor Ferdinand III (Leopold's father) having, contrary to the stipulations of 1648, let six thousand soldiers march across the Empire to reinforce Spain in the Southern Netherlands. In his turn Louis earned the distrust of those preoccupied with German liberties when he, against assurances that had been given, or at least assumed, began pushing his claims in Alsace.[109]

Even greater international concern came over the French attempt to incorporate Lorraine with France. It was true that Lorraine had been occupied for long periods at a time before 1660; it was true that Louis had made a deal with the family that included (and for that reason met opposition from the French princes of the blood) giving the house of Lorraine a share in the heritage of the French crown; but the non-fulfilment of the Treaty of Montmartre from France's side, coupled with its repudiation by the young duke Charles who did not feel tied by his uncle's promises, rendered Louis' case indefensible from the point of view of international morality of the time, and Duke Charles's marriage to the emperor Leopold's sister gave little hope for success in Louis' cherished objective of 'rejoining this province of France to the body and heart of the country'.[110] Louis never gave up hope, however. Lorraine had to be evacuated in

1679 – though with French control of the four military routes through the country; but reoccupation soon followed, and Louis continued with schemes, common enough throughout Europe at this period, for exchanges and equivalents: the dukes of Lorraine (first, Charles V, and after his death, his son, Leopold Joseph) became candidates, if not for vacant thrones as in the case of Augustus of Saxony-Poland between 1706–9 and of James Edward Stuart after 1701 (for whom Poland, Egypt and the Barbary states were at times canvassed), at least for territory thought tempting enough to make them sacrifice Lorraine. The Southern Netherlands, Naples and/or Sicily, the Milanese, and a host of other possibilities, were discussed.[111] The French share of the partition treaties in Italy (which worried English and Dutch competitors for trade in the Mediterranean) were intended as an exchange for the duchy of Lorraine. A successful exchange would enable Louis to make sure of land through which his enemies had entered France in previous times: one of the 'doors' (*portes*) into the heart of the country. The *porte* into France represented by Dunkirk had been secured by purchase from Charles II in 1662, that leading from the Franche-Comté had been closed by Spain's cession of the province in 1678, and that from the Southern Netherlands was bolted in the 1680s: once Vauban's *carré* concept had been adopted, a *frontière de fer* was built which withstood attack in the wars of 1689–1713.[112] Concern for the remaining eastern 'doors' deepened with growing Habsburg power. The hope of closing at least one of them is fundamental to the partition treaties. Naples and Sicily (the French share of the First Partition Treaty of 1698) would, it was planned, be exchanged for the duchy of Lorraine; and when the Second Partition Treaty (of 1700) added to France's gains the duchy of Milan, as well as Naples and Sicily, an exchange of the former with either the duke of Lorraine or (if he refused) with the duke of Savoy was stipulated in a secret article. It is difficult to over-emphasise Louis' and his advisers' concern for the safety of the eastern frontier or their desire to incorporate enclaves inside the territory they considered as 'France'. The most striking illustration came during the Nine Years War when (as Srbik has shown) Louis was willing to renounce for himself, the dauphin and all his heirs, any share in the Spanish succession – and to let this renunciation be registered by the Paris Parlement

– provided France was permitted to retain the gains of Nijmegen in the east and to absorb Lorraine against equivalents. One condition was postulated (not an unreasonable one): in his turn Leopold should promise that the Austrian Habsburg dominions and the Spanish inheritance, which would come with Louis' blessing to the Vienna branch, should never be united under one ruler. The empire of Charles V must not be restored.[113] I shall have more to say of the Spanish succession issue as such in a moment; here I am just stressing what sacrifices Louis – who never relinquished belief in the hereditary legitimate right of his children and grandchildren to the crown of Spain – was willing to make for the security of the eastern frontier. Similarly, Habsburg concern to undo 1648 is illustrated by the immediate refusal of Louis' offer; probably not, as contemporary diplomats believed, because Leopold loved his son Charles better than his son Joseph and hoped to see him restore the empire of Charles V,[114] but because there was in Vienna as genuine a fear of Louis and of French plans for invasion along the Danube valley (did he not hold Strasbourg, the key to the Habsburg House?) as there was of Habsburg designs in Versailles, where Strasbourg was looked upon as the key that turned the lock against invasion. Neither side could give up its attempt, even at the cost of appeal to the dice of war, to obtain a solution favourable to itself.

It has been argued that if Louis had only rested content with the Truce of Ratisbon (Regensburg) of 1684 and refrained from efforts to have it changed to a permanent peace by his aggressive actions in 1688–9, all would have been well.[115] It is an interesting point of view; but it does tend to ignore that Louis at the time was convinced, and so were some of his advisers, that once Leopold had achieved peace with the Turks on his terms, he would turn against France. And the Austrian archives have yielded confirmation of such fears: those in favour of the Turkish war prevailed on the emperor to postpone the reckoning with Louis only because they convinced him that, victorious in the east, he would be better equipped to defeat France.[116]

The vital importance of the eastern frontier can also be illustrated from the War of the Spanish Succession. In his several efforts to obtain peace Louis offered to give up every gain that had come to the Bourbons from his having accepted the will of Carlos II: but he remained firm, even in the darkest hours, that

he could not, and would not, give up Metz, Toul, Verdun nor
the Nijmegen confirmation of sovereignty over the *Décapole* and
the transfer of Franche-Comté, though Strasbourg – gained by
treaty in 1697 when the occupation of 1681 was internationally
recognised – he at times despaired of keeping. And when, after the
breakdown of The Hague conference of 1709, he issued his famous
manifesto to the French people appealing for their support,
the point that loomed so large with the Allies (and with English
historians) – his refusal to give military help to throw his grandson out of Spain – was mentioned only in one sentence, in the
form nearly of an afterthought : 'I pass in silence over the suggestion made to me. . . .'[117] What loomed large in the manifesto
was his explanation that if he surrendered the cautionary towns[118]
that had been asked for as the price of an armistice, the Allies –
unless the suspension of arms were turned into a safe peace,
for which there was no guarantee – would be able to penetrate
to the heart of France and wrest from it the gains of so many
years and so many wars : the nation would be dismembered.

It is my contention, therefore, that despite the aggressive
actions of Louis XIV on the eastern borders of France (where
deeds were perpetrated that, however justifiable from the strategic
point of view and regardless of whether Louis was personally
responsible or not, have been condemned by contemporaries and
posterity), the underlying purpose of defence is part and parcel
of the struggle that took place between Bourbon and Habsburg
over rival interpretations of 1648, and that Louis' actions were
not the prelude to the establishment of control over the Empire
or of universal monarchy.

Where Louis can be labelled 'aggressive' is in an area where
modern French historians have been unexpectedly soft with him,
classing the War of Devolution as 'defensive' or even explaining
it as a 'rectification' of the Treaty of the Pyrenees.[119] The pre-
posterousness of applying private Brabantine law to the realm
of international politics has been stressed, naturally enough, by
historians of the Netherlands; but that issue has been largely
ignored in books written in French, even in a modern *Etude
historique sous les droits successoraux de la Reine Marie-Thérèse
de France.*[120] Nor was there at the time any ground for fearing
that the United Provinces would take offensive action in the
Southern Netherlands; the Dutch, having refused French plans

for partition that would bestow some territorial benefit on both parties while leaving an independent Catholic buffer state between them, were content with the *status quo*. Their attempts during the Thirty Years War to conquer the Southern Netherlands for themselves had failed; the outright partition they had offered France during that war had been declined at a time when Mazarin was negotiating privately with Spain. Now any discussion of change brought fears to the rich towns of the province of Holland, and in particular to Amsterdam, that the river Scheldt might be reopened and Antwerp become a competitor in trade.

Louis XIV's purchase of Dunkirk from Charles II in 1662 had not worried the States General;[121] Louis was their ally, whereas the English were bitter trade rivals. But Louis' precipitate invasion of the Southern Netherlands in 1667 was deeply disturbing to the Dutch. He saw it as a justifiable attempt to improve France's frontiers since Philip IV had refused to annul Maria Teresa's renunciation, even though the term within which her dowry should have been paid had expired.[122] They saw it as an abuse of French power. Louis, when he became aware of their unease, gave Spain the choice of ceding to France either Franche-Comté or certain towns in the Southern Netherlands. Franche-Comté (which the Spaniards thought of as indefensible in the long run and had ear-marked as a bargaining counter to achieve the return of that 'gap in the Pyrenees', Roussillon and part of Cerdagne, which they had sacrificed in 1659) was what Versailles expected Carlos II to cede; but the Spanish king's advisers consciously sacrificed part of the Southern Netherlands to frighten the Dutch Republic sufficiently to make sure of its support in case of renewed French aggression. In Louis' attack on the Dutch in 1672 there is undeniably an element of irritation and annoyance at the manner in which the States General took upon themselves all honour for having arranged the Peace of Aix-la-Chapelle (1668). The war had, however, two basic purposes: to warn the Dutch that France was a serious commercial competitor in Europe and overseas, and to force them to give Louis a free hand in the Southern Netherlands when the Spanish succession issue should be decided. By the partition treaty between Leopold and Louis in 1668 it had been agreed that the Southern Netherlands would fall to Louis' share;[123] and though a secret article in the

Franco-Swedish treaty, which (with many others) belongs to the
diplomatic preparations for the war on the Dutch, guaranteed
that France would respect the integrity of the Southern Netherlands and permit the States General an independent existence,[124]
Louis at this time certainly envisaged a chastened Republic and
the road open to a future incorporation of the Southern Netherlands with France. The greed of the War of Devolution and of
the Dutch War of 1672 was, at least according to my reading
of the *Mémoires* and the instructions of the *Recueil*, regretted by
Louis in more mature years. It might have been poor comfort for
him to reflect that retribution had not been slow in coming:
Leopold, anxious not to lose the leadership of the German mission
and beginning to aspire to the whole of the Spanish succession
for his own house,[125] renounced the partition treaty; the Dutch
War developed into a struggle for the whole eastern frontier of
France; and William of Orange's determination that Louis'
aggression must be resisted at all costs[126] was forged to last his
whole life through.

At the end of the Dutch War Louis accepted that the Republic – which was not the tiny, powerless state[127] of those who
read history backwards – was entitled, since he had begun the
war, to have the *status quo* restored and also to receive some
compensation (given in the form of trade advantages), in contrast
to those rulers, such as Carlos and Leopold, who had declared
war on France.[128] Furthermore, Louis, who did learn from experience, accepted the basic lesson of the war: the impractica-
bility of aspiring to the Southern Netherlands against the wishes
of the Dutch. From 1679 onward Louis had no serious hope of
ever incorporating all or most of the Low Countries with France.
But he was—and to this Dutch historians have paid too little
attention – worried whether the States General might come to
an arrangement with someone other than himself for a partition
or for a government essentially in the Dutch economic interest.
His attempts to persuade Spain to let Charles of Lorraine or Max
Emmanuel, elector of Bavaria, receive the Southern Netherlands
as an independent state (a scheme that would benefit Louis in
that Lorraine could then be incorporated with France, by a
direct exchange in the first case, and by the duke of Lorraine
taking over Max Emmanuel's German lands in the second) met
opposition from all sides: from the Dutch, who feared that either

duke would be tied to French apron strings; from Carlos of Spain, who did not want to dismember his patrimony; from Leopold of Austria, who aspired to the entire Spanish succession to dispose of as he wanted.[129] The Dutch, always frightened of a repetition of 1672, were, for their part, also on the alert for opportunities to checkmate Louis in the Southern Netherlands. At the Peace of Ryswick they wrung from him permission to negotiate with Spain about keeping Dutch garrisons in certain fortresses inside the Southern Netherlands to serve as a barrier against future French aggression : this Dutch 'Barrier' was arranged in 1698,[130] and its security and extension became one of the major aims in Dutch foreign policy from that date.[131] When Max Emmanuel was made governor-general of the Southern Netherlands, the Dutch held conversations with him for the purpose of securing the country against France once Carlos II should die. The secret treaty that France and Europe believed the two parties entered into has recently been shown as much more likely to be genuine than not, in spite of the denials of the elector and the States General when the news leaked out.[132] It was the fear of such arrangements that a French minister used, in confidential conversation with a Swedish diplomat at Versailles, as an explanation for the entry of Louis' troops into the Barrier towns in 1701.[133] The official reason given (which also must be allotted some weight because of the French need to show Spain that Philip V would bring power in his train) was that the new king of Spain, Louis' grandson, had no need of help from the Dutch to defend his own.[134] It was this very entry that reduced William to despair, that he had to witness 'in one day and without a single battle being fought' the loss of the security for which he had worked for twenty-eight years; and it was this entry that decided both William and Heinsius for war.[135]

Great efforts had been made by these two statesmen and by Louis to avoid hostilities over the Spanish succession. Once Leopold's instransigence became known, the Maritime Powers adroitly avoided renewing their promise in the Grand Alliance of 1689 that they would work for the succession going in its entirety to the Austrian Habsburgs; but this did not particularly worry Vienna, where it was argued that in any war over the Spanish inheritance the English and the Dutch would eventually

be drawn to the side that fought against Louis XIV. William's
distrust of the emperor (whose efforts on behalf of the Stuarts in
the Nine Years War were not unknown in Whitehall)[136] and the
general concern at the growth of Habsburg power led to negotiations between William and Louis for a settlement of the succession, in which it was hoped the emperor would eventually join.
The death of Max Emmanuel's son, Joseph Ferdinand – grandson of Philip IV's daughter, Margareta Teresa – shortly after
the signature of the First Partition Treaty was a cruel disappoint-
ment to both monarchs. The candidature of the electoral prince
might, they hoped, have been enforced without recourse to arms,
by moral and diplomatic pressure alone, on Austria as well as on
Spain.[137] The partitioning aspect of the first treaty was relatively
slight: enough concessions for France in Italy to permit Louis
to offer exchanges to either Lorraine or Savoy (which would
realise one or other of the rectifications of the French frontier
discussed above), with hopes also of colonial concessions that
would benefit France's plans for maritime and commercial expansion.[138] The duchy of Milan was to go to Archduke Charles
as compensation for the Austrian Habsburgs. The Second Partition Treaty, by necessity choosing the younger of the emperor's
sons as king of Spain and heir to most of Carlos II's realm, inevitably widened Louis' claims for compensation. Spain would
now lose all her Italian possessions to the dauphin, and Louis
would be put in a position to achieve both the desired exchanges:
Lorraine as well as Savoy might be incorporated with France.[139]

A partition between the two main claimants, even with the
lion's share going to the Austrian Habsburgs, must be hurtful
to Spain's pride and might still not prove acceptable to Leopold.
The emperor had worked against the candidature of his grandson, the electoral prince, in Madrid even when the whole succession was involved; and he proved adamant in refusing accession
to the Second Partition Treaty: the perils of war were far
preferable. In his view he would lose nothing by insisting that
the whole succession should go to the younger of his two sons
since William and Heinsuis would support him, rather than the
Bourbons, in any clash of arms. He bargained also on the influence of Carlos II's German wife, related to the Austrian
house,[140] to have Archduke Charles declared heir to all Spain.
So, it is clear, did William and Heinsius; for when the struggle

for succession inside Spain had produced a will in favour – in the first place – of Louis' grandson, the duke of Anjou (Archduke Charles to be offered the entire monarchy only if the French candidate refused), both these statesmen were taken utterly by surprise. 'I had thought Spain was on our side; I never expected them to call in the French', was the comment of Heinsius.[141] Louis XIV's suspicions that the king of England and the Dutch grand pensionary had not pressed Vienna strongly to bring about acceptance of the Second Partition Treaty seem reasonably well founded. William thought of the partition treaty as a reinsurance that could be used to wring some sacrifices from Leopold once the succession was safe with the Austrian Habsburgs: Louis should be given enough to permit him to keep the peace, and the Maritime Powers would receive rich rewards as mediators.[142] That William did not regard the Second Partition Treaty as one to be enforced on Leopold with arms is evident from his outburst after Carlos's will became known: 'Having made the partition treaty in order to avoid a war, I am not fighting a war to enforce the treaty for France's benefit.'[143] Furthermore, once the offer of all Spain for the duke of Anjou had been accepted – though Louis took care not to let his grandson set foot on Spanish soil till the term given Leopold for entry into the Second Partition Treaty had expired[144] – William and Heinsius looked upon the treaty as one that might serve to wrest concessions both for the emperor and the Maritime Powers from Louis XIV.

Whether such concessions were possible, given the temper of the Spaniards (who had chosen Louis' grandson for their king not out of a love for France but out of a conviction that French power would be able to protect them against partition), is a debatable point. What is clear is that Louis felt he could not let the succession go by default to Austria; that would mean – in view of Leopold's refusal to give an undertaking that the empire of Charles V should not be restored – the certainty of encirclement, the probable loss of the gains of his own reign (the improved northern frontier; the incorporation of Alsace, Franche-Comté, Strasbourg; the four military routes through Lorraine), and the possibility of losing even the gains of 1648 and 1659. Louis, in accepting the will, gambled on peace and a Bourbon family alliance that would give him a friendly neighbour in the south, favourable opportunities for French commerce in the

Spanish empire overseas, and, in the future, exchanges of territory that would improve France's own borders.[145] Above all, he
felt that the balance of Europe would become redressed: the
increase in power and *gloire* that the Turkish wars had brought
to Leopold would now be compensated for by a Bourbon family
alliance in the west. That Louis did not enjoy the peaceful
possession of the Spanish succession was in part due to the accidents of history, such as the death of James II at a particularly
delicate time of Anglo-Dutch negotiations with France. But it
was also due to Louis' own mistakes: he could have made it
much clearer to the Maritime Powers than he did that the
reservation of Philip's rights to the French crown was intended
to keep the Orléans branch of the royal family distant from
succession and was dictated by hopes of keeping Philip, as king
of Spain, in some dependence on a France he might – if death
removed the nearer heirs—rule once he had made alternative
provision for Spain. As it was, he raised the spectre of Charles
V's empire under Bourbon sway. Nor must the insistence of
William and Heinsius that he should not enjoy the peaceful
possession of the will, except at the price of concessions to them
in respect of Barrier towns and overseas trading posts, be forgotten. Louis' inability (quite apart from his unwillingness) to
make immediate sacrifices of Spanish territory, either to the
Maritime Powers or to the Austrian Habsburgs, proved Leopold
right in his analysis of the situation: the Dutch and the English
would be driven to support him rather than Louis in a struggle
over the Spanish succession, provided he took the initiative in
resisting a French candidature. As soon as Philip reached Madrid,
Leopold prepared to send his troops into Italy to take over the
Spanish possessions there for his family. The Grand Alliance
followed in 1701, and general war broke out when the preparations of the Maritime Powers were complete in 1702.

That Louis, after this hardest of all the wars that France had
to fight during his reign, achieved a reasonable compromise
peace in 1713–14, he owed in part to the accidents of history –
such as the change of government in England in 1710 – but also
to his own and his advisers' clever use of the opportunities that
this and other happenings presented, and to the country's grasp
of what was at stake: not Spain, but the security of France.
After the settlements of 1713–14, Philip remained king of Spain

and of Spain overseas; but the areas that had been the particular concern of the partition-treaty negotiations, the Southern Netherlands and the Spanish possessions in Italy, were detached from that crown to move – more or less permanently – into the orbit of the Austrian Habsburgs. Spain also had to give concessions to the English, if not to the Dutch (out-distanced and even cheated by the Tories in the peace negotiations), in respect of trade; and some, at least, of England's claims to Mediterranean possessions – long since postulated[146] – were satisfied by the acquisition of Gibraltar and Port Mahon. France herself had to sacrifice land overseas that she had, in Louis' own reign, taken from England.[147] But the European gains of Louis' reign were safeguarded, and the French maintained their interpretation of 1648. In contrast, the Dutch lost their hoped-for gains from the Thirty Years War : Cleves, and Spanish Guelders – to which the Treaty of Münster had given them a claim – went to Prussia.[148] Charles XII, on his return from Turkey at the end of 1714, fought hard in defence of Sweden's German possessions, Prussia and Hanover having joined the anti-Swedish coalition to obtain, respectively, Swedish Pomerania and Bremen and Verden. To keep Sweden, the fellow guarantor of 1648, in the Empire, Louis entered in April 1715 into a subsidy-treaty with Charles XII. The death of Louis in September of that year certainly weakened Sweden's cause in Germany. By the peace treaties of the Great Northern War, 1719–21 (after the death of Charles in 1718), Sweden was left with Wismar and a small part of Pomerania as footholds in the Empire; but she was no longer a power to be reckoned with in German affairs.

Louis XIV's attitude to his fellow monarchs was, naturally enough, deeply anchored in the past. His policies in respect of the frontiers, the Empire and Italy – even towards the pope[149] – were in general conditioned by those pursued by Richelieu and Mazarin; the technique of the reunions was in the Capetian tradition of his predecessors, as were his efforts (successful in the case or Orange, unsuccessful in the case of Avignon) to absorb foreign enclaves on French soil. He did not, however, slavishly follow established patterns or lines; he tried to avoid what he regarded, in the light of experience, to have been mistakes in the past. To give an example : Louis looked upon Mazarin's alliance with Cromwell as being, in part, responsible

for Charles II's vacillating policy after 1660 – this, it has been
suggested, helps to explain the recognition of James Stuart as
king in 1701 as a form of reinsurance for the future.[150] That
Louis learned from his own mistakes has already been proposed
in our discussion of the Southern Netherlands (though he did not
realise the sensitivity of the Dutch fully enough to avoid further
mistakes in 1701); and he did try to avoid falling into traps that
had proved dangerous in the past. In 1700, when Louis sent
Villars to Vienna to attempt securing Leopold's accession to
the Second Partition Treaty, he warned his ambassador not to
mention the strength and power, the *puissance*, of France, nor
boast of its armed forces or its good finances, lest Vienna should
become frightened and set about forging coalitions against
France – though he was warned not to make France seem so weak
and poor that the dignity of king and country would be impaired.[151] In 1714, to give another example, when Louis sent
a French diplomat to Italy to inspect, discreetly, the future
second wife of Philip V, the envoy was reminded that the
preference of Philip and his first wife for French advisers had
alienated Spaniards, and he was enjoined to lead the new bride
into better ways: in a perceptive instruction Louis summed up
what he had learned from the sometimes strained relationship
of Spain and France during the War of the Spanish Succession.[152]

We are left with the problem of why Louis XIV – were he
as relatively sensible and moderate as this paper has argued –
has had such a bad press. He certainly was insensitive at times
to the reactions of fellow monarchs and other nations, but in
this he was not alone: Professor Kossmann has reminded us
that 'the Dutch had no idea of the intense feelings of jealousy
and fear that their success had aroused in others'.[153] Louis,
like all rulers, at times misjudged situations. His most serious
misjudgement is probably that of the situation in the Empire
after 1689. His dispatches to French diplomats, and in particular
to Avaux in the important years 1694–7, are full of arguments
that he genuinely felt must carry weight with the Swedes and
the German princes: he tried to rouse the king of Sweden
against a Leopold who was becoming so powerful that he might
not only throw France and Sweden out of the Empire but
also subdue the German princes and rob Germany of her liberties.[154] Similar arguments are found in letters to French diplomats

inside the Empire.[155] It does not look as if Louis realised that, in an age of individual ambitious drives among the German princes, the emperor had the upper hand because he was the fountain of honour and titles inside the Empire. One by one the German princes gave Leopold their support: Hanover in 1692 for the electoral title; Saxony in 1697 for support for its prince to be elected king of Poland; Brandenburg in 1701 for the title of 'King in Prussia'; while George I of Hanover–England and Frederick William of Brandenburg–Prussia were kept on tenterhooks, dancing to at least some of the tunes of Charles VI, by their need to obtain imperial investitures for their Swedish conquests.

The accepted view of the consequences for French economic life of the revocation of the Edict of Nantes has recently, by the studies of Scoville and Lüthy, undergone some necessary revision.[156] But on Louis' relations with the Protestant powers of Europe, the evidence that comes to light points to an ever-deepening distrust and horror of Louis after 1685. Geyl has shown how the Dutch, abandoning the cynical 'Tut tut, what does religion matter in state affairs'[157] of the pre-1685 years, entrenched themselves in a belief that Louis plotted not only universal monarchy but also universal religion to be imposed on Europe by his arms. This belief was reinforced by Clause 4 in the Ryswick Treaty which decreed that in the reunions returned by France to their rightful owners the Catholic religion should prevail. Srbik has shown how great a share Leopold and his Jesuit advisers had in this clause;[158] but though some contemporaries blamed Lillieroot, the Swedish mediator, for not preventing the clause,[159] Louis has carried most of the blame. Belief in the plot of resurgent Catholicism has found some support in modern research. Louis and Leopold had a common interest in the Stuart cause and in its concomitant, a Catholic England, which facilitated those negotiations between them that so worried William III during the Nine Years War.[160] A similar Catholic-front element can be discerned in the 1714–15 negotiations between Versailles and Vienna, when Louis was anxious to re-insure against George I restarting the war against France, and Charles VI was alarmed at the growing power of the Protestant princes in the north of the Empire.[161] It is well known that fear of Louis as the instrument of a counter-reformation was

spread by Huguenot refugees. More important, possibly, is the
fact that many Dutchmen and Englishmen, settled as traders
in French ports, felt the full force of the revocation – either because they had become naturalised or because they (though
remaining subjects of their own country) had French wives who,
with their children, were not exempt from the Edict of Fontainebleau. Their bitter complaints aggravated feeling against
Louis in London and at The Hague.[162] William III was also
concerned at the difficulties his restored principality of Orange
encountered as an enclave of tolerance in an intolerant France.[163]
The spread of persecution and brutality to the Savoyard Protestants (instigated by Louis, who objected to French Huguenots
settling across the border in such numbers that they constituted
a threat to the security of France) further alienated European
opinion. Louis' argument is given some support by the fact that
the Allies in the War of the Spanish Succession helped to rouse
the Protestants of the Cévennes (at a time when persecution
had already ceased) against Louis. The tolerant attitude of William
in religious matters and his genuine concern and attempts to help
Protestants in trouble for the sake of their religion (clearly
evidenced in his correspondence with Heinsius)[164] tends to make
him rather than Louis the more acceptable character to a tolerant
age, even when it has been shown that Louis personally was
not the instigator of persecution inside France and was ignorant
of much that happened.[165]

In other and more personal spheres Louis irritated contemporaries – at least in the earlier part of his reign – as well as
posterity. There is a telling comment by one English diplomat
who disliked and feared 'this Great Comet that is risen of late,
the French King, who expects not only to be gazed at but
adored by the whole world'.[166] Most nations struck medals, put
up monuments, or otherwise remembered their victories : France
was annoyed by the Dutch inscription on a medal struck after
the Peace of Aix-la-Chapelle;[167] the English took offence at
Dutch commemoration of their Chatham victories; but a great
many nations felt hurt by the monument in the Place des Vic-
toires which celebrated the Peace of 1679. Rumour even had it
that allies no less than former enemies had been humiliated
in verse and paint on that occasion to enhance the glory of
France.[168] Charles XII, with his aversion to statues of living

rulers, felt a slight contempt for a monarch who praised himself by having statues put up in his own lifetime : such *gloire* should be left for posterity to bestow.

Deeper than such resentments went the distrust of Louis, bred by the progressive interpretation of 1648; by the several occupations of Lorraine which pointed to permanent designs (the Dutch, when Louis' inclination to incorporate Lorraine became apparent, harked back to a statement of his from 1670 specifically denying such designs and told him they would 'rather die' than let him realize his plans); by the memory of the War of Devolution, which rendered Louis suspect in the Palatinate : what might he not do with the claim of his sister-in-law's *immeubles* at a time when the legal heir, as settled by the 1648 treaty, was the father-in-law and supporter of the emperor? From this distrust grew the desire of all who felt threatened to contain Louis by united diplomatic and, if need be, military action : William III's 'indivisibility of the peace' became their slogan, at least as long as fear was strong. Yet, towards the end of Louis' reign relations mellowed between him and Europe. Old enemies died : William III, who had inherited Lisola's mantle as leader of the anti-French coalitions; then Leopold of Austria; then his son Joseph. The new emperor, Charles VI, was both less 'German' and less 'Austrian Habsburg' in the early years of his reign than his father and brother had been. Heinsius and the Dutch were shocked enough at English behaviour in the last years of the Spanish Succession War, and bothered enough by Charles VI's intransigence in the Southern Netherlands over their Barrier, to take a better view of Louis. Saint-Simon noted, with some surprise, that not one adverse comment on Louis was heard from the capitals of Europe when his death was announced.[169]

Louis' relationship with France is being reassessed. As Asher has shown,[170] specialist studies are undermining the image of the all-powerful autocrat at home. The tyrant abroad, the aspirer after universal monarchy, may also diminish somewhat in stature when seen in the proper perspective permitted by new lines of research. The textbook picture of the just downfall of the tyrant, the Louis who after a long reign of aggression in Europe met with utter failure at the end of his life, also needs some realignment. This paper ventures to suggest that Louis XIV was, on the one hand, more frightened than has been realised, and, on the other hand, moderately successful in achieving, after hard struggles, the relatively modest goals he set for himself – or fate set for him. The objectives of 1648 were secured in 1678–9 and not lost in 1713–14;[171] a Bourbon dynasty in Spain helped to safeguard the eastern frontier as completed by 1697 and made possible the later family compacts; the principality of Orange was absorbed;[172] the four military routes through Lorraine were kept, and the incorporation of that duchy – by 1738 achieved in principle along the lines of exchange-equivalents in Italy – was laid down by Louis.[173] The deepest concern of Louis not to lose *gloire* by bringing his country loss of territory and of rights was, at least in Europe, gratified.

NOTES

1 The formal reign after coming of age (1653–1715) is longer than any recorded in Europe till the early twentieth century, when Queen Victoria and Emperor Francis Joseph outdistanced Louis.

2 Louis' blood relationship to his fellow monarchs is traced in A. Lossky's chapter, 'International Relations' in vol. vi of the *New Cambridge Modern History*, hereafter cited as *N.C.M.H.*

3 *Recueil des Instructions données aux Ambassadeurs et Ministres de France . . .* (hereafter cited as *Recueil*) vol. i, *Autriche* (Paris, 1884) p. 158, Mémoire for De Luc, 1715.

4 The formal title of the Dutch Republic was the States General of the United Provinces, often abbreviated to the United Provinces.

5 See Tessé to the Princesse des Ursins, 1 Mar 1701, in *Lettres inédites*, ed. M. C. Hippeau (Caen, 1862) p. 54, for the expression 'se faire république ou être roi'.

6 For England being regarded as a republic in Cromwell's time, see G. Zeller, *Les Temps modernes*, ii, *De Louis XIV à 1789*, 'Histoire des relations internationales', vol. iii (Paris, 1955) pt 2, p. 32.

7 The title of 'Leurs Hautes Puissances' (Their High Mightinesses) was, however, not conceded (or recognised, from the Dutch point of view) till after Louis' death – again at a time of rivalry for Dutch support; see R. M. Hatton, *Diplomatic Relations between Great Britain and the Dutch Republic, 1714–1721* (London, 1950) p. 235.

8 P. Höynck, *Frankreich und seine Gegner auf dem Nymwegener Friedens-Kongress* (Bonn, 1960) pp. 49ff. The prince was Duke Johann Friedrich of Hanover and Leibniz wrote under the pseudonym Caesarinus Furstenius.

9 For Louis' discussion of his motives see M. Grouvelle (ed.), *Œuvres de Louis XIV*, 6 vols (Paris, 1806) i, 69ff (hereafter cited as *Œuvres*); for

expedients to avoid a stop to negotiations on this account see *Recueil*, I, *Autriche*, pp. 7–8, 43ff.

10 For the 1661 incident and the subsequent Spanish apology (since Louis was technically in the right) see Zeller, *De Louis XIV à 1789*, p. 17; cf. *Œuvres*, I, p. 129ff.

11 For the connection of this incident with the prestige quarrel with the House of Habsburg, see C. G. Picavet, *Les dernières années de Turenne* (Paris, 1919) p. 142ff.

12 See G. Spini, *N.C.M.H.*, v, p. 471 for this journey in 1685; cf. Zeller, *De Louis XIV à 1789*, p. 65, for the brilliant reception.

13 For the diplomatic etiquette of the period, see G. C. Picavet, *La Diplomatie française au temps de Louis XIV, 1661–1715* (Paris, 1930) pp. 73–146.

14 C. Wilson, *Profit and Power: A Study of England and the Dutch Wars* (London, 1957) pp. 88–9, 120–1. See H. Woodridge, *Sir William Temple: The Man and his Work* (Oxford, 1940) pp. 110–11, for a shooting incident on this account. The fundamental work on the subject is T. W. Fulton, *The Sovereignty of the Sea* (Edinburgh, 1911).

15 See D. H. Somerville, *The King of Hearts. Charles Talbot, Duke of Shrewsbury* (London, 1962) p. 91.

16 Höynck, *Nymwegener Friedens-Kongress*, p. 27.

17 For Louis' attitude to the imperial title, see *Œuvres*, I, p. 75ff.

18 See, for example, *Recueil*, VIII, *Russie*, I (Paris, 1896) p. 47ff, 54ff, for liberal use, in writings and conversation, of 'le grand seigneur Czar', 'notre affectioné Frère', and 'Sa Majesté le Tsar' in 1657 and 1680. Cf. the difficulties made by Leopold toward Russian rulers, investigated by K. Meyer, 'Kaiserliche Grossmächtigkeit', in *Rossia Externa. Festgabe P. Johansen* (Marburg, 1963) pp. 115–74.

19 *Recueil*, I, *Autriche*, p. 51; cf. P. S. Lachs, *The Diplomatic Corps under Charles II and James II* (New Brunswick, 1966) pp. 110–11, for the solution of a problem of protocol in Paris.

20 Woodbridge, *William Temple*, pp. 172–3.

21 Höynck, *Nymwegener Friedens-Kongress*, pp. 150–1.

22 Public Record Office (hereafter cited as P.R.O.), London, Treaty Papers, vol. 98, has much correspondence on expedients to avoid problems of etiquette, as well as premature recognitions. See, for example, Huxelles to Louis XIV, Utrecht, 6 Feb 1712.

23 See F. Carsten, *N.C.M.H.*, v, p. 447, for this incident in 1701.

24 A distinction can be made between Catholic rulers whose advisers, often Jesuits, encouraged them to put their concern for religion above their word to their fellow sovereigns; but it must not be pressed too far since the personal attitude of each ruler was the decisive factor. H. von Srbik, *Wien und Versailles, 1692–1697* (Munich, 1944) p. 119ff shows the soul-searching of Austrian statesmen when Leopold's signature on a specific document had to be denied to his allies.

25 M. Braubach, *Kurkölnische Miniaturen* (Münster, 1954) pp. 25–7; Höynck, *Nymwegener Friedens-Kongress*, pp. 21–3, 197ff.

26 See letter of Charles (in Swedish, but giving *gloire* in French) of March 1701, quoted in *Sveriges Historia*, IV, ed. M. Weibull, M. Höjer *et al.* (Stockholm, 1881) p. 530; cf. the reference to *heder* in his draft of December 1712 in *Konung Karl XII:s Egenhändiga Brev*, ed. E. Carlson (Stockholm, 1893) p. 393; cf. *Ehre* in the German edition, *Die eigenhändigen Briefe König Karls XII*, ed. E. Carlson (Berlin, 1894) p. 383.

27 See for example Höynck, *Nymwegener Friedens-Kongress*, p. 22, n. 28, for a certain course being 'au préjudice de notre honneur et réputation'.

28 Ibid., p. 78, for William's *Ehre*; see also A. J. Bourde, 'Louis XIV et Angleterre', *XVIIᵉ Siècle*, nos 46–7 (1960) 58, devoted to 'Problèmes de politique étrangère sous Louis XIV'; cf. the character-sketches of William in P. Geyl, *Oranje en Stuart* (Utrecht, 1959) pp. 381–537, and in the same author's *Kernproblemen van onze Geschiedenis* (Utrecht, 1937) pp. 116–34.

29 Srbik, *Wien und Versailles*, p. 105.

30 Picavet, *Turenne*, p. 429, Louis' letter to Turenne of 20 May 1675 ('le bien de mon service et la gloire des vos armes'). For William III's use of *gloire* when discussing the negotiator's craft, see *Œuvres*, VI, p. 519.

31 The clearest expression can be found in Louis' 'Reflections on the Role of a King' of 1679; see the English translation edited by J. Longnon, *A King's Lesson in Statecraft: Louis XIV's Letters to his Heirs* (London, 1924) p. 170. Cf. Louis XIV in *Œuvres*, II, p. 455, for 'le bien et la puissance de L'Etat', and p. 470, for 'la gloire et la sureté de l'Etat'.

32 M. A. Thomson, *Some Developments in English Historiography during the Eighteenth Century* (London, 1957) p. 5, and G. Davies, 'The Control of British Foreign Policy by William III', *Essays on the Later Stuarts* (San Marino, 1958).

33 See P. Geyl, *The Netherlands in the Seventeenth Century*, pt 2, *1648–1715* (London, 1964) pp. 127–38, 147–52, for William's methods in this respect; cf. M. A. M. Franken, *Coenraad van Beuningen's Politieke en Diplomatieke Aktiviteiten in de Jaren 1667–1684* (Groningen, 1966) pp. 261–2, summing up in English his detailed examination of William's relationship to Amsterdam.

34 See Longnon, *Statecraft*, p. 59, for Louis' 'perpetual uneasiness' at praise that he did not feel he had earned. Cf. R. Clark, *Sir William Trumbull in Paris, 1685–86* (Cambridge, 1938) p. 15, quoting Savile's opinion that Louis did not like 'too gross' flattery. William and Charles were also suspicious of flattery.

35 See R. M. Hatton, 'Charles XII and the Great Northern War', in *N.C.M.H.*, VI; cf. Charles's own letters (note 26 above) nos 71–4.

36 Somerville, *Shrewsbury*, p. 115, William to Shrewsbury in July 1696, at a moment of acute financial difficulty: 'If you cannot devise expedients to send contributions or procure credit, all is lost and I must go to the Indies.'

37 For tears at the meeting of ministers in 1709, see A. M. de Boislisle (ed.), *Mémoires de Saint-Simon*, 43 vols (Paris, 1879–1930) XXVII, p. 44

and notes; for tears in the king's private room in the presence of Villars in 1712, see *Mémoires du maréchal de Villars*, quoted in W. H. Lewis, *The Splendid Century* (London, 1953) p. 481.

38 Said to General Schwerin: see document (in Swedish) edited by T. Westrin, *Historisk Tidskrift*, xv (1895) 341–2.

39 William to Heinsius, Hampton Court, 8 Feb 1701, *Archives ou correspondance inédite de la Maison d'Orange-Nassau*, vol. iii, ed. F. J. L. Krämer (Leyden, 1909) p. 407.

40 Srbik, *Wien und Versailles*, pp. 105, 204. Cf. L. André, *Louis XIV et l'Europe* (Paris, 1950) p. 292, that Leopold, on being pressed by Villars to accede to the Second Partition Treaty, reported that there was no war the perils of which would not be preferable to those implied in accession.

41 For an assessment of Louis as a military man, see Rule (ed.), *Louis XIV and the Craft of Kingship*, pp. 196–223, contribution by John B. Wolf.

42 Woodbridge, *William Temple*, p. 118: 'He had one way still left not to see its [his country's] ruin completed, which is to lie in the last dike', and p. 171: he would 'rather die' than make a particular agreement.

43 'Mémoires d'un Suédois qui a servi le roi Charles XII', printed (in the original French) under the title 'Die Erinnerungen Axel von Löwens', ed. A. Adler and S. Bonnesen, in *Karolinska Förbundets Årsbok* (1929) pp. 17–100 (quotation from pp. 25–6).

44 G. Zeller, *L'organisation défensive des frontières du Nord et de l'Est au XVIIᵉ siècle* (Nancy, 1928) p. 50; but see Lewis, *The Splendid Century*, p. 481, for Louis' comment to Villars in the spring of 1712 that – if things went badly – they might scrape up enough troops for a last effort 'in which we will either die together or save the State'.

45 Some of these phrases have been translated into English in F. Bengtsson, *The Life of Charles XII* (London, 1960) e.g. pp. 11–12. Note title of the American edition, echoing one of them: *The Sword Does Not Lie*.

46 E. Kossmann, *N.C.M.H.*, v, p. 297; cf. Geyl, *The Netherlands, 1648–1715*, p. 134.

47 There is much correspondence on this problem in the Archives des Affaires Etrangères (Paris), Correspondance Politique, Suède, vols 70–82; and Public Record Office (London), Foreign Office Miscellanies 31 (several volumes of mainly unused Avaux entry-books, letters received, etc.); see in particular F.O. 95, vol. 576, Louis to Avaux, 20 Sep and 15 Nov 1693.

48 *Nils Reuterholms Journal*, ed. S. Landahl, in *Historiska Handlingar*, 36, 2 (Stockholm, 1957) pp. 80–1 (hereafter cited as *Reuterholms Journal*), where Reuterholm enters a 'relation' from Paris of 10 Oct 1701 which he had been permitted to see in Hanover. This amplifies G. H. Jones, *The Main Stream of Jacobitism* (Cambridge, Mass., 1954) p. 59ff, and C. Petrie, *The Marshal Duke of Berwick* (London, 1951) p. 70.

49 André, *Louis XIV et l'Europe*, p. 320.

50 This is often stated, erroneously, possibly because of the Dutch and

English contemporary nickname for Louis, 'The Christian Turk'; see, for example, the [anon] pamphlet, a copy of which is in the British Museum, *The Most Christian Turk: Or a View of the Life and Bloody Reign of Louis XIV* (London, 1690).

51   See R. R. Betts, *N.C.M.H.*, v, p. 491.

52   Zeller, *De Louis XIV à 1789*, p. 20.

53   V.-L. Tapié, 'Quelques aspects généraux de la politique étrangère de Louis XIV', *XVIIe Siècle*, nos 46–7 (1960) pp. 19–20.

54   See R. Kann, *From Late Baroque to Romanticism* (London, 1960) pp. 38ff, that Italian and German contemporary writers praised Austria as the standard-bearer of the Imperial anti-Islam mission in order to stem anti-Habsburg currents in the Empire. Cf. Spini, *N.C.M.H.*, v, p. 471: 'To strengthen the Empire against the Turks meant also, implicitly, to strengthen the Habsburgs against the Bourbons.'

55   Hippeau, *Lettres inédites*, pp. 46–8, Tessé to Harcourt, letters from Milan, 15, 27 Feb 1702, that people there were infatuated with 'la grandeur de l'Empereur' and everything German was regarded as wonderful. Cf. A. Wandruszka, *Österreich und Italien im 18 Jahrhundert* (Vienna, 1963) p. 16, on the Italians in 1701 shouting 'Viva l'Imperatore!'

56   For Franco-Turkish relations, see K. Koehler, *Die orientalische Politik Ludwigs XIV* (Leipzig, 1907) and J. Stoye, *The Siege of Vienna* (London, 1964) p. 228ff.

57   The visitors of high rank who came to Paris are noted in the memoirs of Beauvillier, who arranged the receptions for them: see M. Langlois, *Louis XIV et la cour* (Paris, [1929]) p. 9ff.

58   See *Œuvres*, VI, p. 65 ff, for letters between 1701 and 1711. Cf. letters quoted in the French studies of the War of the Spanish Succession: A. Baudrillart, *Philippe V et la cour de France*, 5 vols (Paris, 1889–1901) and A. Legrelle, *La Diplomatie française et la Succession d'Espagne*, 4 vols (Ghent, 1888–92).

59   François de Callières, *On the Manner of Negotiating with Princes* (South Bend, Ind., 1963; reprint, with introduction by S. D. Kertesz, of the Whyte abbreviated translation [1919] of the 1716 edition) p. 137.

60   *Œuvres*, VI, pp. 518–20, Callières to the Marquise d'Huxelles, 12 Nov 1697, on the meeting that had taken place on 9 November. For Vauban's disapproval, see A. Rebelliau, *Vauban* (Paris, 1962) p. 134.

61   These can be found in *Letters of William III and of Louis XIV and Their Ministers, 1697–1700*, ed. P. Grimblot, 2 vols (London, 1848).

62   Grimblot (ed.), *Letters*, I, pp. 456–64, Tallard to Louis, London, 8 May 1698; pp. 464–6, William to Heinsius, Windsor, 29 Apr/9 May 1698; pp. 471–5 (p. 474 for the quotation used in text), William to Portland, Windsor, 2/12 May 1698.

63   *Recueil*, II, *Suède* (Paris, 1885) p. 274.

64   H. Rowen, *The Ambassador Prepares for War: The Dutch Embassy of Arnauld de Pomponne, 1669–1672* (The Hague, 1957) p. 8.

65   Grimblot (ed.), *Letters*, I, p. 396, Portland to William, 20 Apr 1698.

66 For the chronology of the *Mémoires*, see P. Sonnino, 'The Dating and Authorship of Louis XIV's *Mémoires*', *French Historical Studies*, III (1964) 303–37.

67 Later implied criticism of himself can also be found, for example *Recueil*, XIII, *Hollande*, II (Paris, 1923) p. 273: 'Chacun peut se tromper dans le choix de la route qu'il croit la plus sûre pour la paix.'

68 See, for example, H. Gillot, *Le Règne de Louis XIV et l'opinion publique en Allemagne* (Paris, 1914); F. Kleyser, *Die Flugschriftenkamp gegen Ludwig XIV. zur Zeit des pfälzischen Krieges* (Berlin, 1935); P. J. W. van Malssen, *Louis XIV d'après les pamphlets répandus en Hollande* (Amsterdam, 1936).

69 The belief, both contemporary and later, in Louis' serious attempts to obtain the imperial title owes much to Mazarin's policy in 1657–8, for which see S. F. N. Gie, *Die Kandidatur Ludwigs XIV bei der Kaiserwahl vom Jahre 1658* (Berlin, 1916); for research into the 1669–70 and the 1679–82 periods, concluding that Louis did not strive for the title, see W. Platzhoff, 'Ludwig XIV, das Kaisertum and die europäische Krisis von 1683', *Historische Zeitschrift*, XXV (1909) 377–412.

70 R. R. Betts, *N.C.M.H.*, V, p. 493; cf. Kann, *A Study in Austrian Intellectual History*, p. 12 ff.

71 W. F. Church (ed.), *The Greatness of Louis XIV: Myth or Reality?* (Boston 1959) p. ix. For a similar judgement see D. Maland, *Europe in the Seventeenth Century* (London, 1966) p. 266: 'The reputed glory of Louis XIV's reign the perpetual warfare to aggrandise his fame and enlarge his territories . . .'. Cf. H. G. Judge (ed.), *Louis XIV* (London, 1965) p. 134.

72 The more recent surveys of the reign are (apart from Zeller, *De Louis XIV à 1789*, and the same author's chapter', 'French Diplomacy and Foreign Policy in their European Setting', *N.C.M.H.*, V, pp. 198–221): G. Pagès, *Les origines du XVIIIᵉ siècle au temps du Louis XIV, 1680–1715* (Paris, 1938); André, *Louis XIV et l'Europe*; R. Mousnier, *Les XVI et XVIIᵉ siècles, 1492–1715*, 'Histoire générale des civilisations', vol. IV (Paris, 1954); Tapié, 'Quelques aspects', is brief but has a balanced analysis; cf. the same author's chapter in *Propyläen Weltgeschichte*, vol. VII, ed. G. Mann and A. Nitschke (Berlin, Frankfurt, Vienna, 1965) entitled 'Das Zeitalter des Absolutismus Ludwigs XIV', pp. 277–348. The brief summary by W. Hubatsch, *Das Zeitalter des Absolutismus* (Braunschweig, 1962) p. 143, is worth noting because it stresses – in contrast to the usual conclusion that Louis' reign ended in total failure – that he died in the knowledge that the *Ansehen* of his country could be maintained.

73 The clearest expression of this is in Tapié, 'Quelques aspects', pp. 24–5.

74 Most strongly stressed by Mousnier, *Le XVI et XVIIᵉ siècles*, p. 280, who argues that up to 1678 the wars were defensive. Contrast this view with William III's comment on being warned by Charles II that the House of Austria ought to be more feared than the France of Louis XIV: he would share such a fear when the Spanish and Austrian Habsburgs began to violate the frontiers fixed by the Peace of the

Pyrenees – 'whenever that should happen, he should be as much a Frenchman as he was now a Spaniard, but not before' (quoted by Höynck, *Nymwegener Friedens-Kongress*, p. 15, n. 1).

75 Mignet was the chief protagonist of the former explanation, Lavisse of the latter. For a Dutch historiographical study of French views on Louis XIV (with a French summary) see P. de Vries, *Het Beeld van Lodewijk XIV in de Franse Geschiedschrijving* (Amsterdam, 1948); for works on the reign in the twentieth century, see J. B. Wolf, 'The Reign of Louis XIV: A Selected Bibliography of Writings since the War of 1914–18', *Journal of Modern History*, XXXVI (1964) 127–47.

76 For the denial of any pattern see Zeller, *De Louis XIV à 1789*, p. 18 ff; cf. André, *Louis XIV et l'Europe*, p. 2 ff.

77 For a summary of Louis' medical history see Rule (ed.), *Louis XIV and the Craft of Kingship*, pp. 132–54, contribution by C. D. O'Malley.

78 Geyl, *The Netherlands, 1648–1715*, pp. 42–3, 99, 164: 'Louis XIV, who even in those years of intoxicating pride of power did not disdain the weapon of moderation'. Cf. J. B. Wolf, *The Emergence of the Great Powers* (New York, 1951) p. 60, that Louis, at the time of the Second Partition Treaty, 'proved reasonable beyond all expectation'.

79 Mark Thomson's articles touching on Louis are reprinted (together with a paper hitherto unpublished) in *William III and Louis XIV. Essays by and for Mark A. Thomson*, ed. Ragnhild Hatton and J. S. Bromley (Liverpool, Toronto, 1968).

80 Srbik, *Wien und Versailles, passim*.

81 See in particular M. Braubach, 'Die Reichsbarriere', *Zeitschrift für Geschichte Oberrheins*, Neue Folge, vol. 50 (Karlsruhe, 1936) pp. 481–530; text and bibliographical notes in the first three volumes of the same author's *Prinz Eugen von Savoyen* (Munich, 1963–4); also contributions by W. Engels, W. Scheur and H. Weber in *Spiegel der Geschichte. Festgabe für Max Braubach*, ed. K. Repson and S. Skalweit (Münster, 1964).

82 Several unpublished theses that may soon appear in print deal with these areas, e.g. those by J. Herley and J. Fayard in France and by J. F. O'Connor in the United States; among published works, note C. Badalo-Dulong, *Trente ans de diplomatie française en Allemagne: Louis XIV et l'Electeur de Mayence 1648–1678* (Paris, 1956) and R. Pillorget, 'La France et l'électorat de Trèves au temps de Charles-Gaspard de la Leyen, II: 1658–79', *Revue d'histoire diplomatique*, vol. 78 (1964) 118–48; cf. below pp. 115–32.

83 F. Ford, *Strasbourg in Transition, 1648–1789* (Cambridge, Mass., 1958).

84 A. Veenendaal, *Het Engels-Nederlands Condominium in de Zuidelijke Nederlanden, 1706–16*, pt I (Utrecht, 1945), has so far carried the study to 1710. Cf. the forthcoming work by J. Rule on Lord Orrery and the Low Countries.

85 D. Coombs, *The Conduct of the Dutch: British Opinion and the Dutch Alliance during the War of the Spanish Succession* (The Hague, 1958). Cf. the study of British opinion of Austria during the same war by H. Kospach, 'Englische Stimmen über Österreich und Prinz Eugen

während des spanischen Erbfolgekrieges', *Mitteilungen des Institutes für Österreich. Geschichtsforschung*, XXIII (1965) 39–62.

86 J. G. Stork-Penning, *Het Grote Werk* (Groningen, 1958) and the same author's 'Het gedrag van de Staten 1711', *Bijdragen voor de Geschiedenis der Nederlanden*, XVIII (1963–4) 193–229.

87 See in particular Jones, *Jacobitism*, n. 48, and bibliography there given.

88 See his *Louis XIV, William III, and the Baltic Crisis of 1683* (Berkeley, Los Angeles, 1954) and 'La Picquetière's Projected Mission to Moscow in 1682 and the Swedish Policy of Louis XIV', *Essays in Russian History: A Collection Dedicated to George Vernadsky*, ed. A. P. Ferguson and A. Levin (Hamden, Conn., 1964). His contribution to Hatton and Bromley (eds), *William III and Louis XIV*, pp. 7–23, contains a more general analysis of Louis' policy in the 1680s ('Maxims of State in Louis XIV's Foreign Policy in the 1680s').

89 For Spain, see the chapter by J. Regla, 'Spain and Her Empire' in *N.C.M.H.*, v; J. H. Elliott, *Imperial Spain 1469–1716* (London, 1963) p. 365 ff; H. Kamen, 'Melchior de Macanaz and the foundation of Bourbon power in Spain', *English Historical Review*, LXXXI (1966) 699–716. For the Austrian Habsburgs see R. R. Betts, 'The Habsburg Lands', in *N.C.M.H.*, v, and Tapié 'Quelques aspects', p. 24. Proof of Habsburg financial power during the War of the Spanish Succession has been given by G. Otruba, 'Die Bedeutung englischer Subsidien und Antizipationen für die Finanzen Österreichs 1701 bis 1748', *Vierteljahrschrift für Sozial und Wirtschaftsgeschichte*, 51 (1964) 192 ff, where the author is, however, too sweeping in his contention that there were no subsidies, only loans, in the War of the Spanish Succession; for payment of arrears of subsidies by Great Britain, see R. M. Hatton, *Diplomatic Relations between Great Britain and the Dutch Republic, 1714–1721*, p. 163.

90 C. Nordmann, *La Crise du Nord au début du XVIIIᵉ siècle* (Paris, 1962) starts after the peace settlements of 1713–14. Since my paper of 1964, an issue of the *Revue d'histoire diplomatique*, 79 (1965) has, in commemoration of the 250th anniversary of Louis XIV's death, been devoted to three articles on his diplomacy, and two of these, by J. Bérenger and Janine Fayard, appear in translation in the present volume.

91 See, for example, Rowen, *Pomponne*, and J. Rule's chapter on Torcy in Hatton and Bromley (eds), *William III and Louis XIV*, pp. 213–36. Of the French studies, L. André, *Michel Le Tellier et Louvois* (Paris, 1942) and G. Livet, *L'Intendance d'Alsace sous Louis XIV, 1648–1715*, 2 vols (Paris, 1954; or 1956, 1 vol.) are particularly relevant for foreign policy.

92 Picavet, *Turenne*.

93 Rebelliau, *Vauban*.

94 Zeller, *Frontières*; see also his 'Politique extérieure et diplomatie sous Louis XIV', *Revue d'histoire moderne*, VI (1931) 124–43.

95 See P. Moraw, 'Kaiser und Geschichtsschreiber um 1700', *Die Welt als Geschichte*, 22 (1962) 162–203, and 23 (1963) 93–136.

96   Kann, *Study in Austrian Intellectual History*, p. 4 ff; A. Wandruszka, *Das Haus Habsburg* (Stuttgart, 1956) pp. 142–57 for Habsburg rulers from 1648 to 1740, with bibliographical references p. 211. An English translation of this book, *The House of Habsburg*, appeared in London in 1964.

97   The best guide to these are, for the pre-1914 period, the footnotes to O. Redlich, *Weltmacht des Barock. Österreich in der Zeit Kaiser Leopold I 1658–1705* (Vienna, 1961; fourth edition of the 1921 work, which was written before the First World War), and H. Hantsch, *Geschichte Österreichs*, II (Vienna, [1950]) with bibliographical notes; for twentieth-century research, see the bibliography and footnotes of M. Braubach's *Prinz Eugen*, vols I–III.

98   See in particular Braubach, I, p. 99 ff for Leopold; II, p. 130 ff for Joseph; and III, p. 56 ff for Charles VI; for Leopold see also Stoye, *The Siege*, p. 53 ff.

99   So will the studies in progress by S. Shapiro (California) on Franco-Austrian relations, 1679–84; W. Slottman (Berkeley) on Paget; A. D. Maclachlan (Cambridge) on the Peace of Utrecht; D. McKay (London) on Anglo-Austrian relations during the early years of Charles VI's reign.

100   For such work, see J. Rule, 'The Old Regime in America: A Review of Recent Interpretations of France in America', *William and Mary Quarterly*, XIX (Oct 1962) 575–600; cf. for European interest in this topic W. Gembruch, 'Zwei Denkschriften zur Kolonial und Aussenpolitik Frankreichs aus den Jahren 1699 und 1700', *Historische Zeitschrift*, 195 (1962) 297–330.

101   The book mentioned in note 7 above is one outcome of this; so are *Charles XII King of Sweden* (London, 1968; New York, 1969); *War and Peace, 1680–1720* (London, 1969); *Europe in the Age of Louis XIV* (London, New York, 1969); *Louis XIV and his World* (London, New York, 1972).

102   See my 'Gratifications and Foreign Policy', *William III and Louis XIV*, pp. 68–94.

103   This series is still in progress; vol. XXVIII, in three parts, dealing with the Empire (ed. G. Livet), appeared in 1962, 1963 and 1966, and vol. XXV, 2, *Angleterre*, 3: *1698–1791* (ed. P. Vaucher) in 1965.

104   *Acta Pacis Westphalicae*, ed. M. Braubach and K. Repgen, of which seven volumes have so far appeared (Munich, 1962 onwards). The first is most useful for our present purpose: see in particular pp. 221–32, 259–300, 477 ff. A fine study by F. Dickmann, *Der Westfälische Frieden*, was published in 1959, at Münster, with a revised edition in 1965.

105   N. Larsson, *Om stadens Bremens ställning till Sveriges krone efter Westfaliska freden*, I (Stockholm, 1847) *passim*; G. Landberg, *Den svenska utrikespolitikens historia*, I: 3 (Stockholm, 1952) pp. 62–7.

106   H. Hantsch, *Reichsvizekanzler Friedrich Karl Graf von Schönborn 1674–1748* (Augsburg, 1929) p. 208.

107   Ford, *Strasbourg*, p. 28 ff. Ford has stressed how late (due to the war with Spain until 1659) France could begin to implement the 1648

treaty, and has analysed (pp. 58–9) the nervously defensive atmosphere in France and the genuine concern at the growing power of the Habsburgs. Cf. *Recueil*, I, *Autriche*, p. 91, Louis XIV's letter of 26 Sep 1681, and *Œuvres*, I, p. 217.

108 Braubach, 'Die Reichsbarriere', pp. 482–3, considers that the time of real opportunity to achieve Habsburg success occurred during the War of the Spanish Succession.

109 See *Reuterholms Journal*, pp. 22–3, for the comments by the Swedish diplomats Von Friesendorff and Snoilsky on Louis' behaviour. Cf. the opening of the English verse (anon.) of 1706 called 'The French Kings Rhodomontade', a copy of which is in the British Museum:

> Lorain a day,
> A week Burgundy won,
> Flanders a month;
> What would a year have done?
> Rochester's prophetic answer:
> Lorain you stole,
> By fraud you got Burgundy. . .

110 Höynck, *Nymwegener Friedens-Kongress*, p. 65 and n. 66; cf. *Recueil*, I. *Autriche*, pp. 119–20, Louis' comment of 22 July 1687.

111 Apart from land in Italy and the Netherlands, the following were at various times discussed as equivalents for Lorraine: the duchy of Mecklenburg, six secularised bishoprics in the Empire, some of the Swiss cantons, the principalities of Moldavia and Wallachia.

112 When Marlborough and Eugène had some success against the French lines in 1710, the political situation in England prevented them from acting boldly.

113 Srbik, *Wien und Versailles*, pp. 124–36.

114 Ibid., p. 156.

115 Tapié, 'Quelques aspects', p. 21.

116 Srbik, *Wien und Versailles*, p. 95 ff; G. Livet, 'Louis XIV et l'Allemagne', *XVIIᵉ Siècle* (1960) pp. 41–2; see below, pp. 60–81.

117 Manifesto, 'To the Governors of the Provinces', translated into English in Petrie, *Berwick*, pp. 235–7. Cf. the Eugène plan to conquer Spain 'in the heart of France': G. Otruba, 'Prinz Eugen and Marlborough', *Österreich und die Angelsachsische Welt*, ed. O. Hietsch (Vienna, 1961) pp. 9–27.

118 For the cautionary towns demanded see Stork-Penning, *Het Grote Werk*, p. 260 ff, and Braubach, *Prinz Eugen*, II, p. 277 ff. Cf. for the 1710 discussion on the same topic Stork-Penning, p. 312 ff and Braubach, II, p. 332 ff.

119 Zeller, *De Louis XIV à 1789*, p. 115.

120 By J. de Stuers, published in Geneva, 1949.

121 In the Franco-Dutch treaty of April 1662 the States General guaranteed the possession of Dunkirk to France. See Geyl, *The Netherlands, 1648–1715*, p. 58, for the Dutch failing to get as firm a guarantee for their occupation of Cleves. For the Dutch eastern frontier after 1648,

see A. C. J. de Vrankrijker, *Die Grenzen van Nederland* (Amsterdam, 1946) p. 101 ff.

122   That such annulment was possible is shown by the Spanish action in 1700.

123   The French share was further to comprise Naples, Sicily, Spain's African possessions and the Philippines.

124   Landberg, *Den svenska utrikespolitikens historia*, p. 168. Cf. for similar assurances in Germany, G. Pagès, *Contributions de la politique française en Allemagne* (Paris, 1905) pp. 38–40.

125   His two sons, of his third marriage, were born in 1678 and 1685. Wandruszka, *Das Haus Habsburg*, p. 152, has stressed the importance of the German marriage of Leopold (to Eleonora of Pfalz-Neuberg) producing sons, and also of the German marriages arranged for Joseph and Charles.

126   See P. Geyl, *History of the Low Countries: Episodes and Problems* (London, 1964) ch. VI, 'William III and the Liberties of Europe'.

127   See E. Kossmann, *N.C.M.H.*, v, p. 286 for the power and riches of the United Provinces at this time.

128   Höynck, *Nymwegener Friedens-Kongress*, p. 28.

129   Leopold had successfully pressed his daughter (Maria Antonia) by his Spanish wife to transfer her claim to the two sons of his third marriage, so that the hereditary right that Joseph and Charles derived from his own Spanish blood should be reinforced.

130   R. de Schrijver, 'De eerste staatse barrière in de Zuidelijke Nederlanden, 1697–1701', *Bijdragen voor de Geschiedenis der Nederlanden*, XVIII (1963–4) 65–90, is the first historian to discuss in any detail the Dutch–Spanish convention: in textbooks it is usually assumed that the Barrier as such formed part of the 1697 peace treaty. Cf. W. Hahlweg, 'Untersuchungen zur Barrierepolitik Wilhelms III von Oranien und der Generalstaaten im 17. und 18. Jahrhundert', *Westfälische Forschungen*, XIV (1961) 42–81.

131   See R. Geikie and I. Montgomery, *The Dutch Barrier* (Cambridge, 1930) *passim*; for maps of the Barrier towns see R. Hatton, *Europe in the Age of Louis XIV*, p. 222.

132   See Schrijver, 'Barrière', p. 77 ff.

133   Portland Papers (deposited Nottingham University Library), PWA 1011: Palmquist to Portland, Paris, 8 Dec 1700, reporting talks with an unnamed French minister and with Torcy. Cf. Krämer, *Archives*, III, p. 343 ff, Heinsius to William, 4 Jan 1701, and p. 515, 26 Apr 1701.

134   Cf. Hippeau, *Lettres inédites*, p. 55, Harcourt to Janson-Forbin, 1 Feb 1701, for Philip V – on being asked by the Dutch envoy to guarantee the security of the garrison troops of the United Provinces – expressing his preference that all such troops should leave the Spanish Netherlands.

135   The correspondence of William and Heinsius in Krämer, *Archives*, shows this conclusively: their constant fear was that Louis, becoming aware of their own preparations for war, should take the initiative (*praeveniren*) before they were ready for hostilities.

136 For these negotiations see Srbik, *Wien und Versailles*, pp. 33 ff, 66 ff, 120 ff. Cf. M. A. Thomson, 'Louis XIV and William III, 1689–97', reprinted in Hatton and Bromley (eds), *William III and Louis XIV*, pp. 26–30.

137 But note that Leopold had been able to have revoked a will made in Madrid in favour of the electoral prince in 1699.

138 Grimblot (ed.), *Letters*, II, p. 482 ff, prints the First Partition Treaty. The French gains would, it was hoped, include also some rectification of the southern frontier with Spain.

139 Ibid., p. 495 ff, for the Second Partition Treaty, and the various possibilities in respect of exchanges left open for Louis.

140 She was Maria Anna of Pfalz-Neuburg.

141 Krämer, *Archives*, III, p. 387, Heinsius to William, 25 Jan 1701.

142 See Grimblot (ed.), *Letters*, and Krämer, *Archives*, for such rewards: for example Grimblot (ed.), *Letters*, I, p. 432, William to Portland, 2/12 May 1698, for the mention to Tallard of Port Mahon, Ceuta and Oran, and the wish for Gibraltar and some places in Spanish America. In the United Provinces the hope was for an extended Barrier and the incorporation of Spanish Guelders (Upper Guelderland): see Geyl, *The Netherlands, 1648–1715*, pp. 312–13.

143 Quoted in André, *Louis XIV et l'Europe*, p. 292.

144 See Grimblot (ed.), *Letters*, II, p. 449 ff for Austrian overtures after the publication of Carlos' will being rebuffed by Torcy.

145 Louis visualised possible exchanges with Spain: e.g. to give Roussillon and Cerdagne (for Spain's desire to reabsorb these territories see J. Regla, *N.C.M.H.*, V, p. 382) as equivalents for land either in the Southern Netherlands or in Italy that could in its turn be exchanged for Lorraine. For the importance of French commercial plans in the period 1700–13 see E. Dahlgren, *Les Relations commerciales et maritimes entre la France et les côtes de l'Océan Pacifique* (Paris, 1909) pp. 237–729; cf. *XVIIᵉ Siècle*, nos 70–1 (1966), devoted to 'Aspects de l'économie française au XVIIᵉ siècle', p. 100 ff. Note Louis XIV's own comment of 1709, quoted in Dahlgren, p. 561: 'Le principal objet de la guerre présente est celui du commerce des Indes et des richesses qu'elle produisent.'

146 The desire of England for a share in the Spanish succession goes back further than William III; in the negotiations for the Treaty of Dover it was suggested that if England gave military help to France to secure the Spanish succession, Louis should be bound to help Charles conquer Minorca, Ostend and places on the American continent: see André, *Louis XIV et l'Europe*, p. 129 ff and M. D. Lee, 'The Earl of Arlington and the Treaty of Dover', *Journal of British Studies*, I (1961) 66. Cf. G. H. Guttridge, *The Colonial Policy of William III in America and the West Indies* (Cambridge, 1922) pp. 44–98, chapter entitled 'The War with France in North America'.

147 Parts of Hudson Bay and Newfoundland (Terre-Neuve) that had been conquered during the war of 1689–97.

148   See Geyl, *The Netherlands, 1648–1715*, p. 313.

149   For a summary of Louis' relations with the papacy, see Rule (ed.), *Louis XIV and the Craft of Kingship*, pp. 240–64, contribution by H. G. Judge.

150   Petrie, *Berwick*, p. 318.

151   *Recueil*, I, *Autriche*, pp. 146–7.

152   *Recueil*, X, *Naples et Parme* (Paris, 1893) p. 170 ff for Albergotti's mission. To the well-known authorities on Franco-Spanish relations during the war (A. Baudrillart, De Courcy, Hippeau and De la Trémoille) might be added Miguel A. Martin, *España entre Inglaterra y Francia 1711–1714* (Panama, 1964), who throws new light on them from documents in the Spanish archives.

153   E. Kossmann, *N.C.M.H.*, V, p. 291; cf. for Sweden's insensitivity in respect of European reaction to her balancing policy, Hatton and Bromley (eds), *William III and Louis XIV*, pp. 93–4.

154   Many examples of this in archive material quoted above, note 47.

155   Cf. *Recueil*, I, *Autriche*, pp. 131 ff, 140 ff.

156   W. Scoville, *The Persecution of the Huguenots and French Economic Development, 1680–1720* (Berkeley, Los Angeles, 1960); H. Lüthy, *La Banque Protestante de la Révocation de l'Edit de Nantes à la Révolution*, vol. I (Paris, 1959).

157   Geyl, *The Netherlands, 1648–1715*, p. 166: Hop, on being warned of the danger to religion unless the Dutch armed against French ambition, answered: 'What religion? Tut, tut, religion.'

158   Srbik, *Wien und Versailles*, pp. 220, 268 ff.

159   *Reuterholms Journal*, p. 317.

160   Srbik, *Wien und Versailles*, pp. 56 ff, 119 ff; cf. Mark Thomson, 'Louis XIV and William III, 1689–97', *English Historical Review*, LXXVI (1961) 38, reprinted in *William III and Louis XIV*, pp. 24–48.

161   M. Braubach, *Versailles und Wien, von Ludwig XIV bis Kaunitz* (Bonn, 1952) p. 45 ff.

162   Clark, *Trumbull, passim*, for English subjects; S. B. Baxter, *William III* (London, 1966) pp. 200–11, for Dutch subjects.

163   See Scoville, *Huguenots*, p. 70, for the principality between 1697 and 1702 being a haven of tolerance to which many French Protestants fled.

164   Archief Heinsius, The Hague, 273, Blathwayt to Heinsius, 28 Apr 1693; and, 546, 6 Nov 1698, on William III's compassion and practical measures. Cf.—from the Nassau Domeinen Archief—N. E. Robb, *William of Orange*, II, *1674–1702*, pp. 236–7, 410.

165   Scoville, *Huguenots*, p. 5 ff.

166   Temple to Ormonde, Jan 1664, quoted from a Bodleian MS. by Woodbridge, *William Temple*, p. 64.

167   See Geyl, *The Netherlands, 1648–1715*, p. 100, for inscription (often wrongly given): 'After having reconciled Kings, preserved the freedom of the seas, brought about a glorious peace by force of arms, and established order in Europe, the States of the United Netherlands had this medal struck: 1668', cf. his comment that the Dutch could hardly

expect England, Spain or France to read this 'with any great pleasure'.

168 P.R.O., F.O. 95, vol. 556, Avaux to Louis XIV, Stockholm, 15 Feb 1696. For modification of the 1686 design for the bas-reliefs after Swedish protests, see the documentary evidence cited in *Les grandes heures de l'amitié franco-suèdoise* (Paris, 1964, publication of Archives de France) p. 85, catalogue entries 241–2.

169 Boislisle (ed.), *Mémoires de Saint-Simon*, XXVII, pp. 379–80; for an English translation see *The Age of Magnificence: Memoirs of the Court of Louis XIV by the Duc de Saint-Simon*, selected by S. de Gramont (New York, 1964) II, p. 184.

170 E. Asher, *The Resistance to the Maritime Classes* (Berkeley, Los Angeles, 1960) p. 94, for the need to penetrate that 'façade of centralized authoritarianism which has long concealed the true nature of the reign'. Cf. the discussion on Louis and absolutism by E. Kossmann, 'Enkele problemen van de Europese Geschiedenis na de Middeleeuwen', *Scientia*, II (1957) 71–107.

171 The aim of Louis, as expressed in *Recueil*, I, *Autriche*, p. 741, to restore the Treaties of Westphalia in all their force, was therefore achieved (Instructions of 8 Sep 1679).

172 Even in the worst days of the War of the Spanish Succession, Louis refused to consider giving up Orange (incorporated into France on the death of William III).

173 In 1738 Louis XV's father-in-law, Stanislas Leszczyński, was made duke of Bar and Lorraine, the duke of Lorraine accepting Tuscany in exchange. It was agreed that Bar and Lorraine, on Stanislas' death, should go to his daughter and her children, and in 1766 they were incorporated with France.

3 Louis XIV and the Germanies*

GEORGES LIVET

The relations between Louis XIV and Germany pose one of
the most challenging problems of the seventeenth century. It
is difficult to view these relations objectively; on either side of
the Rhine we find opposing interpretations, at times motivated
more by emotive national responses than by impartial investigation. From the French point of view some events are represented
as splendid or at least respectable (the Imperial election of 1658,
the use made of the League of the Rhine, and the Strasbourg
coup of 1681), while others are held up as shameful examples
of the use of force for political ends (the devastation of the
Palatinate, the destruction of Speyer and Worms, and the burning of Heidelberg).[1]

The difficulties of our given subject derive from the fact that
the phrase 'Louis XIV and the Germanies' tries to compare
two incommensurable concepts. The first term is easy enough :
Louis XIV represents authority striving for fulfilment, a passion
for ruling, a dedication to a unity embodied in the person of
the king, a desire for order, authority and prestige. It denotes a
hierarchical administration with *intendants* transmitting and
carrying out orders in the provinces, a strictly disciplined army
which had benefited from the reforms of Le Tellier and Louvois,
and a diplomacy where – although the figures of Lionne, Pomponne, Colbert de Croissy and Torcy loom large – Louis XIV
never gave up the smallest part of his authority in a field traditionally the preserve of the kingly office. This is not true of the
opposing term. 'The Germanies' were in part a medieval sur-

* First published in *XVIIe Siècle,* nos 46–7 (1960) under the title 'Louis
XIV et Allemagne'.

vival, that Holy Roman Empire of which Pufendorf said that a political scientist would have to classify it as a malformed body, a 'near monster' – *monstro simile*.[2] Within the Empire we find a collection of states whose territorial sovereignty – 'the *Landesho-heit*' – had been confirmed by the Peace of Westphalia. This territorial sovereignty was recognised 'in ecclesiastical as well as in political matters' and included the right of the state to con-clude treaties with foreign states 'for their preservation and mutual security'. Yet, if the character of the Germanies was thus changed by the virtual independence of the princes, the tradi-tional institutions of the Empire remained : the emperor (whose authority now largely depended on the strength of his hereditary Habsburg lands), the Diet with its three colleges : the college of the electors which (since the Golden Bull of 1356) had the privilege of electing the emperors, and those of the remaining princes and of the Imperial free cities. A chancery (*Kanzlei*), presided over by the archbishop-elector of Mainz, assured the continuity and validity of the transactions of the Diet.

The kings of France and Sweden had guaranteed the treaties of Westphalia – which in effect formed the real constitution of the Empire after 1648 – and German policies after that date had to take into account the separate German states and the Diet. The most important states were those of the electors. The instructions sent to the French diplomats accredited to each of them are therefore especially interesting – to the three ecclesiasti-cal ones, Mainz, Trier and Cologne, and the four lay ones, the Palatinate, Brandenburg, Saxony and Bohemia, the last controlled by the House of Habsburg. The elector of Bavaria had been added to this number in 1648 and the duke of Hanover was awarded an electoral hat by the emperor in 1692, though he did not take his seat in the Electoral College till 1708 due to the opposition of many German princes. Diplomatic relations were also maintained by France with the Diet which sat at Regens-burg in permanent session after 1663. The Diet was a hot-bed of intrigues; the slowness of its deliberations was notorious, but it was also the centre of confrontations between the clients of the Bourbons and those of the Habsburgs. The French residents Gravel and Verjus were the experts in this field (the in-structions sent to them were published by Auerbach in 1912).[3]

But though the Diet was the official theatre of diplomacy, the most important negotiations took place at the territorial courts. That of Mainz, an obligatory stop for French agents on their way to Regensburg, was especially important for France. The instructions for Mainz are therefore extremely revealing for our understanding of the diplomatic, religious, economic and cultural aspects of royal policy in our period. They demonstrate that we should not speak of Louis XIV's policy towards a single Germany, and force us to realise that there are men behind our texts and that what Michelet called 'the shadowy Germany' was still searching for its identity after the great turmoil of the Thirty Years War. The Mainz instructions can be supplemented by the correspondence of the French ministers with other agents in the Germanies and by source material and secondary studies from both sides of the Rhine.[4] In the time at my disposal it is not possible to cover the whole field of the Germanies nor to give a chronological and detailed analysis of all facets of Louis XIV's policy. I will attempt to extract the essential traits of royal policy and put before you the most significant problems of our theme and indicate where we are still searching for answers.[5]

We should note first of all that the policies attributed to Louis XIV, and for which he is held responsible, are, at least up to 1658, the achievement of Mazarin. The term 'achievement' is consciously applied to the Peace of Westphalia: France emerged in 1648 as the power which guaranteed the peace and quiet of the Empire, as the guardian of the Imperial constitution and of the rights of the individual German states in the face of the pretensions of the emperor. For this purpose a novel body was created – the League of the Rhine.[6] In 1657 at the time of the Imperial election caused by the death of Ferdinand III, Mazarin sent a powerful embassy led by Marshal de Gramont and Hugues de Lionne to Regensburg. He tried in vain to prevent the election of Leopold of Austria and to oppose him, underhand, with the candidature of the young king,[7] but succeeded in getting the electoral princes to impose a 'capitulation' which limited considerably the authority of the new emperor. To ensure its execution the French ambassadors encouraged the formation of a confederation, concluded on 15 August 1658, which included two kings, those of France and Sweden, two electors, the archbishops of Mainz and Cologne, and several Imperial princes – Duke Philip Wilhelm of Neuburg (whose capital was at Düsseldorf), the three dukes of Brunswick-Lüneburg and the landgrave of Hesse-Cassel. Concluded for three years in the first place this league – which included Catholic and Protestant princes – had a permanent directory at Frankfurt, a treasury which was amply and regularly filled by France, and hired troops to ensure its purpose : the maintenance of the German liberties which the kings of France had claimed to be defending since the times of Francis I and Henri II. It was renewed on 31 August 1660 and was then joined by the duke of Württemberg and the warlike and formidable bishop of Münster, Bernard von Galen. In August 1661 the archbishop of Trier adhered to it. The landgrave of Hesse-Darmstadt and the duke of Zweibrücken came in at the time of the second renewal of the League of the Rhine in 1663, and were followed by the bishops of Strasbourg and Basel and, finally, the long and much desired accession of the elector of Brandenburg took place in 1665.[8] The various stages of the particular negotiations which produced this remarkable alliance, under the protection of France, an alliance which stretched from the shores of the Baltic to the frontiers of Switzerland, form a fascinating field of study. Here it must suffice to state that the alliance gave the states along the Rhine a respite after the troubles of the Thirty Years War and assured France of the neutrality of the German states at the time of the War of Devolution, 1667–8. But Louis XIV, unlike Mazarin, did not know how to disguise his domination as protection. His actions spoke for themselves and the reaction of Archbishop Johann Philip von Schönborn, 'the Solomon of the North', one of the founders of the League, led to its dissolution after 1667. The League of the Rhine was a striking demonstration of what could be achieved by adroit diplomacy, carried out by skilful agents. Mazarin's skill consisted less in forging the alliance – it first took shape without his participation – than in making excellent use of it to France's advantage. Louis also realised its value but strove in vain to revive it in 1672.

Mazarin also knew how to make the fullest use of the peace

treaties of 1648 and 1659 by stretching their terms to the
uttermost. In both the Westphalia and Pyrenees treaties he had
clauses inserted which appeared vague and ambiguous at the time,
but which might well help France in the future. Such was the
case in the clauses over Alsace. By using terms and phrases like
'the landgravates of Upper and Lower Alsace', 'the protection
of the ten towns', and by admitting clauses which appeared
contradictory, French sovereignty was asserted, although the
ceded territory remained in 'immediate dependence' on the Empire.[9] It must be remembered that France at this time was divided
by the Frondes, and the saying of the Austrian chancellor Volmar
– a wily and far-sighted fox – proved prophetic : 'The stronger
will win' (i.e. impose his interpretation of the clauses of the
treaty). In any case titles to claims were for contemporary rulers
the indispensible complement to titles of possession, a heritage
which any prince eager to practise the art of kingship was duty-
bound not to allow to diminish during his reign; though some
preferred, as did Frederick William of Brandenburg, the Great
Elector, immediate gains to long-term ambitions. After a period of
calm, marked by the conclusion between Louis XIV and Leopold
of the first treaty for the partition of the Spanish succession,[10] and
by the submission of the extent of France's rights in Alsace to
the German princes for arbitration, there followed from 1674
a period of violent Franco-Imperial hostilities when first the
emperor and then the Empire joined the Dutch Republic against
Louis XIV. A fine diplomatic campaign, directed by Lionne
and executed by such distinguished agents as the Fürstenberg
brothers – Prince Wilhelm and his brother Franz Egon, bishop
of Strasbourg – tried in vain to keep the Empire neutral : Gravel's
expulsion from Ratisbon signalled French failure. The double
threat on the Rhine from Brandenburg and the Emperor forced
Louis to make use of his protective rights over the ten Alsatian
towns (the *Décapole*), which included Colmar, Haguenau and
Sélestat.[11] The first stage in the assumption of French control
was marked by the enemy invasion of French Alsace and
Turenne's response, the winter campaign of 1675. The Peace of
Nijmegen of 1679 formally sanctioned the French interpretation
of 1648 : Louis XIV refused to have the validity and extension of
the rights in Alsace questioned.

Next came the *Réunion* decisions pronounced by the French

courts, the parlement of Metz, the *conseil souverain*, and the parlement of Besançon. The debate on the responsibility for this policy, the relative contributions of Louvois and Colbert de Croissy, has been a long one. I have tried to show elsewhere that principle must be distinguished from practice. The principle of 'reunion' was not held only by Louvois : it was shared by Austrian archdukes before 1648, by the French plenipotentiaries at Münster and by the first *intendants* in Alsace. Colbert de Croissy provided the diplomatic skill, notably at Mainz and in Brandenburg,[12] while Louvois' hand can be discerned in the local execution of the plans. The ambitions of Berlin, rather than Vienna, explain the French seizure of Strasbourg.

The *Réunion* decisions have been justifiably criticised. Delivered unilaterally and backed by force, they ensured – as Volmar had predicted – the success of the French interpretation of the treaties of Westphalia. But could anything else have been expected after the failure of the pre-1672 attempts at conciliation, given the lack of any international organs of arbitration such as those envisaged by Erasmus, Sully or the abbé de St Pierre? It should not be forgotten that the *Réunion* decisions over Alsace were accepted, at least in part, by subsequent international treaties : the Truce of Ratisbon of 1684 and the Treaty of Ryswick in 1697. In respect of Strasbourg, that treaty used a formula reminiscent of the 1648 Peace : 'His Sacred Imperial Majesty and the Empire cede to His Sacred and Most Christian Majesty and his successors the town of Strasbourg and all that depends on it on the left bank of the Rhine, with all rights, ownership and sovereignty which belong at present to His Said Imperial Majesty and the Empire.'

From this time onwards Strasbourg was no longer a state of the Empire : the course of a river became a political frontier, and the concept of the Rhine frontier entered the sphere of international diplomacy.[13] The date marks an important stage in relations between France and Germany and signified Louis XIV's success, dearly bought in following the principle laid down at Münster.

The policy of defending German liberties was continued but underwent profound changes. Let us compare the achievement of 1714 with that of 1648.

1648: During the Thirty Years War France, in alliance
with the German Protestant princes, had fought the
house of Austria, the most ardent champion of Catholicism. The two cardinals, Richelieu and Mazarin, resuming the traditional policy of Francis I and Henri
II, had known how to separate, surreptitiously, religious
questions from the political ones with which they were
often intertwined.

1714: The treaties of Rastadt and Baden ended the period of
Franco-German conflict of Louis XIV's reign. The
Empire had been the last belligerent to give up the
struggle in the long and arduous War of the Spanish
Succession. The only princes to stick loyally by the king
of France in bad and good times were the electors of
Cologne and Bavaria, both of the House of Wittelsbach.[14] Both electors were restored to their lands and
dignities by the Treaty of Baden in Argau, signed on
7 September 1714; but since they had been under the
ban of the Empire during the war they had not taken
part in the Imperial election of 1706, which had seen
the accession of Joseph I after the death of Leopold,
nor in that of 1711, when Charles VI became
emperor.

In 1648 we find a firm French alliance with the German
Protestant princes, while in 1714 we note a total break with the
German states and an *entente* limited to two Catholic princes.
How did this change come about? The importance of religious
problems in the seventeenth century was apparent to all. It largely
explains the attitude of the German princes to Louis XIV. We
must not forget that the Peace of Westphalia was a religious as
well as a political peace, which extended to the Calvinist princes
the privileges already ceded to the Lutheran rulers. The failure
of the Catholic church and the House of Habsburg to re-establish
the unity of the Empire brought about a secularisation of European politics, a division of Europe into separate religious camps
and into totally independent states. At the same time it in-
augurated a new international law of mutual respect for divergent
religions and consciences. Louis XIV countered this tolerance, a
forerunner of the modern era, with a resolutely Catholic policy.

He seemed to put on – and lampoons and pamphlets were quick to assert this – the mantle of a champion of Catholicism which the emperors Leopold and Joseph, whether voluntarily or by force of events, had let fall. In his struggle against the Dutch and in his efforts to maintain James II of England, Louis appeared the enemy of Protestantism, ever alert, ever active. His persecution of the Huguenots in France, which culminated in the revocation of the Edict of Nantes (1685), strengthened this view of him, and produced a situation fraught with difficulties for French diplomacy at a time when Frederick William of Brandenburg was setting an example of personal tolerance. The Great Elector was able to rally his Catholic subjects in the duchy of Cleves and the Lutherans of Brandenburg and East Prussia, even though he himself was a Calvinist. He refused to violate the consciences of his subjects, because men's 'consciences belong to God and no power on earth can compel them'. In his *Political Testament*, written in 1667, he told his son, 'Without making any distinctions of faith, you ought, like a true father of your country, to love all the subjects God has put under your authority.'[15] Frederick William replied to Louis' revocation with his own Edict of Potsdam, the preamble of which condemned the persecution of Protestantism in France and promised safety and support in his electoral lands for the refugees. The fourth article of the Treaty of Ryswick, which laid down that Catholicism should be maintained in territories returned to the emperor, annoyed the Protestant states,[16] who turned for protection, now that France had let them down, to the rising star of the elector of Brandenburg. The title of king which the emperor bestowed on the elector in 1701 further increased the prestige of the House of Hohenzollern.

Did Louis' anti-Protestant activities, whether explicable by the king's conscientious scruples or by political necessity, bring him a counterbalancing sympathy in the German Catholic states? At first, as Leibniz put it in his *Mars Christianissimus*, 'the petty Catholic clergy, who had been badly treated by the Protestants, sang his praises as they saw the advance of their liberator'. But soon the flagrant contradiction between Louis' claim to be the eldest son of the church, the upholder of the Catholic faith, and his behaviour towards the pope made them change their tune. In Rome Louis' ambassador acted arrogantly.

Innocent XI took the side of those of the French clergy who condemned the *dragonnades*. The latter in fact helped draw the
Protestants everywhere out of their 'apathy and decreasing piety'.
As J. Orcibal has shown in his studies of the conflict between
Rome and Versailles – sparked off by the declaration of the
four articles in 1682 – this conflict became much more serious
towards the end of the year 1688.[17] Louis XIV ran the risk of
papal excommunication on several counts : the mission of his
ambassador Lavardin, the seizure of the papal enclave of Avignon,
the imprisonment of a *nuncio* and, above all, his appeal for a
general council of the church. Lampoons from the German side
of the Rhine had a field-day in denouncing Louis' actions as
the beginning of a far-reaching design which would lead to the
king of France's becoming as 'absolute at Rome as in France,
reducing the Papacy to a vassal of the *fleur-de-lys*'. Harsh judge-
ments were passed on the Gallican liberties which Louis claimed
to be defending : Leibniz declared on one occasion that 'they
might be liberties as far as the Pope is concerned, but they are
certainly slavery imposed by the King'.

The German situation was directly affected by Louis' relations
with the Holy See. At the death of the elector of Cologne in
1688 Louis needed the support of the papacy to get his own candidate, Cardinal von Fürstenberg, nominated to the post. Louis
XIV's threats merely increased the resolve of the pope to oppose
him, and on 20 September 1688 he nominated Joseph Clement
of Bavaria archbishop of Cologne. To Louis' threats the pious and
obstinate pontiff returned the answer 'that he considered it God's
special grace to let him suffer on this occasion for justice and
to end, if necessary, what remained of his life as a martyr'. The
French king preferred the infinitely more dangerous weapons
of intimidation to the diplomatic moves so dear to Lionne. He
sent troops to install his candidate, besieged Philippsburg, and
sent the pope an ultimatum due to expire in January 1689.
By that date something had happened which upset all Louis'
expectations : the conquest of England by William of Orange,
an event which ruined all the hopes of 'the invincible monarch'.[18]
The burning of the Palatinate produced an outcry of horror
throughout Germany. The Franco-German quarrel generated
a great European conflict – the War of the League of Augsburg
in French parlance or, as German historians call it, the War of

Orléans[19] – in which the Protestants and the Maritime Powers were to be found on the side of ultra-Catholic Austria.

The latter benefited from a revival in her prestige among the German Catholic states as well as the Protestant princes. The emperor had decided to lead a veritable crusade against the Turkish threat to his hereditary lands and to the Empire. The troops of the League of the Rhine, which included those of the king of France, had worked wonders in 1664 in repulsing the Turks at the St Gotthard monastery on the Raab; but in 1683, when the grand vizier Mustapha led an army of 200,000 men to the walls of Vienna itself, Louis sent no help. All Germany was roused. The *Türckenglocke* was rung every day at noon, inviting the faithful to pray for the Empire. On 12 September 1683 Imperial troops, helped by the squadrons of John III Sobieski of Poland, defeated the Turkish army, forcing it to retreat. The reconquest of Hungary began, marked by the victories of Charles of Lorraine, who stormed and took the great fortress of Buda, the shield of Islam. On 11 September 1697 Prince Eugène defeated the Turks at the bridge at Zenta. Two years later at the Peace of Karlowitz Transylvania and all the Hungarian plain, with the exception of the Banat of Temesvar, were restored to the emperor. Prince Eugène, whom much later Frederick the Great of Prussia was to glorify in his *Ode to the Germans*, became a national hero. The emperor's prestige grew and this reinforced his authority in Germany: he had asserted himself as the defender of Christianity and of the Empire, while the king of France, taking advantage of the Empire's troubles, was ravaging its western frontier in virtual alliance with the Infidel. The writers of polemics had a field-day exposing the ambitious Louis, said to be only waiting for the fall of Vienna to resurrect Charlemagne's empire. This was the moment when Mme de Sévigné could speak with a smile 'about our brother the Turk'.[20] After the War of the Spanish Succession the Peace of Passarowitz in 1718 extended the area controlled by the emperor by the annexation of the Banat of Temesvar and northern Serbia: a new empire had been created in the Danube valley.

We must now turn from the political and religious aspects of our investigation to consider the economic and social factors and intellectual and artistic relations – to those aspects which united an area divided by political quarrels.

Economic issues were central to the mercantilist monarchies, and the grand designs of Colbert have their counterparts in some of the German states of the period. The most important areas for our purpose are those of the Baltic and the Rhine. Until 1640 the North German states had been dependent on their commercial ties with the Hansa and the Dutch. Colbert was attracted by the prospect of riches if France could win a share in the Baltic trade because, to quote the words of Jacques Savary in his *Le Parfait Négociant* of 1675, 'there is no finer commerce in all Europe that that of the North'.[21] To achieve his aim Colbert founded a trading company, that of the North, to establish links between the French Channel and Atlantic ports and those of the Baltic.[22]

In 1668 Colbert's correspondents at Danzig, the Formont brothers, convinced him that fairly active commercial relations already existed between France and north-east Germany through the ports of Danzig, Kolberg, Stettin and Hamburg. The proverbially fertile Pomerania and East Prussia, despite their harsh climate, were lands rich in cereals, the veritable granaries of Europe. Cattle and timber were there in abundance. Colbert, ever in fear of French subsistence crises, was keen to buy grain, and also timber which he needed for his shipbuilding programme. To the Baltic France exported wine, salt, textiles, furniture and dyes, trade largely carried on via the town of Königsberg.[23]

The second important field of French commercial activity was the Rhine valley. In Paris it was rumoured in 1667 'that the Dutch are negotiating busily with all princes who have the right to levy tolls on the Rhine to obtain the farming of such tolls for themselves, or to secure considerable decreases in the tolls : in either case they hope to gain control of the wines grown along this river and use them in their own trade instead of French wines.' Colbert, concerned with the harm which would ensue to the wine trade of France, asked the abbé Gravel, French resident at Mainz, to discover :

1. Whether the Dutch were negotiating with the Rhine princes, as rumoured;
2. the number and kinds of tolls levied on the Rhine from

Breisach to where the river entered Dutch territory, the names of the princes with the right to levy tolls, and how much was charged on every hundredweight of goods or tuns of wine;

3. if possible, the number of tuns of wine and other goods which passed through each toll-station per annum;

4. to indicate in his report where the largest vineyards were and to name areas in which the wines were usually consumed.

We have here a typical mercantilist enquiry of the kind Colbert's policy required.[24]

Gravel, having resorted to subterfuge, succeeded in giving Colbert a complete picture of the different tolls on the Rhine: there were fourteen between Mainz and Cologne and thirteen between Cologne and the mouth of the river. A 'malter' of wine bought for a florin in the Palatinate would cost five florins when sold in the Republic, and the Dutch interest in obtaining commercial treaties with the Rhenish princes was therefore understandable. In 1670 Colbert asked Gravel to procure 'a copy of the recent [Dutch] treaty either with the Elector of Mainz or with the Elector of Trier', adding: 'It is important for us to know whether the Elector of Mainz has reached agreement with this envoy [of the States General] on the lowering of tolls, since this Elector's principal privilege is that of the landing place at Mainz: you must find out if he has consented to cut the tolls and let me know.' In fact, the Dutch negotiations did not succeed, as they conflicted with the particular interests of the Rhenish princes. The attention Colbert paid to the Rhine area did not, however, diminish. In November 1679 Dupré, French resident at Cologne, received Pomponne's blessing 'to visit the fairs of Germany, whenever they are held'; he was to let Pomponne know in advance which fairs he proposed to visit and to inform Colbert what went on at the fairs.[25]

Colbert was equally interested in the export of French manufactures to Germany. On 26 October 1669 he wrote to Gravel: 'I would be obliged if you could arrange to be at Frankfurt when the fairs are held, so that you can give me detailed information if there are any French merchants there, what goods they sell and buy there, and, more generally, everything which relates to the German consumption of French goods.' Gravel sent a well-researched report 'about the quantity and quality of French

goods sold in the fairs at Frankfurt', which earned him this
reply from Colbert : 'Your report proves that the sale [of French
goods] is considerable and that this matter needs no further
investigation.'

This was perhaps a rather hasty conclusion at a time when
French exports to Germany were being seriously threatened,
Schröder in Austria and Pufendorf in Brandenburg advocating
the commercial emancipation of the states of the Empire. The
German war against France was also an economic war. In 1688
the emperor Leopold renewed the letters patent of 1674 pro-
hibiting the import of French goods into Austria. In 1691 Wagner
von Wassenfels published in Vienna his *Cry for the Honour of
Germany*; his earlier publications include *Considerations on the
Poverty of Germany and on the Wealth of France, of the Dutch
and the Swiss,* and the *Observations on German Industry*
(1683).[26]

Economic and religious questions were interrelated. The Huguenot refugees welcomed by Frederick William formed in Brandenburg an élite which has been described as 'the yeast which
made the heavy German dough rise'. They introduced hitherto
unknown methods of cultivation, created market gardens and
glasshouses in the vicinity of the capital and set up industries.
The French resident Rébenac reported in 1686, 'They are no
longer upset in Berlin about what happens in France, believing
they can console themselves by the industries they [the Huguenots]
are establishing everywhere' : wool textiles, ceramics, tapestries,
silks, prints and calicoes. It was Louis XIV who created the
essential elements of the Brandenburg armaments industry; he
alone provided Germany with the means by which the Empire
escaped economic dependence on France.

The Huguenot influence in Germany was of course a French
influence. The refugees contributed to the spread of the French
language, customs and civilisation. It is not the least paradoxical
aspect of the period under review that Germany was in intellectual dependence on the very France with which she was
at war.

The phenomenon can easily be explained. The Thirty Years
War – however limited its ravages were in some areas – had un-
fortunate effects on the country as a whole. In Grimmelhausen's
Simplicissimus of 1669 irony and satire are the means whereby

the author tries to rise above the calamities he describes. From the other side of the Rhine the engravings of Callot illustrate the same tragic reality. It is hardly remarkable that, at a time of moral and material ruin following the ravages of war, Germany should turn to the model of France, where the delights of Paris and soon the fairyland of Versailles shone in full splendour. The petty princely courts vied with each other in recreating the pleasures of the enchanted island. The setting for authority had to be French : the trinity of the château built on a grand scale with impeccable symmetry, of the park laid out by Le Nôtre, and of the royal square acting as a show-case for the sovereign's statue. French fashions invaded Germany more assuredly than the armies of Louis XIV. French entertainments followed. The resurrected German theatre – between 1667 and 1693 theatres were built in Nuremberg, Augsburg, Hamburg and Leipzig – soon replaced their improvised farces with comedies in the style of Molière. People became infatuated with French dress : 'Everywhere you see powdered long wigs in the style of Louis XIV, kneebreeches, buckled shoes and hooped dresses'. More importantly, the French language reigned supreme among the German upper classes, and spread to wider circles in the eighteenth century. Leibniz's evidence is significant :

> After the Peace of Münster and that of the Pyrenees nothing could withstand the power of France and the language of France. Our young people, who did not know their own country properly and who admired everything French, took a dislike to their own language. Many of them entered high positions and posts and thus governed Germany for a long time; and, if they did not make her a tributary of French power, they came very near to doing so. In any case they subjected her almost completely to the language, customs and fashions of the French nation.

A contemporary commented : 'To-day everything has to be French : language, clothes, food, music, illnesses. The majority of the German courts live in the French style, and whoever wants to make a career there must know French and above all have been to Paris.'[27]

The social limits of this Gallomania have still to be defined and its extent in urban and rural areas to be ascertained, but

we ought to ask if there was any resistance in the seventeenth
century to this fashion for everything French. The part played
by publicists, pamphlet and lampoon writers in the formation
of public opinion must not be ignored. Louis XIV for one was
lavish in expenditure on propaganda to excuse French actions,
but the writings of agents subsidised by him (Frischmann and
Obrecht among others) did not reach the mass of the German
people as easily as the anonymous lampoons of the German anti-
French writers.[28] The clumsiness – to put it mildly – of the advocate Aubéry in his *Des justes prétentions du Roy sur l'Empire* was
speedily denounced in France.[29] It could justifiably be said of this
pamphlet 'that in German eyes it must look like an official programme of Louis' ambitions'. It maintained that not only was
the French king justified in demanding the Imperial crown,
but that it was lawful for him to regain control of the greater
part of Germany, as this was 'the patrimony and ancient heritage of French princes, having been held by Charlemagne as
king of France'. Such claims were accompanied by extravagant
eulogies on the incomparable greatness of the French monarchy
which the Parisian lawyer proclaimed superior in divinity, in
antiquity and in rank to the German Empire: it was up to
Louis XIV, he urged, to reconstitute the universal monarchy
in his own person or in that of the dauphin. The weapons
Aubéry thrust into the hands of France's enemies were turned
against Louis XIV. Lisola, a native of Franche-Comté, who had
entered the emperor's service, stressed in various pamphlets –
notably in *Le Bouclier d'Etat et de Justice (The shield of the
state and of justice)*[30] – the French king's unlimited ambitions.[31]
He skilfully raised the controversy to the level of a European
question, pretending to maintain the objectivity and breadth of
vision of a 'citizen of the world'.

   In attacking the main principles of French policy, the German
publicists spared neither Louiv XIV's person and agents, nor the
methods of his diplomacy in the Empire. They attacked his pride
in choosing the sun as his emblem and labelled him 'an apocalyp-
tic monster', 'the Christian Suleiman': absolutism was rife in
'French Turkey', the people reduced to slavery and the nobility
in gilded cages at Versailles. The king's ambassadors were casti-
gated: Robert and Jacques de Gravel at Ratisbon and Mainz
respectively, Verjus at Ratisbon, Asfeld at Hamburg, both the

Fürstenberg brothers. The latter were subjected to the fiercest attacks and held guilty of betraying their own country. The French ambassadors, who by the German definition had to be 'crafty rogues who knew how to cheat', had other weapons besides their wits.[32] They held in their hands the famous 'golden key' which permitted the use of bribery in a land where, as one realist said, 'everything is achieved by money'.[33] The influence of money and the extent to which it was used should not, however, be exaggerated. Georges Pagès has published the accounts of Verjus' secret fund, 'income' and 'expenses', at Ratisbon between 1679 and 1688, that is during the particularly critical time of the *Réunions*, of the occupation of Strasbourg, the conquest of Luxembourg from the Spaniards, and the Truce of Ratisbon. What do these accounts reveal? Gratifications averaging from 3000 to 5000 livres for various diplomatic representatives, notably those of the electors of Mainz, Brandenburg and Trier; some presents for wives : Madame de Iéna received a mantle, French gloves and some dress trimmings, in all worth 160 livres (not an excessive sum); some presents for the men : diamond-studded portraits of Louis XIV, gold medallions, silver chocolate pots, and what may seem more useful presents to us, such as mathematical instruments for an Anhalt minister, scientific books and instruments, a finely-bound copy of Confucius, astronomical maps, and globes by Father Coronelli for the Cologne minister. To such presents in kind or money we must of course add the state subsidies which were laid down in formal treaties, notably those concluded with Brandenburg at the Peace of Vossem in 1673 and that of Saint-Germain in 1679. The sums involved were significant and Louis XIV's money was spread throughout Germany. If it delayed some anti-French decisions, it could not prevent two declarations of war, that of 24 May 1674, which was followed by the expulsion of Gravel, and that of 15 December 1688, which was followed by the expulsion of Verjus. More often than not German ministers, princes and states accepted French money when their interests and their ambitions coincided. Personalities and periods have to be distinguished, unwarranted generalisations avoided, and the usages of the time – less strict in this respect than ours – must be taken into account.[34]

The anti-French lampoons have therefore to be examined

critically, truth must be separated from exaggeration, and the picturesque drawing from the crude caricature. Leibniz himself in 1688 declared that he 'could not approve of many of the malicious, badly-reasoned lampoons usually produced by people who have no real knowledge of current affairs, which tear Louis XIV's reputation to shreds and attribute imaginary designs to him. Such satires have a disagreeable effect.' But Leibniz himself surely contributed to creating an unfavourable climate of opinion towards Louis when he accused him of practising rules of justice 'which place him above the laws and morals of this life, and, under the pretext of divine investiture, give him the power to practice a policy which serves his selfish interests and imposes the law of his own pleasure on Europe'.[35] It is generally accepted that men listen more readily to incitement to hatred than to calls to reason.

The historians and diplomats of the seventeenth century were very critical of Louis XIV's policy towards Germany. The case against him, however, is not yet closed. We need to assess and categorise the various influences at work. We must distinguish successive layers of this historic literature, in which synthesis has too frequently preceded analysis : political and nationalist propaganda is one layer; self-justifications and myths (obsession with the Imperial throne, the need for defence of frontiers, the concern for personal glory, the Catholic crusade) form another. Any worthwhile analysis must take into account the paucity and, often enough, the inefficiency of the techniques for adjusting international problems, the diversity of regional particularisms and the inaccuracies attendant on speaking of a homogeneous public opinion.

At a deeper level our period is of interest for the achievement of German unity. It was not by mere chance that Louis XIV dealt less with the Diet than with the German princes : for example, the archbishop of Mainz, the elector of Brandenburg, the archbishop of Cologne and the elector of Bavaria. The German historian Fritz Hartung has indeed remarked that if the ancient body of the Empire kept itself together till Napoleon finished if off, it was more by sclerosis than by vitality. The future lay with the princes, the medieval dream of unity through the emperor having been irretrievably lost. The Great Elector was hailed as a national hero, and the victories of Prince Eugène against the Turks could only fleetingly refurbish the Habsburg coat of arms. The Habsburgs eventually turned away from the Empire in favour of expansion to the east. The changes of frontiers which Louis XIV's wars produced in the west, however unfortunate they might have been for Germany, had little to do with the slow but powerful tremors which threatened to tear the Empire apart. Yet it is too early to talk of an Austro-Prussian dualism in the seventeenth century, and the historians who have done so have been obsessed with the figure of Frederick the Great. The institutions in Vienna and the prestige of the emperor's capital were as useful to Leopold as the victories of his armies against the Turks; and the attempt by the ageing Louis XIV at a *rapprochement* with the Habsburgs in 1714 was justified less by any foreknowledge of the rise of Brandenburg than by religious motives: the desire to stop the rise of the North German Protestant princes, Hanover even more than Prussia.

The Empire at the turn of the century was going through not only a structural crisis but also a crisis of conscience. Louis XIV's France was for Germany both the model to be followed and the enemy to be crushed. It is in this sense that I spoke, at the beginning of my paper, of the opposing tensions implied in the phrase, 'Louis XIV and the Germanies'. At the beginning of Louis XIV's reign both small and large states were eager to recover and to revive after the Thirty Years War. At the end of the reign we find them more concerned with their conscience. In relation to Louis XIV this conscience was aggressive: a hard, bitter, even cruel hostility, which left enduring traces, but which helped Germany to fashion itself into a nation. Such a change had not been achieved by 1715 and much remained to be done, but we must beware of assuming that the emerging Germany was totally in France's debt. We must not forget that this was the time when Leibniz was exploring the world of the unconscious and hoping for European unity, and that the active Pietist movement fostered the genius of a Johann Sebastian Bach. In the *Visionen des Philander von Sittenwald* ('Visions of Philander von Sittenwald') Michael Moscherosch, an enemy of France, none the less paid homage to Paris as the 'town where all go, from which everything comes, capital of the world and of the

Enlightenment'. Should not Paris and France then, for periods even beyond the reign of Louis the Great, be conscious not only of deserving eulogy but ready also to admit that they bear a heavy responsibility?

NOTES

1   For discussions of Franco-German relations in Louis' reign, see G. Pagès, 'L'Histoire diplomatique du règne de Louis XIV: Sources et état des travaux', *Revue d'Histoire Moderne et Contemporaine*, vol. VII (1905–6) 653–80; G. Zeller, 'Politique extérieure et diplomatie sous Louis XIV', ibid. (1931) 124–43: a review article of C.-G. Picavet, *La diplomatie française au temps de Louis XIV, 1661–1715*; G. Livet, 'Louis XIV et les provinces conquises', *XVIIe Siècle* (1952) 481–507.

2   Quoted in B. Auerbach, *La France et le Saint Empire romain germanique 1648–1789* (Paris, 1912) p. xviii.

3   In the series *Recueil des Instructions données aux Ambassadeurs et Ministres de France* (hereafter cited as *Recueil*). The instructions in respect of Austria, Prussia, Bavaria, the Palatinate and Zweibrücken have also been edited; by Sorel and Waddington respectively in the case of the first two states and of the last three by Lebon.

4   See for French works G. Pagès, *Le Grand Electeur et Louis XIV 1660–1688* (Paris, 1905); V.-L. Tapié, *La politique étrangère de la France et le début de la guerre de trente ans 1616–1621* (Prague, 1936); B. Auerbach, *La diplomatie française et la cour de Saxe* (Paris, 1887); for German works see those of Döberl and Preuss on Bavaria, Ennen and Braubach on Cologne, and Schulte on the margrave of Baden. For an attempt at synthesis see G. Zeller, *La France et l'Allemagne depuis dix siècles*, 2nd ed. (Paris, 1948).

5   G. Livet (ed.), *Recueil*, XXVIII, *Etats Allemands*, i, *Mayence* (Paris, 1962); ii, *Cologne* (Paris, 1963); *Trèves* (Paris, 1966).

6   On the League of the Rhine, which has long been a controversial subject, see A. Chéruel, 'La Ligue ou alliance du Rhin', *Séances et travaux de l'Académie des sciences morales* (Paris, 1885); A. Pribram, *Beitrag zur Geschichte des Rheinbundes von 1658* (Vienna, 1887); G. Mentz, *Johann-Philipp von Schönborn* (Jena, 1896); G. Livet, *Le duc de Mazarin* (Strasbourg, Paris, 1954) p. 127.

7   See the instructions sent to the French ministers in the various German courts in A. Pribram, 'Zur Wahl Leopold I, 1654–1658', *Archiv für Österreich. Geschichte*, vol. 63 (1888); J. Preuss, 'Mazarin und die Bewerbung Ludwigs XIV, zum die deutsche Kaiserkrone', *Historischer Vierteljahrschrift* (1904). Mazarin's words to R. de Gravel are worth noting: 'Although you should speak about the King with reserve, if none the less you see the prospect of getting His Majesty elected you should become more open about it'.

8   See the instruction to R. de Gravel at Mainz, for 1655 and 1657, and those to comte de Wagnée and to Gravel at Trier for 1657; see also

Cl. Badalo-Dulong, *Trente ans de la diplomatie française en Allemagne: Louis XIV et l'électeur de Mayence 1649–1678* (Paris, 1956); Auerbach, *La diplomatie française*; M. Huisman, 'Essai sur le règne du prince éveque de Liège, Maximilien-Henri de Bavière', *Mémoires de l'académie royale des sciences, lettres et beaux-arts* (Brussels, 1899). Note that the see of Liège was at this time linked with that of Cologne.

9 G. Livet, *L'Intendance d'Alsace* (Strasbourg, Paris, 1956) p. 114; F. Dickmann, *Der Westfälische Frieden*, 2nd ed. (Münster, 1965) p. 477.

10 See F. Mignet, *Négociations relatives à la succession d'Espagne*, I (Paris, 1888) and A. Pribram, *Franz von Lisola und die Politik seiner Zeit* (Leipzig, 1894).

11 The rest were Kaysersberg, Landau, Munster, Obernai, Rosheim, Turkheim and Wissembourg.

12 See Livet, *L'Intendance d'Alsace*, p. 385; cf. instructions to Foucher at Mainz in 1680, to Tambonneau at Trier in 1681, and to La Vauguyon and Tambonneau at Cologne in 1679 and 1681 respectively. See also Herbert H. Rowen, 'Arnauld de Pomponne: Louis XIV's Moderate Minister', *American Historical Review* (Apr 1956).

13 H. Vast, *Les grands traités du règne Louis XIV*, II, p. 149; Livet, *L'Intendance d'Alsace*, p. 636; H. Ritter von Srbik, *Wien und Versailles, 1692–1697: Zur Geschichte von Strassburg, Elsass und Lothringen* (Munich, 1944).

14 The elector of Cologne, 1688–1723, Joseph Clement, although elected instead of Cardinal Fürstenberg in 1688, proved amenable to Louis XIV's subsidies. His brother, Maximilian II, elector of Bavaria, was annoyed at the court of Vienna for its attitude towards him during the preliminary negotiations for the Spanish succession. Louis XIV for his part saw Bavaria as a natural counterbalance to Austria: 'It is in France's interest to increase the power of the Elector of Bavaria in Germany and to oppose the House of Austria with a power strong enough to put a brake on its plans': A. Sorel (ed.), *Recueil*, I, *Autriche* (Paris, 1884) p. 121. This policy, which proved a delusion, persisted until the Peace of Füssen of 1745 and left traces even into the nineteenth century.

15 Pagès, *Le Grand Electeur*, p. 563.

16 H. von Srbik has shown that the clause in fact originated with the emperor rather than with Louis XIV: see his *Wien und Versailles, 1692–1697* (Munich, 1944) pp. 220, 268 ff (*ed.*).

17 J. Orcibal, *Louis XIV et les Protestants* (Paris, 1951) p. 127 and the same author's *Louis XIV contre Innocent XI: les appels au futur concile de 1688 et l'opinion française* (Paris, 1949) p. 48.

18 Leibniz realised that this was a 'turning point' of the reign.

19 English and Dutch historians now prefer the more neutral 'Nine Years War'.

20 Louis XIV was convinced that if he did not profit from the emperor's troubles, the latter would turn against France as soon as he had overcome the Hungarian revolt and the Turkish invasion. Cf. his comment to his envoy in Vienna, Sébeville, on 26 September 1681, *Recueil*, I,

Autriche, p. 92, 'You are quite right to think that the Emperor will contemplate waging war on the Rhine as soon as he is free of the struggle which is keeping his principal forces in Hungary'. See also A. Gaedeke, *Die Politik Österreich in der Spanischen Erbfolgefrage*, 2 vols (Leipzig, 1877); A. Arneth, *Prinz Eugen von Savoyen*, 3 vols (Vienna, 1858–9); M. Braubach, *Prinz Eugen*, 5 vols (Vienna, 1963–5) and the same author's *Versailles und Wien von Ludwig XIV bis Kaunitz* (Bonn, 1952).

21 English title, *The Complete Merchant*.

22 P. Boissonnade, *Histoire des premiers essais de relations économiques directes entre la France et l'Etat prussien pendant le règne de Louis XIV, 1643–1715* (Paris, 1912).

23 For the activities of this port see P. Jeannin's article in *Bulletin de Société d'histoire moderne*, XII, no 5 (1954).

24 M. Braubach, 'Eine Wirtschaftsenquête am Rheim im 17. Jahrhundert', *Rheinische Vierteljahrsblätter*, XIII (1949); Livet, *L'Intendance d'Alsace*, p. 506; Badalo-Dulong, *Trente ans de diplomatie*, p. 239.

25 Archives des Affaires Etrangères, Correspondance Politique, Cologne, vol. 14, f. 33.

26 These German titles have been translated into English.

27 This contempt for and abandoning of the national language is a more serious sign than the mere transfer of territory: L. Levy-Brühl, *L'Allemagne depuis Leibniz* (Paris, 1890) p. 3. See ibid., p. 6 for the contention that the idea of a common country, Germany, had been stifled by the religious hatreds let loose in the Thirty Years War.

28 H. Gillot, *Le règne de Louis XIV et l'opinion publique allemande* (Nancy, 1914).

29 The author was imprisoned by Louis XIV, whether as a punishment for work done badly or work done without authorisation is still debated (*ed.*).

30 English title of the 1667 Lisola pamphlet printed in Brussels.

31 Up to 1679 there is a remarkable continuity in Louis XIV's claims to the Empire: the treaty of 2/12 April 1664 with Saxony contained secret articles by which the elector John George promised in case of an Imperial election to vote 'according to the good intentions of the King'; the treaty of 17 February 1670 with Bavaria contained a secret article proposing the election of Louis XIV as German emperor after the death of Leopold while reserving the title of king of the Romans to the elector; in the treaty with Brandenburg of 25 October 1679 the elector promised to do his utmost to get His Most Christian Majesty elected emperor, 'because of his great and heroic qualities and because of his ability to sustain the Imperial crown and to re-establish the Empire in its ancient splendour and to maintain it in all its dignity and to defend it against the proximity and the always very dangerous undertaking of the Turks'. Cf. H. Vast, 'Des tentatives de Louis XIV pour arriver à l'Empire', *Revue Historique*, LXV (1897) 1–45; G. Zeller, 'Les rois de France candidats à l'Empire', *Revue Historique*, CLXXIII (1934) 521–34.

32 The ambassador *more gallico*, the 'French servant', was in German eyes: 'Always merry, never sad, a fine fellow who is always whistling, dances one *courante* after another, and conceals a black satanic soul under a carefree and goodnatured appearance'. France also took care, it was held, to match its envoys to the character of their opposite numbers in the diplomatic game: 'They have assigned to the courts of Germany hefty fellows who can take their wine and are able to make a good impression at the table of the princes to whom they are accredited . . . ' Gillot, *Le règne de Louis XIV*, p. 95.

33 Another favourite expression of the writers should be noted: 'money is a saddle which will fit any horse'.

34 G. Pagès, *Contribution à l'histoire de la politique française en Allemagne, Note sur le rôle de l'argent dans la politique française en Allemagne sous Louis XIV* (Paris, 1905) p. 66.

35 More interesting, because they are constructive, are Leibniz's ideas on the need for the advancement of science and the arts; see his *The foundation of an academy or society in Germany for the development of the arts and sciences* of 1669. In 1711 Thomasius began to lecture in German at the University of Leipzig, and in a review of 'Monthly Topics' in the German language he tried to disturb the apathy of his compatriots and the pedantry of his colleagues. He also reformed the teaching in the law faculty. The foundation by George II, king of England and elector of Hanover, of the University of Göttingen in 1737 may thus be said to have been prepared in advance.

4 Louis XIV and the Jacobites*

CLAUDE NORDMANN

Although Jacobitism played a lesser role in the second Hundred Years War between England and France than has often been thought, its significance should not be ignored.[1] The prospect of a Stuart restoration influenced both the will-power of the French court during the Nine Years War and the War of the Spanish Succession and the determination of the British to defend the rights and liberties they had won through the Glorious Revolution of 1688. Irrespective of the ups and downs of the Jacobite movement in Great Britain itself, it acted as a permanent source of Anglo-French discord and coloured the ideological conflict between the two states.[2] Louis XIV and the majority of his people wanted to defend the Catholic faith and the just cause of the legitimate Stuart kings. But the doctrine of Bossuet was the complete opposite of that propounded by Locke in England. With Ireland humbled after the battle of the Boyne and Scotland divided the Stuart cause had little chance of succeeding, and the supporters of James II and the Old Pretender failed to make the most of any opportunities that came their way. Louis XIV had solid good sense enough to realise this better than his own advisers, but he took a pride in defending to the last the interests of a house allied to his by ties of blood. For its part, the Jacobite diaspora, scattered across Europe, maintained contacts and organised pressure groups which ensured the survival of Jacobitism even after the death of its sincerest champion, the *Grand Roi*, although the Jacobites never managed to rally France's Catholic enemies to their counter-revolutionary crusade.[3]

James II had not listened to Louis XIV's sensible advice

* Specially commissioned for this volume.

before November 1688. He failed to prevent the landing of his
son-in-law, William of Orange, in England and was forced to
follow his wife, Queen Mary of Modena, and the young Prince
of Wales to France.[4] As in the 1640s the French court offered
the exiled Stuarts a royal asylum, this time at Saint-Germain-
en-Laye.[5] Madame de Sévigné commented, 'The King's mag-
nanimous soul enjoys playing this grand role. What could be
more in keeping with the image of the Almighty than standing
by a king who has been expelled, betrayed and abandoned
like this one.'[6] From January 1689 the Stuarts built up a small
court and government, relations with Versailles being the responsibility of the earl of Melfort, James's principal private secretary.
The close ties between the Stuarts and the government of the
Most Christian King (the ruler who had revoked the Edict of
Nantes), and their dependence on his subsidies and good offices,
undoubtedly did serious harm to their cause in England and
throughout Protestant Europe.[8] James II seemed a mere tool
in Louis XIV's hands; and Louis himself continued to ascribe
to James II, as to his son later on, all the attributes of majesty,
including the right to touch for the king's evil, the very symbol
of divine grace.[9]

James II and his supporters intended to re-establish their
power in the three kingdoms as quickly as possible by expelling
the 'usurper' William III. They counted at first on Catholic
Ireland where the lord-lieutenant, Richard Talbot, earl of
Tyrconnel, had stayed loyal. He promised to raise nearly 40,000
men, though he asked for 500,000 crowns from Louis XIV to
support his troops who were threatened by famine. Louvois
opposed a campaign in Ireland, but Seignelay was inclined to risk
a landing. Louis XIV tried to balance between the two, but
remained reluctant to sanction a sea-borne invasion as he had no
experience of such ventures. Madame de Maintenon, who had
been completely won over to the Stuart cause, supported Seignelay; and – as a compromise decision – the military engineer, the
marquis de Pointis, was sent to Tyrconnel to promise French
help, limited to arms and money, and to report on the Irish
loyalist troops.

Having communicated his plans to the Holy See and to
Vienna, James II, accompanied by Melfort, the comte d'Avaux
(accredited by Louis XIV as his ambassador to Ireland), and

D

some French officers, embarked from Brest and arrived at Kinsale
on 22 March 1689.[10] There he found close on 40,000 men at his
disposal, including 7000 French troops sent in exchange for
5000 Irish.[11] All he did, however, was to blockade Ulster and lay
siege to Londonderry. He ought to have moved speedily either
into Scotland or England to rally the Jacobites there; but his
general staff was divided and the French commander, Rosen
(a Livonian by birth), was a rough character who did not work
well either with James or with his advisers. Londonderry was saved
by the arrival of William's ships, and the Protestant victory of
the Boyne (1 July 1690 O.S.) confirmed the English ascendancy
over the *Gaele Erinn*.[12] Nine days later James II was back at
Brest. All sections of French society had followed events in Ireland with as much interest as if they had taken place in France
itself.[13] The Jacobites and the French still held on to Limerick.
But the prudent Chamlay, a disciple of Louvois, advised Louis
XIV to keep the Irish happy with promises rather than give
them effective help. On his advice the king decided against
sending money and troops to Ireland. In any case French com-
mitments in the war on the Continent made it impossible to send
the 10,000 troops asked for by the Jacobites, though 30,000
crowns and some arms were sent to make sure that William
of Orange would have to keep soldiers in Ireland.[14]

Without reinforcements Limerick had to give in to the English
on 13 October 1691. The capitulation terms, however, permitted the defenders to leave for France to serve James there.
The 12,000 who did so formed the core of that brave Irish
phalanx, 'the wild geese', who fought for the Bourbons right
up to the end of the Ancien Régime.[15] But in Ireland the victorious English subjected the Catholics to penal laws, the harsh
effects of which have been felt down to the present day.[16]

James II returned to Saint-Germain and sought consolation
for his defeat in devotional exercises and periodic retreats to the
monastery at La Trappe. Louis XIV had more pity than esteem
for him and seemed determined, for the time being, to do nothing
to further his cause beyond giving him an annual pension of
600,000 livres. Despite its victory at Beachy Head, the French
fleet limited itself to a demonstration off Exeter where twelve
English ships were burnt.[17]

Scotland, however, and the Highlands especially, was still

a promising area for a Jacobite campaign. Although the ablest Highland chief, Dundee, had fallen in the summer of 1689 at Killiecrankie where a victory had been won through his own leadership, the lairds and their clans were not prepared to accept the Orange régime. In the western Lowlands a strong minority demurred at the abolition of the Episcopalian church and was able to rally others discontented with the course of events. Louis XIV and his court believed that disorders and risings were endemic in the British Isles with its multitude of Protestant sects. Jacobite agents, who went to and fro between France and Great Britain, maintained that discontent was now general, not only among the Catholics and the High Churchmen but even among such men as Marlborough, Godolphin and Admiral Russell: they had played an active part in the Revolution but were now entering into correspondence with the Stuarts.[18] Louis XIV also counted on jealousy between the Maritime Powers. For all these reasons, in the winter of 1691 and early spring of 1692, he authorised preparations for an expedition against England. A transport fleet was fitted out, with an escort squadron commanded by Tourville. On 21 April 1692 James II travelled to the coast of Normandy and advertised his hopes of success in a printed manifesto which was distributed in England. Twenty-four thousand men were concentrated in the Cotentin, but contrary winds prevented Tourville's ships joining up with the transports. Eventually the admiral was instructed by Pontchartrain to sail out of Brest, and his fourty-four ships of the line ran straight into a combined fleet of seventy-nine English and Dutch ships commanded by Edward Russell off La Hougue. On Louis XIV's express orders Tourville engaged the enemy in an action which began on 29 May and continued for six days along the coast between Barfleur and La Hougue, resulting in a defeat for the French.[19] The Sun King did not blame either Tourville or the fleet: the damage did not seem irreparable and hope was not abandoned of future successful actions against Britain.

From this time onwards, however, the prestige of the Jacobites at the French court declined. Their initiatives, like their promises and assurances, became suspect. Their ranks were infiltrated by spies and adventurers and leaks of information, of which the English government and its allies took advantage, multiplied.

Quite apart from this, the British had brought the art of inter-cepting dispatches to a fine art.[20]

Louis XIV therefore turned down an invasion plan, presented to the *conseil du roi* in January 1694 by Sir Theophile Ogle-thorpe and Sir James Montgomery, which urged several landings in Britain and in particular at Dover, where the governor was expected to surrender the port.[21]

At this time Croissy wrote to James II in Louis' name, advis-ing him to accept the harsh pre-conditions of Middleton and the English royalists for his return : recognition of the established laws, respect for the Protestant religion, and security for the lives and property of his subjects.[22] But Middleton was com-promised when the British government discovered his and other gentlemen's correspondence with James II, and he had to flee to France, reaching Saint-Germain in April 1693. The former sec-retary of state was presented to Louis XIV at Versailles on 16 April, but did not succeed in persuading the French king to invade the British Isles until 1695.[23]

While waiting to support the Stuart cause with ships and troops, Louis XIV did his best to win other European courts for James II and genuinely believed that his guest could count on sympathy from Catholic princes. His first move was to let it be known that any monarch making peace with France would have to engage himself, if not to help Louis restore James II, at least not to oppose such a venture. In 1692 and 1693, negotia-tions over peace terms between Vienna and Versailles showed that the emperor Leopold I favoured the Stuart cause. Influ-enced by his Jesuit adviser, Leopold suggested that James II's son, Prince James Edward, ought to succeed William III and Mary if – as seemed certain – they should die without a male child of their own, and that until his accession James II and his family should be paid a pension; William III would also have to promise complete toleration to English Catholics. Leopold was the author also of the strange proposal that France and the Maritime Powers should jointly conquer one of the Barbary states, or Egypt, as a kingdom for James II.

The Franco-Austrian negotiations broke down before mid-1693. On 28 June 1693 Pomponne presented Louis XIV with a memorial proposing eventual French recognition of William III, and that meanwhile French diplomats abroad (though stressing that Louis, by friendship and alliance, was bound to support his relative James II) should urge the powers to whom they were accredited to help James II and William III to come to an agreement along the lines suggested by Leopold.[24] This was accepted by Louis XIV, and the comte d'Avaux, the French ambassador to Sweden, accordingly informed chancellor Oxenstierna of his master's views. He added that Louis XIV was not tied by any formal treaty to James II, but that it would detract from the French king's glory to cause James II public shame and humiliation by a too speedy recognition of William as king of England. As Ragnhild Hatton has stressed, Louis XIV was somewhat dogmatic and legalistic in his attitude towards the House of Stuart.[25] Avaux went on to suggest that one way out would be for William and Mary to be persuaded to declare James II's son their successor (if they had no heir of their own), and to give the Stuarts a pension. Oxenstierna passed on this proposal to the Dutch envoy in Stockholm and went out of his way to stress that the Stuart succession was a problem which merited discussion among the powers. Denmark and the United Provinces were approached along similar lines by Louis XIV. The French king suggested a pension of a million crowns for the Stuarts plus repayment of what was due to Mary of Modena, and demanded that the English parliament should recognise Prince James Edward Stuart as heir-presumptive. This last condition was roundly rejected by the Dutch grand pensionary Heinsius; and William III declared that, even if he were to consent to give his father-in-law a pension, he could not possibly agree to recognise James II's son since English public opinion denied his legitimacy. For his part James II refused to renounce his rights in favour of his son during his own lifetime,[26] while the court of France neglected to keep him fully informed of their negotiations on behalf of his son. In 1695, a year when the Assembly of the French Clergy sent a deputation to Saint-Germain to express their devotion to James and his queen and when Brulart de Sillery, bishop of Soisson, and Fléchier, bishop of Nîmes, praised the virtues of the house of Stuart and predicted its impending restoration, James II felt unsure enough of Louis XIV's support to send the earl of Perth to Pope Innocent XII to beg him to oppose any peace which did not ensure James's restoration. His belief that his cause and that of European Cath-

olicism was indivisable, was not accepted. The Holy Father, as
in 1689, responded with platitudes and seemed unwilling even
to give refuge to James II, as William III had suggested, in
Rome.[27]

As peace negotiations broke down and the campaign in the
Low Countries achieved little, Versailles became interested once
more in various projects for a descent on the British Isles.[28] Queen
Mary had died on 7 January 1695 (N.S.) and her death revived
hopes of the Jacobites, who also counted on England's difficulties
at this time, especially her financial ones.[29] In Scotland the massacre of Glencoe had destroyed any chance of reconciliation
between the Highlands and the government in London. The
former episcopalian clerics who were dissatisfied with William
contributed to Jacobite nostalgia. Even the Cameronians appeared
willing to join their implacable Jacobite enemies in support for
James II.[30] Louis XIV now authorised extensive preparations
at Dunkirk and Calais to help James II return home. Some
16,000 men were sent there and put under the command of
the marquis d'Harcourt. On the pretext of reviewing these troops
in the north of France, James's illegitimate son, the duke of
Berwick, secretly crossed to England to assess the real strength
of the English Jacobites who were pressing for a Stuart invasion.
His main contact in London was their agent, James Simpson.
A former officer in James II's household cavalry, the Scot Sir
George Barclay, was sent to England to get in touch with the
Nonjurors. The projected rising was to be led by Sir John
Fenwick, a member of an old Northumberland family, who
was, however, both careless and of little influence. The leading
Jacobites planned to facilitate the invasion by seizing and
assassinating William III on 15 February 1696, near Turnham
Green as he returned from Richmond; but the government dis-
covered what was afoot and arrested all the conspirators except
Berwick and Barclay who escaped to France.[31] James II reached
Calais on 1 March[32] and proceeded to Dunkirk to inspect the
ships under the command of Nesmond and Jean Bart. Louis
XIV had forbidden his forces to move before those in charge
of the expedition had definite news of a rising in England; while
on the other side of the Channel the Jacobites were equally
determined not to rise until after the French had made a successful landing. The result was that Louis' soldiers remained en-

camped around Calais throughout the rest of the winter of 1696–7, while his ships were kept in port due to contrary winds and an English blockade. For his part James II had, on 15 May 1696, already returned to Saint-Germain.

Although Louis XIV promised the Stuart court that he would support James II in the 1697 season,[33] he was at the same time trying hard to achieve peace with the allies. Secret conversations had been going on at Maastricht for some years and these were, from May 1696, pursued more actively between the French plenipotentiary Callières and two Dutch negotiators, Dijkvelt and Boreel. But they continually came up against the same obstacle, namely Louis XIV's persistent refusal to recognise William III. The Dutch demanded an effective barrier in the Low Countries and the immediate recognition of William of Orange as king of England, 'without any conditions, restrictions or reservations', as a preliminary to any agreement. Louis XIV, no longer dominant in Europe, was willing to return Luxembourg or an equivalent and even proposed restoring Strasbourg to the Empire; he agreed moreover to tolerate Protestant religious services in Dutch consulates in France, but he refused categorically to recognise William III before the signature of peace.[34]

William III was determined to bring these preliminary negotiations to a successful conclusion, in spite of Austrian resistence. His resolve was strengthened when the duke of Savoy defected to Louis XIV in the hope of obtaining Milan on the death of Carlos II. Mutual Franco-Dutch concessions brought agreement on the more essential points; and in May 1697 a peace congress opened at the palace of Ryswick, near The Hague, with Sweden acting as mediator.[35] A protest by James II, dated 8 June 1697, against the Franco-Dutch negotiations, and against any peace terms which did not recognise his legal right to the English crown, precluded any compromise solution in favour of his son.[36] Whether such a solution could have been found is unlikely, as William III thought the time ripe to rob the Jacobites of all French support and to consolidate the succession of his wife's sister Anne and her children.

Meanwhile a solution to the *impasse* seemed to present itself in Eastern Europe. The Polish king, John Sobieski, died and some Polish magnates wished to offer the Polish–Lithuanian crown to the ex-king of England. The French ambassador in

Poland was quick to inform Louis XIV, and the king immediately sent Pomponne to Saint-Germain to elicit James II's
response. James, however, declared that he did not want the
Polish crown as he had no claim to it : to accept a crown which
did not belong to him would amount to a renunciation of the
one which did.[37] Thus he rejected an elective crown at the very
time his adversary was safeguarding the English crown for his
Protestant successors through the will and ratification of the
English parliament. The recognition of William's kingship by
Louis XIV marked the official fall of the House of Stuart.

The talks between the Dutchman Bentinck, now Lord Portland, and Marshal de Boufflers, French commander in the Low
Countries, proved more significant in clearing the way for an
Anglo-French settlement than the discussions at Ryswick. The
French king dropped his demand for an amnesty for the Jacobites
and the return of their possessions; William III in return gave
'his word secretly' not to shelter French Protestants in his prin-
cipality of Orange. Without formally undertaking to abandon
James II and expel him from his kingdom, Louis XIV agreed
not to assist, directly or indirectly, the enemies of the king of
England, i.e. of William III and his successors.[38] The Peace of
Ryswick was signed on the night of 20 September 1697.[39]

The French plenipotentiaries had been concerned to get financial justice for the Stuarts. They succeeded in having a clause inserted whereby Mary of Modena's jointure, originally fixed by
an act of parliament at £50,000 a year, should be paid in the
future – a measure which, it was hoped, would ease the burden
on French finances.[40] In return William III hoped to achieve
the expulsion of the Stuarts from French territory and to exile
them to Avignon or Italy, but this Louis XIV refused absolutely.
In December 1698, in his instructions to Tallard, named French
ambassador to London, Louis explained that 'H.M. is in honour
bound not to refuse asylum to a king who has demanded it and
has so far enjoyed it with him, and it is therefore impossible for
him to satisfy the King of England on a point which has been
raised but refused so many times before'.[41] In recognising William
III Louis XIV had greatly strained his religious and political
principles, and he intended to show the legitimate king respect
and affection by abiding by the laws of civilised hospitality. On
7 December 1697 James II and his queen attended the wedding

of the duke of Burgundy, the dauphin's eldest son; at supper Mary of Modena was seated between the two kings.[42]

The death of Princess Anne's sole surviving heir, the young duke of Gloucester, in 1700, removed a rival to the Prince of Wales and revived Jacobite hopes. But an act of parliament was speedily passed which recognised Sophia, the dowager electress of Hanover, a granddaughter of James I, as the next Protestant heir to the English crown. This Act of Settlement of 1701 named the Hanoverian dynasty as successors to the Stuarts, and stipulated that 'whosoever shall hereafter come to the possession of this Crown shall join in communion with the Church of England as by law established'.

In March 1701 James II suffered a stroke, was paralysed down one side and had not long to live. As Chateaubriand put it : his kingdom was no more of this world; power gave place to piety.[43] He and his queen went to take the waters at Bourbon, where the marquis d'Urfé on Louis' orders received James as a monarch, but nothing could arrest his illness. On 13 September Louis XIV visited him and assured him in the presence of his suite that he would protect all his family and would consider his son 'king of England'. On 16 September 1701 James II died at Saint-Germain.[44]

The Grand Alliance had been signed on 7 September 1701 and on the seventeenth Louis XIV, against the advice of the majority of his ministers, recognised James III as king of Great Britain and Ireland. Too much can be made of this recognition of the Stuart pretender, which the English considered not only an insult but a breach of the Treaty of Ryswick. Louis XIV held 'once a king always a king'. Mary of Modena had argued that while William III was *de facto* king of England James Francis Edward had to remain a private individual, but that if his royal title was refused him this would be tantamount to a denial of his legitimate birth.[45] In fact France's economic policy, demonstrated by Louis' purchase from a Portuguese company of the unexpired portion of their slave contract – the *asiento* – and the decree of 6 September 1701 which prohibited the entry of English textiles into France, probably alienated Great Britain more than the recognition of James III.[46] William III himself died on 18 March 1702. But the Whigs, the moneyed men, controlled the City of London and did well in the local elections.

D*

Parliament voted subsidies for raising troops and proclaimed Anne queen.

The parliamentary régime and the Protestant succession seemed safe from the Jacobites, but the English declaration of war of France on 15 May 1702 gave renewed hope to James III's followers and endangered what had been gained by diplomacy in 1697. The young Stuart prince was at the centre of rather ineffectual intrigues, planned in correspondence with the Jacobites and Nonjurors in England.

While the more fortunate adherents of James III played a distinguished role in Louis XIV's armies and navies (or in those of other European rulers), a large number of half-starving, mainly Irish, refugees were reduced to misery, forced to live in almshouses or to accept the charity of English and Scottish colleges, convents and monasteries in France.[47] The religious duty of succouring the poor was strong in France and sympathy for these Jacobites lasted for a considerable time, though eventually it gave way to indifference, irritation and suspicion.[48] Was it not an Irish hot-head who had dared to throw a stone at Louis XIV's carriage?[49] In 1703–4 the Paris police made a determined search for all Jacobite agents newly arrived from Scotland, Ireland and England. When the duke of Perth sent Torcy a signed recommendation on behalf of a Scot called Mackenzie, its effect was to land Mackenzie in the Bastille.[50] The Lovat affair finally discredited the projects of Saint-Germain in the eyes of Louis XIV's government. A Scottish captain, Simon Fraser, who called himself Lord Lovat, had been sent in 1703 on a reconnaissance mission to Scotland to prepare for a landing of 5000 men and to encourage a rebellion of 12,000 Highlanders. But this double agent betrayed the Jacobite plans to the duke of Queensbury, and several of James's British followers were arrested. When Fraser returned to France, Louis XIV had him imprisoned at Bourges and later (23 July 1704) at the Château d'Angoulême. Legrelle assumed that the 'Lovat Affair' was a plot hatched in London to facilitate the absorption of Scotland into the United Kingdom,[51] but this is to read too much into routine British wartime intelligence.

The question of a possible diversion in Britain was seriously considered at Versailles. Two memoirs put forward in 1704 on 'the Scottish venture' stressed that such a diversion would cause the English government more serious embarrassment than the British-financed revolt in the Cévennes was causing France.[52] The failure in 1704 of the Darien Company, which had brought economic and financial difficulties in its train, gave some hope that Scotland was now ripe for revolt against English domination.[53] The two missions of Torcy's agent, Colonel Nathaniel Hooke, in August 1705 and April 1707, should be seen in this context. The French War Office archives and Foreign Ministry archives supplement the evidence already available about these secret missions,[54] and show that they were prepared by the court of France and that Saint-Germain was not fully informed. The minister for war, Chamillart, had intended to offer the Scots only a few thousand guns and pistols and a couple of mortars; but when Hooke returned from his second mission he was supported by the duc de Chevreuse, one of the advisers Louis XIV took seriously. There was a great deal of contact between the *dévôt* party at the French court and James III; Elizabeth Hamilton, Comtesse de Gramont, whose two brothers were to take part in the coming expedition, had been a pupil of Fénelon.[55] Hooke proposed that James III should land in Scotland and claimed that 25,000 Scottish infantry and 5000 cavalry would immediately march on England, where they would be joined by a considerable number of English Jacobites with whom the Scottish nobility were in correspondence.

It will be easy enough to seize Newcastle. London depends so heavily on the coal from this town for its heating that if it were deprived of it for six weeks the capital would be reduced to great straits. The Scots, their numbers increased by those who are merely discontented as well as by the rightful king's loyal subjects, plan to make themselves masters of the greater part of England and even to take London – possession of which decides who holds the crown – before Princess Anne can get her troops transported from Flanders across the Channel.

Ireland, he claimed, was only waiting for Scotland to lead the way; the Scottish lairds for their part wanted 5000 of the Irish troops serving in France to be sent to Scotland – the duke of Berwick to be their commander – and 600,000 livres to support the campaign.[56]

When Hooke, on 29 July 1707, sent his report to Chamillart, he accompanied it with a declaration signed by thirteen of the more powerful Scottish lairds who declared that they had no confidence in the court of Saint-German and would only trust the French government. The Scottish Presbyterians among them wanted the Pretender to promise, first, never to agree to the Act of Union (passed in March 1707) and, secondly, to protect the Protestant religion. Hooke had also, through Ker of Kersland, made contact with the Cameronians of western and southern Scotland. They had promised to join a Jacobite revolt, but insisted on a landing near Edinburgh and the rapid seizure of the capital with all its economic and financial resources. The landing, all agreed, ought to take place in August or September 1708 when the Anglo-Dutch fleets would be off Spain or Portugal; Dunkirk was suggested as the best port of embarkation. When he reached Scotland, James III, it was suggested, should free all vassals from lords who had declared for the Union. Scotland, Hooke ended his report, was short of money, in part because of the fiscal demands of the English, in part because of five years of poor harvests which had forced them to buy grain in England and Ireland. Money had also been taken out of the country by the great Scottish nobles who now sat in parliament in London.[57] Hooke's report tells us much of Scottish grievances at the time of the Act of Union, a union which had been passed to ensure that the unity of Great Britain would not be endangered by the eventual change of dynasty.[58]

The greatest of all the Scottish nobles, James, fourth duke of Hamilton, had, however, been reserved in his talks with Nathaniel Hooke. He was a cautious man, who was suspected – not without reason – by Lockart of Carnwath and Ker of Kersland of wanting the Scottish crown for himself. Most Scottish lairds gave assurances that they would bury their differences for the sake of Scotland and the legitimate king, and urged James III to act speedily since delay would be fatal.[59] Hamilton, however, in a letter addressed directly to James, stressed that without the support of a strong French army (which he argued that Louis XIV could spare because of his victory at Almanza) the chances of a Stuart restoration were small. James, he pointed out, must not count on Godolphin or Marlborough in England. They had been in favour of the Union of 1707; it was a pity that there had not been enough money available to buy votes in the Scottish parliament to prevent the ratification of the Act of Union.[60] Hamilton also let James know that the British government was aware of Hooke's mission.[61] His letter thus sounded a clear and perceptive warning of the risks involved in the project of a Stuart invasion.

The duc de Chevreuse, when he sent Hooke's report to Torcy and Chamillart, had come out in favour of French aid for the Jacobites and had supported the invasion of Scotland. He stressed that the Maritime Powers would not make peace as long as Spain and the Indies remained under a French prince. They believed it was in their power to impose on France a peace on the lines they desired : the only way, therefore, to keep Philip V on the Spanish throne was by a Scottish descent 'to keep Princess Anne's forces'[62] busy on that side of the water and force her to a reasonable peace. The Dutch on their own would be unable to continue the war. The establishment of two sovereign powers in Great Britain (i.e. the separation of Scotland and Ireland from England) might in fact please the Dutch, who were by now exhausted and jealous of the power and arrogance of the English in commercial matters, an arrogance which France had also experienced. The money for the Scottish descent could be found from contracts recently concluded with the tax farmers and financiers, and a suitable cover would be to announce that the sums were needed to increase the subsidies due to Charles XII.[63]

The duc de Chevreuse easily won his brother-in-law Beauvilliers, Desmarets and the elder and younger Pontchartrain for the plan. Samuel Bernard provided a million livres which Dugué de Bagnola, the intendant of Flanders, passed on to the intendant of coastal Flanders at Dunkirk, Berbières. The merchants of Dunkirk, who included important Irish and Scottish shipowners,[64] advanced a further 300,000 livres.[65]

At the end of February 1708 six thousand Franco-Jacobite troops embarked at Dunkirk on several privateering ships under the command of the general Comte de Gacé, who had been appointed ambassador to James III, and Marshal de Matignon. A quantity of arms and munitions was also taken on board and Forbin was put in charge of the fleet. 'The King of France has judged the time ripe to crown his services of nearly twenty years

past for the late King of England and for the King, his son, and
to revenge the insults suffered by the monarchy by the last revolution in England.' But, in Louis XIV's opinion, James III must
remain satisfied with Scotland alone during the lifetime of Queen
Anne; after her death he should reign over all three kingdoms
and be succeeded by his sister, the young princess Louise Mary,
if he died without heirs of his own body.[66]

The expedition was delayed first by James Stuart's catching
measles and then by the dilatoriness of the French naval and
war departments. Having set sail, Forbin's tiny squadron was
unable to effect a landing at or near Edinburgh. On 23 March
Forbin found the Firth of Forth barred by Admiral Byng's fleet,
and there was nothing else he could do but return to Dunkirk.
The area of south-east Scotland was a bad place for a landing:
the local population was indifferent,[67] being more interested in
preserving commercial relations with the Dutch than in helping
the Stuarts. Berwick had advised a landing in the west of Scotland, but he was not listened to by Louis XIV nor consulted
by the French military experts.[68] All the same, Berwick, like
Chevreuse, remained of the opinion that an invasion of Scotland
ought to be attempted once more since it might lead to a Stuart
rebellion and speed up the peace. The following year it was
Torcy who advocated the Scottish descent plan, 'to put a fresh
complexion on things'. He was then supported by Marshal Villars,
who offered to lead an expedition in person,[69] and managed to
convince Louis XIV, overcoming the king's reservations.[70] This
time the expedition was to sail from Brest, and not from Dunkirk
which was alive with British spies. Louis put Marshal d'Estrées
in charge of the invasion force but was willing to provide only
a limited number of men. Towards the end of the autumn of
1709 Torcy discussed the venture with Queen Mary, Middleton
and Berwick, after which he felt bound to warn Louis that
success was doubtful because of the weakness of the Pretender's
position. Louis then decided to abandon the project, using the
excuse that his navy would be unable to carry it out 'without a
safe port in Scotland, without fortresses and possibly without information which could be depended on'. The chevalier de Saint-
Georges' Christian virtues, which impressed Fénelon, were not
accompanied by the qualities of a statesman or soldier.

Unable to achieve a military solution, the French court had

to seek a diplomatic settlement of the problem. The Tories, who had been in power in England since 1710, wanted to win Louis XIV's confidence; and they accompanied their peace overtures with vague proposals for restoring Anne's half-brother (described as Mr Montgoulin in their correspondence) to the Stuart throne after her death. The earl of Jersey, who was used by the Tory ministers in the peace negotiations, was known to be pro-Jacobite. The mission of Gaultier in January–February 1711 is too well known to need discussion here. Undoubtedly the death of the emperor Joseph I in April 1711 radically changed the situation, as Great Britain had no intention of fighting to reconstitute the empire of Charles V for the benefit of Charles VI. But as St John reminded the French agent Mesnager, in October 1711, the House of Commons had forbidden negotiations with any prince who sheltered the Pretender in his territories.[71]

When, on 19 January 1712, the Utrecht peace congress opened, the English government sent a memorial to Versailles through the abbé Gaultier in which they demanded that the Pretender leave France.[72] In November Louis XIV sent the duc d'Aumont as ambassador to England to make an accurate assessment of the strength and influence of the various parties. He reported that 'The King of England's [i.e. James III's] party has regained much of its strength over the past few years, and because of the divisions between the Tories and the Whigs this prince has won several friends among the former. But everyone is afraid to declare himself. No friend can be trusted when it is a matter of losing your head and property.'[73] Despite the revival of Jacobitism in Great Britain at this time, one must not forget the divisions among the Jacobites, nor that there were many shades of Jacobites. R. C. Jarvis has pointed out that the Jacobite fervour of the Lancashire Catholics went little further than toasting the 'King over the water'; largely, it seems, because of their gradual assimilation into county society, which in turn made their Protestant friends reluctant to search their homes for arms.[74]

At the beginning of 1713, after strong British pressure through Prior on the French government,[75] James Stuart retired to Lorraine, where Duke Leopold offered him the palace of Bar as a residence.[76] The Maritime Powers agreed to sign the Treaty of Utrecht with France on 11 April 1713, Article 4 of which contained Louis XIV's promise to recognise the Protestant succession and never to allow James's return to France. By Article 5 Louis engaged himself never to disturb the queen of Great Britain, her heirs and successors nor to help the enemies of the Protestant succession.[77]

Despite the difficulties Louis XIV had experienced in obtaining peace after the long War of the Spanish Succession, he ordered Iberville, his first envoy extraordinary to England after Utrecht, to find out if the Tories wanted the return of their rightful king. It was assumed that the member for Oxford University who had just been made a minister, William Bromley, would be in favour of James III.[78] Torcy also renewed his contacts with those Jacobites in France who believed they could count on Robert Harley, Earl of Oxford, although he was in fact drawing closer to the Whigs, the dissenters and the Low Churchmen. What would happen when Queen Anne died? The prospect of her death posed problems and induced hopes in Jacobite hearts. The queen, like Oxford and Bolingbroke, held that the Pretender's Catholicism would make any plans for his return look like a counter-reformation backed by the papists.[79] But James III refused to accept Anglicanism and he was supported in this by Torcy.[80] The French court became increasingly realistic in respect of James's chances and tried to pour cold water on Jacobite hopes. In spite of this, Jacobite ambitions and activities revived once Iberville in January 1714 reported the queen's serious illness.[81] Louis XIV warned James III that the only help he could give him was his good wishes.[82] He could come as far as Pontoise but was not to show himself in Paris.[83]

Queen Anne's death on 12 August 1714 seems to have taken her half-brother's supporters by surprise. Louis XIV let Prior, the British minister in Paris, know that he would not support any venture by the Jacobites.[84] But Torcy had already promised the Pretender that France would put two armed frigates at his disposal at Le Havre, and an embarrassed Louis XIV seems to have accepted this.[85] But, when James III reached Paris to consult his mother and his supporters there, Louis XIV declared that it was impossible for him to help: he did 'not wish to break his given word'.[86]

The divisions in the Tory party made it impossible for the Tories to agree among themselves and to proceed to action. In the summer of 1714 Jacobitism was limited to Scotland, Ireland and the north and west of England. Consequently the friends of the House of Hanover, that is mainly the Whig commercial classes, had no difficulty in welcoming the elector of Hanover who, having been proclaimed king of Great Britain on 1/12 August, landed at Greenwich on 18/29 September 1714. The Pretender's supporters were neither capable nor decisive,[87] and the accession of the new dynasty marked the culmination of the Glorious Revolution.

The situation, however, did seem to favour the Jacobite émigrés in France and the enemies of the Anglo-Hanoverian régime in Britain. Although George I's personality and achievement merit historical rehabilitation,[88] there is no doubt that his reign at the outset was unpopular not only in Scotland but in most of England. Violent demonstrations and riots began in Bristol in October 1714[89] and spread throughout the country.[90] Iberville reported to Torcy that the Jacobite gentry of the west and north of the country were about to show their true feelings.[91] Even in London public opinion turned against the dull German prince. Louis XIV, however, maintained his policy of caution. The old king was tired of war and told the Stuarts so. Although he allowed Torcy to keep in touch with them, he himself now intended to 'preserve the peace and the European balance'.[92]

The threatening attitude of parliament towards his own person made Bolingbroke go over to the Stuarts. It seems that it was his idea rather than Berwick's that a combined Franco-Spanish-Swedish expedition should overthrow George I and the Whigs. He had been in touch with the princesse des Ursins via Iberville and Sir Patrick Lawless, James III's Irish agent in Madrid,[93] and managed to leave England for Paris in April 1715.[94] When he at last met the Pretender at Commercy he was, from the very first, disappointed in him. In Paris he had to fight the hesitations of Marshal d'Huxelles and the blundering schemes of the Irish Jacobites. His mistress, Mme de Tencin, confided to him that 'no strenuous resolution is possible here because of the age and poor health of the King'.[95]

The so-called Marly project finally took shape as a result of talks in June 1715 between Berwick, Torcy and Sparre, the Swedish ambassador in France. Louis XIV used the excuse of his own advanced age and the exhaustion of France for refusing

to break his engagements undertaken at Utrecht. But he did
acknowledge that the time was ripe for an expedition to restore
the Stuarts 'because of the present mood of the English nation'.
He therefore asked his grandson Philip V of Spain to give James
III 100,000 gold crowns. As Charles XII of Sweden was in
Stralsund, holding off a coalition of Baltic powers which included Hanover, he might well have agreed to take part in a
landing in the north of England against the elector of Hanover
who had occupied his duchies of Bremen and Verden. Swedish
ships from Gothenburg might seize Newcastle and land seven
to eight thousand men there.[96] In the event, the Spanish court
agreed to send the Jacobites 428,520 French livres, and Antoine
Crozat donated a much larger sum in return for a promise of a
title of nobility. Torcy and Pontchartrain signed orders putting
the commissioners of the French navy at Rouen and le Havre
at their disposal.[97] But despite the urgings of Sparre and the
earnest requests of the French ambassador, Croissy (who was
with Charles at Stralsund), the Swedish king replied that though
he realised the importance of the affair he could not spare any of
his troops. Moreover, even though he had a quarrel with Hanover, that was not cause for him to behave in a hostile manner
to England.[98]. He had no intention of giving Norris's fleet an
excuse to take action against him in the Baltic.

Although there is little doubt that a Swedish Protestant prince
would have been able to rally more supporters in England than
the Catholic king of France,[99] nothing was done to receive the
Swedish troops in Great Britain, even if rumours about them
were rife.[100] A rising had, however, been prepared in the west
of England by the duke of Ormonde, who intended seizing
Bristol and Plymouth as suitable places for James Edward Stuart
to land. A leading Anglican, Ormonde was very popular and
his importance had increased after the church riots of the summer
of 1715.[101] Scared of his influence, the Whig ministers Stanhope
and Townshend tried to have his friend Monteleón, the Spanish
ambassador in London, convince him that only a written pro-
fession of allegiance to George I and temporary exile could save
his life, honour and property. They assumed that Monteleón
was unaware of the preparations made by the court of Madrid
on behalf of the Pretender, and of the support of the French
court for the Jacobites, and expected him to send home a

pessimistic report on the chances for Jacobite success.[102] In fact, however, Monteleón had already reported the strong discontent in England; he also knew of the projected alliance between France, Spain and Sweden against George I from Ernst Vellingk, Charles XII's chamberlain, whom he had met in secret.[103] When Ormonde realised that there would be no landing of foreign troops, he took fright and in August 1715 fled to France. Now rid of the principal Tories, the British government took energetic measures against a Jacobite invasion which many thought imminent. Although Louis XIV assured the English government that 'it was all a false alarm'[104] (and had in fact forbidden Berwick to accept a command either in England or Scotland),[105] Byng was put in charge of the Channel fleet and told to watch the French ports, and all suspected Jacobites were rounded up.[106]

On 1 September 1715 Louis XIV died. The Stuarts' best support left the scene before the 'Fifteen' rising. Bolingbroke wrote, 'The King was the best friend the Chevalier had. My hopes sank as he declined, and died when he expired.'[107]

The Sun King's affection for the Stuarts, his respect for a cause dogged by so much bad luck (but which for a Christian was a particular way of achieving salvation), is not in doubt. But though Louis XIV on the whole had a sounder appreciation than his entourage of Jacobite prospects, he was not well versed in the political facts of life in Great Britain. To quote David Ogg, if neither Louis XIV nor James II had changed, England – after the Glorious Revolution – had. The nation, after the Nine Years War, had no intention of becoming a dependant of the France of Louis XIV; and this would certainly have been the case if James II had been restored. A restoration would have brought the repudiation of the millions of pounds lent to the British crown. These investments were certainly the greatest obstacle to a successful invasion, for William's government paid interest on its debts fully and on time. We must also take into account the political experience of the English, which increased over the years, and produced a state of mind which the courts of Versailles and Saint-Germain hardly understood. British public opinion was also deliberately incited against the Sun King, who was represented as leading a papist crusade paid for by the Jesuits and Rome.[108] If James II or James III were to restore

Catholicism in England with the support of Louis XIV, all ministers and officials would be forced to accept the Catholic religion. The economic struggle against France and the fight for a religion better suited to the spirit of capitalism had led to the Revolution of 1688.[109] The attempt to destroy France's formidable commercial and colonial position followed.

Dominated by merchants and an aristocracy who had lost their liking for wars and were drawing close to the bourgeoisie, England was moving further and further away from the House of Stuart. The Hanoverians ensured their attachment by opening up the German market through Bremen and Verden.[110]

It would be wrong to assume that Jacobitism for France was nothing more than a weapon in her struggle against English power in the seventeenth and eighteenth centuries. We are still uncertain just how far French support for the movement itself went. Did Louis XIV hope to restore the Stuarts to all the crowns of England, Scotland and Ireland, or to only one of them?[111] There can be no definitive answer to this question as the surviving documents only allow tentative conclusions. In any case, as Mary of Modena told her son, one crown was better than none. French public opinion was not unanimous on the advisability of sheltering the Stuarts in France. Some Frenchmen believed that Louis' protection of James II and James III worsened relations between France and the European Catholic rulers, by ensuring that these remained within the Protestant alliance, and made it more difficult to obtain peace. They shared the view of some of their English Jacobite contemporaries that it would have been better for the Stuarts to move to Avignon, Lorraine, Bern or the electorate of Cologne. The papacy advocated they leave France, much to the delight of the British government and its allies.[112]

The death of Louis XIV did not end French support for the Stuarts. French foreign policy paid a heavy price for this support. The image of France in Europe, at a time when the Continent was passing through an intellectual crisis,[113] was harmed by its association with the unfortunate Stuarts. On the credit side, one important consequence of the Jacobites settling in Louis XIV's France was the cross-fertilisation of French culture with that of the United Kingdom.

NOTES

1   M. A. Thomson, review of G. Hilton Jones's basic study *The Main Stream of Jacobitism* (Cambridge, Mass., 1954) in *English Historical Review* (1955) 672. Note that works cited in Hilton Jones's book are not listed in the notes to this article in order to save space. See also R. Walcott, 'The later Stuarts (1660–1714). Significant works of the last twenty years (1939–1959)', *American Historical Review* (1962) 352–70. To these should be added R. H. George, 'The Financial Relations of Louis XIV and James III', *Journal of Modern History* (1931) 392–413; E. Chapman, *Mary II Stuart* (London, 1953); J. Prebble, *Glencoe, the Story of the Massacre* (London, 1966); A. C. Addington, *The Royal House of Stuart*, (3 vols London, 1972).

2   Cf. G. Ascoli, *La Grande-Bretagne devant l'opinion française au XVIIe siècle*, 2 vols (Paris, 1930); W. H. Greenleaf, *Order, Empiricism and Politics 1500–1700* (London, 1964); J. Truchet, *La Politique de Bossuet* (Paris, 1966); J. Béranger, *Les hommes de lettres et la politique en Angleterre de la Révolution de 1688 à la mort de George Ier* (Bordeaux, 1968). For this debate see also R. Hatton, *Europe in the Age of Louis XIV* (London, 1969) pp. 78–9, 188, 202.

3   The Jacobite diaspora in Europe, from the Iberian peninsula to Scandinavia, has not as yet been studied in its entirety. Jacobite contacts with freemasons are touched upon in studies of freemasonry, the role of the financiers in H. Lüthy, *La Banque protestante en France de la Révocation de l'Edit de Nantes à la Révolution*, vol. I (*1685–1730*) (Paris, 1959). My seminar paper on 'Les Jacobites en France aux XVIIe et XVIIIe siècles' delivered at the Institute of Historical Research, London, will appear in article form in a forthcoming issue of the *European Studies Review*.

4   M. Ashley, 'King James II and the Revolution of 1688. Some reflections on the historiography', *Historical Essays, 1660–1750, presented to D. Ogg* (London, 1963) pp. 185–202; see also René Durand, 'Louis XIV et Jacques II à la Veille de la Révolution de 1688', *Revue d'Histoire Moderne et Contemporaine* (1908) 28 ff.

5   J. Dulon, *Jacques II Stuart, sa famille et les Jacobites à St. Germain-en-Laye* (St Germain, 1897); Du Bosq de Beaumont, *La Cour des Stuarts à Saint-Germain-en-Laye* (Paris, 1912); A. Joly, *Un converti de Bossuet, James Drumond, duc de Perth* (Lille, 1934).

6   Mme de Sévigné to Mme de Grignan, Paris, 24 Dec 1688 and 10 Jan 1689: *Lettres de Mme de Sévigné*, ed. Gérard-Gailly (Paris, 1957) p. 310.

7   Jones, *Main Stream of Jacobitism*, p. 7 ff.

8   Sir Charles Petrie, *The Stuarts*, 2nd ed. (London, 1958) p. 265, is of the opinion that the Stuart family would have done better to choose the Spanish Netherlands as a place of residence.

9   Marc Bloch, *Les rois thaumaturges* (Paris, 1961) p. 392.

10   See the memoir for the instruction of Comte d'Avaux, dated 11 Feb 1689 at Marly, in Jusserand (ed.), *Recueil des Instructions aux*

Ambassadeurs de France en Angleterre, vol. II (Paris, 1929) pp. 425–32 (hereafter cited as *Recueil*).

11 A. Dillon, *Observations historiques sur l'origine, les services et l'état civil des officiers irlandais au service de la France* (Paris, 1792).

12 See P. Coquelle, *Les projets de descente en Angleterre* (Paris, 1902) and, for a more recent treatment, J. G. Simms, *Jacobite Ireland, 1685–1691* (Dublin, 1969) p. 52 ff; see also J. Stevens, *The Journal of J. Stevens, Containing a Brief Account of the War in Ireland (1689–1691)*, ed. R. H. Murray (Oxford, 1912).

13 Ascoli, *La Grande Bretagne*, vol. I, p. 173 ff.

14 Vincennes: Archives de la Guerre; A I 2654, ff. 321–2, Chamlay to Louis XIV, 5 Aug 1691. For the strained relations between the French and the Jacobites in Ireland see Dalrymple's *Memoirs* (1771) pp. 451–2, and C. Rousset, *Histoire de Louvois*, IV (Paris, 1863) p. 191 ff.

15 A. Corvisier, *L'Armée française de la fin du XVIIᵉ siècle au ministère de Choiseul: le soldat*, I (Paris, 1964) pp. 147–8, 261–3, 270 ff.

16 Cf. J. G. Simms, *The Williamite Confiscation in Ireland 1690–1703* (Dublin, 1956).

17 Thomas Lediard, *Histoire navale d'Angleterre*, III (Lyon, 1751; translated from English edition of 1735) p. 28 ff.

18 For Dundee, see C. S. Terry, *John Graham of Claverhouse, Viscount Dundee* (London, 1905); for the history of Scotland, T. C. Smout, *A History of the Scottish People 1560–1830* (London, 1970).

19 Lediard, *Histoire navale*, III, pp. 89–101; Sir George Clark, 'The Nine Years War 1688–1697', *New Cambridge Modern History*, vol. VI (1969) pp. 243–4.

20 See the old, well-documented article by A. Desbans, 'Une affaire d'espionnage maritime à Marseille en 1696', extract from *La Revue Maritime* (Paris, 1906); and also S. P. Oakley, 'The Interception of Posts in Celle 1694–1700', in Ragnhild Hatton and J. S. Bromley (eds), *William III and Louis XIV. Essays by and for M. A. Thomson* (Liverpool, 1968) pp. 95–116.

21 Coquelle, *Les projets de descente*, p. 3.

22 Jones, *Main Stream of Jacobitism*, p. 29.

23 G. Hilton Jones, *Charles Middleton. The Life and Times of a Restoration Politician* (Chicago, 1967) p. 265.

24 M. A. Thomson, 'Louis XIV and William III, 1689–1697', in Hatton and Bromley (eds), *William III and Louis XIV*, pp. 24–32.

25 R. Hatton, 'Louis XIV and his Fellow Monarchs', in Rule (ed.), *Louis XIV and the Craft of Kingship* (Columbus, Ohio, 1969) p. 161, and above, pp. 22–3.

26 M. Haile, *Queen Mary of Modena, her Life and Letters* (London, 1905) p. 330.

27 F. W. Head, *The Fallen Stuarts* (Cambridge, 1901) p. 55. For relations between the Stuarts and the papacy, see Bruno Neveu, 'Jacques II médiateur entre Louis XIV et Innocent XI', *Mélanges d'Archéologie et d'Histoire* (l'Ecole française de Rome) 79 (1969) 699–764.

28 E. Dubois, *La famille des Stuarts* (Rouen, 1874) pp. 140–1; A. Hassal, *Louis XIV* (London, New York, 1895) pp. 277–8.

29 P. G. M. Dickson, *The Financial Revolution in England, 1688–1756* (London, New York, 1967) *passim*.

30 D. Ogg, *England in the Reign of James II and William III 1685–1702* (London, 1955) pp. 270–6; P. Jeannin, *L'Europe du N.O. et du Nord, aux XVIIᵉ et XVIIIᵉ siècles* (Paris, 1969) p. 184; J. Prebble, *Glencoe, the Story of the Massacre* (London, 1966).

31 Ogg, *England in the Reign of James II and William III*, pp. 426–7, 435–6; Head, *The Fallen Stuarts*, p. 77; Claudine S. Boulanger, 'La vie quotidienne chez les ducs de Fitz-James au XVIIIᵉ siècle', unpublished thesis, University of Paris, Nanterre, 1971.

32 A. de Wismes, *Jean Bart et la guerre de course* (Paris, 1965) p. 161.

33 Cf. Hist. MSS. Comm., *Trumbull Papers*, i, 2 (London, 1924) p. 709.

34 Thomson, 'Louis XIV and William III', p. 36 ff.

35 A. Legrelle, *Notes et documents sur la paix de Ryswick* (Lille, 1894); for the Swedish mediation see R. M. Hatton, *Charles XII* (London, 1968) pp. 72–85.

36 Jones, *Main Stream of Jacobitism*, p. 52.

37 Dubois, *La Famille des Stuarts*, pp. 142–3. For the Polish question the old work by M. Topin, *L'Europe et les Bourbons sous Louis XIV*, 4th ed. (Paris, 1881) is still useful; see also A. Gieysztor, Stefan Kieniewicz et al., *Histoire de Pologne* (Warsaw, 1971) pp. 276–7 and A. Larangé, 'L'élection d'Auguste de Saxe au trône de Pologne', unpublished thesis, University of Lille, 1972.

38 Haile, *Queen Mary of Modena*; Thomson, 'Louis XIV and William III', p. 46.

39 H. Vast, *Les grands traités du règne de Louis XIV*, ii (Paris, 1893) p. 202 ff.

40 Jones, *Main Stream of Jacobitism*, p. 52.

41 Instruction to Comte de Tallard, Dec 1698, in P. Vaucher (ed.), *Recueil*, iii (Paris, 1965) p. 45.

42 Duc de la Force, *Louis XIV et sa Cour* (Paris, 1956) p. 152.

43 Chateaubriand, *Les quatre Stuarts* (Paris, 1833) p. 204; see also *La correspondance inédite de l'abbé de Rancé et de Jacques II*, ed. M. L. Serrant (Paris, 1905).

44 'Voyage du Roi et de la Reine d'Angleterre à Bourbon (1701): Journal de voyage et lettres', Archives Nationales, K. 1302, no 6; 'Acte de décès de Jacques II, roi d'Angleterre, d'Ecosse et d'Irlande (16 Sept 1701)', from Registre paroissial, Archives Communales St-Germain-en-Laye, in *Souvenirs du Collège des Ecossais* (1962) p. 43; 'Lettres de lord Perth à l'abbé de Rancé (17 Sept. – 9 Oct. 1701)', Arch. Nat. K. 1717, no 26; 'Lettres du duc de Bourgogne au roi d'Espagne Philippe V et à la Reine', ed. Baudrillart and Lecestre, *Société de l'Histoire de France*, i (1912) 6–7. For popular belief in the miraculous power of his corpse, see *Stuart Papers*, ed. Falconer Madan, i (London, 1889) p. 211, and ibid., ii, pp. 515–24; F. G. Alger, 'The Posthumus Vicissitudes of James II', *The Nineteenth Century* (1889) 104–9.

45 See Hatton; 'Louis XIV and his Fellow Monarchs', p. 23 above; cf. Baudrillart and Lecestre (eds), 'Lettres du duc de Bourgogne', pp. 8–9, which adopts Louis XIV's point of view, and the anti-Louis testimony of Saint-Hilaire, in his '*Mémoires*', ed. L. Lecestre in *Société de l'Histoire de France*, III (1903–16) pp. 86–9. Note A. Lossky, in Rule (ed.), *Louis XIV and the Craft of Kingship*, p. 344, n. 33: 'Louis, however, maintained that this step involved neither a withdrawal of his recognition of William III nor any design to help the Pretender to establish himself in England', based on Archives des Affaires Etrangères, Correspondance Politique, Danemark, vol. 66, ff. 393–4, Louis XIV to Chamilly, 15 Sept 1701.

46 Claude-Frédéric Lévy, *Capitalistes et pouvoir au Siécle des Lumières* (Paris, The Hague, 1969) p. 171.

47 Ascoli, *La Grande Bretagne*, vol. I, p. 460 ff; J. C. Dufermont, *Les collèges anglais, écossais, irlandais, à la mort de Louis XVI*, unpublished thesis, University of Lille, 1967.

48 Ascoli, *La Grande Bretagne*, vol. II, pp. 166–8.

49 See J. Saint-Germain, *La vie quotidienne en France à la fin du Grand Siècle* (Paris, 1965) p. 21. For James III being closely supervised, possibly for his own protection in 1706, see ibid., pp. 268–9.

50 A. Legrelle, *La diplomatie française et la Succession d'Espagne*, vol. IV: *La solution 1700–1725* (Ghent, 1892) pp. 300–1; see also Sir Charles Petrie, *Berwick* (London, 1953) p. 170.

51 Petrie, *Berwick*, p. 303; Jones, *Main Stream of Jacobitism*, pp. 67–9.

52 Archives de la Guerre, Projets et Mémoires de Chamlay, A¹. 1698.

53 Henry Hamilton, *An Economic History of Scotland in the Eighteenth Century* (Oxford, 1963) pp. 251–2, 291–3; G. S. Pryde, *Social Life in Scotland since 1707* (London, 1934).

54 Archives de la Guerre, A¹ 2017, A¹ 2089, Y2d 1464; A.A.E., C.P. Angleterre, vol. 250; Mémoires et Documents, Angleterre, vol. 75 (Stuarts, vol. I); Archives Nationales: Archives de la Marine, B² 33, B² 205.

55 Lévy, *Capitalistes et pouvoir*, p. 309; Claire E. Engel, preface to Antoine Hamilton, *Mémoires du Chevalier de Gramont* (Paris, 1958) pp. 35–6.

56 Nathaniel Hook to Chamillart, 29 July 1707: Archives de la Guerre, A¹ 2019, ff. 209 ff.

57 Ibid., 'Mémoire des seigneurs écossais'; cf. Jones, *Main Stream of Jacobitism*, p. 78 and W. D. Macray, *Correspondence of Col. Nathaniel Hooke, 1703–1707* (London, 1871) vol. II, pp. 256–62, but note that this edition has sufficient errors to make consultation of the original documents worth while: hence citations to these throughout my article.

58 See Hamilton, *An Economic History of Scotland*, T. C. Smout, *Scottish Trade on the Eve of the Union (1660–1707)* (London, 1963) and W. Ferguson, 'The Making of the Treaty of Union of 1707', *Scottish Historical Revue* (1964).

59 Archives de la Guerre, A¹ 2019, 'Lettres des Seigneurs écossais au Roi Jacques III d'Angleterre': Stormont, from Scone, 1 May 1707

and the marquess of Drummond, from Drummond, 8 May 1707; Panmure, from Panmure, 12 May 1707; the duke of Gordon, from Gordon, 16 May 1707; the count of Errol, from Slains, 27 May 1707; cf. Macray, *Correspondence of Col. Hooke*, vol. II, pp. 262–8.

60 Archives de la Guerre, A¹ 2019, letter of James, duke of Hamilton to James III, 19 May 1707 (in cypher); cf. G. S. Pryde, *The Treaty of Union of Scotland and England 1707* (London, Edinburgh, 1950) pp. 8–34. For the duke himself having distributed 20,680 francs (put at his disposal by the Pope) among the Scottish deputies see Head, *The Fallen Stuarts*, p. 130.

61 For the espionage of John Ogilvie, employed by Harley in Edinburgh, see Hist. MSS. Comm., *Rep. XV, App. IV*, pp. 464–6, also Jones, *Main Stream of Jacobitism*, p. 79.

62 Until Louis XIV recognised Anne as queen at the Peace of Utrecht she was referred to in French correspondence as Princess Anne.

63 Lévy, *Capitalistes et pouvoir*, p. 310.

64 J. Teneur, 'Les commercants dunkerquois à la fin du XVIIIᵉ siècle et les problèmes économiques de leur temps', *Revue du Nord* (1966) 22, 33, 35, 36. For James Rutlidge, the son of the strongly Jacobite Irish privateer Walter Rutlidge, see R. Las Vergnas, *Le Chevalier Rutlidge, 'gentilhomme anglais'* (Paris, 1932), especially ch. 3, 'Le milieu irlandais en France', pp. 46–57.

65 Archives de la Guerre, A¹ 2019, nos 207–8.

66 Ibid., A¹ 2089 no 72, 'Mémoire de Charles Fleming à Chamillart sur l'Ecosse', instruction au Comte de Gacé of 8 Mar 1708; no. 73, Gacé to Chamillart, Dunkirk, 9 Mar 1708. The English blockade, in which twenty four ships took part, evidently delayed the operation even before James's illness: see ibid., no 80. Forbin's letter to James III, 10 Mar 1708.

67 Ibid., A¹ 2089, the intendant Bernières to Chamillart, Dunkirk, 29 Mar 1708.

68 David Ogg, 'The Emergence of Great Britain as a World Power', *New Cambridge Modern History*, vol. VI, p. 257; Sir Charles Petrie, *The Jacobite Movement* (London, 1959) pp. 164–5.

69 John C. Rule, 'France and the Preliminaries of the Gertruydenberg Conference, September 1709 to March 1710', in R. Hatton and M. S. Anderson (eds), *Studies in Diplomatic History* (London, 1970) pp. 100–2.

70 Archives de la Guerre, A¹ 2151, Villars to Louis XIV, 1 July 1709; Louis XIV to Villars from Versailles, 2 July 1709: 'The descent on Scotland and Ireland is difficult to put into operation as long as our enemies have 140 ships at sea, while I for my part have not been able to make proper preparations for the descent'.

71 C. de Sèze, 'Comment Louis XIV a perdu Tournai', *Revue du Nord* (1964) 517–24.

72 'Extracts from Papers of l'Abbé Gaultier', *Edinburgh Review*, vol. LXII (1835) 1–36; see also A.A.E., Mémoires et Documents, Angleterre, vol. 75.

73   Instruction for the duc d'Aumont, Marly, 6 Nov 1712, in Vaucher (ed.), *Recueil*, pp. 126–7.

74   R. C. Jarvis's articles in *Transactions of the Lancashire and Cheshire Antiquarian Society* and *Transactions of the Cumberland and Westmorland Antiquarian Society* from 1944 onwards (now republished as *Collected Papers on the Jacobite Risings*, 2 vols, Manchester, 1971–2); see also his book *The Jacobite Risings of 1715 and 1745* (Cumberland C.C. Record Series I, 1954).

75   For Prior's mission see L. G. Wickham Legg, *Matthew Prior, a Study of his Public Career and Correspondence* (London, 1921), Charles K. Eves, *Matthew Prior, Poet and Diplomatist* (London, New York, 1939) and J. C. Rule, 'King and Minister, Louis XIV and Colbert de Torcy' in Hatton and Bromley (eds), *William III and Louis XIV*, pp. 233 ff.

76   See H. Baumont, *Etudes sur le règne de Léopold duc de Lorraine et de Bar* (Paris, Nancy, 1894) pp. 234–7.

77   For the Congress of Utrecht and the treaties signed there see Gaston Zeller, *Les Temps modernes* II, *De Louis XIV à 1789*, 'Histoire des Relations Internationales' (Paris, 1955) pp. 94–101. For the Spanish side of the peacemaking, see Marianne Cermakian, *La Princesse des Ursins* (Paris, 1969).

78   See the *Mémoires* for the instruction of d'Iberville, 26 Sep 1713 and 31 Oct 1713, in Vaucher (ed.), *Recueil*, pp. 145–6. Louis XIV was willing to make commercial concessions in order to promote a reconciliation between Queen Anne and her brother James: ibid., p. 156, note 11. In fact Bromley was a non-juror, but leant towards Hanover, sending his son there in February 1714: see E. Gregg, 'The Protestant Succession in International Politics 1710–1716', unpublished thesis, University of London, 1972.

79   Jones, *Main Stream of Jacobitism*, p. 94 ff. For Queen Anne's personality see N. Connell, *Anne, the Last Stuart Monarch* (London, 1937).

80   A.A.E. Angleterre, Mémoires et Documents, vol. 75, ff. 56–7, Torcy to James III, 18 Apr 1714, in which Torcy declares that he has had long discussions on this topic with Father Lewis Inese, principal of the Scottish College in Paris. For criticism of Father Inese and the college see J. Gordon, *Mémoires* (London, 1738).

81   A.A.E., Mémoires et Documents, Angleterre, vol. 75, ff. 53–4, Iberville to Louis XIV, 10 Feb 1714.

82   Ibid., f. 62, Torcy to James III, 12 Aug 1714.

83   James had wished to seek out at Passy the duc de Lauzun, who had taken him to France in 1688 and fought for him in Ireland in 1690: ibid., ff. 64–5, James III to Torcy, 15 Aug 1714, and Torcy to James III, 16 Aug 1714. According to Mathieu Marais' *Journal et Mémoires*, I, ed. de Lescure (Paris, 1863) pp. 147–8, 'Our king of England' had already visited Passy in June 1712.

84   A.A.E., Mémoires et Documents, Angleterre, vol. 75, ff. 67–9; Iberville to Louis XIV, 16 Aug 1714, Louis XIV à Iberville, 22 Aug 1714. Informing Louis of Queen Anne's death, Iberville told him that 'all sensible Jacobites held that the interests of the king of France, of

Europe and James III himself demanded that he keep quiet for the moment, for there has not been the smallest demonstration in his favour while the Elector of Hanover has been proclaimed in London and the whole country'. He concluded that the Jacobites wished to avoid civil war. Cf. H. L. Snyder, 'The Last Days of Queen Anne. The Account of Sir John Evelyn Examined', *Huntington Library Quarterly* (1971) 268–9.

85 A.A.E., Mémoires et Documents, Angleterre, vol. 75, ff. 48–50; Torcy to James III, 21 Oct 1713. It is worth noting that Torcy had not taken Father Inese into his confidence about the Le Havre project.

86 Ibid., ff. 70–2; Louis XIV to Iberville, 16 and 22 Aug 1714; Louis XIV to Philip V, 25 Aug 1714, in Courcy, *L'Espagne après la paix d'Utrecht 1713–1715* (Paris, 1891) p. 191; J. B. Perkins, *France under the Regency* (London, 1892) pp. 373–4.

87 See M. A. Thomson, 'The Safeguarding of the Protestant Succession 1702–1718', in Hatton and Bromley (eds), *William III and Louis XIV*, p. 248; J. B. Wolf, *The Emergence of the Great Powers 1685–1715*, new ed. (London, 1962) p. 120.

88 See R. M. Hatton, 'George I as an English and European Figure', in P. Fritz and D. Williams (eds), *The Triumph of Culture. 18th Century Perspectives* (Toronto, 1972) pp. 191–209 for work in progress on George as elector and as king: see, for a fine analysis of the Tory and Whig parties, J. H. Plumb, *The Growth of Political Stability in England 1675–1725* (London, 1967) pp. 159, 161–2, 168–72; cf. also K. Kluxen, *Das Problem der Politischen Opposition* (München, 1956).

89 J. H. Jesse, *Memoirs of the Pretenders and their Adherents* (London, 1901) pp. 22–3.

90 Sir Charles Petrie, *The Four Georges*, new ed. (London, 1946) pp. 32–3; J. H. Plumb, *The First Four Georges* (London, 1966).

91 A.A.E., Mémoires et Documents, Angleterre, vol. 75, ff. 79–80: Iberville to Torcy, London, 22 Apr 1715.

92 G. Zeller, *Aspects de la politique française sous l'Ancien Régime* (Paris, 1964) p. 181.

93 Claude Nordmann, *La Crise du Nord au début du XVIIIᵉ siècle* (Paris, 1962) p. 39.

94 See Bolingbroke's letter from Dover of 7 April 1715 to Lord Landsdowne in Grimoard (ed.), *Lettres historiques, politiques de Henri Saint-John Lord vicomte Bolingbroke depuis 1710 jusqu'en 1736*, II (Paris, 1808) pp. 427, 428; cf. Walter Sichel, *Bolingbroke and his Times*, I (London, 1901) pp. 525–6; and the letter of 12 Apr 1715 from Paris, E. Sparre to Müllern, cited in Nordmann, *La Crise du Nord*, p. 40, n. 33.

95 Jean Sareil, *Les Tencin, Histoire d'une Famille au XVIIIᵉ siècle* (Geneva, 1969) pp. 50–2; Plumb, *Growth of Political Stability*, pp. 164–6.

96 Nordmann, *La Crise du Nord*, pp. 40–1 and 249–50.

97 A.A.E., Mémoires et Documents, Angleterre, vol. 75, ff. 108–15: Torcy to Berwick, 14 July 1715; Pontchartrain to Champigny, intendant of the Navy at Le Havre, 15 July 1715; Torcy to James III,

16 July 1715; Inese to Torcy, 16 July 1715. See also Dom H. Leclercq, *Histoire de la Régence*, I (Paris, 1921) p. 250.

98   G. de Lamberty, *Mémoires pour servir à l'Histoire du XVIIIᵉ siècle* (The Hague, 1730) p. 23; Nordmann, *La Crise du Nord*, p. 42 and n. 43.

99   R. M. Hatton, *Charles XII* (London, 1968) p. 416.

100 Plans for gaining Swedish help for the Stuarts were not new. In 1712 it had been suggested that Princess Louise Marie, daughter of James II, should marry Charles XII to gain his help for the Jacobite cause; but before this plan could be mooted she died, twenty years old, on 10 April of that very year. Cf. Petrie, *The Jacobite Movement*, p. 174. For Louise Marie Stuart, see B. Saint-John, *La Cour de Jacques II à St-Germain-en-Laye* (Paris, 1913) pp. 52–7.

101 J. H. and Margaret Shennan, 'The Protestant Succession in English Politics, April 1713 – September 1715' in *William III and Louis XIV*, ed. Hatton and Bromley, pp. 266–8.

102 M. Carpio, *España y los últimos Estuardos* (Madrid, 1952) pp. 13–14.

103 Carpio, *España*, pp. 9–10; Nordmann, *La Crise du Nord*, pp. 43–4. The Shennans, on p. 268 of the article cited above (note 101), erroneously share the British government's assumptions in respect of Monteleón.

104 P. Purcell, 'The Jacobite Rising of 1715 and the English Catholics', *English Historical Review* (1929) 418–32.

105 A.A.E., Mémoires et Documents, Angleterre, vol. 75, ff. 130–5: D'Iberville to Louis XIV, London, 12 and 13 Aug 1715; Louis XIV to d'Iberville, Versailles, 22 Aug 1715. Even so there existed, after 11 July 1715, a semi rupture of diplomatic relations between France and Great Britain, since George I's ambassador, Lord Stair, was forbidden to seek audiences with Torcy: Leclercq, *Histoire de la Régence*, I, p. 249. For troops having been collected in the Boulogne region see L. André, *Louis XIV et l'Europe* (Paris, 1950) p. 343.

106 Petrie, *The Jacobite Movement*, p. 250.

107 Bolingbroke, *Letter to Sir William Wyndham of 1717* (London, 1753); Jesse, *Memoirs of the Pretenders*, p. 25; P. Baratier, *Lord Bolingbroke, ses écrits politiques* (Paris, 1939) p. 154; C. S. Terry, *The Jacobites and the Union* (Cambridge, 1922) p. 57. The 'Rising of 1715' might benefit from being reconsidered in the perspective of recent studies of 'risings', such as those of Mousnier and Porchnev: the tendency of the gentry towards Jacobitism in a period of economic difficulties is worth exploring.

108 Ogg, *England in the Reign of James II and William III*, pp. 427–8; Wolf, *Emergence of the Great Powers*, pp. 113–14. For the role of the British press see E. S. De Beer, 'The English Newspapers from 1695 to 1702' in Hatton and Bromley (eds), *William III and Louis XIV*, pp. 117–29.

109 Roland Mousnier, *Les XVIᵉ et XVIIᵉ siècles. Les progrès de la civilisation européenne et le déclin de l'Orient 1492–1715*, 4th ed. (Paris, 1965) pp. 308–9.

110 Nordmann, *La Crise du Nord*, p. 247. For the advantages stipulated for British commerce in 1720 in Sweden–Finland see Claude Nordmann,

Grandeur et liberté de la Suède 1660–1792 (Paris, Louvain, 1971) pp. 220–1.

111 See Petrie, *The Jacobite Movement*, p. 253. Jeffrey Hart in his *Viscount Bolingbroke, Tory Humanist* (London, 1965) p. 45 argues that French policy was more subtle than often assumed and directed more at promoting unrest in Britain than at a restoration of the Stuarts.

112 Haile, *Queen Mary of Modena*, pp. 426–7; Coissac de Chavrebière, *Histoire des Stuarts* (Paris, 1930) p. 278.

113 Paul Hazard, *La crise de la conscience européenne 1680–1715* (Paris, 1935).

Part II

CASE-STUDIES

5 Louis XIV and the Electorate of Trier 1652-1676[*]

RENÉ PILLORGET

In the seventeenth century the elector of Trier could not really hope to play a major role in the politics of the Holy Roman Empire. His electorate was neither rich nor extensive; it was about twice the size of the present duchy of Luxembourg. To try and describe briefly what were the precise frontiers of the electorate would be somewhat foolhardy, because of the numerous enclaves and territories where sovereignty was shared with other overlords. But one vital feature is clear even from a cursory glance at the map: apart from a few excrescences, the territory of the elector of Trier, stretching from Lorraine to Coblenz, consisted essentially of the valley of the Moselle. This position was at one and the same time advantageous and dangerous.

It was advantageous because a large part of the electoral revenues derived from its geographical situation – the tolls on the Moselle compensated for the mediocre resources of the rest of the state. The danger came from the close proximity of the Spanish Netherlands whose frontiers ran along the western side of the electorate. Trier itself, although a capital city of the Empire and thus possessed of a certain prestige, was of minor military importance. Far more significant were Coblenz and Ehrenbreitstein, a powerful fortress controlling the confluence of the Rhine and the Moselle; these were the key points of the electorate. The small state stood in fact at the crossroads of two great military routes. One led from the Empire and the heredi-tary lands of the Habsburgs to the domains of their cousins in

[*] Specially commissioned for this volume.

E

the Spanish Netherlands. The other, leading northwards from France, followed the axis of the Moselle and intersected with the first. Depending on whether he allowed free movement of troops from east to west or from south to north, the elector was in danger of making an enemy either of the king of France, in the first case, or of the Habsburgs in the second. Caught between the pull of the political and moral ties binding him to the Empire, and the threats of powerful neighbours who coveted his fortresses and bridges, the elector could do no more once war had broken out than watch, from the heights of Ehrenbreitstein, as his lands were ravaged by both friend and foe. He was far too weak financially to be able to defend them on his own.

After the Peace of Westphalia, with France and Spain still at war, the question of his relations with the former power took on a particular importance for the elector. His decision whether or not to allow the free passage of Imperial reinforcements on their march to the Spanish Netherlands might well seal the fate of the electorate, against which France was now in a position to concentrate most of its forces. The elector's policy would be determined in part by personal factors and in part by the play of influences to which he was subjected.[1]

THE ACCESSION OF KARL-KASPAR VON DER LEYEN TO THE ARCH-BISHOPRIC OF TRIER

For a quarter of a century the archbishopric of Trier had been held by Philipp-Christoph von Sötern, who was also bishop of Speyer. He had been the German prince most favourably disposed towards France,[2] and several secret treaties had made him a French client and pensioner. He was well aware of his financial and military weakness; and although the occupation of his lands by French troops might be unpleasant, at least it would save his subjects from being invaded by the heretical Swedes. It would not be correct to say that Philipp-Christoph's actions were determined solely by base motives, but there can be no doubt that material considerations went a long way towards deciding his political alignments. As he grew older he became dominated by one obsession: to reconstitute his family's patrimony. To this end he bought or redeemed lands which he wished to entail into a *fideicommis*, heritable only according to certain rules and conditions fixed by the testator. In 1633 and 1634, once he was sure of French protection, a series of legal decisions of dubious validity allowed him to 'recover' feudal rights and lands which he claimed had been detached illegally from the possessions of his family. This brought him into conflict with the Metternich family, perhaps the richest in the electorate, several members of which were canons in his chapter, and with whom he had already been in bitter dispute over an inheritance. The prince-archbishop's lawyers now laid claim to his rivals' estates, and later to those of other canons, with the result that they all closed ranks behind the Metternich family. Moreover, hereditary loyalty made the latter the leaders of the pro-Habsburg party within the electorate.[3] In 1635 they appealed to Spain for assistance. The governor of Luxembourg sent troops into Trier, and a member of the Metternich family serving in the Spanish army arrested Philipp-Christoph and handed him into the custody of the emperor. This was the pretext on which France declared war on Spain, and the incident also brought about a state of war between France and the emperor.

In 1645, when Ferdinand III was beginning to accept the necessity of making peace, France refused to open negotiations until its client had been set free and restored to his state. Thus Philipp-Christoph in November of that year returned to Trier and resumed his former policies, using French support to bring his great project, the *fideicommis*, to fruition. On 19 July 1646 a new treaty was signed with Louis XIV. A French garrison was placed in Philippsburg, patterned on the Imperial occupation of Ehrenbreitstein during his absence.[4] Almost at once the Metternich family, and all the canons except one, fled to Cologne. For the next three years Philipp-Christoph governed autocratically. He divested the hostile canons of their positions and in a parody of an election, on 24 April 1649, provided himself with a coadjutor of his own family, Baron Reiffenberg. The exiles immediately reacted to this challenge, feeling free to do so since the French crown was preoccupied by the Fronde of the Parlement. From the Spaniards they obtained a few hundred men, and led by one of the canons, still in his thirties – Karl-Kaspar von der Leyen, nephew of Johann-Philipp von Schönborn, the elector of Mainz – they marched on Trier and without much difficulty took possession of the town on 31 May. Philipp-Christoph became a virtual prisoner in his palace. Mazarin, at the *Exekutions-*

tag (or Assembly at Nuremberg), charged with implementing
the Peace of Westphalia, protested in vain at the outrage perpetrated on Philipp-Christoph.[5] Next he attempted with the help
of Johann-Philipp von Schönborn to arrange a reconciliation
between Philipp-Christoph and his chapter and to replace the
Imperial forces in Ehrenbreitstein with those of the elector-
archbishop of Mainz. The Fronde of the princes caused the
collapse of these schemes : the French troops sent to the electorate
to support Schönborn's mediation had to be withdrawn, and
soon not even a French diplomatic representative could be found
in Trier.

Accordingly in June 1650 the fifteen canons of the chapter
met to elect a coadjutor to Philipp-Christoph of their own choice.
Von der Leyen seemed the obvious choice as he was supported
by his uncle, the archbishop of Mainz, and also by the Metternich family, to which he was related. His sponsors decided to
divide Philipp-Christoph's benefices. Von der Leyen was to be
coadjutor for the archbishop of Trier only, while Speyer would
remain in the sole charge of Philipp-Christoph but pass after
his death to a Metternich. With this bargain struck, Karl-Kaspar
was elected coadjutor with nine votes, against six for his rival
candidate, Cratz von Scharffenstein. Mazarin had not intervened
because of the domestic situation of France. In any case he
preferred von der Leyen to Scharffenstein. Although the former,
a connection of the Metternichs, was open to Habsburg influence,
he was also the nephew of Schönborn and might therefore be
won over to the French side; while Scharffenstein was by French
observers considered inaccessible to French influence.[6] In July
1650 the emperor's troops evacuated Ehrenbreitstein, formally
handing over the fortress – as the words of the peace settlement
of 1648 had stipulated – to the 'Archbishop and his Chapter' –
though in reality to the chapter alone. When Philipp-Christoph
died (4 February 1652) Karl-Kaspar succeeded him, and a few
days later the canon Lothar-Friedrich von Metternich was elected
archbishop of Speyer.[7] Schönborn had once remarked that Karl-
Kaspar was 'a blank sheet of paper' on which 'one might write
whatever one wished'; but, as a French agent lamented, 'since
that time the Spaniards have written all over that sheet'.[8] Ehrenbreitstein had now been handed over to a prince friendly to
the Habsburgs; the Spanish Netherlands continued to receive

reinforcements from the emperor; and the Franco–Spanish war continued until 1659.

As long as the French Frondes lasted, Karl-Kaspar maintained his friendly relations with the emperor. The most notable consequence of this was his assistance in electing at Augsburg, on 31 May 1653, the son of Ferdinand III as king of the Romans. As soon as France recovered its full strength, Mazarin began to draw all the Rhineland electors into his orbit: they would be useful not only in the event of an Imperial election but also in French military operations against the Spanish Netherlands. Between 1654 and 1658 he laid the groundwork both for French intrigues at the next Imperial election and for the future League of the Rhine.[9]

Mazarin and Brienne did not hold Karl-Kaspar's earlier hostility against him, but sought to win him over by friendly attentions. In this they were partially successful. When the king of the Romans died, his younger brother Leopold was not made his successor: this had been agreed at a meeting of the three ecclesiastical electors, held at the instigation of France, in 1654 at Kärlich in the territory of Trier. Mazarin thereupon redoubled his professions of amnity for Karl-Kaspar, and the announcement of the emperor's death in April 1657 came at a particularly good moment in the relations between France and Trier.[10] In the period which elapsed between the emperor's death and the election at Frankfurt, three separate and differing stages may be discerned in the relations between Karl-Kaspar and Mazarin.

The first stage, in June 1657, was the period of great expectations, centring on the mission of the comte de Wagnée to Trier. Mazarin, building on the concept of 'the Germanic liberties' of the treaties of Westphalia and – more immediately – on the amity of Johann-Philipp von Schönborn, entertained, if only for a few weeks, the hope of seeing Louis XIV as a candidate for the Imperial throne.[11] But the attitude of Karl-Kaspar, a particularly important elector since it was the Trier incumbent who traditionally voted first, proved insufficiently favourable for precise overtures to be made to him.

The second stage was one of ticklish manœuvres conducted by Robert de Gravel, the French resident at Frankfurt. Mazarin instructed him to remind Karl-Kaspar of the 'noble action of one of his predecessors', the elector of Trier who had supported Francis I's candidature, in a speech that had been greeted by 'universal applause'.[12] Karl-Kaspar recalled that France still owed him 60,000 *Reichstaler* but did not proceed to negotiations. In August Schönborn warned Mazarin, with due formality, that the general attitude of the Electoral College was not favourable to Louis XIV's candidature: there was no hope of his ascending the Imperial throne. Karl-Kaspar let it be known that he would only vote for the king of France if, prior to the election, he were given proof that four other electors were ready to vote for Louis XIV. He would gladly make 'the fifth from four', but nothing could persuade him to start a schism in the Electoral College by adding his vote to three others. It is possible that Karl-Kaspar had already made up his mind; but though he might believe in ultimate success for Leopold, he wished to leave himself a loophole in case the selection did not turn out as expected. By December, despite French efforts to persuade first Ferdinand-Maria of Bavaria and then Philipp-Wilhelm of Neuburg to offer themselves as candidates, Leopold's success seemed inevitable. Johann-Philipp von Schönborn now came out openly in his support but was determined to secure, in return, first, a 'capitulation' of precise promises to be sworn by the emperor; secondly, an alliance of princes to see that the capitulation was observed; and finally, the conclusion of a general peace settlement.

January 1658 saw the beginning of the final stage of the French efforts. Mazarin had by now recognised that 'our plan to take the Imperial dignity away from the House of Austria, which has such deep roots in Germany . . . would be rather like trying to defeat a whole navy with two or three brigantines'.[13] Gravel made a last visit to Coblenz and spoke firmly to Karl-Kaspar, but only of the need to impose a strict capitulation on Leopold. The elector of Trier tried to extract as great a monetary reward for this service as for that previously held out as compensation for the projected 'exclusion' of the Habsburgs. Gravel was annoyed: the capitulation was in the German princes' own interest, and there was no reason for France to pay them for supporting it.[14] On 23 March Karl-Kaspar arrived at Frankfurt, four days after Leopold. With the baron von Metternich closely watching him he naturally acted in the interests of the Habsburgs. He even went so far on 13 and 15 May as to vote against the capitulation, as did the electors of Saxony and Bavaria (whose attitude can be explained, however, by the proximity of their states to those of the Habsburgs), while the four remaining independent electors had voted as desired by France. On 18 July Leopold was elected emperor, but only after swearing to observe the following capitulation : 'We promise not to provide arms, money, soldiers, provisions or other commodities to foreigners at war with the Crown of France, on whatever pretext it may be.' French diplomats were pleased with the result and planned optimistically ahead. 'The capitulation has been arranged to our satisfaction. It would seem as if the king of Hungary[15] will observe it, and in any case the League that is to be established . . . will force him to do so.' This league, which had been taking shape during the last year, was now in the process of actual formation, with the electors of Mainz and Cologne as its linchpins.

Thus ended an election that at times has been assessed as no more than a 'brilliant fiasco' for France. It is true that some of those involved (including Mazarin himself) may at first have had an exaggerated idea of what French diplomacy could achieve.[16] They had placed an unwarranted faith in their power and their gold, when in fact pensions and gratifications proved only of secondary importance. This is clear in the case of Karl-Kaspar; though in need of money, he still seems to have been the virtual prisoner of the Metternich family throughout his stay at Frankfurt. What counted more was the situation in Germany and Europe as a whole, the overall balance of forces, and – most of all – the weight of tradition. The negotiations also reveal the empiricism of Mazarin's methods. If the cardinal had judged it possible to obtain Louis XIV's election as emperor, there can be no doubt that he would have seized the glorious opportunity. But when his first testing of the political climate proved unfavourable for Louis' candidature, and having failed to procure any alternative German candidate, Mazarin fell back on positions he had prepared well in advance : a strict capitulation to be imposed on the newly-elected emperor and, more important, a league of German princes to enforce it.

KARL-KASPAR VON DER LEYEN AND THE LEAGUE OF THE RHINE

It is not quite correct to say that during the seventeenth and eighteenth centuries, 'with the exception of [Philipp] Christoph von Sötern, Mainz and Trier remained in the Habsburg camp, in spite of all the danger and devastation this spelt for the Archbishop-Electorate'.[17] Karl-Kasper's political alignment only corresponds in part to this pattern. For, quite apart from the fact that his successor proved accommodating towards France, it must be emphasised that for six years Karl-Kaspar was a member of the League of the Rhine, largely the creation of Mazarin. The first steps towards this alliance, taken in the years between 1651 and 1654, certainly derived from a purely German initiative, in which Trier played its part.[18] The project orginated with Johann-Philipp von Schönborn and is known as the 'Irenic system', since it envisaged a new and wider alliance of a number of German princes regardless of their religion. France, Sweden and even the Habsburgs would be asked to join in the hope of neutralising them and thus promoting a general pacification (i.e. to put an end to the Franco-Spanish war in which the emperor materially helped Spain). The French diplomats' skill lay in shaping Schönborn's ambitious scheme into an instrument of French policy. The motives behind the League of the Rhine were transformed into a political expedient to prevent military co-operation between the Spanish and Austrian Habsburgs. The German princes who agreed to join the league did not consider this French purpose incompatible with their own interests : the upholding of 'Germanic liberties' against the emperor, and ensuring peace for the Rhine valley. But within the league, just as during the election at Frankfurt, Karl-Kaspar played the Habsburgs' game. First he opposed the inclusion of France in the projected alliance. Next, shortly after the signature of the treaty establishing the league (14 August 1658) he refused to become a member.[19] Terrified by his own boldness (prompted by the so-called 'Austrian' party in the electorate which consisted of the chancellor Anethan and the Metternich family), Karl-Kaspar feared that the French army would take revenge on his territories. His fears were ungrounded. France could afford to tolerate an outpost of Spanish influence on the eastern border of the Netherlands. The electorate of Trier was a weak state and was, after the league had been formed, cut off from the rest of the Empire by a chain of small and medium-sized states linked firmly together.

After the peace of the Pyrenees Karl-Kaspar began to draw closer to France. The emperor had disappointed him; of the money promised him at Frankfurt he had only received a part. Moreover, he hoped that in return for his joining the League of the Rhine, France would recognise his metropolitan jurisdiction over Metz, Toul and Verdun.[20] Yet he proved hesitant to commit himself. To put an end to his vacillations, Louis XIV ordered the occupation of the castle of Montclair, the possession of which was shared – along with the territories of Merzig and the Saargau – between France and the elector. This threatened the road to Trier itself. Karl-Kaspar agreed to become a member of the league, but only after an agreement had been signed to settle remaining disputes between himself and Louis. A treaty to that effect was signed at Fontainebleau on 9 August 1660, but the elector still delayed his entry into the league in the hope of obtaining further advantages. A second treaty was concluded, also at Fontainebleau, on 12 October. The price exacted was the evacuation and dismantling of Montclair; and, more significantly, French formal recognition of Karl-Kaspar's metropolitan jurisdiction over the Three Bishoprics.[21] In return the elector joined the League of the Rhine and recalled his deputy at the Diet of Regensburg. To round off the bargain Louis 'promised the Elector a pension of 45,000 livres, the first year to be paid in advance, besides other pensions to be paid to a few of his relatives and ministers'.[22] In spite of such rewards Karl-Kaspar carried out his obligations under the Treaty of Fontainbleau with extreme reluctance. He did not enter the League of the Rhine until February 1662, having delayed his open alignment with France and its allies for as long as possible.[23] The next few years were peaceful for the electorate; relations with France were good and Karl-Kaspar supported French interests in the Holy Roman Empire.[24]

Not until 1665 did it become evident that the League of the Rhine was in decay. Louis XIV was unable to secure its renewal, despite the distribution of pensions and gratifications. The interplay of forces inside Germany, which was a factor of far greater significance than French gold, was now acting in a direction opposite to that of the previous decades : the Rhineland princes

saw the gravest threat to Germanic liberties to come no longer
from the emperor but from the king of France. After the collapse
of the league prudence became the guiding principle of Karl-
Kaspar's policy. During the War of Devolution, he declared –
. as did his uncle Schönborn – that he would oppose any movement of troops across his state in the direction of the Spanish
Netherlands, and obtained a ready assurance of complete respect
for the neutrality of his state from France.[25] But a period of peace
was now clearly drawing to a close. It had given the electorate
time for recovery and had favoured the extension of French
influence. Presents, favours and personal courtesies had apparently
diminished the influence of the so-called 'Austrian' party; but
throughout this period, when Karl-Kaspar was a pensioner of
France, he had continued to show signs of independence. From
1668 onwards these grew more and more striking until he finally
changed sides in 1673.

COBLENZ AND TRIER : THE STRATEGIC POINTS

Karl-Kaspar's letters to Louis XIV in the years from 1668 to
1673 contained frequent protestations of devotion. But the elector
was in reality moving gradually into the Habsburg camp. On 8
August 1668 his plenipotentiaries met Castel-Rodrigo, the governor
of the Spanish Netherlands, with whom they signed a treaty of
alliance between Trier and Spain. Supposedly secret, this treaty
was soon known in Paris.[26] Next the elector embarked on a series
of diplomatic moves whose anti-French character became increasingly apparent. When a number of princes met at Limburg
to discuss a defensive alliance, with Trier, Mainz and Lorraine
as a nucleus, Karl-Kaspar – acting almost as an agent of Spain –
made his participation subject to the condition that Mainz would
join him in his efforts to 'have the Burgundian Circle included in
the [general] guarantee of the Empire'. The outcome of such
a guarantee would be a declaration of war against Louis XIV
by all the German states if the French king were to attack
Franche-Comté or the Spanish Netherlands.[27]

The elector's policy during the succeeding years followed
similar lines. In 1670 at a meeting with his uncle Schönborn he
suggested that Spanish garrisons be placed in Mainz and Trier.
In 1671 he worked hard, if in vain, to form an alliance between
the emperor, Mainz and his own state.[28] At this time Louis XIV

and his ministers were preparing for the Dutch war. Karl-Kaspar could not refuse a French request for permission 'to transport a few guns and munitions from Metz to Bonn, along with the transit of some infantry and cavalry' since the operation was represented to be for the assistance of the archbishop-elector of Cologne.[29] All through the spring of 1672 boats – laden with provisions and ammunition – travelled down the Moselle without paying tolls, a fact which irritated Karl-Kaspar greatly.[30] His protests had no effect.[31] Worse still, a body of French troops marched down the Moselle valley, covering the right flank of the main army bound for Aachen and the Dutch border via the Meuse valley. When the marquis de Dangeau arrived in September to warn the embittered Karl-Kaspar of Louis XIV's displeasure 'should he afford the right of transit or asylum in his states' to any enemies of France, the elector showered him with verbal assurances of loyalty. But three months later, in his fortress at Ehrenbreitstein – in which he was destined to live for the rest of his life – he signed a treaty with Spain renewing the alliance of 1668; and on 31 December at Montecuccoli's headquarters his envoy signed a treaty of alliance between the United Provinces, Brandenburg and the Austrian Habsburgs. In return for his accession to the alliance Karl-Kaspar was to receive six thousand *écus* a month to maintain his fortresses and some troops. The two treaties were supposed to be secret, and Karl-Kaspar continued to treat French diplomats to professions of undying amity long after their contents were known to Louis XIV.[32] In May 1673 Imperial troops occupied Coblenz and Ehrenbreitstein,[33] and when Karl-Kaspar's deputy at the Diet of Regensburg launched a violent attack on France[34] there was no longer any doubt which side he had chosen.

The Empire now made ready for war, the first in which the German states as a whole joined forces against France. Louvois took counter-measures which, although well justified from a military standpoint, destroyed the last hopes of preserving peace. The *Décapole*, the 'Ten Cities of Alsace' (see glossary), were occupied and the Palatinate invaded. To safeguard French communications along the Moselle it was decided to place a garrison in Trier. The inhabitants of the town resisted vigorously: a week's regular siege with guns and mines was necessary before its capitulation on 7 September 1673.[35] The shock of this siege was widely felt – not only at Coblenz, where a French attack was feared to be imminent, but throughout the whole Empire. An Imperial capital city had been besieged and profaned by the French without a declaration of war; the German pamphleteers had a field day.[36] A circular letter from Karl-Kaspar to the German princes helped stir up anti-French feelings on the eve of the Imperial declaration of war against Louis XIV which followed on 28 May 1674.

Karl-Kaspar's dominant – or rather sole – political aim now became the desire to recover possession of his capital. He arranged a meeting with Montecuccoli and drew still closer to the elector of Mainz.[37] Yet, from his refuge at Ehrenbreitstein, he had to witness helplessly the unrolling of events disastrous for his subjects: the march of armies, the pillaging and destruction of the electorate.[38] In August 1675 a victory by the duke of Lorraine over Créqui, at Conz-Saarbrucken, where the Saar joins the Moselle, gave him a short-lived moment of hope,[39] but by the time Karl-Kaspar died on 1 June 1676 the French had recovered the initiative.

To a French observer the elector's policy appeared foolish. This it certainly was when he refused to join the League of the Rhine in 1658 and when he delayed his ratification of the second treaty of 1661. His fateful choice in December 1672 seems nearly incredible, considering the proximity of France and the military might of Louis XIV. Karl-Kaspar's decision did indeed bring misfortunes on his state and his people. His actions can in part be explained by his inflated ideas of the power represented by an alliance of Spain and the Empire. Believing that he could safely count on solid military support, he felt that he could defy Louis XIV with impunity. He did not realise how much his anti-French appeal annoyed Louis and that king's ministers. While French troops were besieging Trier, Gravel wrote on 5 September 1673, 'His Highness the Elector will have all the time in the world to repent of having been so eager to cut a figure in great affairs.'[40] Because of his hectic and over-ambitious diplomatic activity, which contrasted so sharply with his financial and military weakness, Karl-Kaspar in French eyes was no more than an incompetent mischief-maker with delusions of grandeur.

Even when Louis XIV was offering him subsidies and friendship, Karl-Kaspar had been hostile. Was this, as Jakob Lehnen argues, because loyalty to the emperor was his guiding principle and the determining factor in his policy? That assertion would seem to need considerable qualification. As we have seen, Karl-Kaspar at times listened to French proposals and for several years he received French subsidies. It should also be noted that the emperor meant less to him than the Empire, and in particular his neighbours, the Rhineland princes. This can best be seen in the years between 1668 and 1672 when Karl-Kaspar devoted far more energy to concluding alliances with his neighbours than with the emperor. Finally, and most significantly, it must be stressed that Lehnen's thesis is founded on a distortion of perspectives. He holds that Karl-Kaspar, like many other princes, was sandwiched between *two* hostile potentates, Louis XIV and the emperor. In fact the elector of Trier was caught between *three* major powers: the Bourbons, the Austrian Habsburgs and the Spanish Habsburgs in the Southern Netherlands. The two branches of the House of Habsburg often disagreed and failed to co-operate. But contemporary diplomats who referred to the 'Austrian' or 'Spanish' faction within the electorate, without differentiating between them, have helped to create and perpetuate the assumption that allegiance to one side of the Habsburg family implied loyalty to both. This assumption is false. In fact, from his accession until 1661 Karl-Kaspar was the client of Spain, not of the emperor; and, after a few years of reluctant participation in the League of the Rhine, he renewed his ties with Spain in 1668. Although he was to become the emperor's ally on 31 December 1672 – six years after his initial pact with Spain – this was because the two branches of the Habsburgs had now drawn closer together after years of comparative separation and were on the point of uniting in a formal alliance. Karl-Kaspar's policy is explicable by a geopolitical factor: the length of his common border with the Spanish Netherlands, Trier and Coblenz being closer to Brussels than to Vienna.

If the 'idealist' theory – that Karl-Kaspar's policy was decided by fidelity to the emperor – is not a sufficient explanation for Karl-Kaspar's conduct, the view that he was motivated solely by venal considerations is even less satisfactory. It is true that he attached a good deal of importance to the things of this world – pensions, tolls and dues. But this characteristic he shared with the other Rhineland princes: their avidity for money seems only to have been matched by their greed for men. The Elector Palatine's use of his right of *Wildfang* (see glossary), for example, amounted to an excuse to seize peasants from the land of his neighbours. This greed is understandable if seen against the frightful devastation of the Thirty Years War along the left bank of the Rhine, by the slow pace of recovery and by the persistence of unfavourable economic conditions. The Rhenish princes were all hard up. Once he had been forced – however reluctantly – into the French alliance in 1661, Karl-Kaspar was not above reaping what profits he could. But if money had been his only preoccupation, he would have continued to support Louis XIV, who was well known as a better and more regular paymaster than the king of Spain or the emperor.

The real motivation behind Karl-Kaspar's policy must therefore be sought outside the realm of 'loyalist idealism' or 'mere venality'. Nor can his attitude be explained by a fear of being kidnapped by the Spaniards (though this had held good in his predecessor's reign). What needs to be stressed is that from his accession until his death, he remained in close contact with the Metternich family. He was related to them, and it was largely through their support that he had obtained the archepiscopal throne. At every crucial moment in his reign a member of that family can be see at his side; at Frankfurt in 1658, as at Coblenz in 1673, it was a Metternich who guided his steps. So great was the family's ascendancy over Karl-Kaspar that he was their virtual prisoner. For complex reasons, among which family solidarity and common interest must have counted, Karl-Kaspar took their advice and was dominated by their influence, which was always anti-French even though the anti-French note varied in stridency. To understand what made the Metternich influence effective – and thus to fathom the secret of their power over the elector – one would have to delve into the internal workings of the electorate, conduct a study of the great families of the Rhineland, draw up a list of their possessions, scrutinise their mutual ties and assess the importance of their systems of clientage. Once the results – even if incomplete – of this kind of enquiry are known, the diplomatic history of these unsettled and sometimes tragic years will be greatly illuminated.

NOTES

1 The only complete history of the electorate of Trier is the old work by Johann Leonardy: *Geschichte des trierischen Landes und Volkes* (Trier, Saarelouis, 1870). For Franco-German relations in this period the most useful study is that by Bertrand Auerbach, *La France et le Saint-Empire romain germanique depuis la Paix de Westphalie jusqu'à la Révolution française* (Paris, 1912). Relations between Louis XIV and the elector of Trier form the subject of the thesis of Jakob Lehnen, *Beiträge zur kurfürstlicher-trierischen Politik unter Karl-Kaspar von der Leyen, 1652–1676* (Strasbourg, 1913; Trier, 1914). Though brief (89 pp.) it is well documented, based on research in the archives of Coblenz and Vienna. Lehnen did not however use the French documents of the Bibliothèque Nationale, nor the important Correspondance Politique, Trèves, of the Ministère Français des Affaires Etrangères, Quay d'Orsay, Paris. I have tried to fill this gap in my articles 'La France et l'Electorat de Trèves au Temps de Charles-Gaspard von der Leyen, 1652–1676', *Revue d'Histoire Diplomatique* (1964) 7–34, 118–47, and 'Jean-Hugues d'Orsbeck, Electeur de Trèves, et la Politique des Réunions, 1678–1688', ibid. (1965) 315–37. I have in the process modified some of Lehnen's conclusions, notably his thesis that loyalty to the emperor constituted the mainspring of the elector's political activity. In the above contribution I have made use also of a recent, but already classic work, Georges Livet's *Recueil des Instructions données aux Ambassadeurs et Ministres de France depuis les Traités de Westphalie jusqu'à la Révolution française*, xxvIII, *Etats Allemands*, vol. 1, *Mayence* (with an excellent introduction), and vol. 3, *Trèves* (Paris, 1962 and 1966 respectively).

2 Hermann Weber, *Frankreich, Kurtrier, der Rhein und das Reich, 1623–1635* (Bonn, 1969); cf. the same author's 'Richelieu et le Rhin', in *Revue Historique* (1968) 265–80.

3 It should be stressed that the large estates which the Metternichs possessed in Bohemia constituted a guarantee of their fidelity to the Habsburgs: at the least sign of a wavering in their loyalty, or of an intrigue with France, the emperor could confiscate their lands: Archives des Affaires Etrangères, Correspondance Politique, Trèves, vol. 3, f. 425. For this form of political pressure being expected of the Habsburgs, see ibid., f. 430; cf. note 6 below.

4 The text of the treaty is in Johann-Nikolaus von Hontheim, *Historia Diplomatica et Pragmatica*, III (Trier, 1750) p. 504. Philipp-Christoph benefited especially from Article xi by which the king of France promised 'to protect against all enemies' not only the elector himself and his heirs, but also 'all those possessions, legally held, and which shall be acquired by the *fideicommis* of Sötern, of whatever nature and wherever they may be'. For the stipulation in the *Instrumenta Pacis Westphalicae* that Ehrenbreitstein was to be handed over to the archbishop and his chapter together, see the edition of this text in the

Quellen zur neueren Geschichte, published by the History Seminar of the University of Bern (Bern, 1949) pp. 84, 158.

5 For these 'important and often neglected negotiations', see Livet (ed.), *Recueil*, XXVIII, vol. 1, p. 16, n. 1. Cf. also Bibliothèque Nationale, MSS. 4225–9 in the *Fonds Français*.

6 Scharffenstein exhibited 'a great deal of aversion' for France. His family, which had not proved sufficiently loyal to the emperor, had had all its lands within the hereditary domains of the Habsburgs confiscated. His ostentatious Francophobia was 'perhaps based on the fear of losing all his estates in Bohemia': A.A.E., C.P., Trèves, vol. 3, f. 430.

7 On the bishopric of Speyer, see Franz-Xavier Remling, *Geschichte der Bischöfe zur Speyer*, 2 vols (Mainz, 1852–4).

8 A.A.E., C.P., Trèves, vol. 3, f. 425.

9 It was at this time that the Fürstenberg brothers, influential at Cologne, began their significant shift into the service of France. See Max Braubach, *Kurköln. Gestalten und Ereignisse aus zwei Jahrhunderten rheinischer Geschichte* (Münster, 1949) pp. 20–6.

10 A.A.E., C.P., Trèves, vol. 3, ff. 437–9, 449, 450, 451, 458, 460.

11 On this topic, which has been the subject of a number of studies, see the bibliography in Suzanne Pillorget, 'Louis XIV, candidat au trône impérial, 1658', *Revue d'Histoire Diplomatique* (1967) 1–13.

12 B.N., Mélanges Colbert, vol. 51 A, f. 64.

13 A.A.E., C.P., Allemagne, vol. 140, f. 315.

14 *Lettres de Mazarin*, ed. A. Chéruel, vol. VIII (1894) p. 327: letters of 11 and 25 February 1658.

15 Leopold had been recognised as elector-king of Bohemia and king of Hungary before the Frankfurt election.

16 Cf. the confirmation of this in Brienne's *Mémoires*, ed. J. F. Michaud and J. J. F. Poujoulat, vol. III (1838) pp. 154–5.

17 Nikolaus Irsch, 'Die Stellung des trierischen Raumes in mittelrheinischen Gebiet', in *Archiv für mittelrheinische Kirchengeschichte* (1952) 16–23.

18 On these alliances, see J. Dumont, *Corps diplomatique du Droit des Gens* (Amsterdam, The Hague, 1728) vol. VII, pt 2, pp. 97, 113; Erich Joachim, *Die Entwicklung des Rheinbundes vom Jahre 1658* (Leipzig, 1886); and Roman Schnur, *Der Rheinbund von 1658 in der deutschen Verfassungsgeschichte* (Bonn, 1955). The first projects for the league, as the league itself, confirmed the *Landeshoheit* (stipulated in Article 67 of the Treaty of Münster) of the princes and the cities – their right to conclude alliances among themselves, and if they so wished, with foreign powers. On this crucial political concept, see T. Kurschner, *Die Landeshoheit der deutschen Länder seit dem Westphälischen Frieden unter dem Geschichtspunkt der Souveränität* (Heidelberg, 1938).

19 B.N., 'Cinq-Cents de Colbert', vol. 328, f. 563; A.A.E., C.P., Trèves, vol. 3, ff. 520, 531. For the functioning of the League of the Rhine, besides the works of Joachim and Schnur cited above, see A. Chéruel: *Etude sur la Ligue ou Alliance du Rhin* (Paris, 1884); and A. F. Pribram, 'Beiträge zur Geschichte des Rheinbundes vom Jahre 1658', in *Sitzungsberichte der Wiener Akademie* (Vienna, 1887). On the relations

between the league and Duke Eberhard of Württemberg, see F. L. Carsten, *Princes and Parliaments in Germany from the Fifteenth to the Eighteenth Century* (Oxford, 1959) p. 78 ff.

20 Its restoration had been stipulated at the Peace of Westphalia: see A.A.E., C.P., Trèves, vol. 3, f. 439. On the international repercussions of this ecclesiastical jurisdiction question, see ibid., vol. 4, ff. 78, 90; also R. Folz: *Le concordat germanique et l'élection des évêques de Metz* (Metz, 1931) pp. 140–3.

21 For the two successive treaties, see A.A.E., C.P., Trèves, vol. 4, ff. 23, 38, 43, 121, and ibid., C.P. Allemagne, vol. 123, f. 109; see also Hontheim, *Historia Diplomatica*, vol. III, p. 738; Dumont, *Corps diplomatique*, vol. IV, pt 2, p. 382; A. M. de Boislisle, *Les mémoriaux du conseil pour 1661*, 3 vols (Paris, 1905–7) II, p. 116, n. 3.

22 A.A.E., C.P., Trèves, vol. 4, ff. 40, 50; Boislisle, *Mémoriaux du conseil*, vol. III, p. 28, n. 4, and p. 29.

23 On the implementation of the Treaty of Fontainebleau, see B.N., 'Mélanges Colbert', vol. 26, f. 302; A.A.E., C.P., Trèves, vol. 4, ff. 49, 58, 66, 70–1, 73, 84; ibid., Allemagne, vol. 123 (120), f. 111 v.

24 Ibid., Trèves, vol. 4, ff. 66, 95, 103–4.

25 Ibid., ff. 140, 142. We should remember that Louis XIV and Leopold I (first cousins and brothers-in-law) enjoyed good relations for about a decade. Leopold did not intervene in the War of Devolution, despite appeals from Spain for him to do so, because of his negotiations with Louis XIV for a treaty to divide the Spanish inheritance. The discussions began in 1665 and did not conclude until 19 January 1668, with the signing of a secret treaty at Vienna. For these negotiations see the contribution in this volume by J. Bérenger.

26 A.A.E., C.P., Trèves, vol. 4, ff. 147, 219.

27 Ibid., ff. 147, 150.

28 He did not know of the secret treaty between Louis XIV and Leopold signed at Vienna on 1 November 1671, which had been negotiated by the French ambassador Grémonville. By its terms the emperor promised to remain neutral in the event of war between France and the United Provinces, so long as hostilities remained 'outside the Circles and fiefs of the Empire'.

29 A.A.E., C.P., Trèves, vol. 4, f. 163.

30 Ibid., f. 185.

31 Ibid., f. 171.

32 Ibid., f. 219.

33 *Lettres inédites des Feucquières, Tirées des Papiers de la Famille de Madame la duchesse Decazes*, ed. E. Gallois, 5 vols (Paris, 1845–6) II p. 153.

34 Though not producing any tangible results, these protests caused Gravel much trouble during his mission: see Auerbach, *La France*, pp. 180–2. For the devastation caused by the French troops in the electorate, see A.A.E., C.P., Trèves, vol. 4, f. 226, 234, 242, 246–7.

35 G. Pagès, *Le Grand Electeur et Louis XIV* (Paris, 1905) pp. 336–7; A.A.E., C.P., Trèves, vol. 4, f. 251.

36 For the question of whether this flood of pamphlets was a genuine

expression of public feeling, and to what extent it helped to create a collective mentality, see Henri Gillot, *Le Règne de Louis XIV et l'Opinion publique en Allemagne* (Paris, 1914).

37 Gallois (ed.), *Lettres des Feucquières*, vol. ɪɪ, p. 287; Auerbach, *La France*, p. 182.

38 J. Buschmann, *Die Zerstörung des trierischen Stiftes St. Paulin durch die Franzosen im Jahre 1674* (Trier, 1880).

39 For the military events see A. Janke, *Die Belagerungen der Stadt Trier in den Jahren 1673–1675 und die Schlacht an der Conzer-Brücke* (Trier, 1890); Gottfried Kentenich, *Geschichte der Stadt Trier* (Trier, 1915) p. 513 ff; R. Welschinger, 'Créqui dans Trèves (12 aout 1675)', in *Revue des Etudes Historiques* (1925) 371–84.

40 Gallois (ed.), *Lettres des Feucquières*, vol. ɪɪ, p. 243.

6 An Attempted *Rapprochement* between France and the Emperor: the Secret Treaty for the Partition of the Spanish Succession of 19 January 1668*

JEAN BÉRENGER

This chapter is concerned with a little-known aspect of French diplomacy during the personal rule of Louis XIV: an attempted *rapprochement* between France and Leopold, one much earlier than the famous instructions given to the comte du Luc in 1715 when France resumed normal diplomatic relations with the emperor after the War of the Spanish Succession.[1] It was this same problem of the Spanish succession which led the two courts to try to define their respective rights to the inheritance of Spain and to agree on a partition of Carlos II's dominions in a way which would avoid conflict and spare both a long war.

From 1660 onwards the chancelleries of Europe were preoccupied with the problem of the Spanish succession, since the ageing and sick king of Spain, Philip IV, had only two daughters (the infantas Maria Teresa and Margareta Teresa) and a very young and physically weak son, Don Carlos, who was not expected to survive. When Philip IV died in 1665 the situation had

* First published in *Revue d'Histoire Diplomatique* (1965) under the title 'Une tentative de rapprochement entre la France et l'Empereur; le traité de partage secret de la succession d'Espagne du 19 Janvier 1668'.

scarcely improved. The infanta Maria Teresa had in theory renounced her rights to Spain when she married Louis XIV, but her renunciation, published in the Peace of the Pyrenees, was tied to the payment of a dowry which in fact was never paid. Consequently the validity of the French queen's renunciation was suspect. The infanta Margareta Teresa was betrothed to the emperor Leopold, but the Spanish court was reluctant to send the young princess to Vienna at a time when the House of Habsburg was going through a serious dynastic crisis: after the death of Archduke Sigismund of the Tyrol, the young emperor Leopold and the infante Carlos II were the only surviving males in the family. For Leopold marriage was a necessity to ward off the danger of the Austrian branch of the House of Habsburg dying out. The gravity of this dynastic crisis should not be underestimated at a time when the good or poor health of ruling families was a basic factor in the stability of states, and when a minority government was liable to lead to domestic disturbances and foreign wars.

The Spanish crown linked together several autonomous states: Spain and the Indies on the one side, the Netherlands and the Spanish possessions in Italy on the other. If the senior branch of the House of Habsburg were to die out, the succession would certainly be contested by foreign princes with claims of varying validity, and the local governments would be likely to break away from Madrid once they considered themselves free from their obligations to a legitimate sovereign.

As early as 1665 the French minister in Vienna, Grémonville, in his 'state of negotiations for an eventual partition' analysed the dangers threatening the integrity of the Spanish monarchy:[2]

1. The Spaniards might choose a native king, for example Don John of Austria, Philip IV's illegitimate son.
2. The papacy might try to seize the states of Naples and Sicily which were its fiefs, under the pretext of sequestering them.
3. The emperor might attempt to sequester Milan but could do so only with the consent of its Spanish and Swiss garrisons.
4. The Spanish Netherlands might be tempted to assert their independence.
5. There was some risk that the Indies might try to secede.

It was thus important to maintain the dynastic link which was in fact the only guarantee of subjects' loyalty in an age when respect for the legitimate sovereign was very strong. The patrimony of the House of Habsburg also had to be preserved. The question was not one of a private succession but of the future of a great European power; and no settlement could be made without the agreement of other princes, nor against the wishes of states belonging to the Spanish crown.

The death of Carlos II could therefore lead not only to the dissolution of the monarchy but also to war between the principal European rulers, especially between the emperor as head of the House of Habsburg and the king of France as husband of a possible heir and ruler of the greatest power in Europe. It did indeed seem obvious that Louis XIV, at a time of great personal glory, would try to prevent the resurrection of the empire of Charles V; and that the emperor Leopold, despite his poor resources, would not allow himself to be robbed of his share of the inheritance. Europe could only escape war by a compromise solution agreed on by the emperor and Louis XIV, and this was attempted by the secret treaty for the partition of the Spanish monarchy signed at Vienna on 19 January 1668 between French and Imperial plenipotentiaries.

The first suggestion for a partition of the Spanish monarchy between the principal heirs had come from the court of the elector of Mainz, Johann Philip von Schönborn, as early as 1663, even before the death of Philip IV. 'After he [the elector] had conveyed his thoughts to von Saal, Great Dean and Governor of the Electorate of Mainz, and to his brother Baron von Schönborn . . . they all agreed that the best solution would be an eventual partition between the King of Spain's sons-in-law, the King [of France] and the Emperor.'[3]

This initiative, which might seem surprising at first, can be explained by the geographical position of the electorate of Mainz which, sooner or later, would become a battlefield for the French and Imperial armies if war broke out. The suggestion was in fact an expression of the Rhenish princes' wish for peace, since they (as the elector Palatine and the elector of Mainz) considered that their first priority was to rebuild their states after the destruction caused by the Thirty Years War.[4]

Schönborn and his successors usually achieved their policy of

preserving peace by an alliance with France, though for them it
was less a question of defending France's interests than of safeguarding peace in the Empire. From the legal standpoint the
elector's initiative was bold, for partition would imply recognition
of the rights of the queen of France and thus ignore the enact-
ments and treaties which tied the two branches of the House of
Habsburg together. At his abdication in 1556 Charles V had
in effect divided the House of Habsburg into two branches, a
Spanish and an Austrian. The Spanish branch had, however,
received the prerogatives of a senior branch : for example, only
the king of Spain could confer the order of the Golden Fleece.
The links between the two lines had been strengthened by
numerous marriages and confirmed in 1617 by the Oñate treaty,
concluded between Ferdinand of Styria and the Spanish ambassador to the emperor Matthias. The clauses of this document
had been kept secret, Grémonville had in vain used financial
inducements to obtain a copy, but he assumed that if the senior
branch died out the treaty provided for the cadet branch, that
of Vienna, to inherit all the dominions of the Spanish crown.
In this case the emperor Leopold would be the heir not as Philip
IV's son-in-law, but as head of the Austrian branch of the
Habsburgs. This was indeed the argument of the Spanish court
and of some of the ministers at the Imperial court. Partition
negotiations must therefore be delicate, and the very idea of partition would inevitably meet opposition from Spain. Grémonville
warned Louis XIV on 4 June 1665 :

> There are members of the Emperor's Council so passionately
> devoted to the concept of an inseparable union of the two houses
> of Spain and Austria that they would take measures in Spain
> as well as trying to persuade His Imperial Majesty that his
> honour and dignity demand that he never give up Spain, if
> they perceived the slightest sign that Your Majesty intended
> to contest the succession or wanted to settle it by partition.[5]

France's position in law was not sound since the French queen
could only claim a share of the Spanish possessions and even then
only if her renunciation could be proved invalid because of the
non-payment of her dowry. In fact, however, France was strong
enough to use force; and in 1667 it was easy enough to find legal
experts who maintained that the Law of Devolution justified a

French attack on the Spanish Netherlands.[6] In short one could say that Leopold had the right and Louis XIV the power, but that any negotiation for partition of the Spanish monarchy would be unwelcome to the Spanish government which would only agree under duress. The first attempt to start negotiations for a partition, that of the elector of Mainz, miscarried. The elector broached the subject first to the emperor, who in the autumn of 1663 came in person to the Diet of Regensburg to ask the German princes for help against the Turks. Leopold did not welcome the overtures, being afraid of annoying the court of Madrid at a time when he was pressing Spain to let him marry the infanta Margareta Teresa : quite apart from his personal inclination for a Spanish bride, the marriage of the infanta to someone outside the Habsburg family would have complicated the succession issue by giving a third party a valid claim to a share of Carlos II's dominions. The emperor therefore wished to avoid complications and to have the marriage negotiations completed as soon as possible, but in the end he consented to the elector of Mainz sending an exploratory mission to Madrid. An untoward incident robbed the elector's plans of their essential secrecy. The head of his council, the intelligent and ambitious Johann Christian von Boyneburg, had lost his master's favour as he wished to pursue a policy too favourable to the interests of Louis XIV. To get his own back Boyneburg communicated the elector's project to the French, having first informed the Imperial minister, Prince Auersperg – who led the pro-Spanish party at Vienna – and the papal nuncio, Cardinal Caraffa.[7] The elector's secret became widely known and when in the spring of 1664 the Spanish ambassador in Paris, Marquis de la Fuente, reported it to his government,[8] all the principal parties were informed of the elector's partition initiative. Nonetheless the elector persisted, sending an experienced diplomat, the Franciscan Don Cristobal Rojas y Spinola, to Spain; he was unlikely to attract much attention as clerics often moved from place to place in their work.

The son of a good Spanish family settled in Flanders, Rojas had run a seminary at Cologne since 1650 which aimed at bringing Protestants back to the Catholic church. A convinced champion of reconciliation between Catholics and Protestants, with an interest in political economy, he played a significant role in Germany and at the Imperial court. He was particularly

favoured by the emperor Leopold, who made him titular bishop
of Stephania in Bosnia and provided him also with more substantial benefices. Despite his personal qualities, which were appreciated, Rojas had a cool reception in Madrid on his arrival
in July 1664. He was allowed to attend the *Konferenz,* but his
mission failed, in part possibly because of the lack of secrecy.

The emperor himself believed the matter had been raised
prematurely. After Rojas' return Leopold wrote to the elector
of Mainz : 'You will recall what I said about this when I was
at Regensburg, and I still find the negotiations premature and
dangerous.'[9] Beyond the political difficulties loomed Leopold's
conscientious scruples over agreeing to the partitioning of the
dominions of a living relative.

Louis XIV's aggression against the Spanish Netherlands in
early 1667 revived plans for a partition. The initiative for negotiations was once again taken by one of France's Rhenish allies,
the elector of Cologne, who in the summer of 1667 sent his
brother Count Wilhelm von Fürstenberg to Vienna.[10] The similarity of outlook among the Rhenish princes can be explained by
their anxiety to prevent the war spreading to their own states;
it was this concern which made them willing to suggest France
having a share in the Spanish succession. But however good
the cause might be from the Rhenish point of view, it was this
time promoted by a bad advocate : the court of Vienna did not
conceal its hostility to the pro-French Fürstenberg family and
believed that Louis XIV was behind the overture.[11]

The would-be negotiator failed. The emperor refused to receive him and Fürstenberg had to make do with communicating
his mission via Leopold's grand chamberlain and *Konferenz*
minister, Count Lamberg. Louis XIV was not particularly upset,
preferring to wait for an initiative from the emperor himself.[12]

This initiative was in fact provoked by the Flanders campaign
of the summer of 1667. The French attack on the Spanish
Netherlands caused intense diplomatic activity at the Viennese
court between April and September 1667. The Spanish ambassador, the marquis de Malagon, worked for Leopold's direct
military intervention on Spain's side, or at the very least for
auxiliary troops to be sent to the Netherlands on the pretext of
Imperial help for an Imperial circle. Grémonville, for his part,
tried to delay troops being raised. The emperor had disbanded

some of his army after the signature of peace with the Turks in 1664 and would have to bring existing regiments up to strength before any military action could be taken. Numerous meetings of his ministers took place but Leopold was slow to put his forces on a war footing, much to Malagon's disgust. A relieved Grémonville was able to report to France :

> The Spanish ambassador has renewed his instances, or rather his insolent demands, for help. To satisfy him a long Conference, the eleventh on the same matter, has been held. The next day a War Council met, at which the Emperor was present; Count Montecuccoli and other generals were called in to examine how the collapse of the [Spanish] Netherlands could be staved off. Many of those present wanted war, to please the Spaniards and to further their own interests. Nothing was said at that Council about a public declaration, discussed in the most secret Council but put off till next spring; for the reasons I have already explained the War Council only discussed a preliminary plan to make a diversion into Alsace and to begin recruiting fresh troops which may be sent to the Netherlands.

If the emperor had enough determination and the means to go to war, France would be in real danger, but Grémonville was convinced that the ruling circles in Vienna were divided and that the emperor was too short of money for Louis to be worried by the prospect of war with Leopold. To raise troops and put the regiments on a war footing the emperor needed contributions from the Estates throughout his territories, as his ordinary resources would not suffice : 'Bohemia, Silesia and Bavaria have actually refused outright the loan asked from them and are still making difficulties over increasing the number of troops . . . not so much because of the expense and trouble involved, but because they are afraid it might bring war on them.'[13]

The Estates also feared that the regiments raised would not be dispatched to Flanders immediately. In the meantime their being quartered on the hereditary lands would require subsidies to maintain them, and the population would have to put up with all the inconvenience of billeted soldiers. The people of the Austrian provinces of Tyrol and Breisgau, which were furthest from Vienna and had the greatest autonomy, refused categorically to

permit quartering in their territories. Even garrisons were unpopular, as Grémonville reported: 'The places near to Alsace
have refused to accept the garrisons the Emperor wanted to
send there, offering instead to raise money for increasing the
army.'[14]

It is interesting that the emperor's subjects in his Czech lands
were the most reluctant to become involved in a war for the
benefit of the family and dynastic policies of the Habsburgs; as
in the Rhineland, these lands wished at all costs to maintain the
peace and to get on with the work of reconstruction.

The general feeling of unease expressed itself in a three-way
split among Leopold's ministers and advisers, explained by
Grémonville as follows. Count Lamberg, the grand chamberlain,
and Prince Auersperg hold 'that the Emperor should openly
declare that he will defend the Netherlands if Your Majesty
wants more than what the mediators judge right for him';
Prince Lobkowitz, who at this time was head of the council,
was reluctant to act without the approval of the Imperial princes:
he thought it unrealistic to rely on the Spaniards alone and
wanted the German princes to consider 'defending the Netherlands as part of the Empire'.[15] Finally Prince Schwarzenberg
and Prince Auersperg hold 'That the Emperor should openly
and of the War Council, advocated military preparations to
enable Austria to defend the Empire if it were attacked by
France.[16]

The emperor in the end decided in favour of the Schwarzen-
berg-Gonzaga policy, though it entailed the abandonment of a
dynastic policy in favour of one for the benefit of the Empire
and the hereditary lands. This essential change of approach
made possible a dialogue between Leopold and Louis XIV since
the former was now ready to buy peace at the expense of his
claim to the Spanish succession; for negotiating a partition
amounted to recognising the latter's rights, even though Louis'
claim, as we have seen, was debatable. The War of Devolution
thus provided the spur for the partition negotiations, and the
armistice of September 1667 made the discussions between the
two powers easier. Lionne wrote to Grémonville on 28 October:

As matters stand the King and the Emperor are agreed over
a partition of their future rights and to please him [the em-

peror] His Majesty will be satisfied for the time being with what his armies have occupied in Flanders in this campaign and will sacrifice all the great things he had hoped for purely for the sake of the peace of Christendom.[17]

It is difficult to determine who initiated this policy in Paris, but it would seem that the impetus came from Lionne himself.[18] He had made the first approaches to the Imperial *chargé d'affaires* in Paris, Vicka, during a reception to celebrate the birth of Leopold and Margareta Teresa's first child, the archduke Ferdinand.[19] The idea met with a favourable reception in Vienna despite the difficulties involved : success depended on a speedy and secret agreement between the king and the emperor and on the latter's agreeing to confront Spain with a *fait accompli*.

Lionne wished Grémonville to negotiate with Prince Lobkowitz, who was known to favour a reconciliation with France; but Grémonville held that prince too vulnerable to intrigues from the Spanish party and suggested that Prince Auersperg, who was well thought of by the Spaniards and was hoping to become first minister, should be approached first.[20]

Prince Auersperg came of an old Austrian family and had the solid qualities of a statesman, but he had suffered a semi-disgrace after the death of Emperor Ferdinand III. The young emperor disliked him, as he was too sure of himself for Leopold, and had named his tutor, Prince Portia, first minister. At the latter's death in 1665 Leopold imitated his cousin Louis XIV and refused to name a first minister, although he gave wide-ranging responsibilities to Prince Lobkowitz. The rivalry between Auersperg and Lobkowitz was notorious : Lobkowitz wanted a *rapprochement* with France, while Auersperg still championed the traditional dynastic alliance with Spain. Lobkowitz was using all his wits to outstrip Auersperg; Auersperg was trying to win a cardinal's hat as he thought this might help him become first minister more easily.[21]

Grémonville made skilful use of this ambition in his first talk with Auersperg. His report to Louis was favourable : 'In his [Auersperg's] opinion the thing seemed feasible, particularly after I had persuaded him that his great aim of obtaining a cardinal's hat would come as a by-product of our plan, since the Pope would be very willing to give him the hat if he achieved a peace which would bring glory on his pontificate.'[22]

From this point on the three principal negotiators were Grémonville, Prince Lobkowitz and Prince Auersperg : 'Without going about it this way round, we would have no chance of success, as that man [Auersperg] would have opposed us in everything and paid court to the Spaniards. As it is, the negotiation has been started without his being able to stop us.'[23]

These roundabout procedures might appear unnecessary, but they were dictated by the indecisive character of the emperor. He was susceptible to the influence of his entourage and especially to that of the powerful Spanish party which consisted of all the attendants he had brought from Spain. The Spanish ambassador would always try to make up any lost ground with the help of the *camerera mayor*, the marquis d'Eril. The Spaniards had to be kept outside the negotiations, because, as Grémonville was told in Vienna, 'The Emperor is not like your King who looks into and does everything himself. He is like a statue which can be carried where one wants and set up at one's pleasure.'[24]

Lobkowitz was undoubtedly a strong character who sought a lasting *rapprochement* with Louis, not out of pro-French feeling but from his analysis of the respective strengths of Austria and France. A Bohemian noble, a devoted servant of the House of Austria, he had fought the French in the Thirty Years War before becoming president of the War Council and, in 1665, grand master of the court and leading minister. In the Privy Council he was called up to give his views first, and he undoubtedly had some influence on the emperor.[25] He realised that the hereditary lands, poorer and with a smaller population than France and also threatened by the Turks, could not wage war in the Netherlands without the help of all the European rulers. He therefore wanted to preserve the peace, like the electors of Mainz and Cologne and his predecessor, Prince Portia. His contemporaries and some German historians have accused him of corruption. But his large personal fortune ensured his independence, and his conduct of Imperial policy in respect of the French alliance was motivated by his concern for the public good. The emperor himself, concerned for the prosperity of his territories, could not but approve of Lobkowitz's approach, even though it harmed his dynastic interests.

The third protagonist in these negotiations is as interesting as the Habsburg ministers. Son of a president of the parlement of Rouen, Jacques Bretel, chevalier de Grémonville, was the youngest of a *noblesse de robe* family, who had embraced a military career. He served first in the Champagne regiment and then, commanding a regiment of his own as a lieutenant-general, went into Venetian service at Candia. Because of his connection with Hugues de Lionne, Louis in 1664 sent him to Vienna, where he stayed without a break till 1673. His fluent Latin and Italian, knowledge of military questions and Ottoman problems, together with his quick intelligence and proved skill, soon made him a redoubtable figure in Vienna. He knew every court intrigue. His dispatches were models of their kind, written in a lively style, with a wealth of reliable information. He kept his ear to the ground and considered himself a soldier in the king's service. His tireless energy certainly contributed much to the conclusion of the secret partition treaty.

The full powers given to both Grémonville and Auersperg were for a limited period only, so that the negotiation would have to be carried out quickly. Here is the full power given to Auersperg :

I empower the Duke of Monsterberg, Prince of Auersberg and member of my Council of State to negotiate, conclude and sign with the Chevalier de Grémonville, lieutenant-general in the French army, as representative with full powers from His Majesty the King of France, my Brother and very dear Cousin, as many articles as necessary of a peace treaty in respect of the differences that His Most Christian Majesty has with the crown of Spain as well as an eventual accommodation over the differences which might occur between me and His Most Christian Majesty over claims to the future succession.[26]

On 18 January 1668 Grémonville proposed two alternatives for the partition of the succession. The first would give Leopold Milan, Finale, the Balearic and Canary Islands, the Indies and all Spain except for Navarre and the fort of Rosa. The second would give Leopold Milan, all Spain except for Navarre, Sicily, Naples and Sardinia; while Louis would receive not only the Netherlands and Navarre but also all the overseas possessions in the Indies, the Spanish towns in Africa and the Balearic Islands.[27] This second alternative would permit France to develop her commercial and maritime power, while allowing the emperor to extend his power in Italy and practically reconstitute the empire of Charles V.

No record has so far come to light of the discussions in the *Konferenz* which the emperor convened the same day to choose between the proposed alternatives. But we know that, after a long and difficult discussion, Leopold finally chose the first alternative and accepted the treaty which we know about through its instrument of ratification. The most important part of it is Article III :

If the Most Serene Catholic King of Spain, their well-beloved relative, allied by marriage to them both, should die prematurely without children of a lawful marriage . . . a partition of the whole inheritance of the Spanish monarchy shall then, in case of that eventuality, be made, and be effective, in the following manner – To his Sacred Imperial Majesty and his children, heirs, and successors, there shall go as their portion of the inheritance, the Kingdom of Spain (except those to be excepted, respecting which explanation will be made below), the West Indies, the Duchy of Milan, with the right which pertains to it of giving the investiture of the duchy of Siena, Finale, the ports called Longone, Ercole, Orbitello, and the other ports which are subject to the law of Spain, on the shore of the Ligurian Sea, commonly called the Sea of Tuscany, along to the borders or territory of the kingdom of Naples, the island of Sardinia, the Canaries, the Balearic Islands, commonly called Majorca, Minorca and Ibiza.

And to His Sacred Royal Most Christian Majesty, and to his children, heirs and successors there shall fall and accrue as the portion of their inheritance, all of Flanders which Spain possesses (under which is also comprehended Burgundy, called Franche-Comté), the Philippine Islands in the East, the kingdom of Navarre with its dependencies, such as are so regarded today, Rosa, with its dependencies, the places situated on the coasts of Africa, the kingdom of Naples and Sicily, with its dependencies and adjacent islands, which pertain to it today . . .

investiture by the Supreme Pontiffs is necessary for obtaining possession of the said kingdom of Naples and Sicily.

Although the emperor would have liked Naples, he finally chose the first alternative which left him with the kingdom of Spain and its American possessions, the Canaries, the Balearic Islands, the presidencies of Tuscany and the duchy of Milan. In this way the House of Habsburg kept the essentials of the Spanish empire together : it would have been difficult to admit to the Castilians that both the Indies and the freedom of communication between the Spanish possessions and those of the House of Habsburg in Central Europe had been lost. Milan and the port of Finale were essential parts in this link between Spain and Austria. Moreover the court of Vienna could increase its influence in Italy through the exercise of Imperial sovereignty in northern Italy. It is interesting to note that the negotiations did not break down over the question of the kingdom of Naples which was highly prized by both sides : by France because the possession of Naples would assist contact with the Levant and allow her also to increase her influence in the western Mediterranean (French interest in the presidencies of Morocco must be understood in the same light); by the emperor because Naples would give him Italy, a dream which was to be realised in Charles VI's reign (the Treaty of Rastadt of 1714). Italy's cultural and economic reputation was still great and it is understandable that the European rulers should have wanted political control of the country. The attraction of Italy was even greater for the Viennese Habsburgs if one remembers that Italian was still the language used at court, that its newspapers were printed in Italian, and that many of the administrators were of Italian origin. It needed all Grémonville's tenacity, together with Auersperg's unbounded ambition, to achieve the partition of Spanish Italy.[28]

The treaty provided for Leopold to become king of Spain or to designate one of his children as such. Although France had not excluded the possibility of Charles V's empire being rebuilt, she had received solid compensation by having her claims to the Burgundian and Navarre inheritances recognised. Stronger than in the preceding century, France was now trying to repair the injustices she had suffered in the past, especially the loss of her sovereignty over Flanders at the time of the signature of the Treaty of Madrid (1526). Louis XIV, as heir to the house of Albret, would also recover the Navarre provinces annexed by Spain. The partition treaty was therefore valuable on two counts : it maintained a balance of power between France and the House of Habsburg, and it rested on dynastic traditions which could justify transfers of sovereignty. Finally, in leaving Spain's colonial empire intact it stood more chance of not offending Spanish national feeling and made possible a future agreement with the Spanish government. Spain had been kept in the dark during the negotiations, but her acceptance of the principle of partition would have to be won.

It was a good time to exert pressure on Spain. Louis and Leopold decided to act jointly in the hope of speedy success, and the partition treaty thus amounted to an alliance between them. Leopold undertook to look after the diplomatic side while Louis XIV agreed to provide military pressure. The emperor entrusted his task to the marquis de Grana[29] and, unusually for him, Leopold moved quickly. Only eight days after the signature of the preliminaries, on 28 January 1668, Grana was handed twenty-two pages of instructions in a cipher which has so far defied deciphering.[30] In the margin there is an amendment *en clair* in French of 4 February 1668, which reveals the emperor's attitude to Spain :

> If Spain wants to carry on the war alone, although the Emperor does not think it advisable to involve himself in it at the moment he [Grana] can give His Catholic Majesty to understand that I might be willing to raise a considerable number of troops on terms which would reflect the zeal which I have and must have for the House of Habsburg and that I would prefer to give rather than sell him my services.[31]

But the essential part of Grana's instructions was given to him orally to prevent any leakage of information by loss of documents. The need for secrecy was also the reason why Vienna did not use the normal diplomatic channels.[32] Grana was a Spaniard from the Netherlands, who had been in the emperor's service for a long time and whose membership of the Aulic council linked the Burgundian circle with the court of Vienna.[33] It was assumed that he stood the best chance of getting the Spaniards to accept the secret partition treaty, and this was the chief aim of his mission.[34]

On his arrival he immediately contacted the Imperial ambassador in Madrid, Count Pötting. Together they worked out a plan whereby Spain would make peace with France at the congress of Aix-la-Chapelle and at the same time accept the secret partition treaty. Through Father Neidhart, the Jesuit confessor to the queen regent and her closest political adviser, they hoped to overcome Spanish national opposition led by Don John of Austria, Philip IV's illegitimate son. Don John was a member of the council and an advocate of war to the death with France. He counted on the support of the Imperial army and declared to Grana on 4 March 1668: 'Only His Imperial Majesty can save this monarchy. Unless he acts, the Netherlands are irretrievably lost.'[35]

Don John would certainly never agree to the dismemberment of the monarchy, and it is quite possible that he hoped to get himself declared king if Carlos II died and Leopold could be accused of consenting to a partition. Grana tried to reason with a more moderate minister, the cardinal of Aragon, explaining to him that the emperor did not have the means to fit out a large army and that a body of five to ten thousand men would not be enough to halt the French. He stressed the exhausted state of the emperor's hereditary lands, the persistence of the Turkish danger and, finally the great distance which separated Austria from the Netherlands and rendered sustained military help difficult. But the cardinal of Aragon would not accept his arguments.

The negotiation seemed likely to fail since the Spaniards were reluctant to yield to French military pressure. Louis' winter campaign against the Franche-Comté was undertaken to force Spain to accept peace and the possibility of partition, and can only be properly understood in the light of the new alliance between Louis and Leopold.

In gratitude for the Emperor's having, by the treaty, yielded the kingdom of Naples, the King agrees that the Spaniards need not accept either of the alternatives for a settlement before the end of March – as provided for in the treaty – but will let them have till the middle of May. Furthermore, if he makes

F

any conquests from them in the Franche Comté, he will not insist on keeping them.[36]

The French armies' advances into Burgundy served Grana's arguments admirably: 'When the ministers here could no longer doubt the progress of the King of France in Burgundy, I magnified the disasters as greatly and as skilfully as possible.'[37]

He was now able to speak to the Spanish government with some effect. And though several ministers clung to the hope that the Maritime Powers would offer to mediate, the Council of State, after an exchange of correspondence with the marquis de Castel-Rodrigo, governor of the Netherlands, agreed to the suggested partition and also to the cession of the fortresses conquered[38] by the French armies in Flanders during the campaign of the summer of 1667.[39]

The marquis de Grana's mission was thus successful. Spain accepted the possibility of a partition of the monarchy in return for the king of France keeping only some places in Flanders. It was therefore not the triple alliance of The Hague which halted Louis XIV, but rather the prospect of a more forward-looking policy based on French reconciliation with the emperor. Louis XIV certainly recognised the danger to French power from the alliance of the United Provinces and England, but he did his best to isolate them by reconciling himself with the emperor – thus foreshadowing the policy put forward in his instructions to the comte de Luc in 1715 and only fulfilled in 1756. His alliance with Leopold prevented a *rapprochement* between the emperor and the Maritime Powers. Prince Auersperg told Grémonville in confidence that 'this treaty put an end to and broke up the general union which was being contemplated against His Majesty, and that the Emperor had been on the point of concluding in eight or ten days time four very important treaties, but that now all the ministers would be very surprised.'[40]

The real significance of the 1668 treaty must now be assessed. Was France concerned only to get a quick peace and the recognition of her claims to a share in the Spanish succession?

The secret partition treaty remained unknown to the other powers,[41] thanks to the many precautions taken, and was only discovered in the last century when Mignet published Grémonville's correspondence.[42] The emperor has been criticised by a number of historians[43] because he sacrificed his credit with the court of Spain. Grana related on his return to Vienna that all the Spanish ministers

> had told him bluntly that they would, for the future, be far less resentful against France than against the Emperor. They threatened that when he found himself embarrassed by rebellions, as had happened in the past, they would abandon him. They much deplored his lack of energy and affection for his House. especially since they had let him know that they had reason to hope that England and the United Provinces would declare for them as soon as he moved. . . .[44]

The change in Leopold's policy was based on two premises: first, that Carlos II would soon die (it was rumoured in Vienna that he would not live to see his tenth birthday); and, secondly, that Louis XIV sincerely wanted peace and did not intend to misuse his military and diplomatic supremacy. But as early as 1670 the *entente* between the two rulers began to weaken. Louis XIV occupied the Imperial fief of the duchy of Lorraine in that year and claimed, with evident dishonesty, that Lorraine was his.[45] Though Leopold could sacrifice his own family's interests to maintain the peace, he could not sacrifice those of the Empire or the basic rights of his vassals. A split was therefore inevitable despite the efforts made by Grémonville to breathe life into the alliance.

The failure of the French alliance policy was signalled in Vienna by the disgrace of Prince Lobkowitz, who in 1674 had to retire to his estate at Roudnice in Bohemia. By then his policy was already discredited: in 1673 the emperor, who had hesitated thoughout the 1672 campaign, had joined the Dutch in their struggle against Louis XIV.

The partition treaty of 1668 is interesting if seen as a first attempt at a *rapprochement* between the houses of Bourbon and Habsburg.[47] It shows that war was not inevitable between them, but also that in 1668 the situation was not yet ripe for friendship despite the sacrifices made on both sides. The final failure of the policy of reconciliation can be explained in particular by France's attitude: while Louis XIV was pleased with the *rapprochement*, he proved unwilling to make the necessary concessions to preserve peace between France on the one hand and

the emperor and the Imperial states on the other. It is clear
that the change in French policy, inspired by Hugues de Lionne
and helped by the existence of a pro-French party in Vienna,
did not outlive its inspirer. After Lionne's death other ministers,
surer of France's power, suggested a policy to the king which
was to lead to the alliance of the emperor and the Maritime
Powers, the very basis of the two later coalitions against France.

NOTES

1   *Recueil des Instructions données aux Ambassadeurs*, vol. I, *Autriche* (Paris,
    1884) hereafter cited as *Recueil*; 'Memorial to serve as instructions for
    Comte du Luc', pp. 154–83: the peace 'will be the basis of a new union
    to be established between the House of France and the House of
    Austria'.
2   Archives des Affaires Etrangères, Correspondance Politique, Autriche,
    vol. 23, f. 24, Grémonville to the king, 24 May 1665.
3   A.A.E., C.P., Autriche, vol. 23, f. 23, 31 May 1665, 'State of the
    negotiations for an eventual partition'.
4   See H. Hassinger, *Johann Joachim Becher* (Vienna, 1951) *passim*.
5   A.A.E., C.P., Autriche, vol. 21, f. 188, Grémonville to the king, 4 June
    1665.
6   *Traité des Droits de la reine très chrétienne sur divers états de la monarchie
    d'Espagne* (Paris, 1667).
7   Samuel J. T. Miller and John P. Spielman, *Cristobal Rojas y Spinola,
    1626–1695* (Philadelphia, 1962) p. 24 ff.
8   Ibid., citing despatch of 20 Apr 1664 from the archives of Simancas,
    Estado legajo E.K. 1388–89, f. 57.
9   Translation, by Grémonville, of Leopold's letter of 31 May 1665, in
    'State of the negotiations for an eventual partition': A.A.E., C.P.,
    Autriche, vol. 23, f. 35.
10 See A. M. A. Mignet, *Négociations relatives à la Succession d'Espagne*, 4 vols
    (Paris, 1835–42) II, pp. 324–33.
11 A.A.E., C.P., Autriche, vol. 27, ff. 168–70, Grémonville to the king,
    Vienna, 15 Sep 1667. For the general direction of the Fürstenberg
    brothers' policy see especially G. Livet (ed.), *Recueil*, vol. XXVIII,
    Cologne (Paris, 1961).
12 A.A.E., C.P., Autriche, vol. 26, Hugues de Lionne to Grémonville,
    Saint Germain, 25 Mar 1667: 'His Majesty does not want this negotia-
    tion pushed any further either by you or by anyone else. If Vienna
    wishes to take it up again and they speak to us about it first, His
    Majesty would like you to write for his information what they have to
    say to you.'
13 Ibid., vol. 27, f. 114, Grémonville to the king, Vienna, 18 Aug 1667.
14 Ibid., f. 293, Grémonville to the king, 3 Nov 1667.

15 Ibid., ff. 270–1, Grémonville to the king, Vienna, 27 Oct 1667.

16 For the weakness of the Spanish army in the Netherlands see H. Pirenne, *Histoire Belgique*, v (Brussels, 1926) pp. 14–25. The situation is well summed up in a letter from Castel-Rodrigo, governor of the Netherlands, to the queen regent, Brussels, 16 Mar 1667, published in translation by Mignet in *Négociations relatives*, II, pp. 52–5: 'if [the French] attack us this spring I cannot see how the Netherlands can be saved except by a miracle. Your Majesty is aware that I have cried out and protested for a long time; and I believe that if a Spanish province was demanded of us to avoid a rupture this year it would be politic to give it to win time to put us in a proper state of defence'.

17 A.A.E., C.P., Autriche, vol. 27, H. de Lionne to Grémonville, Paris, 28 Oct 1667.

18 Ibid., vol. 28, H. de Lionne to Grémonville, Saint-Germain, 5 Feb 1668.

19 This son died almost at once, on 13 January 1668 (ed.).

20 A.A.E., C.P., Autriche, vol. 28, Grémonville to the king, Vienna, 17 Nov 1667.

21 See Grete Mecenseffy, *Fürst Weikhard Auersperg, im Dienste Drei Habsburger* (Vienna, 1950).

22 A.A.E., C.P., Autriche, vol. 28, Grémonville to the king, Vienna, 24 Nov 1667.

23 Ibid., Grémonville's despatch of 22 Dec 1667; for Lobkowitz's share see A. Wolf, *Wenzel Fürst Lobkowitz* (Vienna, 1873).

24 A.A.E., C.P., Autriche, vol. 28, Grémonville's despatch of 22 Dec 1667.

25 See Wolf, *Wenzel Fürst Lobkowitz*, pp. 247–8.

26 A.A.E., C.P., Autriche, vol. 27, f. 466, deciphered. Grémonville's full powers are in Mignet, *Négociations relatives*, II, pt iii, p. 314.

27 For the alternatives see Grémonville's despatch of 18 Jan 1668: A.A.E., C.P., Autriche, vol. 29, ff. 84–5. For details of the negotiations see Mignet, *Négociations relatives*, II, pt ii , who also prints, pp. 441–9, the French version of the secret treaty. The Latin text which I have used is from the Haus-, Hof- und Staatsarchiv of Vienna, Frankreich, 117 (translated pp. 44–5 from the Latin into English by D. McKay).

28 When the negotiations seemed to have reached an *impasse* over the kingdom of Naples, Grémonville declared to Auersperg, 'Allow this article if you want to be the cardinal of the peace and to be regarded as the greatest minister in the courts of the European princes': Mignet, *Négociations relatives*, II, pt iii, p. 435.

29 Mignet did not know about Grana's mission, which was of course in line with the provisions of Article 2 of the secret Austro-French treaty. I am much obliged to Dr Hans Wagner, archivist of the Haus-, Hof- und Staatsarchiv, Vienna, for having drawn my attention to the existence of a file relating to Grana's negotiations in the records of Leopold I's secretary of state, Abele von Lilienberg: Österreichische Staats Registratur, Repertorium N, which will be cited henceforth as H.H. Sta., Repertorium N.

30 H.H. Sta., Repertorium N., fasc. 56, pars prima, 'Instructions for

Reichshofrat Cammerer . . . Otto Heinrich, Marquis de Grana, Count of Milesimo, for what he is to do at the royal Spanish Court to which he is being sent'.

31 Ibid., 'Instructions'.

32 Ibid., Grana's despatch to the emperor, Madrid, 9 Mar 1668: 'So that I could discover verbally, as if witnessing it with your Majesty's own eyes, the situation here and their basic intentions.'

33 Ibid., despatch of 9 Mar 1668.

34 Ibid., Grana to the emperor, 29 Mar 1668.

35 Ibid., Grana to the emperor, 9 Mar 1668.

36 A.A.E., C.P., Autriche, vol. 28, f. 239, Instructions from the king to Grémonville, Paris, 6 Feb 1668.

37 H.H. Sta., Repertorium N., fasc. 56, pars prima, Grana to the emperor, Madrid, 21 Mar 1668.

38 See G. Zeller, *Les Temps Modernes*, ɪ, p. 99 (vol. ɪɪ of 'Histoire des relations internationales', ed. P. Renouvin, Paris, 1953).

39 H.H. Sta., Repertorium N., fasc. 56, pars prima, Grana to the emperor, Madrid, 2 Apr 1668: 'I have only to report that confirmation has come from the Marquis de Castel-Rodrigo on the alternative accepted. . . . The Queen has come to an agreement with the Privy Council on choosing the way to make peace, namely that the places lost in the last campaign should be surrendered in return for the restitution of the Franche-Comté.'

40 A.A.E., C.P., Autriche, vol. 29, f. 125, Grémonville to the king, Vienna, 22 Jan 1668.

41 The Venetian ambassador in Vienna, who was vaguely aware of important negotiations going on, was never able to discover their purpose. Cf. Archives of Venice, Dispacci di Germania, despatches for Jan 1668.

42 Mignet, *Négociations relatives*, ɪɪ, ch. iii (Paris, 1835).

43 See, for example, Miller and Spielman, *Cristobal Rojas y Spinola*, who label the treaty 'stupid'.

44 A.A.E., C.P., Autriche, vol. 30, f. 6, Grémonville to the king, Vienna, 3 May 1668.

45 Ibid., vol. 44, f. 12. Copy of the king's declaration to the emperor's envoy, Count Windeschgrätz, on the Lorraine affair: 'Lorraine is mine. And no one today has a better right than I have because of the convincing reasons that I have given you.'

46 For Lobkowitz's disgrace see Wolf, *Wenzel Fürst Lobkowitz*.

47 It amounted to a veritable alliance since it provided in Article 4 for help and mutual assistance to ensure the execution of the partition, H.H. Sta., Vienna, Documents Frankreich, 117: '. . . it is agreed that the one party shall aid and assist the other party, which asks for reciprocal aid where and whenever necessary by land and sea to obtain possession of its inheritance, with counsel, action, forces, arms, ships, and finally with a sufficient army . . .'

7 Louis XIV and the Dutch War*

PAUL SONNINO

Louis XIV fulfilled the image of the ideal young king to his own perfect satisfaction. A firm believer in the efficacy of dedication and reason, he took special pride in conquering youthful passion and impetuosity. Louis had shown his mother that he could be a firm master of the royal family (as, for example, when he disgraced the duke and duchess of Navailles in 1664), and this proof was more than sufficient for the queen, Maria Teresa, for his brother, the duc d'Orléans, and for the king's mistress, Mlle de La Vallière. Louis had demonstrated by arresting Fouquet that he would brook no over-mighty minister in his *conseil d'en haut*, nor was this lesson lost on the secretary for war, Le Tellier, the controller-general of finances, J. B. Colbert, and the secretary for foreign affairs, Lionne. The king had, with their aid, restored order at home and contented himself with some periodic sabre-rattling abroad. The emphasis on domestic matters, however, was merely the basis for more glorious excursions into the realms of foreign policy and war, aimed chiefly at the Spanish branch of the House of Habsburg. The first of these, the War of Devolution in 1667, was intended to conquer the bulk of the Spanish Netherlands and was blocked by the English, the Dutch and the Swedes banding together in the triple alliance. Louis responded with more of his restraint and accepted the compromise Peace of Aix-la-Chapelle in 1668. His *Mémoires for the Instruction of the Dauphin*, written around this time, eloquently confirm his pride in his entire conduct until then.

The king, however, was weighing the past by a different set of standards than he meant to apply to the future. He felt with

* Specially commissioned for this volume.

ever-growing intensity that the method and patience so extra-ordinary for a man in his youth did not retain the same distinction in one who was entering the prime of his career, unless they were accompanied by imposing results. For all the power he enjoyed over his entourage, he sensed their desire for him to show them his mettle and to be quick about it. It mattered little that most of his intimates demanded no additional signs of him. The queen accepted Louis unconditionally. The duc d'Orléans had other amusements. La Vallière was giving way to Montespan. Le Tellier, whose young son the marquis de Louvois was taking over the ministry of war, had most to gain from a bellicose policy, but also much to lose; while Colbert and Lionne harboured very mixed feelings about any developments that accelerated the rising star of Louvois. The king thus became a driven man after 1668, goading and pushing the very persons he wanted to impress in a determined effort to fulfil his self-image.

It is easy enough to tie this intense and insecure young man to some ambitious war of aggrandisement or revenge, but it is another matter to connect him specifically with the war that he declared against the Dutch Republic in 1672. Why, to begin with, did Louis, whose original goal had been the Spanish Netherlands, choose to attack the far-away Dutch? What, for that matter, did he expect an invasion of that republic to achieve? Did he consider at all that the Dutch might flood their dykes and turn to the prince of Orange, or that the emperor, the elector of Brandenburg, and Spain, might come to their aid? And what was the relation between his war aims and the final outcome of the Peace of Nijmegen?

The king himself is well worth consulting on these questions, although it takes some doing to track him down and to put his responses in the proper perspective. He wrote a good many *projets*, letters, and marching orders during the war, papers of the moment that cannot afford to lie. Systematically arranged, they begin to form a pattern. He also worked on his military *Mémoires* or rather, *Mémoires for the History of the Dutch War*, during this same general period, documents of display whose function it was to describe his ultimate triumph.[1] Carefully identified, these outline his search for a most elusive victory. Woven together, these fragmentary sources lay him bare in a manner that no polished work could do, at the very time when he was making his bid for immortality.

Louis was faced with two choices if he wanted to acquire the Spanish Netherlands: the first was to declare war against Spain and confront the entire triple alliance with all its sympathisers; the second was to isolate the impudent Dutch Republic and remove it as a threat while Europe watched. The king chose the more moderate alternative, with its redeeming overtones of putting the upstarts in their place, but still it was no easy task. Louis met with his *conseil d'en haut*, Le Tellier, Colbert and Lionne, in order to achieve this goal, and they were quickly beset by false starts and vacillations. The first problem they faced was that of turning England from an opponent into an ally, for Colbert de Croissy, French ambassador in London, found in Charles II a consummate procrastinator.[2] The second problem was that of continental alliances. Prince Wilhelm von Fürstenberg, a French agent in Germany and councillor of the elector of Cologne, might well induce his eccentric master and the warrior bishop of Münster to attack the Dutch,[3] but would Spain, the emperor, the elector of Brandenburg, the dukes of Brunswick, and Sweden sit idly by as the pivot of the European balance of power was summarily removed from the scene? These difficulties are reflected in the first piece that the king wrote specifically on the Dutch War, a little note, or *feuille*, that he jotted down around January 1670.[4] The first entry noted confidently, 'English Treaty', since Colbert de Croissy was then making some slight progress with Charles II.[5] Another entry indicated expectantly, 'Sending of Prince Wilhelm to the Elector[s] of Cologne and Brandenburg, the Bishop of Münster, and the Dukes of Brunswick'; but Fürstenberg, after some success with his own master, had a cool reception in Berlin which augured badly for the future of this key negotiator.[6] Louis was trying everyone, including Portugal, Sweden and the House of Lorraine, in a succession of frustrating negotiations. He just did not seem to be taken seriously.

The king did achieve some notable successes, but these were nevertheless accompanied by increasing vacillations and sudden reversals of policy. He managed, in the course of 1670, to secure Charles II of England as an ally in a war against the Dutch, but aside from the tractable elector of Cologne and the always

F*

willing bishop of Münster, the problem of the other continental
states persisted, and it proved impossible to begin the war in
1671. Louis, moreover, seemed to be of two minds about its
scope. Early in 1671, he and his *conseil d'en haut* began very
assiduously to collect as many allies as possible, but Lionne
gradually adopted the more modest policy of seeking fewer allies
and many benevolent neutrals. Lionne also sent written assurances to Spain about the security of its possessions in the Netherlands.[7] On the other hand, the king's and Louvois' frequent
voyages into this area, accompanied by large numbers of troops,
and the continuous incidents on the frontier hardly seemed intended to lull the Spanish to sleep.[8] Louis' two minds became
one when Lionne died in September 1671, the king's vast ambitions coming to the fore the moment that the environment
became more congenial. Louis appointed Louvois as interim
foreign minister until the arrival of Lionne's successor, Pomponne, and the new *conseil d'en haut* of Le Tellier, Colbert and
Louvois immediately reversed Lionne's Spanish policy, doing
everything possible in order to bully and frighten Spain into
declaring for the Dutch.[9] It was at this juncture, around October
1671, that the king picked up his pen to write a second *feuille*
on the Dutch War.[10] The first entry noted happily, 'continuation
of contacts with England to attack and ruin the Dutch'. Another
entry meandered, 'plans to engage many princes – changes of
mind'. Others referred to a 'paper sent to Spain' and to 'incidents
in Flanders', but the last one rang with the excitement of the
moment : 'efforts to keep Spain from joining the Dutch and then
to make them join'. Yet the moment passed. Louvois must have
begun to worry about the dangers of involving Spain, and it was
easy enough for him, in conjunction with Le Tellier, to prevail
upon Louis to reverse his decision.[11] The king was denied.

Louis thus acquired a more adventurous *conseil d'en haut*
on the eve of the Dutch War. It was a council much more indul-
gent of the king's ambitions, even though it was still compelled
to curb them. But, dominated by Louvois, who combined his
vital responsibilities with the assured support of his father, it
was hardly disposed to challenge Louis' assumption that a bril-
liantly executed military demonstration, supported by England
and by two petty German princes, would turn the frantic Dutch
burgers into eager betrayers of the Spanish Netherlands. There

was no thought of the dykes of the great cities being flooded or of any threat from that untried youth, the prince of Orange.

The king was completely immersed in the advancing preparations for the war when Pomponne entered the *conseil d'en haut* early in 1672, in full sympathy with Lionne's conception of a limited war against the Dutch Republic that would not alarm the benevolent neutrals. Pomponne must have been more disturbed by Louis' great expectations, by Le Tellier's and Colbert's tacit approbation and by Louvois' continued presence in the council and involvement in foreign affairs, than by the actual policies being followed. The auspices, moreover, looked favourable. On the eve of the war, the king managed to strengthen his alliances with Cologne and Münster and even secured the benevolent neutrality of Sweden, which promised, in very evasive terms, to intervene should the emperor or the elector of Brandenburg come to the aid of the Dutch.

Louis might have wished for more allies and enemies, but he still went off to war at the end of April 1672 like a hero to his victory. He left the queen at home to govern the state with the advice of the two elder statesmen, Le Tellier and Colbert, while the duc d'Orléans, the prince de Condé, the vicomte de Turenne, Louvois and Pomponne followed him into the field. The king's conception of generalship was not limited to strategy and tactics. It ranged from writing his own marching orders[12] to keeping a *Journal* of the campaign for himself and for his court.[13] Everyone expected him to begin by attacking Maestricht. He responded on 29 May in his first entry, 'It has appeared so important to me for the reputation of my arms to begin my campaign with something of great brilliance that I have not deemed that the attack on Maestricht would suffice for this. I have esteemed it more advantageous to my plans and less common for glory to attack all at once four strongholds on the Rhine . . . Rheinberg, Wesel, Büderich, and Orsoy.' The cities fell with amazing ease between 2 and 6 June, although we do not have the entry that describes their fall. On 9 June Louis announced, 'I advance early this morning to hasten by my presence the orders that I gave yesterday for the passage of the Rhine'. This crossing, however, should not be confused with the more celebrated passage of the Rhine that the king narrated on 12 June in an enthusiastic entry that concludes happily, 'affairs are in such good state that

I have every reason to praise God for this undertaking'. Indeed, as Louis' armies spread out over the Dutch provinces of Overijssel, Gelderland and Utrecht, they outran their supplies, a clear indication that their success was exceeding all expectations. On 18 June the king sent out a lieutenant-general, Rochefort, with a detachment of cavalry that even managed temporarily to seize Muiden, the town that controlled the dykes of Amsterdam, but Louis' campaign was simply not geared to the taking of Amsterdam, as the missing entries for this period would probably confirm. The Dutch, moreover, were already flooding their dykes when their deputies appeared before the king's ministers near Doesburg on 22 June, hinted broadly at some extraordinary concessions, then sent back one of their number for further instructions. They again approached Louis' ministers on 28 June in Amerongen, pushed their negotiations a little further, then disappeared without a trace. Louis was in no rush, confidently noting on 7 July, 'The deputies of Holland told Louvois and Pomponne that the States had given them power to accept generally everything I desired and wanted to retain from my clemency what I would please to cede to them.' The king put the final stamp of approval on his planning and execution of the war about a week later, 'It's a good thing that I have prepared as I have for so long, for nothing has been lacking in my undertakings . . . I am in a position to instil fear in my enemies, to cause astonishment to my neighbours, and despair to the envious.' It was on this happy note that Louis adjourned his campaign, hardly disturbed by the fact that the great cities of the Republic were temporarily secure behind their waters or that his ally, the bishop of Münster, was bogged down in an unsuccessful siege before Groningen.

The king had scarcely returned to France, however, when his entire project began to crumble. In August the prince of Orange came to power in the Dutch Republic, while the emperor and the elector of Brandenburg moved their armies to its assistance, without officially entering the war. But Louis was not particularly distressed at the gradually shifting situation. It merely provided more grist for his mill. He increasingly relished the idea of the duc de Luxembourg hemming in the Dutch while the vicomte de Turenne entered Germany and disposed of the new threat once and for all.[14] The king also counted on his diplomats enrolling a few greedy or frightened allies under his banners. Louis could not complain in October when the inexperienced prince of Orange tried to take Woerden and the duc de Luxembourg made a dashing march to relieve the city, but the king was less than delighted with Turenne, who insisted on keeping his own counsel and manœuvring in all directions instead of dutifully and obligingly dispersing the enemies.[15] The diplomats, for their part, were managing to make some expensive and tepid alliances. Louis' greatest challenge, however, came in December, along with his greatest visions. The stubborn prince of Orange, aided by Spanish auxiliaries, suddenly appeared before Charleroi. The excited king was not prepared to forfeit the city, even if it had obtained for him a kind of Spanish intervention. He proceeded to act as his own minister of war, dispatching Louvois to Flanders to plan for the relief. During this period we meet again the man of the *feuille* for 1671, stubbornly pursuing his *idée fixe*, yet incapable of executing it alone. Around 19 December he wrote a *Mémoire* for the distant Louvois.[16] Louis was thinking of establishing himself at Lille that very winter, 'to fall upon wherever I might think I could do something'. In any case, 'Flanders must be my principal dedication, once war is declared with the Spanish.' Why not take Franche-Comté while they were at it? He added, 'The undertaking against Burgundy could be executed easily.' But Louvois, initially just as bellicose, was beginning to feel the effects of winter, writing to the king in regard to Charleroi on 21 December,[17] 'The weather is so bad that I fear that a part of the cavalry will be ruined on the march', and adding cautiously, 'The Spanish undoubtedly believe that they are not making war against Your Majesty when they attack strongholds in conjunction with the Dutch.' Louis would not relent and grew even more enthusiastic when Charleroi's spirited defence forced the prince of Orange to raise the siege. The king wrote to Louvois on 27 December,[18] 'I confess that I would find it grand if while the Emperor, Spain, Holland, and Brandenburg try to stop my projects, one saw M. de Luxembourg enter Holland over the ice, M. le Prince take part of Burgundy, and me in Flanders clearing all their troops and taking some stronghold if it were possible.' But he hastened to add reassuringly, 'We will see each other before executing anything.' Louis' visions scarcely materialised. The duc de Luxembourg did try to enter Holland over the ice, but it melted too quickly, and on Louvois' return, the war against Spain idea was scrapped. The king was denied again.

Louis' plans for 1673 are fairly clear and surprisingly tangible. He would personally lead an army against the great fortress of Maestricht, while the prince de Condé hemmed in the Dutch and the vicomte de Turenne held off the Germans. The Spanish were cowed by the failure of the siege of Charleroi, and a peace congress was to assemble in Cologne. If the king took Maestricht while Europe watched, two bright prospects opened up before him : one was that the Dutch would make peace and in the process sell out the Spanish Netherlands; the other was that Spain would in desperation come openly to the aid of the Dutch and give him an additional pretext to attack the Spanish terri-tories. Louis received an unexpected lift in March, when the sluggish Turenne turned on the Brandenburgers, forcing the elector to sue for peace and the Imperialists to scurry home to Bohemia.

The king treated his good fortune as if she were a harlot. On 1 May he left Saint-Germain, Louvois and Pomponne in his suite. Louis first manœuvred his army through the Spanish Netherlands, encouraging the suspicion that he intended to fall on one of its great cities. Everyone also expected that once a treaty was signed with Brandenburg, Turenne would be with-drawn from Germany. On 22 May the king delightedly strength-ened the first suspicion by writing a marching order that brought his army to the vicinity of Ghent, but on the same date he casually ordered Turenne to march further into Germany and remain until such time as the emperor promised not to come out again.[19] Louis thus invested Maestricht on 6 June with the help of reinforcements from Condé's and Turenne's armies, amidst a growing clamour of friend and foe over his German policy. Pom-ponne arranged an audience with the king for Fürstenberg in an effort to reverse the policy, but it was to no avail.[20] Louis was more interested in the day-to-day details of the siege of Maes-trict which he inserted into a *Journal* and, with Vauban directing the operations, the city surrendered on June 30. The king then slowly wended his way to Lorraine, redistributing his troops and waiting for his plans to bear fruit. He also took advantage of the lull to expand his *Journal* into a *Mémoire* which would describe the great siege and its aftermath to posterity.[21] We lack the first few sheets, which might have confirmed for us the motives of the operation, but we do have an enthusiastically long-winded account in which Louis recapitulates every step of the siege, every reinforcement received, every rumour of relief, and proudly praises his troops as 'the best in the world'. As the king wrote, however, it gradually became evident that the magnificent siege of Maestricht had neither ended the war nor prompted Spain to enter it; but Louis was not disappointed. He simply trotted out his old plan, slightly sharpened for the occasion – declare war on Spain, attack Franche-Comté that very year. Louvois supported it. Pomponne did not matter. As the king hinted to one of his lieutenant-generals, the duc de Navailles, at Thionville on 24 July, 'I am in for a long war'.[22] Louis got himself ready for it by attacking Trier at the end of August. He was in Nancy by September, where he was shocked to learn that the prince of Orange had broken out of his defences and surprised the town of Naarden; but the king could assuage his indignation by preparing a *projet* for the campaign of the following year.[23] Louis would again have an army hemming in the Dutch and another holding off the Germans, while he himself would besiege one or two of the greater cities of the Spanish Netherlands. As Louvois wrote to his friend Courtin at Cologne on 22 September,[24] 'The king believes that if the affairs of all his enemies together were to go as well as they have gone badly up to now, it would take them many years to retake what His Majesty has conquered from them.' Louvois personally composed the declaration of war on Spain, scheduled for 24 September,[25] but the old story repeated itself. Louvois must have begun to fear the consequences of attacking Spain and prevailed upon Louis to suspend the plan. The king had been denied thrice.

Louis might at least have expected on his return to France at the end of September to see the curtain falling on the *status quo*. On the contrary, the Spanish waited until they could no longer be attacked that year, then declared war. The Imperialists surprisingly outmanœuvred the renowned Turenne and joined the prince of Orange in taking Bonn. The king suddenly saw his petty German allies abandon him and was obliged to withdraw from his great conquests of 1672. Louis celebrated these catastrophes by falling into a deep silence.

The king could not have been very happy with himself or with his entourage at the beginning of 1674. He had to renew the war virtually from scratch, presiding over a divided *conseil d'en haut* in which Le Tellier watched over Louvois apprehensively, Colbert played the overburdened servant, and Pomponne counted reversals with prophetic glee. The prince de Condé and the vicomte de Turenne came in from the field, blaming Louvois for the disasters and demanding his disgrace.[26] But Louis was too closely tied to his minister of war's policies to condemn them outright, and found it much more convenient to conclude that it was Turenne who had precipitated the setbacks. Le Tellier also aided his son by reconciling Condé, thus leaving Turenne isolated. The king had to patch up his council, send off his grumpy generals to their armies, and bear patiently as England abandoned him, the peace congress at Cologne broke up, and as the emperor and the Empire officially declared war against him. The brightest prospect for 1674 was the hastily planned conquest of Franche-Comté, the afterthought of previous years.

The campaign of 1674 did, however, have the merit of accomplishing its objective. Louis left Versailles on 19 April. Louvois, Pomponne and a number of generals accompanied him; Le Tellier and Colbert, as was their habit, remaining behind. The king wrote a few marching orders on the way to the campaign,[27] but he had neither the time nor, apparently, the inclination to record his triumphs for posterity. The first siege, Besançon, lasted from April 25 to May 22. Louis simply wrote to Colbert at its conclusion, 'It's a great accomplishment and more difficult than it appeared.'[28] The king then moved on to Dôle and informed Colbert on June 4, 'They are putting up a stiffer defence than expected.'[29] Dôle fell two days later, but Louis still neglected to record his victories. He was at the very least learning not to jump to conclusions about them.

The king was back in France by the end of June and had to watch respectfully while the old generals defended the very frontiers of the monarchy. Condé was less than brilliant in August, when he barely defeated the prince of Orange at Senef, although Turenne regained his reputation with some classic little actions at Sinsheim and Enzheim. As for Louvois, he must have wondered how long he could count on Louis' support while offering him such meagre satisfactions and may well have cast a glance in the direction of the king's manuscripts, hoping for some sign of Louis' renewed pleasure in the war and pride in the face of posterity. Other ministers, moreover, were gaining strength. A revolt had taken place in Messina against Spanish rule. Colbert and the navy stood to gain from a successful intervention. The Swedes were about to honour their treaty and invade the Empire. Here was a feather in Pomponne's diplomatic cap. Louvois desperately needed control over the king's disposition in the midst of so many enemies, and the first step was to surround him with his creatures. Louvois had been grooming one such person in the marquis de Chamlay, a *maréchal général de logis* of the French army, who, with his inseparable assistant, François de La Prée, had served in every campaign of the war. Chamlay had made a fine impression on Condé and Turenne through his skill in preparing marching orders and in planning the movement of troops. He also rose in the estimation of Louvois and of the king by providing exactly what the generals did not : long, detailed reports of every slight movement of the army. By the end of 1674, Louvois was ready to throw Chamlay into the breach, and it was not a moment too soon.

Louis seems to have lost a sense of purpose in the war by 1675. Louvois offered him a modest little campaign in the area of the middle Meuse, aimed at taking some strongholds, such as Dinant, Huy and Limbourg, which would strengthen the communications with Maestricht. The king may have been relying on the diversionary moves and alliances to turn the tide for him. Louvois appears to have had less confidence in them. It was all the more reason to tighten the reins around Louis.

The campaign of 1675 had all the qualities of a pleasure outing. The king left Versailles on 11 May with the duc d'Orléans, the prince de Condé, Louvois and Pomponne in his entourage. When he left Compiègne on 14 May two more had joined the party, Chamlay and the shadowy La Prée. Louis immediately accepted the agreeable services that they offered him. We see his hand mixed with theirs on the marching orders, the king choosing the password of the day and filling in other details of the beautifully planned marches.[30] Louis managed in this delightful manner to take Dinant, Huy and Limbourg before leaving for France on 17 July. Louvois had provided the king with a campaign that made war a joy.

Louis had barely returned to France, however, when a series of calamities began. On 27 July, Turenne, reconnoitring a position near Sassbach, Germany, was struck by a cannon ball and killed. His army withdrew across the Rhine in confusion. Several weeks later, Marshal de Créqui, bringing up another army to relieve the city of Trier, was completely routed by an enemy force. Taking refuge in Trier, he was forced to surrender by the mutinous garrison. It took Condé, rushed – with Chamlay and La Prée – to assume command of Turenne's army, and Rochefort, who rallied the remnants of Créqui's to preserve the frontier. The diversionary moves and alliances, moreover, bore little fruit. The French had some successes in Sicitly, but the Swedes proved unable to hold their own in the Empire. As for Louvois, whatever personal satisfaction he may have felt at the passing of Turenne or at the inefficacy of his colleagues' wars was far outweighed by the humiliations to the armies under his control. The only recourse now was to surround the king with the illusion of victory. Louvois again called upon Chamlay. When Chamlay and La Prée returned to France in December 1675, they quickly resumed their duty of embellishing the war. We see them working on what they called the *Livre du Roi*, carefully collecting the marching orders of Louis' campaign, drawing up the appropriate maps for each march, and writing several drafts of a straightforward little history of the operation.[31] It sounded very much like one of Chamlay's letters, heavy on movements, reasuring in its monotony : 'The thirtieth His Majesty stopped over at Ham, where he already found a rather large body of troops camped on the other side of the Somme below the castle.' Chamlay describes the sieges of Dinant, Huy and Limbourg in similar style and informs us that 'His Majesty left Vellaines the seventeenth with his musketeers, in order to return to Versailles.' The account concluded by mentioning the death of Turenne, but did not deal at all with the disasters that followed. The intent of the work is clear. It was designed to keep alive in the king's mind the memory of his own agreeable campaign, while events elsewhere fell into oblivion. And Louis was willing to play the game. Chamlay presented the final draft of his little history to the king, and where it mentioned that His Majesty had returned home with his musketeers, Louis punctiliously added in his own hand, 'and the quarter of his guards, gendarmes, and

light horse that he ordinarily keeps at his side'. Chamlay and La
Prée then collected everything in a beautifully bound and illustrated book destined for the king.[32] Louis must have wiled away
many a winter evening contemplating the graceful and orderly
movements of his troops.

The king's approach to the campaign of 1676, moreover,
showed that a remarkable transformation had taken place. He
picked up his pen on a number of occasions to prepare *projets*
on the first operation, the ambitious siege of Condé.[33] Louis corresponded happily with Louvois, who had gone ahead with
Chamlay and La Prée to prepare the way. He wrote enthusiastically to Louvois on April 5, 'Let me know every day exactly
what happens.'[34] The enemy was unbowed and a peace congress
was assembling at Nijmegen, but the king seems to have found a
new goal for the war : establishing defensible frontiers in Flanders
and holding on to Franche-Comté. He had, at that point, little
choice but to seek some kind of compromise peace, for even if
his armies resumed their spectacular successes, these very successes were likely to push England into joining the ranks of his
enemies and bring the long war to a new and costlier *impasse*.

The campaign of 1676 conveniently provided an opportunity
to come out of the war with considerable honour. Louis left Versailles on 16 April with the duc d'Orléans and Pomponne in his
entourage and arrived at Condé on the twenty-first to find the
city invested. The siege operations, conducted by Vauban,
were so successful that Condé fell on 26 April with the prince of
Orange not even making an effort to relieve it. The king then
sent the duc d'Orléans to besiege nearby Bouchain, while he himself guarded the approaches against possible relief. Louis was
at Heurtebise, in the vicinity of Valenciennes, on 10 May when,
to his amazement, he saw the much smaller army of the prince
of Orange come into view. It was the chance of a lifetime. The
king was eager to attack. He skilfully placed his troops in battle
position and fired three shots at the enemy to invite them to
battle, but Louvois and a number of generals strongly advised
Louis against attacking an enemy protected by the guns of
Valenciennes, particularly since his primary duty was to cover
the siege of Bouchain.[35] The king gave way and the armies stood
at arms for the entire day. By the eleventh the enemies had piled
so much earth in front of them that they had disappeared from

view. On the twelfth Bouchain fell. Louis fired three more shots
at the enemy to apprise them of the event and withdrew from the
field.

The king's attitude when he returned to France suggests that
he was completely impervious to what had happened at Heurtebise. The undaunted prince of Orange decided to try his luck
before Maestricht, and it looked as if he might succeed. Louis
once more decided to become his own minister of war, sending
Louvois to Flanders to take another city, Aire, in compensation.
The old relationship of the king pushing the minister re-emerges
in the correspondence between them. Louis wrote on 21 July,[36]
'It seems that you believe that we must content ourselves after
the siege to rest the troops and to prepare for the coming year
. . . I confess that I would think it opportune to do something
more afterwards which would, along with Aire, replace in some
manner the [probable] loss of Maestricht.' And on 27 July, hearing that the governor of the Spanish Netherlands was trying to
relieve Aire, the man of Heurtebise wrote,[37] 'We must fight if
possible, for I can't help but think that we would have a great
advantage.' Louvois did very well for the king. He brought back
Aire, some minor strongholds, and he even managed, against all
expectations, to save Maestricht, but he still did not forgo the
benefits of an official interpretation. When Chamlay and La
Prée returned to France in October 1676 they put together a
considerably more ambitious *Livre du Roi*.[38] La Prée took over
the writing, bringing new eloquence to the work, making the
points more sharply, and expanding it to cover the entire year.
He specifically underscored the services of Louvois. The king had
sent Louvois to Flanders, 'deeming that his presence would
advance everything'. The taking of Condé 'was all the more
glorious for the king in that in no other stronghold is relief
easier, the circumvallation more difficult, the separation of quarters greater'. He heaped contempt on the prince of Orange, who,
'must have been extremely upset to have stood in the presence of
his enemy for three days only to be the witness of his glory'. The
account ended with the inevitable contrast of the fall of Aire with
the relief of Maestricht. La Prée must have been floating with
the tide. Chamlay would never have approved the specific references to Louvois' services if he did not know that the compli-
ments confirmed Louis' own appreciation. And would Chamlay

have permitted the criticism of the prince of Orange for standing in the presence of his enemy without fighting if he were not aware that the king had somewhere lost the capacity to turn the reproach upon himself?

Louis was again convinced of his military prowess by 1677, but he was less sure about the endurance of his subjects. The king could look forward to another successful campaign in the Spanish Netherlands, hoping to take Valenciennes, Cambrai and perhaps even Saint-Omer. Louvois, accompanied by Chamlay and La Prée, went ahead in February to ensure that everything would be ready. The choice of these three cities, however, indicates that Louis was still rounding out his frontiers and interested in a compromise peace. And his *conseil d'en haut* was happy to procure it for him. Le Tellier and Louvois looked forward to the prospect of a respite from obligatory victories, Colbert desired nothing more than a break in the extraordinary taxation, and Pomponne eagerly grasped the opportunity to come into his own as the architect of the Peace of Nijmegen. Pomponne believed that if Louis made his terms clear and disclaimed any designs on the entire Spanish Netherlands, England could be dissuaded from joining the ranks of the enemies and peace would be assured.

The trouble with the campaign of 1677, however, was that it proved to be too successful. The king left Saint-Germain on 1 March, with the duc d'Orléans and Pomponne following, and arrived at Valenciennes three days later. The siege, directed by Vauban, was proceeding according to plan when on 17 March the incredible happened. A French detachment following hard upon the heels of the withdrawing garrison troops pursued them through an open gate right into the city, thus taking it by storm. Louis understood the significance of such events. As he wrote to the archbishop of Paris on March 22, 'God, who sees my good intentions, has wanted to bless their execution.'[39] The king then moved on to besiege Cambrai while the duc d'Orléans turned against Saint-Omer. Louis had just sent some reinforcements to his brother when opportunity again presented itself. The irrepressible prince of Orange attempted to relieve Saint-Omer and the duc d'Orléans came up to meet him at Mt Cassel. It seemed initially like a repetition of the previous year. On 10 April the two armies faced each other for the entire day, but there the similarity ended. On the eleventh, just as the prince of Orange seemed about to give battle, the effeminate duc d'Orléans ordered an attack on the enemy and routed him with heavy losses. Louis could not have missed the contrast, but he showed no signs of grasping it. As Louvois wrote to Courtin, now in England, on April 13, 'The first thing the King said to me on receiving this important news was that he hoped the blow would dispose his enemies to agree to a peace.'[40] But Louis was soon master of Cambrai and Saint-Omer, the enemy army was in pieces, and nothing stood in the way of proceeding to the conquest of the rest of the Spanish Netherlands except the uncertain endurance of his subjects, the enigmatic will of God, and the ambiguous threats of the English. The king still insisted on bowing before these three manifestations of a single force, yet his submission showed a tell-tale sign of doubt, pride and defiance. He announced his plans to return to France and give no more alarm to his enemies, but he would first visit his Channel ports and ensure their readiness for defence again any naval power. Pomponne did not like this bellicose gesture, but he was less effective at curbing his master than Louvois had been.[41]

Louis' return to France intensified his dilemma. He was personally committed before his entire *conseil d'en haut* to the compromise peace that was within his grasp, but he was increasingly haunted by visions of the glorious peace that might have been and that could still be. It is little wonder that we find him, in the latter part of 1677, beginning to ponder over the past by resuming his *Mémoires* and expanding them into a history of the Dutch War. It is evident from this work that the war had exacted a heavy toll on him and that he was struggling desperately to buttress his ego against the moderate peace that was looming at Nijmegen. The king first picked up and revised his old *Mémoire* on the siege of Maestricht.[42] He began by recalling the situation in the latter part of 1672, and his introductory words advanced for the first time an extraordinary new thesis on the expansion of the war. 'The advantages that my armies had just gained over the United Provinces having surpassed everyone's expectations,' he wrote, 'had at the same time excited the hatred and jealousy of my neighbours.' He went on, 'I noted on all sides leagues forming against my progresses.' Louis was thus propounding the theory that it was no mistake of strategy or diplomacy, but his great successes that had turned all Europe against him. The king then proceeds to introduce another new theme into his writing, the countermotif of the scapegoat. He waxes enthusiastic over the duc de Luxembourg's dashing relief of Woerden and his winter march over the ice into Holland, but is lethargic and sloppy as he describes Turenne's manœuvres in Germany against the emperor and the elector of Brandenburg. It almost seems as if Louis had buried with Turenne the memory and responsibility for the great reversals in the war. The amazing thing is that the king will even juggle facts in order to save the mounting enemies theory and detract from the services of Turenne. He casually mentions right in the middle of Turenne's campaign in the latter part of 1672, 'having detached' the elector of Brandenburg 'in some way from the interests of the Emperor and Holland', an event of March 1673! But of course, if Louis had inserted the defection of the elector of Brandenburg in the correct place, he would have had to explain why, once the maligned Turenne had disposed of the Germans, the brilliant siege of Maestricht had not finished off the Dutch. The king seems to reach a new level of self-adulation in the *Mémoire*. When he gets to the year 1673, he describes how his best troops were in the Republic and in Germany, how his enemies were mounting, and how his options were reduced to besieging Maestricht with raw recruits. He seems to have forgotten that at this point his enemies were cowed, that Condé and Turenne had sent him reinforcements, and that he had personally dubbed his troops 'the best in the world'. But the mounting enemies thesis was well worth a little playing with the facts. It was not just a convenient explanation of the past, it was even more useful for the present, for what theory could better justify the current policy of a compromise peace guaranteed by defensible frontiers? Chamlay and La Prée were always sensitive to Louis' feelings. When they returned to France in November 1677, they devoted themselves to preparing a beautiful new *Livre du Roi*,[43] Chamlay affixing his name to a work that the faithful La Prée had conceived and executed. La Prée exhaustively praised the king for his paternal concern with the frontiers of the monarchy and employed the remaining encomiums to assure Louis that it was his own foresight in sending reinforcements that had enabled the duc d'Orléans to gain the battle of Mt Cassel.

The king was again obliged in 1678 to give his enemies a token both of his invincibility and of his moderation. Louis had a number of great cities to choose from : Luxembourg, Namur, Mons, Brussels and Ghent. He selected Ghent, a city whose conquest would demonstrate his capacity to conquer the entire Spanish Netherlands and once again threaten the territory of the Dutch Republic. The conquest of Ghent, however, would be accompanied by offers to restore the city at the peace. The enemies had the choice of attempting to reverse the tide militarily or agreeing to reverse it diplomatically. Louvois prepared the siege of Ghent, but Pomponne's touch is evident in the tantalising alternative presented to the opposition.

The campaign of 1678 turned out to be a classical exercise in seventeenth-century warfare. Louis left Saint-Germain early in February, Louvois, Pomponne, Chamlay and La Prée following him into the field. By 22 February he was at Metz. During that entire month his troops manœuvred mysteriously both in the Spanish Netherlands and on the borders of the Empire. No one knew where the blow was going to fall. Suddenly, at the end of February, five cities in the Spanish Netherlands – Ypres, Bruges, Namur, Luxembourg and Charlemont – were invested in quick succession, and on 1 March Marshal d'Humières surrounded Ghent, finding the great city reduced to a garrison of some 700 men. The king arrived three days later, and on 8 March the city surrendered. The conquest was so easy that Louis could not resist the temptation of moving on to take Ypres, which fell on the twenty-fifth. The king, however, still willing to put Pomponne's diplomacy into effect, returned to France, offered to restore Ghent, and promised to suspend all operations until 12 May. Yet he was beginning to chafe under the restraint. He told a merry gathering at Saint-Germain that 'he was in a fair way to be master of Flanders if his last offers of peace should be refused', and that 'the people of England would never contribute towards the war for three years together'.[44] Louis did not get the opportunity to test his predictions. Back in the field, he received a visit from a Dutch ambassador, Van Beverningk, who informed him that the Republic was amenable to his terms but needed time to impose them upon the Spanish. It seemed as if the war was truly coming to an end, and the king's thoughts carried him back once more into the past. He turned to Chamlay and asked him to prepare a *Mémoire* on the campaign of 1672. Chamlay obliged with a rather straightforward account of the origins of the war and of the great campaign.[45] Louis then proceeded to write his own *Mémoire* for 1672, but he needed more than straightforwardness in order to explain the war to himself.

The king returned to France at the end of May and waited patiently while the Dutch forced the hesitant Spanish monarchy to accept the peace in September. It was during this period that Louis hammered out the bulk of his *Mémoire* for 1672.[46] The king began on solid enough ground, claiming that the origin of the war lay in the 'ingratitude' of his old allies, the Dutch, who when 'most of the best strongholds in the Netherlands had submitted to my obedience', had forced him to make the Peace of Aix-la-Chapelle in 1668. He also describes his diplomatic and military preparations, revealing that he only expected his alliances to last while he reduced the Dutch into submitting to a shameful peace. Louis then launches into a lively and proud description of the campaign itself, referring to his *Mémoire* as a history of the Dutch War and obviously sensitive to the presence of the reader. The troublesome question arises in the course of this account as to whether the whole whirlwind campaign of 1672 had actually been a failure, since, of course, it did not achieve its stated objective. The king, however, sidesteps this issue in a variety of ways. He resumes his familiar refrain. It was no error of strategy or diplomacy, but 'the great and surprising progresses of my armies' that ultimately reduced the Dutch to the desperate act of flooding their dykes. Louis also cultivates the fantasy that he had specifically ordered Rochefort to seize Muiden, the town that controlled the dykes of Amsterdam, although he implies quite correctly that Rochefort's unsuccessful raid was not a major operation. The king's greatest delusion, however, is that he did get the Dutch where he wanted them in 1672, claiming that he had numerous opportunities for making a glorious peace, but that he was always held back by a secret premonation that he would go on to more useful conquests. Indeed, his central struggle in this *Mémoire* is to convince himself that the terms he imagines he could have obtained in 1672 were not as useful to him as those he was obtaining at Nijmegen. He does not entirely succeed, but he admits no error, just that 'ambition and glory are always pardonable in a prince, particularly in a prince as young and as blessed by fortune as I was'. Even the unsuccessful siege of Groningen Louis attributes to his 'indulgence' in following the poor advice of another scapegoat, the bishop of Münster. When the king gets to the latter part of 1672, he overlaps his *Mémoire* of the previous year and does a considerably better job of describing Turenne's campaign in Germany against the first of the jealous enemies, the emperor and the elector of Brandenburg. For example, he drops all mention of the elector's defection. However, he incredibly places at the end of 1672 the prince of Orange's seizure of Naarden, an event of September 1673! It is a curious pattern of errors. In 1677 Louis misplaces a favourable event that preceded the siege of Maestricht. In 1678 he misplaces an unfavourable event that followed it. And the king can only have been deluding himself, for he could hardly have expected to delude posterity with such errors.

Between 1678 and 1679 Louis watched the diplomats come and go as the last major enemies, the emperor and the elector of Brandenburg, came to terms. During this same period, the king also succeeded in bringing his own interpretation of the war to a precarious conclusion. He did this in a final revision of his *Mémoire* for 1673,[47] in which he shortened the beginning and composed an extremely important addition for the end of the year. The shortened beginning pretty much reiterated the old themes, and Louis failed to take this new opportunity to insert the defection of the elector of Brandenburg in the proper place; but the addition for the end of the year contributes both positively and creatively to his pattern of errors. The king mentions, for example, returning to France to achieve among other things the 'making treaties of alliance'. Louis, of course, made no such treaties at the end of 1673; he must have been thinking of late 1672! The purpose of the king's unconscious shifting of setbacks and advantages thus becomes abundantly clear. He keeps manipulating events in order to make the mounting enemies theory flow more smoothly and to isolate the siege of Maestricht from the advantages that preceded it and the catastrophes that followed it. One recollection that Louis does not succeed in effacing is the prince of Orange's taking of Bonn, but he dismisses this event, which cost him his petty German allies and doomed his conquests of 1672, with the words, 'it wasn't much'. The king is considerably more eager to report that 'The Spanish declared war on me about that time, and I planned to make progresses against them that would be more advantageous to me than those that I had made until then.' Once again, and perhaps with greater confidence, he is weighing the gains of 1672 against the Peace of Nijmegen! He finally culminates his entire thought-process as he concludes : 'I therefore finished that year not reproaching myself for anything and not believing that I had lost a single occasion to assure and extend the limits of my kingdom.' Louis thus had successfully managed to forget that the original purpose of the war had been to secure the Spanish Netherlands and could unabashedly conclude that his policy had been a masterpiece of opportunism directed at gaining whatever advantages presented themselves and at strengthening the frontiers of the monarchy.

The psychological environment, however, shifted with the coming of the peace. There were no more excited preparations for a promising new campaign, no more ominous threats from potentitl new enemies. The king had little to do except to steer the experts of the *conseil d'en haut* through their accustomed paces or through some carefully cultivated minor crisis. Louis needed a friend to occupy his leisure and he found one in Chamlay, who now became the constant companion of the king. We can imagine the two men fondly reminiscing about the war, Chamlay ingratiatingly showering Louis with admiration and deftly introducing a word of praise for Louvois here, a gesture of contempt for the enemies there. La Prée was meanwhile sitting obscurely in Paris, busily compiling the last magnificent *Livre du Roi* of the war, devoted to the grandiose theme of war and peace.[48] It began with an elaborate contrast between the unity of the French body politic and the disunity that had characterised the enemies, proceeding to describe at length the glorious sieges of Ghent and Ypres. But even La Prée was forced to admit that the king did everything to facilitate the peace, 'which he seemed to wish with no less passion than the vanquished themselves'. Chamlay presented this work to Louis, and the king responded with an even greater token of regard. In the summer of 1679, Louis sent Chamlay on a secret mission to Bavaria to obtain an impression of its princess, a possible bride for the dauphin.[49] The king must have cherished the latest *Livre du Roi* all the more in his friend's absence, and it was around this time that Louis decided to write his own *Mémoire* for 1678.[50] It is hard to compare the two works without noting the king's increasing dependence on the forms and conventions of Chamlay and La Prée. Louis' theme is also war and peace. He presents himself as a great conquerer who could only surpass his previous exploits by taking Ghent and Ypres, and he heartily congratulates himself for magnanimously granting a peace to enemies who did not want it. And in terms of his own personal struggle, the king still expresses satisfaction with his behaviour and with his opportunism, 'I was overjoyed at my good fortune and my good conduct, which had made me profit from every occasion to extend the limits of my kingdom at the expense of my enemies.'

La Prée, who was still in Paris in the latter part of 1679, also found time weighing heavily upon his hands. He proceeded to occupy himself by writing a series of summaries, or *abrégés*, on each year of the war, covering parts of the campaign of 1672 and the entire campaigns of 1674, 1675, 1677 and 1678.[51] It is difficult to tell whether this new project was consciously related to Louis' own writings. However, it appears as if Chamlay became a kind of literary middleman between the king and the retiring La Prée around this time. Louis may have given some of his own *Mémoires* and marching orders to Chamlay, who forwarded them to La Prée; and when the king asked Chamlay for a summary of the campaign of 1674 in order to continue his own *Mémoires*, Chamlay conveniently procured for him La Prée's *abrégé* for that year. Louis swallowed this *abrégé* almost whole. First, he dutifully took notes on it, inserting a few additional details, but carefully adhering to its organisation. Then he slavishly followed these notes in preparing his own *Mémoire* for 1674, expanding them chiefly for a brief introduction reminiscent of the previous *Livre du Roi* and for a laboured description of the siege of Besançon.[52] It almost seems as if the king was losing interest in recording his military triumphs as he cast his eyes on what, exactly, they had procured for him. Louis was about to relate the siege of Dôle when a fortuitous event brought his conflict into full consciousness.

In the earlier part of November 1679, Colbert de Croissy, now a French ambassador at Munich, dispatched a special courier to the king on the principal issue of the day, the Bavarian marriage. The courier arrived at court on the night of the fifteenth, just as Pomponne had departed for a two-day sojourn on his country estate. The courier, however, also carried some private communications for J. – B. Colbert, who dutifully, or perhaps maliciously, let Louis know of their arrival.[53] The king began to simmer inside at Pomponne's apparently lackadaisical attitude toward this vital negotiation, his anger growing with each passing moment. It was no time to reminisce about the siege of Dôle. It was the opportunity to explode again Pomponne and lay upon him the blame for what now seemed like a succession of wasted victories.

On 16 November, or perhaps the seventeenth, Louis picked up his pen and wrote a passionate little piece that has become known as the *Reflections on the Craft of Kingship*. It could more aptly be considered as the culmination of his *Mémoires for the History of the Dutch War*.[54] We meet here the same self-righteous and wilful man who had prodded his hesitant ministers into the war. 'The craft of kingship', he waxes, 'is grand, noble, and delicious to one who feels worthy to acquit himself well of his engagements.' But we also meet the confused and torn person who had been struggling for over three years to reconcile his ego with the Peace of Nijmegen. 'Uncertainty', he admits, 'is sometimes exasperating, and when one has passed a reasonable time in examining an affair, one must make a decision and take one's stand.' Convinced, with the help of Louvois, Chamlay and La Prée, that he had won the war militarily, Louis now concluded that he had lost it diplomatically. He seems to have forgotten how eagerly he had desired the compromise peace, blaming it all on his indulgence for the new scapegoat Pomponne who, unfortunately for himself, did not have a coterie of creatures or an illustrated diplomatic history to plead his case. 'I have suffered for many years from his weakness, his obstinacy, his laziness, and his incompetence', the king wailed. 'He has cost me dearly and I have not profited from all the advantages that I could have had. I must finally order him to withdraw.' Thus did Louis salvage his ego from the ruins of the Peace of Nijmegen and discover a new fund of self-righteousness with which to attack the future.

NOTES

1 For the arrangement and identification of these documents, see Paul
   Sonnino, 'Louis XIV's *Mémoires pour l'histoire de la guerre d'Hollande*',
   French Historical Studies (spring 1973) 29–50.
2 See the Archives des Affaires Etrangères, Correspondance Politique,
   Angleterre, vols 92–6.
3 A.A.E., C.P., Cologne, vol. 6.
4 Bibliothèque Nationale, Manuscrit Français 10329, f. 23, published in
   Œuvres de Louis XIV, ed. Ph. A. Grouvelle (Paris, 1806) II, pp. 450–1
   (hereafter cited as Grouvelle (ed.)).
5 A.A.E., C.P., Angleterre, vol. 97.
6 A.A.E., C.P., Cologne, vol. 6, ff. 342–4, 346–60, Fürstenberg to
   Lionne, 15 Jan, 3 Feb 1670.
7 A.A.E., C.P., Allemagne, vol. 247, ff. 408–10, Mémoire pour servir
   d'instruction au Sr. de Verjus, 2 Feb 1671 published in *Recueil des
   Instructions données aux Ambassadeurs et Ministres de France, Prusse*, pp.
   163–8. For the vacillation of policy, see A.A.E., C.P., Prusse, vol. 7,
   ff. 155–7, Louis to Verjus, 15 May 1671. For the efforts not to alarm
   Spain, see A.A.E., C.P., Espagne, vol. 60, f. 158, Ecrit envoyé à M.
   l'arch. de Toulouse pour remettre à la Reine d'Espagne, 27 Apr 1671.
8 See, for example, Archives de la Guerre, Série A^1, vol. 259, no. 143,
   Humières to Louvois, 23 Aug 1671; vol. 256, f. 261, Le Tellier to
   Lionne, 24 Aug 1671, and ff. 283–4, Louvois to Humières, 25 Aug 1671.
9 A.A.E., C.P., Espagne, vol. 60, ff. 263–5, Mémoire du Roi au Sr Du
   Pré, 19 Sep 1671, and ff. 267–8, Louvois to Du Pré, 19 Sep 1671.
10 B.N., MS. Fr. 10329, ff. 30–1 (published in Grouvelle (ed.) II, pp.
   451–2).
11 A.A.E., C.P., Angleterre, vol. 102, ff. 269–70, Louis to Colbert de
   Croissy, 25 Oct 1671, and f. 295, Louvois to Colbert de Croissy,
   25 Oct 1671.
12 B.N., MS. Fr. 10329, *passim*, published in Grouvelle (ed.) III, pp.
   133–44.
13 We have this *Journal* only through fragments scattered among various
   sources. *29 May*: B.N., MS. Fr. 10249, ff. 32–3, published in Grouvelle
   (ed.) III, pp. 183–4; in J. J. Champollion-Figeac, *Mélanges historiques*,
   II, pt 2 (Paris, 1843) p. 521; and in *Lettres, instructions, et mémoires de
   Colbert*, ed. P. Clément (Paris, 1861–82) VI, p. 298. *9–10 June*: Public
   Record Office, State Papers Foreign, France, vol. 134, ff. 98–100,
   Perwich to Arlington, 18 June 1672, published in *Despatches of William
   Perwich*, ed. M. B. Curran (London, 1903) pp. 224–5. *12 June*: Grouvelle (ed.), II, pp. 195–8. *7 July*: Bibliothèque de l'Arsenal, MS. 3567,
   ff. 21–2. *Final statement*: B.N., MS. Fr. 10329, ff. 2–3, published in
   Grouvelle (ed.), III, pp. 130–1.
14 A.G., A^1 269, ff. 117–18, Louvois to Turenne, 13 Oct 1672.
15 Archives Nationales, R^2 58, v, Louvois to Turenne, 7 Nov 1672.
16 A.G., A^1 282, n. 141, 'Mémoire de la main du Roi pour M. de Louvois

que Sa Mte avait fait dès Saint-Germain', published in Grouvelle (ed.), III, pp. 261–9.

17 A.G., A¹ 270, ff. 301–3.

18 A.G., A¹ 282, n. 204, published in Grouvelle (ed.), III, pp. 293–8.

19 B.N., MS. Fr. 10329, ff. 98–9, published in Grouvelle (ed.), III, pp. 307–8; A.G., A¹ 304, pt. I, pp. 183–5, Louvois to Turenne.

20 *Mémoires du Marquis de Pomponne*, ed. J. Mavidal (Paris, 1860) vol. I, pp. 297–8.

21 The *Journal* is in the Archivo Segreto del Vaticano, Nunziatura de Francia 149, ff. 576, 579, 12 June; ff. 577–8, 14 June; f. 575, 18 June; ff. 575, 580, 19 June; and f. 592, 21 June. The *Mémoire* is in B.N., MS. Fr. 10330, ff. 35–136, published in Grouvelle (ed.), III, pp. 327–99.

22 *Mémoires de Chouppes et de Navailles*, ed. C. Moureau (Paris, 1861) pt II, p. 176.

23 B.N., MS. Fr. 10330, ff. 203–19, 'Projets pour la campagne 1674', published in Grouvelle (ed.) III, pp. 426–41.

24 A.G., A¹ 306, ff. 276–7.

25 A.G., A¹ 306, ff. 324–6, 327–9; *Mémoires du Marquis de Pomponne*, I, p. 142.

26 See Turenne's letter to Louis, Jan 1674, published in Grouvelle (ed.), III, pp. 424–5.

27 A.G., Don de Bontin, II.

28 *Lettres, instructions, et mémoires de Colbert*, VI, pp. 319–20.

29 Ibid., pp. 321–2.

30 A.G., Don de Bontin, III.

31 Ibid.

32 B.N., MS. Fr. 7891.

33 B.N., MS. Fr. 10329, ff. 143–7, published in Grouvelle (ed.), III, pp. 404–9, and 10331, ff. 6–7, 1, published in Grouvelle (ed.), IV, pp. 46–7, 48–50. It should be noted that the first of these projects is erroneously attributed to the siege of Maesricht in 1673 and the last one is published with the page reversed. B.N., MS. Fr. 10331, ff. 4–5, 'Mémoire pour camper', published in Grouvelle (ed.), III, pp. 51–3.

34 Grouvelle (ed.), IV, pp. 70–1.

35 See A.G., A¹ 499, n. 153 for the official account. See also J. B. Wolf, *Louis XIV* (New York, 1968), pp. 249–53, for a sympathetic analysis of the decision-making process.

36 Bibliothèque de l'Arsenal, MS. 6613, ff. 170–3. See the copy sent in A.G., A¹ 506, n. 124, published in Grouvelle (ed.), IV, pp. 84–6.

37 A.G., A¹ 506, n. 141.

38 A.G., Don de Bontin, IV; B.N., MS. Fr. 7892.

39 B.N., MS. Fr. 4800, f. 206, published in Grouvelle (ed.), V, p. 561.

40 A.G., A¹ 520, ff. 233–4.

41 A.G., A¹ 520, ff. 265–6, Louvois to Courtin, 15 Apr 1677.

42 We have this revision only in a typewritten copy in A.G., Don de Bontin, VI.

43 A.G., Don de Bontin, V; B.N., MS. Fr. 7893.

44 P.R.O., S.P.F., France, vol. 142, ff. 287–8, Montagu to Williamson, 9 May 1678.

45 Archives du Département de l'Yonne, Legs Niel, carton 5.

46 We have this *mémoire* only in Chamlay's copy in A.G., A¹ 1112. published in C. Rousset, *Histoire de Louvois* (Paris, 1861–3) I, pp. 515–40,

47 B.N., MS. Fr. 10330, ff. 1–34, published in Grouvelle (ed.) III, pp. 256–8, 303–27; ff. 137–41, published in Grouvelle (ed.), III, pp. 399–403. These, joined to the earlier folios 35–136, published in Grouvelle (ed.), III, pp. 327–99, constitute Louis' final text for 1673.

48 B.N., MS. Fr. 7984; A.G., Don de Bontin, VI.

49 *Mémoires du Marquis de Pomponne*, I, pp. 250–1.

50 B.N., MS. Fr. 10331, ff. 47–95, published in Grouvelle (ed.), IV, pp. 143–76.

51 B.N., MS. Fr. 7984; A.G., Don de Bontin, I (1672) II (1674), III (1675), and VI (1678). I have reason to believe that La Prée also wrote an *abrégé* for 1676.

52 B.N., MS. Fr. 10330, ff. 223–9, 247–75, published in Grouvelle (ed.), III, pp. 444–52, 453–72.

53 B.N., Manuscrit Italien 1888 (copies of dispatches of the Venetian ambassadors), ff. 78–84, Foscarini to Doge, 22 Nov 1679.

54 B.N., MS. Fr. 10331, ff. 125–30, published in Grouvelle (ed.), II, pp. 453–9.

8 Louis XIV and the Outbreak of the Nine Years War*

GEOFFREY SYMCOX

The crisis which overtook Louis XIV in 1688 was the outcome of his aggrandisement during the earlier part of his reign, but it took him by surprise and found France unprepared for war. He had completely failed to understand the effects that his aggressive policies had produced, he did not realise that his own actions had united his enemies against him as nothing else could have done. Self-delusion is the occupational disease of absolute monarchs; and although Louis was normally less afflicted than some of his fellow-rulers, in the decade between the Peace of Nijmegen and the outbreak of the Nine Years War he succumbed to this dangerous disease. In fact Louis could no longer rely on the overwhelming military superiority which had assured him the triumphs of his early years. Slowly, in the decade after Nijmegen, the balance of power began to tip in favour of Louis' enemies, while he continued to act as if nothing had changed. The economic base of French power began to be eroded; French military superiority began to be challenged by the resurgence of Habsburg Austria, whose armies were tempered in the harsh school of the Turkish wars; French diplomacy no longer checked and outwitted William III's efforts to build up a European alliance. In the years just before the outbreak of war some signs of misgiving did begin to appear in French government circles. Louis began to show unwonted restraint in his dealings with other powers; serious attention was paid to the economy; projects of military reform were in the air. The growing power of the emperor, backed by several of the German princes, was identified as the principal threat, and some thought was given to the possibility of a permanent settlement with the emperor which

* Specially commissioned for this volume.

would allow Louis to retain what he had already acquired. But
this aim was not pursued with great energy; the threat was still
considered distant.

The Peace of Nijmegen had left France in a very favourable
position. By adroit diplomacy Louis XIV had divided his enemies,
first making terms with the Dutch so that they incurred the
lasting mistrust of their allies. This legacy of discord haunted
the attempts of Louis' enemies to rebuild the alliance against
him, and greatly facilitated French aggrandisement in the next
few years. The peace treaties also left France with a more
defensible frontier than before. To the north, territorial exchanges
eliminated most of the salients and enclaves which had bedevilled
the defence of that frontier, and a major step had been taken
towards achieving what Vauban termed the *pré carré*, a militarily
logical frontier which could be defended with the minimum of
effort. Following the peace Vauban worked ceaselessly to construct a great double line of fortifications from Dunkirk to the
Ardennes, barring the traditional invasion route towards Paris.[1]
On the eastern frontier the problem was more complex. France
had merely *de facto* control of Lorraine, since its duke had
refused to accept the terms on which the peace treaties would
have restored him; he preferred to live in exile at the Imperial
court, leaving French garrisons in the strong points of his duchy.
French sovereignty over Alsace was dubious, because of the deliberate ambiguity of the terms under which the emperor had
ceded it in 1648 : one clause of the treaty admitted full French
sovereignty while another denied it.[2] The Treaty of Nijmegen
had again left the issue in abeyance, despite the eagerness of
the imperial negotiators to raise it, and France retained the
disputed province. But the Imperial claims were not forgotten,
and were given renewed urgency by the extension of French
administrative control over Alsace in the period after the peace.
Louis XIV was well aware that the emperor remained unrecon-
ciled to the loss of Alsace, and his attention was continually
focused on the problem of guarding his eastern frontier. During
the war German armies had twice invaded and ravaged Alsace,
and in the period after Nijmegen the threat that they would
do so again bulked larger and larger. In June 1684 Louvois
wrote to Vauban that 'the Germans must from now on be considered our real enemies', and from that time French policy

was increasingly aimed at securing this vulnerable eastern frontier.[3]

Three principal fortresses guarded the routes into Alsace across the Rhine – at this time a turbulent and undomesticated river, and a serious obstacle to an invading army – at Breisach, Strasbourg with its fort of Kehl and Philippsburg. Breisach, along with Freiburg-im-Breisgau, remained in French hands after the peace, but Strasbourg was a free city outside French control, and the emperor retained Philippsburg which he had conquered in the course of the war. Louis XIV thus held only one of the three keys to Alsace. The programme of *Réunions* can be seen as an effort to rectify this and straighten the eastern frontier into another *pré carré*, since the peace treaty had not achieved this aim in the east.[4] The defects of the treaty were gradually made good : in August 1680 the *Chambre de Réunion* at Breisach declared the whole of Alsace to be under direct French suzerainty; southward, the county of Montbéliard was annexed, linking Alsace with the newly acquired Franche-Comté; to the north, the duchy of Zweibrücken and some parts of the Palatinate were taken over as bastions covering Lower Alsace. In Lorraine the French-held fortresses were strengthened. The Parlement at Metz laid claim to territories stretching northward along the Moselle : the ultimate objective here was Luxembourg, blockaded intermittently since 1681, and finally taken after a short war with Spain in 1683-4. Strasbourg naturally figured largely in any plan for improving the defences of the eastern frontier, and after being subjected to increasing French pressure it was occupied in September 1681 : this bold *coup de théâtre*, stage-managed by Louvois in person and timed to coincide with the acquisition of Casale in northern Italy, alarmed the whole of Europe.[5] The occupation of Strasbourg, along with the important gains made by the *Réunions*, greatly improved the defensive position in the east. But as long as Philippsburg remained in the emperor's hands there was a gap in the line threatening Lower Alsace which defensive works inside the frontier could not really cover.[6]

The *Réunions* were only part of a generalised policy of aggression characteristic of the years immediately following the Treaty of Nijmegen. These were the years when the French fleet, armed with a new offensive weapon, the bomb-ketch, laid in ruins the infidel cities of Chios and Algiers, and more efficiently, the

Christian city of Genoa.[7] In this same period Louis XIV's dispute
with Pope Innocent XI came to a head with the publication
of the four Gallican Articles of 1682, which would have reduced
papal authority over the French church to nothing. Innocent
rejected the articles, and counter-attacked by refusing bulls of
investiture to clerics preferred to bishoprics by Louis XIV, if
they had taken part in the assembly which drew up the articles.
An increasing number of sees were thus left without bishops,
which troubled Louis' growing piety and created difficulties in
the internal administration of the country. But rather than compromise, the king's thoughts turned more and more to measures
of compulsion : to the possible seizure of Avignon, or an invasion
of the Papal States.[8]

Relations with the papacy were further embittered by Louis
XIV's *entente* with the Turks, and his indifference to the crusade
which was the pope's principal interest. Louis refused to take
part in the defence of Vienna in 1683 : he had known well in
advance that the Turkish attack was planned and had encouraged it to be directed against the Austrian Habsburgs, rather
than against other Christian powers. But Louis was not actually
allied to the sultan, as contemporary pamphleteers believed.
There is evidence of French assistance to the Turks, but it was
scarce and unofficial.[9] The Turkish pressure on the emperor's
eastern frontier served Louis' purposes very well : as long as the
Habsburg forces were involved in war in the east they could
not intervene to check French expansion in the Rhineland, or
towards Luxembourg. French pressure on this Spanish possession
led Carlos II to declare war in October 1683, in the hope that
the emperor's recent victory over the Turks at Vienna would
allow him to send aid. But the emperor could spare no forces,
and in any case preferred to follow up his success in the east
rather than listen to the promptings of family loyalty. William
III, Spain's other ally, was prevented from intervening by the
opposition of the States party in the States-General; all he
could do was to send token forces, and the French were able
to take Luxembourg in June 1684. This important conquest
was sealed by the truce of Ratisbon concluded in August of the
same year, to which the emperor also acceded. French acquisitions since 1678 were recognised, but not permanently : this was
not a full peace treaty, but a truce for twenty years.[10]

The emperor had agreed to this settlement in order to have his hands free for the Turkish war, and also because of the equivocal attitude of several of the German princes – particularly the elector of Brandenburg – who retained close ties with France.[11] From this point Louis XIV's policy centred on trying to convert the truce into a permanent settlement which would allow him to keep Strasbourg, Luxembourg and the territories acquired under the *Réunions*. A more defensive tone begins to pervade French policy : a new note of restraint starts to appear.[12] The situation was no longer so favourable to Louis XIV. The Imperial armies began to make vast conquests from the Turks and the Hungarian rebels who supported them. In September 1686 Budapest fell to the Habsburgs. Next year the Turks were routed on the historic field of Mohács; the fortresses of Essek and Peterwardein fell, and the Habsburg armies penetrated into Serbia. Nearly all the kingdom of Hungary was now under Habsburg control, and to symbolise this the emperor's son Joseph was crowned hereditary king of Hungary in December 1687. The Imperial armies were growing larger and more effective every year, and Louvois began to study their arms and equipment with close concern. As the emperor's power and prestige rose the German princes drew closer to him, sending contingents to the Turkish war and loosening their ties with France. Bavaria and Brandenburg led the way in this reversal of the traditional princely hostility to any extension of Imperial power.[13] In these circumstances neither the emperor nor the Diet was willing to consider converting the Truce of Ratisbon into a permanent peace. The growing weakness of the Turks and the decline of French influence among the German states removed the traditional counterpoises with which Louis XIV had kept the emperor in check. The king and his ministers grew increasingly anxious that the emperor would soon be able to finish the war in the east and turn his victorious forces towards the Rhine. Peace on France's eastern frontier depended upon maintaining the Turkish diversion.

As the threat from the Habsburgs became more pressing, other enemies of France started to raise their heads, led by William III, the most skilful and implacable of Louis XIV's antagonists. Up to 1684 Louis had successfully countered William's efforts to build up a European coalition. But the cumulative effects of French territorial aggrandisement and the revocation of the Edict of Nantes in 1685 combined to change William's diplomatic position. The revocation alarmed all the Protestant powers, coming as it did so soon after James II's accession and the failure of Monmouth's rebellion in England. This final stroke led the elector of Brandenburg to ally with the emperor and William III, disarmed the opposition to William in the States-General, and prompted the English opposition to draw closer to William as the Protestant claimant to the throne.[14] Nor did the revocation compensate for these losses by drawing the pope and the Catholic powers closer to France. The pope still refused any compromise in the matter of the Gallican Articles, and observed that Christ had not found it necessary to use armed apostles to spread the gospel. Carlos II and the emperor were likewise unimpressed. The net result of the revocation was to add religious tension to the political factors already polarising Europe, and to isolate France still further.

From about the time of the truce of Ratisbon and the revocation of the Edict of Nantes the balance of power began to incline in favour of Louis XIV's enemies. At the same time the resources which had underlain French military superiority began to dwindle, as the result of an economic depression which affected France particularly in the later 1680s.[15] It is no longer fashionable to regard the Revocation of the Edict of Nantes as a factor contributing to the economic malaise, but the revocation affected the military situation in a crucial area: that of trained soldiers and sailors. By 1688 close on nine thousand Huguenot seamen had fled abroad, principally to the United Provinces, while an even greater number of Protestant soldiers, of whom Marshal Schomberg was the most illustrious, had also taken service with Louis XIV's enemies.[16] In addition, the revocation created a severe problem of internal security. As the Venetian ambassador was to note, 'il re per voler fare dei buoni cattolici ha fatto dei pericolosissimi sudditi'.[17] The shortage of military manpower and the problem created by a fifth column of Huguenots in touch with the Allies were dramatically revealed in the measures taken at the outbreak of war to cover the coasts against a landing by William III and raise troops from any available source, including the *arrière-ban* and the militia.[18]

There are signs that the economic situation was causing the

government some concern.[19] Under Colbert's successor, Le Peletier, taxation was kept at a low level and government expenditure was reduced. But in the later 1680s a serious agrarian crisis made itself felt, and in 1687–8 the government embarked on an inquest into the causes of rural poverty. Meanwhile the Colbert clan was conducting its own semi-official investigations, and Seignelay took measures of his own to succour trade. In the economic sphere, as everywhere else, the factions within the government often worked at cross-purposes: their efforts raised hopes of reform while preventing a unified direction of policy. Since Colbert's death the conduct of economic affairs had become the subject of debate, which soon broadened into criticism of the whole theory and practice of absolute monarchy. This debate about the purpose of government reached its climax under the stress of military and economic disasters in the 1690s; but dissension was already in the air, and the government's response was curiously hesitant and ambivalent. This was perhaps due to a crisis in its administrative structure, traceable in part to Innocent XI's continued refusal to approve the nomination to bishoprics of any clergy who had taken part in the assembly of 1682: by 1688 nearly forty sees were without bishops, and many of these were in the south, where the government's authority was weakest, and the Huguenots strongest.[20] At the same time Louis XIV himself, nearly fifty, plagued by illness and growing increasingly devout, no longer exercised so close control on the functioning of the government.[21] As the king aged the bureaucratic system grew more complex and unresponsive, ministerial rivalry continued unchecked, and the power of one minister, Louvois, grew at the expense of others. Louis XIV's government was becoming increasingly confused and inflexible while the problems facing it grew more serious and complex. In these circumstances the government cast about in vain for a solution to the economic crisis, and continued to conduct foreign policy largely on the assumptions which had been valid before, but which no longer corresponded to the shift in the balance of power.

Gradually a realisation of the magnitude of the internal problems and a dawning awareness that France could no longer count on unchallenged military superiority began to affect the conduct of affairs; but not quickly enough.[22] Evidence of growing moderation can be seen in the desire to convert the truce of

1684 into a permanent peace, and in Louis XIV's caution in the dispute over the Palatine succession. Here the death of the elector Karl II in May 1685 left the succession open to Philip-Wilhelm of Neuburg, duke of Jülich-Berg, a prince closely allied with the emperor and hostile to France. A dangerous neighbour was thus installed just across the border from Lower Alsace, at the most vulnerable point on the frontier. Louis XIV could not prevent the Neuberg claimant from taking over the Palatinate, but he put forward a claim to certain parts of the inheritance on behalf of his sister-in-law the duchess of Orléans, 'Madame Palatine', the sister of the defunct elector.[23] But this claim was not pressed by force : instead Louis sought and accepted papal mediation, and allowed the dispute to drag on inconclusively until the outbreak of war.

A further indication of the defensive orientation of French policy was the acceleration of the programme of frontier fortifications. After 1684 the eastern frontier received first priority : each threatening sign from Germany led to a fresh spate of fortress-building. In Vauban's correspondence these fortresses were always considered as purely defensive works, not, as before, as bases from which to achieve further conquests.[24] After the truce Vauban rebuilt Luxembourg and strengthened Belfort and Hüningen to cover the Upper Rhine and Franche-Comté. In July 1686 the League of Augsburg was formed by the emperor and several of the German princes together with the kings of Spain and Sweden. This increased Louvois' anxiety for the Rhine frontier: in October of that year Vauban was sent to examine the area around Strasbourg, and in January 1687 work began on a new fortress on an island in the Rhine, Fort-Louis, intended to shield Strasbourg from an attack launched via Philippsburg, which remained the weak point in the French defences.[25] In April 1687 Vauban was despatched to the Moselle to plan a new fortress covering Trier, at Mont-Royal, on territory occupied since 1681 under the *Réunions*.[26] This was to secure the electorate of Trier as an advanced post covering Luxembourg and Lorraine, and keep its archbishop-elector within the French orbit. The quest for security was forcing Louis XIV to push his outposts further and further afield, to the consternation of his neighbours. In August 1687 the news of the Turkish defeat at Mohács provided fresh evidence that the threat from the east was increasing.

Louvois wrote to Vauban: 'The news which the king has just received of the defeat of the Turkish army has made him judge it necessary to bring his frontier towards Germany to the last stage of perfection.'[27] The weakest point in the whole frontier was still Lower Alsace, because of Imperial control of Philippsburg. In November 1687 Vauban began work on a fortress at Landau to block the route from Philippsburg into Alsace: but this fortress was still far from complete when war came next year.

It is important to note that Louis XIV's answer to the mounting threat to his eastern border was primarily defensive. He built fortresses rather than increase his army. The number of troops remained at the peace-time level until the middle of 1688, and expenditure on the army and fortifications remained below 50 million livres a year for the period 1685-7, compared to 89 million livres for 1689, the first full year of war. Expenditure on the navy was similarly restricted.[28] This financial stringency was part of the general curbing of government expenditure under Le Peletier, and was due in part to the worsening economic situation. The armed forces were maintained at a peace-time level, and were even allowed to run down. Many of the troops were employed in building fortresses, on the various royal building projects – Louvois had taken over the *surintendance des bâtiments* after Colbert's death – and on such grandiose projects as diverting the river Eure to run the fountains at Versailles. This latter project in particular had a serious effect on the health and discipline of the troops involved.[29] The fleet was also kept at a low level of preparedness.[30] And at the same time the French forces were beginning to lose the technical superiority in weapons and logistics which had played a major role in the victories of Louis XIV's early years. Relatively few warships were built in the period before 1688, and the secret of constructing bomb-ketches, a French innovation, was soon passed on to the Dutch and English by Huguenot émigrés.[31] By the end of 1687 the improvements in the armament and organisation of the Imperial forces in the east were causing Louvois serious disquiet. He questioned officers who had served with the emperor's army and began to look for ways of increasing the French army's firepower. Vauban suggested the adoption of the socket bayonet in place of the pikes which were still used by the French infantry, and urged the substitution of the flintlock for the more cumbersome musket. Louvois had hardly started to experiment with these new weapons when war overtook the French army and changes were frozen : the flintlock and bayonet were not finally adopted until after the Peace of Ryswick in 1697. Thus at the outbreak of war the edge of technical superiority enjoyed by the French army had been severely reduced; a fact of which the government was slowly becoming aware.[32]

The crisis of 1688 overtook the French government at a time of economic difficulty, when the assumptions on which policy had been founded were coming under attack, and when the emphasis of that policy was slowly shifting from offence to defence. In addition Louis XIV was caught with part of his frontiers unguarded and his forces unprepared. He had assumed that war was not imminent. Europe was enjoying one of its rare intervals of relative peace. If the Turks held out for a year or two more the *frontière de fer* in the east would be finished and proof against any attack from the direction of Germany. But the signs of impending collapse in the Ottoman empire could not be ignored : the Turkish armies were breaking up and the whole state was falling into anarchy. Louis therefore grew increasingly anxious about his defences on the Rhine. To make his frontier there more secure he had extended his influence among the German border-states, especially the ecclesiastical principalities from Speyer to Cologne.[33] Here territorial fragmentation and military weakness made penetration easy, particularly when backed by the distribution of subsidies and gratifications. From the French point of view the most important of these statelets along the *Pfaffenstrasse* was Cologne, the most northerly. Its geographical position made it an important gateway into north Germany, and a base from which to threaten the United Provinces. If Louis XIV controlled Cologne he could dominate the other ecclesiastical principalities to the south, which in turn afforded access to the Palatinate. Cologne was also a Catholic enclave in Protestant territory, and its archbishops stood in constant need of protection against the encroachments of the Dutch or the north German princes. Since 1648 they had played an important role in French policy. The archbishop of Cologne was a key member of Mazarin's League of the Rhine in 1658, and his alliance provided the French army with their main avenue into the United Provinces in 1672. Furthermore the archbishop was always faced with opposition from the local estates and the city government of Cologne, and needed French help to keep control of the principality. The archbishop at the time, Maximilian-Henry of Wittelsbach, had also acquired the bishoprics of Liège, Münster and Hildesheim, so that Cologne formed the nucleus of an important group of petty states extending from the French frontier into north Germany. Maximilian-Henry himself, never a man of outstanding ability or decisiveness, and by now well advanced in years, was kept loyal to Louis XIV by his chief adviser, William-Egon von Fürstenberg, bishop of Strasbourg and a pensioner of France.[34] As long as Maximilian-Henry lived and Fürstenberg remained in actual control of Cologne, French influence was secure.

To keep his hold on Cologne Louis XIV planned to have Fürstenberg elected as successor to Maximilian-Henry. Early in January 1688, with French backing, Fürstenberg was elected co-adjutor to the ailing archbishop, the first step towards securing his election as archbishop once Maximilian-Henry died. The emperor's efforts to block Fürstenberg's progress were unsuccessful, and when the cathedral chapter voted on the coadjutorship he received nineteen votes out of a total of twenty-four. But papal confirmation was necessary to make the election valid, and since his relations with Louis XIV were deteriorating Innocent XI was unlikely to give his approval. Fürstenberg was therefore not secured in undisputed succession to the archbishopric. This was a definite setback for Louis XIV: he could not afford to lose the struggle for Cologne and the other Rhineland statelets to which it was the key.

This deadlock was the result of a worsening in Louis' relations with the papacy. The pope had long been concerned at the lawlessness prevalent in Rome, and in order to deprive criminals of an inviolable refuge he had persuaded the powers with embassies at Rome to renounce the general immunity protecting the 'quarters' around their embassy buildings. Every country except France had given up this much-abused privilege. Louis XIV however refused, hoping to extract concessions from the pope in return for renouncing the immunity of the quarter. To force the pope's hand Louis ordered his new ambassador, Lavardin, to enter Rome at the head of an armed retinue in November 1687. This and other provocations led Innocent to excommunicate the ambassador, and in January 1688 this sanction was extended, in secret, to Louis himself.[35] The king was worried by this, but there was little he could do. Pamphleteers were allowed to denigrate the pope as a senile bigot pursuing a personal vendetta against the dutiful eldest son of the Church, and the *procureur-général* of the Paris Parlement appealed the excommunication of Lavardin to a future council of the Church as a higher authority than the pope. But the secret excommunication of Louis XIV remained in force, and his dispute with the pope was further than ever from settlement. Once again Louis' thoughts began to turn towards military action against the temporal possessions of the papcy, for the situation at Cologne made it imperative to bring the pope to heel at once.[36]

The problem of his relations with Innocent XI and the allied question of Cologne were Louis XIV's main preoccupations in the early months of 1688. But there were other problems to be confronted, notably in the Baltic where the duke of Holstein–Gottorp, backed by Sweden, was resisting renewed Danish claims to suzerainty over his state. This dispute was potentially dangerous since Louis XIV was pledged to support Denmark, while the Dutch might ally with Sweden. In the hope of preventing the polarisation of the Baltic situation, and to offset a possible move by William, Louis contemplated arming a squadron of warships to be sent to the Baltic in the spring; he also tried to interest James II in this venture.

The overtures to James were part of a long series of attempts to woo him out of his friendly neutrality and into direct alliance with France.[37] Since James's accession Louis and William III had been competing for his support. The odds favoured Louis: James's religion and his personal and familial inclinations tended to make him pro-French. But his aim was to maintain neutrality and not embroil himself in continental affairs, lest this lead to instability at home, jeopardising his great ambition to reclaim England for the Catholic faith. He consequently tried to preserve an uneasy independence sympathetic to France, as his brother Charles II had done more skilfully before him. William III had seen for a long time that the alliance of England was essential if he was to build up a coalition able to hold its own against France. His marriage to James's elder laughter Mary had made him an important candidate for the English succession, on which he already possessed a claim through his mother, while at the same time he was careful to keep close ties with the leaders of the English opposition. But his efforts to obtain an alliance with Charles and James had either met with indifference, or been checkmated by French diplomacy. James's accession improved William's chances of succeeding to the English throne, for James had no son. Encouraged by some of the leaders of the opposition, William had probably contemplated the possibility of ousting James for some time, but he did not make any overt move until the early summer of 1687 when he sent his close associate Dijkvelt to sound out the opposition: Dijkvelt returned with pledges of support from some of the leading political figures in England. James did not consider that his son-in-law constituted a serious threat, and disregarded warnings that William might be planning to overthrow him. The most insistent warnings came from Avaux, the French ambassador at The Hague, who had been aware of the drift of William's ambitions for years. Late in 1687 Avaux began to report that William was fitting out a large number of ships, ostensibly for service in the Baltic; he was also raising troops with money voted by the States-General for the avowed purpose of improving frontier fortifications. The States-General had by now ceased to offer serious resistance to William, for the final blow had been dealt the pro-French deputies when in the autumn of 1687 a new discriminatory tariff severely reduced Dutch trade with France.[38] This renewal of earlier tariff conflicts by Louis XIV alarmed Dutch opinion, especially as it coincided with a demand on the part of James II, encouraged by the offer of French subsidies, for the return of the English troops serving in the United Provinces. To William III and the leaders of the anti-French party all this came as confirmation of their fears that the Anglo-French alliance of 1670 was being revived, while this attempt by James to increase his forces at home seemed to the leaders of the opposition to be another step towards the establishment of popery and absolutism by force. Just at this point it became known that James's queen was pregnant. The possibility that James might have a Catholic heir changed the whole basis of William's relations with his father-in-law; he could now no longer afford to wait for James to die peacefully.

    Louis XIV knew in a general way of William's intrigues with the English opposition and of his designs on the throne. But he

had no definite indication that William planned to strike in the
near future: indeed William seems not to have made up his
mind to invade England until the last moment. Avaux reported
regularly on the build-up of men and ships, but was not certain
when or where they would be used: for a long time he felt they
might be sent to the Baltic to help William's Swedish allies.
Louis therefore concluded that William posed no immediate
threat and that James could be left to look after himself. In any
case James did not respond favourably to Louis' suggestion that
the English and French fleets collaborate to keep the peace in
the Baltic, although this offer was baited with the promise of
subsidies and accompanied by warnings of William III's naval
preparations. James evaded the demands for a naval alliance until
April 1688, when the tension in the Baltic began to subsidise, and
intervention was no longer necessary.[39] A further French offer of
joint naval action in June was also declined. Louis XIV therefore
did not fit out any ships for service in the Channel: a decision
which was to have disastrous consequences both for himself and
for James before the end of the year.[40] But faced by James's con-
fident rejection of his proffered help, and confronted with more
pressing problems elsewhere, Louis could hardly have done otherwise.

The ships that Louis did send to sea in 1688 were concentrated
in the Mediterranean. Detachments cruised in the western Mediterranean to cover trade, while a large punitive expedition bombarded Algiers in July.[41] This operation was part of the normal
peace-time activities of the French fleet. But because the available
French ships were in the Mediterranean, Louis XIV was unable
to block the Channel later in the year when William III sailed
for England. At the end of July the squadron from Algiers
headed back to its base at Toulon. For a time Louis XIV contemplated directing it to Brest instead, where it could have been
kept in readiness, but finally decided against this.[42] Once the
ships were back at Toulon it would have taken them a long time
to fit out again and sail to the Channel; Louis' decision in fact
meant that he had renounced the opportunity of intervening in
the Channel that year.

In the early months of 1688 Louis XIV had no reason to
think that the various disputes in which he was involved would
swiftly coalesce into a major crisis and force him into war. The

first element of crisis was provided by the death of Maximilian-Henry of Cologne on 3 June. The importance of the electorate for French policy made it essential to secure the succession of Fürstenberg, and envoys were at once despatched to ensure that the cathedral chapter would vote for him, as it had done in January. Envoys from William III and the emperor meanwhile converged on the chapter to try to block his election. So as to leave nothing to chance, and to back up the efforts of his agents at Cologne, Louis XIV ordered 4000 cavalry from their camp on the Saône to the region of the upper Meuse, and rumours began to circulate that Fürstenberg planned to introduce French troops into the key points of the electorate.[43] Fürstenberg was also working to secure election to the other sees which had been held by Maximilian-Henry, at Liège, Hildesheim and Münster; but the French government realised that he had little chance of keeping this bloc intact, and therefore made the main effort on his behalf at Cologne. The chief obstacle however remained the attitude of the pope, who would have to confirm any election. Fürstenberg was already bishop of Strasbourg, and to be eligible for the see of Cologne he needed a papal dispensation. Innocent still had not approved Fürstenberg's election as coadjutor in January, and did not seem disposed to grant the required dispensation. Without it Fürstenberg could only be 'postulated' to the archbishopric by two thirds of the votes of the chapter, and even then would require papal confirmation.

The other candidate was Joseph-Clement of Bavaria, the seventeen-year-old brother of the elector Maximilian. His principal claim to the see was that it had been held continuously by members of his family since 1580 and could almost be regarded as a Wittelsbach apanage. Despite his youth and lack of clerical vocation Joseph-Clement already possessed two bishoprics; he needed papal dispensations on account of this, and also because he was not of canonical age for election. Initially his candidacy laboured under some disadvantages: Fürstenberg was at Cologne, and by vote of the chapter acted as temporary administrator of the state. He thus controlled the troops and revenues of the electorate, and could call in French help at any time. But for the present he preferred to avoid any overt reliance on Louis XIV, and the king tended to concur in this.[44] Gradually Fürstenberg's position began to deteriorate, however. The pope granted a dispensation to

Joseph-Clement, thus allowing him to be elected by a simple
majority of the chapter, and refused a similar concession to
Fürstenberg.[45] Pressure by the agents of William III and the
emperor began to have its effect on the chapter. Early in July
Louis XIV decided that further measures might be required to
secure his protégé's election: the situation was by no means
critical as yet, but it would be as well to reach some understanding
with the pope, as an insurance against mishaps.

On 6 July Louis therefore drew up a highly secret instruction
for the marquis de Chamlay, a trusted adviser of Louvois:
Chamlay was to go to Rome incognito and negotiate a settlement
with the pope by offering concessions in the affair of the ambassadorial quarter.[46] It was assumed that Fürstenberg would obtain
the two-thirds majority needed for postulation, and that therefore
papal confirmation would be all that was required. The proffered
concessions were in fact minimal, although they did represent a
change when compared with the inflexibility of Lavardin's instructions a year before. As an afterthought, and in the face of
strong opposition from Louvois, Chamlay was empowered to
offer a further concession: Louis XIV would make all the
bishops who had taken part in the 1682 assembly write a humble
apology to the pope. Chamlay proceeded to Venice to await the
outcome of the Cologne election, scheduled for 19 July. The
result when it came was completely unexpected: Fürstenberg
received thirteen votes, or less than the required two-thirds
majority, and Joseph-Clement eight, or less than a simple
plurality. The election was inconclusive, and the decision therefore passed to the pope. On 22 July Croissy redrafted the orders
for Chamlay in the light of the changed situation, and a note
of warning now appeared. Chamlay was to stress Joseph-
Clement's youth and inexperience, and urge the pope to confirm
Fürstenberg as the more suitable candidate with Joseph-Clement
as his coadjutor:

> all the more since any refusal by His Holiness to grant the
> necessary Bulls would only serve to set off a war in the Empire
> which it would be hard to end, and which would cause
> Christendom to lose all those advantages which have been
> secured only because I have not wished to profit from favour-
> able circumstances to press the claims of my Crown against

neighbouring states, and those of my brother [Orléans] on the Palatine succession, while the Emperor's forces were occupied in Hungary. . . .[47]

The same day Louvois wrote separately to Chamlay: 'You should greatly exaggerate to the pope the imminent war which he will cause between His Majesty and the Emperor, if he grants Bulls to Prince Clement, assuring him that His Majesty will uphold the rights of Cardinal Fürstenberg by force. . . .'[48]

Louis XIV was not the only ruler who saw the Cologne dispute as the distant signal for war. Since the death of Maximilian-Henry William III's diplomatic activity in Germany had intensified: his aim was to obtain contingents of troops and build up a system of alliances to supplement the League of Augsburg.[49] At the end of June William set up a camp at Nijmegen and began to gather his forces there: Nijmegen was chosen because it was within reach of Cologne, while from there troops could just as easily be moved down river to embark on the fleet waiting in the Channel ports to sail for England if William so decided. James II's queen had given birth to an heir on 20 June so that William was obliged to dispose his forces so as to be able to move in either direction – down the Rhine to Cologne, or across the Channel to England. On 30 June he concluded an important agreement with the new elector of Brandenburg, which provided him with a detachment of troops under the old marshal Schomberg. This force was stationed at Wesel, an enclave of Brandenburg territory on the Rhine about fifty miles from Cologne.[50] From The Hague Avaux reported these troop movements, so that Louis XIV began to fear the possibility of a coup against Cologne.

But William was not yet committed to any course of action; he could keep his forces together at Nijmegen until he saw how the situation was developing, and then make his move. He was as much interested in the situation in England as in the developments at Cologne. Avaux from The Hague reported signs of hostility to James following the birth of the prince of Wales: prayers for the royal infant were suspended in William's chapel, rumours began to circulate that he was a suppositious child, and work on the fleet was stepped up. Early in July, about the time that Admiral Herbert arrived in the United Provinces with the famous invitation to William from the leaders of the English opposition, Avaux learned that William was asking the States-General to raise another 8000 sailors. All these indications pointed to an invasion of England, but as time passed Avaux became less certain about William's real intentions : as autumn approached the likelihood of an expedition that year receded. At the same time William's negotiations with the German princes seemed to pose a more immediate threat to France.[51] Louis XIV shared his ambassador's uncertainty. He felt that the well-publicised negotiations for the combination of the English and French fleets, which were still going on dilatorily, would be enough to dissuade William for that year, even though in fact there were no French ships actually available in the Channel to support James's fleet. William's move in the direction of Cologne seemed far more menacing.[52]

The failure of his plans to secure Fürstenberg's election concentrated Louis XIV's attention on this problem. To secure Cologne and forestall a coup there by William III and his German allies it was essential to obtain the pope's consent to the election which had, after all, given Fürstenberg a simple majority. Following the election Fürstenberg and his partisans had retained control of most of the electorate, with the exception of the city of Cologne itself which was controlled by its own burgomasters.[53] Everything now hinged on Chamlay's mission to Rome. Pursued by couriers from Versailles he reached Rome on 3 August, to be confronted by a total *impasse* : the pope refused to grant him an audience. After a series of fruitless efforts to see the pope, Chamlay was forced to admit defeat and leave Rome. On 20 August he wrote bitterly to Louis that any attempt to reach an understanding with the pope was futile. Louis had already reached this conclusion for himself, and on the eighteenth had ordered Chamlay to break off negotiations and return.[54] Unable to overcome the pope's obstinacy by what he regarded as concessions, Louis XIV now turned to force. This was in fact the decisive moment at which he committed himself to war.

After the failure of Fürstenberg's bid for election in late July Louvois had ordered a force of troops under Boufflers to move close to Luxembourg to await developments.[55] No positive action was taken while there was still a chance that Chamlay might succeed in winning over the pope, and while Fürstenberg was still campaigning for election to the see of Liège. Nonetheless Louvois began to make preparations to raise an extra 16,000 men early in August.[56] By the middle of the month it was clear that Chamlay's mission had failed, and on the eighteenth came news that Fürstenberg had been defeated in his attempt to win Liège.[57] Louis XIV's response was to recall Chamlay, promise to back Fürstenberg's claims on Cologne, and activate his forces. The troops at Maintenon were ordered to the frontiers. One force was earmarked for the defence of the electorate of Cologne, while another was to cover the border with the Spanish Netherlands in case of a surprise attack by William III: at this stage Louis still considered that he posed a greater threat on the Continent than to England. On 21 August orders were issued for a naval expedition against the Papal States: Innocent XI was to be chastised for his obstinacy.[58] It was thus the failure of Louis' plans to retain his hold on Cologne which led him into the initial decision to use armed forces.

But there was another important factor behind this decision. At the same time as news came of Chamlay's failure at Rome Louis received despatches from his ambassador at Constantinople, warning him that the Turks were about to make peace, and had already sent envoys to Vienna.[59] The situation in the east was extremely grave: the Ottoman empire was racked by revolt, its armies were on the verge of collapse, and the Imperial army was besieging Belgrade. It thus became essential for Louis XIV to undertake some action to distract part of the Imperial forces and relieve the pressure on the Turks, and the intervention at Cologne formed the basis of this diversion. It was also vital for him to secure the gaps in his frontier, in case the emperor came to terms with the Turks and quickly moved his forces to the Rhine. Already on 23 August there were rumours that the king intended to seize Philippsburg.[60] The plan for intervention at Cologne thus immediately broadened into a general operation to cover the Rhine frontier. Louis XIV was not planning the major war that in fact followed; he intended a localised conflict, like the others over the past decade, to secure limited but necessary gains. The aim was basically defensive: a pre-emptive strike to prevent the emperor from taking advantage of the weakness of France's eastern frontier. The miscalculation lay in underestimating the hostility that previous operations of this kind had aroused, and

the ability of France's enemies to respond promptly, effectively
and with determination. Louis XIV might be planning a painless
little war, but his enemies were out for revenge, and were now
stronger and more united than before.

By the time he replied to the despatch from Constantinople,
on 22 August, Louis XIV's plans for a series of limited actions
along the Rhine had already taken shape. He was therefore able
to assure his ambassador that a war would soon break out which
would ease the pressure on the Turks. His forces were ready
to move into Cologne and the Palatinate – in the latter case to
prosecute the Orléanist claims on the Palatine succession. Another force was being sent to Italy. The king observed:

> You may easily judge what effects this will produce, and that
> the Emperor will be forced to withdraw his troops from Hungary
> in order to send them to the Rhine and even into Italy. I leave
> it to your discretion to make use of this information . . . in the
> way that you deem best for my service; the Imperialists have
> every reason to fear that if the Turks were truly aware of the
> weakness of the Court of Vienna, they would easily recover
> all that they have lost in the recent campaigns and a minister
> as astute as the Grand Vizier . . . could profit very well from
> such a favourable situation as the affairs of Europe present
> to him at present. . . .[61]

Disentangled from the diplomatic rhetoric, Louis XIV's intentions were plain enough. A strike in the Rhineland would encourage the Turks to go on fighting, while not involving the
French forces in more than a limited conflict. This operation
would also allow Louis to settle his accounts in the Palatinate and
at Cologne, and place him in possession of a chain of frontier
posts from Cologne southward along the Rhine, thus securing
Alsace. In any case the size of his forces limited the scale of any
offensive he planned. With his army still essentially on a peace-
time footing Louis XIV did not have the troops to intervene
wherever he might wish, and he had to choose what seemed the
most important objective. In fact there was little he could do
about the danger posed by William III's designs on England,
beyond warning James II and urging him to build up his forces.
From the French point of view William's designs on Cologne constituted a more immediate threat, and one which could be dealt

with by prompt military action.[62] As autumn approached the chances of a naval expedition by William III against England receded, while the danger posed by the unfinished fortifications on the eastern frontier remained as great as ever. In the circumstances Louis XIV's decision to commit his forces to a limited offensive in the Rhineland was correct: only in retrospect can it be said that he should have concentrated on deterring William III from attacking England.[63]

From now on the king and Louvois were constantly occupied in assembling troops for the invasion of the Palatinate and the siege of Philippsburg. Preparations went forward in the greatest secrecy so that when the offensive began the opposing forces should be taken by surprise. By the end of the month the disposition of the French armies had been determined: a force under Sourdis was to move into the electorate of Cologne to garrison Bonn and Kaiserswerth; the army under d'Humières would cover the northern frontier; a third force would assemble under the command of Duras in Alsace and the Franche-Comté. This last army would co-operate with the main striking force which would besiege Philippsburg and at the same time overrun the Palatinate, aiming first at Kaiserslautern, thereby securing the weakest point in the frontier. This army would be under the nominal command of the dauphin, an indolent and obese young man whose achievements up to this time had been confined to dozing through meetings of the *conseil d'en haut* and exterminating the wolves in the neighbourhood of Versailles at the head of his pack of hounds. His lack of military aptitude was to be made good by a staff of competent officers, among them Vauban, who was to supervise the operations at Philippsburg. But the choice of the dauphin indicates how important Louis XIV considered this operation to be: the capture of Philippsburg would close the last serious gap in the *frontière de fer*.[64]

A month elapsed between the decision to go to war and the actual opening of operations. The delay was caused primarily by the need to assemble and deploy the various armies. Further troops had to be raised: early in September it was decided to increase the new levies from 16,000 to 58,000 men.[65] Another cause for delay was the attitude of Fürstenberg, who now developed cold feet and balked at admitting French troops to Cologne. Louvois wrote impatiently to him, urging him to cease this prevarication since he was now committed to using force to maintain himself. This hesitation had a serious result: the troops under Sourdis did not enter the electorate until mid-September, and could not secure the city of Cologne, which admitted Schomberg's troops on the twenty-third.[66] Meanwhile the quarrel with Innocent XI continued. On 6 September Louis XIV wrote to Cardinal d'Estrées at Rome outlining his side of the dispute and justifying his impending attack on the Papal States: the despatch was then published as a manifesto. The pope had acted like a temporal prince, not as the common father of Christendom, in systematically opposing the reasonable demands of Louis XIV in the affair of the Gallican Articles, and in the election at Cologne: because of his obstinacy and vindictiveness in this latter question, the pope was to blame for the war which was about to engulf the Christian nations. A French army was being sent to Italy to force the pope to fulfil his obligations to France's ally the duke of Parma, under the Treaty of Pisa of 1664, which he had consistently evaded.[67] D'Estrées read this diatribe to the pope on 18 September, without visible effect, and two days later Innocent sealed the bulls conferring the see of Cologne on Joseph-Clement. Louis XIV's attempt to browbeat the pope had failed, but for a time he continued his policy of coercion: orders were issued for the occupation of the papal territory of Avignon, and on 27 September a fresh appeal was directed to a future council of the whole church.[68] But the attack on the Papal States never took place: the rapid extension of the war forced Louis XIV to use the ships and men elsewhere.

The manifesto addressed to the pope was part of a diplomatic campaign to justify Louis XIV's actions and if possible neutralise potential antagonists. Rébenac, the new ambassador at Madrid, was kept busy trying to assure Carlos II of his master's desire to maintain friendly relations with Spain, and convince him that the impending conflict was essentially one of religion, in which the Catholic powers must stand united against William III and his German allies.[69] This contention became a familiar leitmotiv of French diplomatic argument in the opening stages of the war. A special envoy was sent to warn Gastañaga, the governor of the Spanish Netherlands, not to co-operate with William III and to maintain strict neutrality.[70] Villars was sent to Munich to try to prevent the elector of Bavaria from joining the German princes leagued against France, and the French representatives elsewhere in Germany strove to prevent the formation of an effective alliance.[71] The diplomatic campaign came to a climax on 24 September with the publication of Louis XIV's manifesto to the emperor, explaining the reasons which had forced him to take up arms once more.[72] This was timed to appear just before French troops moved into the Palatinate, and came shortly after news was received of the fall of Belgrade to the Imperial army under the command of the elector of Bavaria. This document has usually been taken as a classic statement of Louis XIV's hypocritical Machiavellism. It is full of contradictions and misleading statements, a curious mingling of threats with promises of pacific intentions, and its very inconsistencies make it a good indication of Louis XIV's confused state of mind at this time. Louis presented his decision to go to war as essentially defensive, prompted by the fear of a hostile league forming against him, and aimed at obliging his enemies to turn the truce of 1684 into a lasting settlement. He was reluctant to start hostilities while the emperor was occupied with the Turkish war – an interesting admission – but the intrigues of his enemies, especially in the matters of the Palatine succession and the election at Cologne, left him no choice. The real blame for the outbreak of war lay with the emperor, the pope and the Protestant princes who were in league against France. But Louis was not out for unlimited aggrandisement: all he sought was justice in certain specific disputes. Any further conquests which he might make would be returned once a permanent peace had been negotiated; his enemies had until the end of January 1689 to agree to realistic negotiations.

Like the earlier manifesto to the pope, this one is laden with self-justification and casuistry, but it deserves to be examined carefully, for it represents the culmination of Louis XIV's efforts over the past few years to convert the truce of 1684 into a final peace. Despite its self-righteous tone the manifesto was a clear plea for peace negotiations, and the claim of a defensive purpose behind the resumption of hostilities was not insincere. At this point Louis XIV saw himself as pursuing limited objectives with limited means: he still hoped perhaps to repeat his successes of the previous decade, when a show of force had been sufficient to obtain his ends. But this time he had misjudged the situation and the forces arrayed against himself. To couch the plea for peace in the form of an ultimatum was a bad move, since now the ultimatum was no longer backed by overwhelming force. The aggressive tone, carried over from the time when France enjoyed unchallenged military superiority, no longer rang true. The emperor's hands were no longer tied by the Turkish war and he was ready to assume the leadership of the coalition forming to resist any further French demands. Consequently both emperor and Diet rejected the manifesto and prepared for war.

In the last week of September the French armies began operations at Philippsburg and in the Palatinate, meeting very little resistance at first, save at Philippsburg itself. But the offensive in the Rhineland, although successful, tied down the available forces and prevented action elsewhere. In effect Louis XIV surrendered the initiative to William III in order to secure his primary objective of covering the vulnerable eastern frontier. By this time Louis XIV felt that William did not pose an immediate threat. In the last days of August he had feared for a moment that William was about to invade England. In a last-minute endeavour to parry this threat and awaken James II to his danger Louis XIV despatched a special envoy, Bonrepaus, to negotiate a naval treaty with England, evidently calculating that reports of the negotiations would be enough to dissuade William III, even though no French ships were available for service in the Channel. But in little over a week Louis XIV and Seignelay changed their minds, possibly because of fresh intelligence from the United Provinces, and ordered Bonrepaus to wind up the negotiations without concluding a formal treaty.[73] At the same time Louis XIV tried another piece of bluff: on 2 September he ordered Avaux to warn the States-General that any attack against England would be interpreted as an act of war, since James II was the ally of France. Avaux made this démarche on 9 September, only to find that it backfired.[74] The States-General saw this as confirmation of their suspicions that there was an Anglo-French alliance against them, and drew closer to William III. From London James II sent an immediate disclaimer and assured the Dutch of his peaceful intentions, thereby confirming their belief in his weakness, and revealing to Louis that any attempt to aid him was futile. This conviction that James II was beyond help, and a growing belief that William III could not in fact mount his invasion that year, combined to make Louis believe that he could leave this area alone and concentrate on the more immediate problem in the Rhineland.[75]

By the time he launched the attack on Philippsburg in the last days of September Louis XIV had good reason to believe that James II was safe for the remainder of the year at least; in any case there was nothing more that could be done to help him. There was still a chance that William's fleet might be used for a landing on the French coast to raise the Huguenots in revolt, and measures were taken to garrison the ports and coastal fortifications. Shortage of troops made this a difficult task : most of the troops were in fact raw local levies, with only a sprinkling of regulars. At Cherbourg the unfinished fortifications had to be dismantled to prevent them from being used in the event of a landing, since there were no men to garrison them.[76] But despite these alarms William's ambitions were directed elsewhere. The news of the siege of Philippsburg was received with relief in the United Provinces : William and the States-General could now be sure that they would not be attacked that year.[77] On 8 October William disclosed his plans for the invasion of England to the States-General, which voted to support him. No dissenting voices were heard : the opposition so carefully nurtured by Avaux had been completely overwhelmed. On 11 November William's fleet sailed, and in just over a month he had run James II out of his kingdom. Louis XIV was powerless to intervene, with no fleet in the Channel and his available forces committed on the Rhine, and any hopes that he may have entertained that William would be caught up in a long civil war in England were dashed by the rapidity and finality of James's overthrow.

William III's victory completely altered the diplomatic and military situation on the continent. On the Rhine the French armies had made steady progress. Philippsburg fell on 29 October, and within the next weeks Kaiserslautern, Mannheim, Heidelberg and Heilbronn, placing most of the Palatinate under French control. Speyer and Mainz accepted French garrisons : Coblenz did not and was subjected to a heavy bombardment. Although Cologne itself was lost, French forces at Bonn and Kaiserswerth controlled much of the disputed electorate, while others overran the archbishopric of Trier to the south in order

to maintain communications.[78] Within less than two months
Louis XIV had seized most of the strong points on the Rhine
from Cologne to the border of Alsace and secured his primary
objective : from this point the eastern frontier was secure. As the
war progressed some of the outlying conquests were lost or abandoned, but the eastern frontier as a whole was not breached by
invading armies as it had been in the 1670s. But these successes
could not offset the effects of William III's triumph in England
and break up the alliance forming against France. At the end
of October some of the leading German princes met at Magde-
burg to form an alliance which would replace the League of
Augsburg.[79] Very soon the French began to encounter the
advance guards of a large army which the princes were assembling to defend the Rhineland provinces. Their resistance was
encouraged by the news from England, and by the attitude of
the emperor and the king of Spain. At the end of December William III wrote to Carlos II and Leopold to announce his victory
and to assure them that, contrary to French propaganda, he had
no intention of persecuting the Catholics in his new realm.[80] This
assurance, coupled with the knowledge that William would bring
England into the war, helped decide the Habsburg sovereigns
to commit themselves to the anti-French coalition. Negotiations
were begun early in 1689 and led to the conclusion of a league
headed by William and the emperor on 12 May.[81]

It soon became clear to Louis XIV that his show of force had
not attained its other objective : to prevent his potential enemies
from combining against him. The hope of turning the truce of
Ratisbon into a permanent peace receded as the coalition formed
on the other side of the Rhine. Louis' response followed the pattern of his earlier actions : he intensified his effort to cover his
frontier before the coalition could mobilise its full strength. The
means he chose to do this further accelerated the formation of
the hostile coalition and increased its enmity towards him.[82]
During December 1688, faced by growing resistance on the Rhine
and unsure that they could hold all the places captured so far,
Louis XIV and Louvois began to order the destruction of some
of the fortresses they had seized. Their aim was to deny the use
of these fortresses to the enemy in the event of a counter-attack.
But the strategy was dictated by the shortage of troops, and by
their evident decline in quality. From the beginning of the cam-

paign Louvois had been worried by the inadequacy of the forces available, and by the end of December it was clear that no further large operations could be undertaken until the new levies were ready. On 30 December Vauban wrote to Louvois : 'There can be no thought of starting a siege in the beginning of this winter or next spring, as we were accustomed to do formerly; furthermore this could only be done at the cost of completing the ruin of our infantry, which is very different from that which we had during the first four or five years of the Dutch war.'[83] This was the period at which the militia began to be formed, to supplement the regular troops and free some of them for service at the front. At the same time, to economise the forces already engaged, Louis XIV and Louvois began to withdraw from the more exposed positions and shorten their defensive perimeter. As the French armies withdrew they were ordered to exact heavy contributions and ravage the countryside so that it would not be able to support an invading army. The devastation of the Rhineland cities and the Palatinate was defensive in aim : it was in fact the last and most extreme stage of the defensive measures undertaken by Louis XIV to meet the crisis which had burst upon him. But in this, as in his earlier actions, Louis XIV failed to foresee the consequences of what he ordered : the result of the ravaging of the Palatinate was to unite the bickering German princes solidly behind the emperor and so extend the war still further. The thoroughness with which the programme of destruction was carried out seemed something new : to contemporaries it was a violation of the normal customs of war. Between the end of December 1688 and May 1689 Heidelberg, Mannheim, Trier, Speyer, Oppenheim, Worms and a host of smaller places were systematically razed.[84] In tactical terms the policy achieved some success : the German forces were hampered by the lack of supplies and bases in the next campaign in the Rhineland. But this final demonstration of French aggressiveness completed the process of uniting Louis XIV's enemies and was politically disastrous.

Louis XIV's progress towards all-out war was accomplished in several stages, each one arising out of the one before, and the whole motivated by a sense of urgency stemming from the knowledge that the forces available were inadequate and unprepared. The underlying purpose was defensive, but because the crisis

took him by surprise and found him without sufficient forces
Louis XIV felt that he had to move first and forestall his enemies,
thus giving himself the appearance of being the aggressor. The
initial triggering action was taken to deal with the crisis at
Cologne, but developed almost immediately into a general covering action to protect the gaps still open in the Rhine frontier,
when the news of the collapse of the Turks gave warning that
the emperor might soon be free to move westwards. By the end
of September 1688 Louis XIV's armies were committed and he
had no means of preventing William III from invading England
and dethroning James II. William's success accelerated the formation of a coalition against France and stiffened the resistance
that the German princes had begun to offer, so that Louis XIV
was confronted with a far more serious conflict than he had bargained for. It was clear that his offers of peace would not be
accepted, and he had to plan for a longer war. The inadequacy
of his forces obliged him to shorten his defensive line : to protect
it still more he followed a scorched-earth policy which although
reasonably successful in military terms completed the process of
uniting his enemies against him. In this final step the faults of
his earlier policy can be seen : a failure to estimate accurately
the temper of his antagonists, an over-readiness to use force, a
certain arrogance and contempt for weaker states. This final
show of force undertaken with a blatant disregard for the usages
of war completed the process begun when Louis decided to turn
to armed force, and transformed a limited crisis into a general
war.

NOTES

1　See Vauban's memorandum on the Flanders frontier, Nov 1678, in
　　A. D. Rochas d'Aiglun, *Vauban, sa famille et ses écrits*, ɪ (Paris, 1910)
　　pp. 189–91; G. Zeller, *L'organisation défensive des frontières du nord et de
　　l'est au XVIIᵉ siècle* (Paris, 1928) p. 69.

2　See G. Livet, *L'intendance d'Alsace sous Louis XIV* (Paris, 1956) pp.
　　114–23.

3　Louvois to Vauban, 28 June 1684, quoted in Zeller, *Frontières*, p. 85;
　　cf. Louis XIV to Sébeville (ambassador at Vienna) 26 Sep 1681, in
　　G. Livet, 'Louis XIV et l'Allemagne', *XVIIᵉ Siècle* (1960) 41, n. 17, for
　　similar sentiments. (The translated Livet article is in this volume,
　　pp. 60–81.)

4   For the adverse long-term effects of the *Réunions*, see V.-L. Tapié, 'Aspects de la politique étrangère de Louis XIV', *XVIIᵉ Siècle* (1960) p. 15. Cf. Tapié's translated article from the *Bulletin of the Académie des Sciences Morales et Politiques* in this volume, pp. 3–15. The *Réunions* in general are surveyed by B. Auerbach, *La France et le Saint Empire Romain Germanique, depuis la paix de Westphalie jusqu'à la Révolution Française* (Paris, 1912) p. 200 ff.

5   For the fall of Strasbourg and its effect in Germany, see B. Erdmannsdörffer, *Deutsche Geschichte vom Westfälischen Frieden bis zum Regierungsantritt Friedrichs des Grossen*, I (Berlin, 1893) p. 658.

6   Louis XIV's anxiety to recover Philippsburg can be seen in his offer as early as October 1681 to return Freiburg to the emperor if Philippsburg were given back to the archbishop of Speyer, its rightful owner: J. T. O'Connor, *William-Egon von Fürstenberg and French Diplomacy in the Rhineland prior to the Outbreak of the War of the League of Augsburg in 1688* (University of Minnesota Ph.D. thesis, 1965) p. 71; cf. Zeller, *Frontières*, p. 82.

7   On the development of the bomb-ketch, a small vessel with heavy mortars for bombarding coastal targets, see C. de la Roncière, *Histoire de la marine française*, 6 vols (Paris, 1899–1932) v, p. 716.

8   J. Orcibal, *Louis XIV contre Innocent XI, les appels au futur concile de 1688 et l'opinion française* (Paris, 1949) p. 3 ff.

9   For French policy in the east, see F. R. Place, *French Policy and the Turkish War 1679–1688* (University of Minnesota Ph.D. thesis, 1966) p. 72 ff.

10   Auerbach, *La France*, pp. 227–30. For William III's policy at this time see S. Baxter, *William III* (London, 1966) pp. 187–91; P. Geyl, *The Netherlands in the 17th Century*, 2 parts (London, 1961) pt 2, pp. 163–8.

11   For Brandenburg, see Erdmannsdörffer, *Deutsche Geschichte*, vol. I, pp. 690–2.

12   The view of 1684 as a turning-point is held by C. Rousset, *Histoire de Louvois*, 4 vols (Paris, 1863) III, p. 287; Tapié, 'Aspects de la politique étrangère', pp. 19–21.

13   Bavarian policy is covered by Erdmannsdörffer, *Deutsche Geschichte*, vol. I, p. 700; see also *Recueil des Instructions données aux Ambassadeurs de France depuis la Paix de Westphalie jusqu'à la Révolution* (hereafter cited as *Recueil*) vol. VII, ed. A. Lebon, *Bavière, Palatinat, Deux-Ponts* (Paris, 1889) pp. xiv–xvi. In July 1685 the young elector Max-Emanuel married the emperor's daughter Maria-Antonietta, with the stipulation that he receive the Spanish Netherlands as his part of the inheritance after Carlos II's death. This was opposed by Louis XIV: he intervened at Madrid to prevent the nomination of Max-Emanuel as governor of the Netherlands, which was the first step towards his being given complete control of the province: see R. Dollot, *Les origines de la neutralité de la Belgique et le système de la barrière* (Paris, 1902) pp. 274–80.

14   On 7 April 1688 Rébenac, then French envoy at Berlin, wrote: 'les affaires de la religion ont entièrement éteint l'inclination que M. l'Electeur s'accoutumoit depuis quelque temps à avoir pour la France';

quoted in A. Waddington (ed.), *Recueil*, vol. xvi, *Prusse*, p. xliv. For the effect on Dutch opinion see Geyl, *The Netherlands*, pp. 169–70; for William III and the English opposition, see Baxter, *William III*, pp. 215–18.

15 Tapié, 'Aspects de la politique étrangère', pp. 10, 15.

16 See Vauban's memorandum on the recall of the Huguenots, Dec 1689, in Rochas d'Aiglun, *Vauban*, ii, pp. 465–77, which is confirmed by the figures in R. Mémain, *Matelots et soldats des vaisseaux du Roi* (Paris, 1936) p. 122 ff. See also E. Spanheim, *Relation de la Cour de France in 1690*, ed. C. Schefer (Paris, 1882) p. 350.

17 N. Barozzi and G. Berchet (eds), *Relazioni degli stati Europei lette all Senato dagli ambasciatori veneti nel secolo decimocettimo*, ser. 2, *Francia*, vol. iii (Venice, 1863) p. 467.

18 The militia, originally 25,000 strong, was formed in November 1688, and the *arrière-ban* was called out in 1689. The orders for the defence of the coasts can be found in Archives de la Marine (hereafter referred to as Marine) ser. B2, vol. 66; cf. G. Toudouze, *La défense des côtes de Dunkerque à Bayonne au XVIIᵉ siècle* (Paris, 1900) p. 222; Rousset, *Histoire de Louvois*, iii, p. 505.

19 L. Rothkrug, *Opposition to Louis XIV, the Political and Social Origins of the French Enlightenment* (Princeton, N.J., 1965) pp. 211–34. Comparative tables of expenditure are in A. M. Boislisle, *Correspondance des contrôleurs généraux des finances avec les intendants des provinces*, 2 vols (Paris, 1874) i, pp. 583–99.

20 E. Lavisse (ed.), *Histoire de France illustrée depuis les origines jusqu'à la révolution*, 9 vols (Paris, 1911) viii, pt 1, p. 292.

21 Barozzi and Berchet (eds), *Relazioni, Francia*, iii, pp. 445, 471–2. The vicissitudes of Louis XIV's health can be followed in J.-A. le Roi (ed.), *Journal de la santé du Roi Louis XIV de l'année 1647 á l'année 1711, écrit par Vallot, d'Aquin et Fagon* (Paris, 1862).

22 M. Braubach, *Versailles und Wien* (Bonn, 1952) p. 13.

23 A. Lebon (ed.), *Recueil*, vol. vii, *Bavière, Palatinat, Deux-Ponts*, pp. 397–405, prints the instructions for the envoys sent to the Palatinate in 1685. Cf. M. Immich, *Geschichte des europäischen Staatensystems von 1660 bis 1789* (Munich, Berlin, 1905) pp. 122–5.

24 Vauban's attitude in the later 1680s contrasts with that expressed, for instance, in his memorandum of November 1678 on the Netherlands frontier, where fortresses are specifically described as having both offensive and defensive purposes. Now only the defensive function appears.

25 Zeller, *Frontières*, pp. 86–91; Rousset, *Histoire de Louvois*, iii, p. 343.

26 Zeller, *Frontières*, pp. 92–3. Vauban now began to fear that too many fortresses were being built, in a defensive war such as France would now have to fight they might provide the enemy with useful bases: see his letter to Catinat, 7 Apr 1687, in Rochas d'Aiglun, *Vauban*, ii, p. 278. On the value of Trier see G. Livet (ed.), *Recueil*, vol. 28, *Etats Allemands*, pt 3, *L'Electorat de Trèves*, pp. ci–cii.

27 Louvois to Vauban, 25 Aug 1687, in Rousset, *Histoire de Louvois*, III, pp. 345–7.

28 Ibid., p. 287. After 1684 army expenditure was reduced, and the effectives fell to 160,000 (on paper) compared with 280,000 for the war year 1678. Boislisle, *Correspondance*, I, p. 598, gives these figures for expenditure on the army including fortifications: 1684, 55.8000 livres; 1685, 48.3000; 1686, 47.1000; 1687, 48.2000; 1688, 64.2000; 1689, 89.1000. The cost of the navy and galleys was: 1684, 10.1000; 1685, 9.7000; 1686, 9.1000; 1687, 9.4000; 1688, 10.2000; 1698, 18 million. D. Neuville, *Etat sommaire des archives de la marine antérieures à la révolution* (Paris, 1898) p. 610, gives somewhat higher figures for naval expenditure.

29 *Mémoires*, ed. J. F. Michaud and J. J. F. Poujoulat (Paris, 1836) pp. 211, 213; Rousset, *Histoire de Louvois*, III, pp. 411–14; Marquis de Dangeau, *Journal*, ed. A. Soulié *et al*, 19 vols (Paris, 1854) II, p. 144. Cf. below, n. 86.

30 See for instance 'Etat des radoubs à faire aux vaisseaux à Brest', Mar 1688, in Marine, ser. B3, vol. 57, ff. 329–63. Many ships needed major repairs involving use of the dry-dock.

31 Pepys's 'Abstract of the State of the Royal Navy', 18 Dec 1688, gives three bomb-ketches; quoted in J. Charnock, *An History of Marine Architecture* 3 vols (London, 1802) II, p. 432.

32 R. Fester, *Die armirten Stände und die Reichskriegsverfassung* (Frankfurt am Main, 1886) p. 33; Rousset, *Histoire de Louvois* III, pp. 325–30; P. Daniel, *Histoire de la milice française*, 2 vols (Paris, 1721) II, pp. 590–4. Place, *French Policy*, pp. 164–5, notes that the French failure to modernise was in part due to an underestimation of the effectiveness of the Imperial armies, and an assumption of superiority based on past experience. It was also due to innate military conservatism extending to the king himself.

33 See the introduction to G. Livet (ed.), *Recueil*, vol. 28, *Etats Allemands*, pt 2, *Cologne* (Paris, 1963).

34 Fürstenberg's career is described by O'Connor, *W.-E. von Fürstenberg*.

35 Orcibal, *Louis XIV contre Innocent XI*, p. 11. Lavardin's orders are in G. Hanotaux (ed.), *Recueil*, vol. VI, *Rome*, pt 1 (Paris, 1888) pp. 287–363. See also C. Gérin, *Innocent XI et la révolution anglaise de 1688* (Paris, 1876).

36 Rousset, *Histoire de Louvois*, IV, p. 64.

37 Louis XIV's English policy can best be followed in the documents in the Archives des Affaires Etrangères, Correspondance Politique, Angleterre, vols 164–6. The view that Louis XIV intended to embroil James II and William III, put forward by O. Klopp, *Der Fall des Hauses Stuart und die Succession des Hauses Hannover in Gross-Britannien und Irland*, 14 vols (Vienna, 1875–88) IV, p. 1 ff, does not accord with the evidence of this correspondence.

38 Louis XIV's relations with the United Provinces are best followed in A.A.E., C.P., Hollande, vols 154–7, and in the summary of this by Avaux in A.A.E., Mémoires et Documents, Hollande, vol. 45.

William's relations with England are discussed in Klopp, *Der Fall des Hauses Stuart*, IV, pp. 36–8; Baxter, *William III*, p. 218 ff.

39 Louis XIV to Barrillon (ambassador in England), 6 May 1688, A.A.E., C.P., Angleterre, vol. 165, f. 271. For the Baltic crisis see G. Landberg, *Den svenska utrikespolitikens historia 1648–1697* (Stockholm, 1952) pp. 235–7.

40 Klopp, *Der Fall des Hauses Stuart*, IV, p. 34; Rousset, *Histoire de Louvois*, IV, p. 100.

41 De la Roncière, *Histoire de la marine française*, VI, p. 15; Marquis de Quincy, *Histoire militaire du règne de Louis le Grand*, 7 vols (Paris, 1726) II, pp. 146–7

42 Rousset, *Histoire de Louvois*; Dangeau notes (*Journal*, II, p. 157) that word was received of the return of the ships on 4 August.

43 O'Connor, *W.-E. von Fürstenberg*, pp. 237–8. Dangeau, *Journal*, II, p. 145, confirmed by Marquis de Sourches, *Mémoires sur le règne de Louis XIV*, ed. G.-J. de Cosnac and E. Pontal, 13 vols (Paris, 1882) II, p. 173. For another contemporary view of the Cologne crisis, see G. Burnet, *History of my own Times*, 3 vols (Oxford, 1897–1902) II, p. 481 ff.

44 O'Connor, *W.-E. von Fürstenberg*, pp. 238–40.

45 J. Hanoteau (ed.), *Recueil*, vol. XVII, *Rome*, pt 2 (Paris, 1911) p. 3, n. 1; T. Bouille, *Histoire de la ville et pays de Liège*, 3 vols (Liège, 1732) III, p. 482.

46 Printed in Hanoteau (ed.), *Recueil*, vol. XVII, *Rome*, pt 2 (Paris, 1911) pp. 4–20.

47 Ibid., p. 22.

48 Ibid., p. 20, n. 2; cf. Rousset, *Histoire de Louvois*, IV, pp. 76–9, for Louvois' letter to Le Peletier, 22 July 1688: 'Cette affaire-ci me paroit bien épineuse . . . car le prince de Bavière, Electeur de Cologne et apparemment évèque de Liège ou de Munster, soutenu par le duc de Juliers, l'Electeur Palatin, l'Empereur et les Hollandois me paroitroit un mauvais voisin, et particulièrement si les Espagnols faisoient M. L'Electeur de Bavière gouverneur des Pays-Bas . . .'.

49 See William's correspondence in N. Japikse (ed.), *Correspondentie van Willem Bentinck, eersten Graaf van Portland*, 5 vols in 2 (The Hague, 1927) I, pt 1, p. 36 ff.

50 Erdmannsdörffer, *Deutsche Geschichte*, II, p. 17.

51 Avaux's despatches for this period are in A.A.E., Mémoires et Documents, Hollande, vol. 45, ff. 336 ff.

52 Louis XIV to Barrillon, 14 July 1688, A.A.E., C.P., Angleterre, vol. 166, f. 27; cf. ibid., letter to Barrillon, 3 Aug, ff. 77–8; see also Louis XIV to Avaux, 5 Aug, A.A.E., C.P., Hollande, vol. 155, f. 249, in which he concurs with Avaux that William is unlikely to move until next year.

53 O'Connor, *W.-E. von Fürstenberg*, p. 274.

54 Rousset, *Histoire de Louvois*, IV, p. 87.

55 O'Connor, *W.-E. von Fürstenberg*, p. 261.

56 Louis XIV to Cardinal d'Estrées, 9 Aug 1688, quoted in Place, *French Policy*, p. 173.

57 Sourches, *Mémoires*, II, p. 202.

58 Louis XIV to Barrillon, 19 Aug 1688, A.A.E., C.P., Angleterre, vol. 166, f. 106: d'Humières was to command the army on the Netherlands frontier. Louvois ordered d'Huxelles to break camp at Maintenon on 20 August: Rousset, *Histoire de Louvois*, III, p. 413; on 21 August he wrote to Fürstenberg to urge him to stop hesitating about admitting French troops to Cologne: ibid., IV, p. 89. The orders for the naval expedition against the papal states are in Marine, ser. B2, vol. 67, f. 194 *bis*, ff.

59 Girardin to Louis XIV, 29 June 1688, A.A.E., C.P., Turquie, vol. 20, ff. 171–86. This arrived at Versailles about 15 August: Place, *French Policy*, p. 173. Cf. the entry by Sourches for 16 Aug in his *Mémoires*, II, p. 201.

60 Dangeau, *Journal*, II, p. 161.

61 Louis XIV to Girardin, 22 Aug 1688, A.A.E., C.P., Turquie, vol. 20, ff. 188–91.

62 Louis XIV to Barrillon, 26 Aug 1688, A.A.E., C.P., Angleterre, vol. 166, ff. 121–4: warnings from Avaux indicated that William would soon attack James II. But on 2 September Seignelay wrote to Avaux that it seemed unlikely that William could attack that year: see Marine, ser. B2, vol. 66, f. 115.

63 Avaux had urged Louis XIV to invade the Netherlands in order to deter William III, but this was rejected; see Louis XIV to Avaux, 14 Oct 1688, quoted in L. André and E. Bourgeois (eds), *Recueil*, vol. XXI, *Hollande*, pt 1 (Paris, 1922) p. 395, n. 2. For a summary by A. de St-Léger of the arguments for and against this proposal see Lavisse (ed.), *Histoire de France*, VIII, pt 1, p. 16, n. 1.

64 The orders for assembling these forces can be found in P. Griffet, *Recueil de lettres pour servir d'éclaircissement à l'histoire militaire du Règne de Louis XIV*, 8 vols (The Hague, 1760) V, *passim*. On the system of command for this campaign, where the Dauphin's part was largely nominal, see J. Wolf, *Louis XIV* (New York, 1968) p. 446 ff.

65 Louis XIV to Barrillon, 10 Sep 1688, A.A.E., C.P., Angleterre, vol. 166, f. 154.

66 Schomberg to Bentinck, 15 Sep 1688, and Danckelmann (minister of the elector of Brandenburg) to Bentinck, late September, in Japikse (ed.), *Correspondentie van Willem Bentinck*, I, pt 2, pp. 139, 158. Fürstenberg's attitude is covered in O'Connor, *W.-E. von Fürstenberg*, pp. 272–5.

67 Orcibal, *Louis XIV contre Innocent XI*, pp. 25–6.

68 Rousset, *Histoire de Louvois*, IV, p. 91.

69 Rébenac's mission at Madrid is described by A. Legrelle, *La mission de M. le comte de Rébenac à Madrid 1688–1689* (Paris, 1894).

70 Louvois to Boufflers, 13 Sep 1688, in Griffet, *Recueil de lettres*, V, p. 154.

71 Villars' orders are in A. Lebon (ed.), *Recueil*, vol. VII, *Bavière, Palatinat, Deux-Ponts*, pp. 92–4. The mission was doomed from the first because French opposition to Joseph-Clement's candidacy at Cologne had

completed the process of driving the elector of Bavaria into the Imperial party. Cf. Marquis de Vogüé (ed.), *Mémoires du maréchal de Villars*, 6 vols (Paris, 1884–1904) I, pp. 41–2.

72   Printed in J. Dumont, *Corps universal diplomatique du droit des gens*, 8 vols (The Hague, 1731) VII, pt 2, pp. 170–3. The confusion of thought evident in this manifesto is graphically paralleled in the drafts of correspondence from this time; they are full of erasures, corrections and re-writing.

73   Bonrepaus' orders are in J. Jusserand (ed.), *Recueil*, vol. XXV, Angleterre, pt 2, pp. 405–9. Seignelay's letter to Bonrepaus, 8 Sep 1688, is in Marchesa Campana de Cavelli, *Les derniers Stuarts à St. Germain-en-laye*, 2 vols (Paris, 1871) II, p. 254. The incomplete draft of the naval treaty, dated 13 September, is in A.A.E., C.P., Angleterre, vol. 166, ff. 214–16.

74   A.A.E., Mémoires et Documents, Hollande, vol. 45, ff. 355–8.

75   Ibid., ff. 332, 350 describes the failure of Seignelay's agents to penetrate William's plans.

76   Toudouze, *Défense . . . de Dunkerque à Bayonne*, p. 222; N.-J. Foucault, *Mémoires*, ed. F. Baudry (Paris, 1862) p. 257.

77   Burnet, *History of my own Times* II, p. 491; Baxter, *William III*, p. 235.

78   The campaign can be followed in Wolf, *Louis XIV*, p. 446 ff.

79   Immich, *Geschichte des europäischen Staatensystems*, p. 138; Erdmanns-dörffer, *Deutsche Geschichte* II, p. 10; Fester, *Die armirten Stände*, pp. 70–1.

80   Klopp, *Der Fall des Hauses Stuart* IV, p. 199.

81   For these negotiations, see H. M. Sutton, (ed.), *The Lexington Papers, or some Account of the Courts of London and Vienna at the Conclusion of the Seventeenth Century . . .* (London, 1851) p. 327 ff.

82   Wolf, *Louis XIV*, p. 455.

83   Rochas d'Aiglun, *Vauban*, II, p. 306. For similar complaints about the quality of the troops, see Chamlay's memorandum on the events of 1678–88, quoted in Rousset, *Histoire de Louvois* III, pp. 413–14; cf. St-Pouange to Louvois, 7 and 10 Oct 1688, and Louvois' reply, 13 Oct, in Griffet, *Recueil de Lettres* V, pp. 25, 62, 64; Madame de la Fayette, *Histoire de Madame Henriette d'Angleterre* (Paris, 1853) p. 223.

84   Details in Rousset, *Histoire de Louvois*, IV, p. 155 ff; de Quincy, *Histoire militaire*, II, p. 138 ff; Erdmannsdörffer, *Deutsche Geschichte* II, pp. 9–17.

9 Attempts to Build a 'Third Party' in North Germany, 1690-1694[*]

JANINE FAYARD

Louis XIV had hoped that the conflict which broke out between France and the Empire in 1688 would be brief : his aim was to transform the Truce of Ratisbon of August 1684 into a definitive treaty as quickly as possible, thus forcing his enemies to recognise the *Réunions*. A year later all hope had vanished of hostilities ending in the near future. The so-called War of the League of Augsburg, the 'Nine Years War' of English and Dutch history, had proved an abortive *Blitzkrieg*. If horror over the devastation of the Palatinate did not produce the alliance against France in 1689, the general condemnation of Louis helped to forge it into a solid coalition. On 12 May the Dutch States General allied with the emperor, Victor Amadeus of Savoy joined them on 3 June, and England committed herself definitely in December. This was the 'Grand Alliance of Vienna', also known as the First Grand Alliance.

At the end of 1689 Croissy, the French secretary of state for foreign affairs, had to take on the difficult task of breaking France's diplomatic isolation. He looked to the north, hoping to find some states willing to stay at least neutral. In past struggles with the Habsburgs France had often been able, with the help of one or other of the Scandinavian powers, to exploit the quarrels between the Imperial princes and the head of the House of Austria.[1]

* First published in the *Revue d'Histoire Diplomatique* (1965) under the title 'Les tentatives de constitution d'un tièrs party en Allemagne du Nord 1690–1694'.

Diplomatic relations between Louis XIV and Charles XI of Sweden had been broken off when the *Chambre de Réunion* at Metz declared that the duchy of Zweibrücken, the king of Sweden's personal possession, was a fief of the bishopric of Metz. Consequently Croissy would have to proceed cautiously if Louis was to reach an agreement with Sweden. As to the German princes, the most Croissy envisaged was to oblige them, through treaties with France, to give the emperor no more than the military contingents they owed him under the Imperial constitution.[2] If several could be kept more or less outside the conflict they would form a neutral bloc, a 'third party', which could be used to exert pressure on the belligerents to make peace. Croissy was prepared to use French money and the skill of French agents to build such a neutral bloc.

In November 1689 he sent Benoît Bidal, Baron d'Asfeld, to Stockholm. He was the sixth son of a Parisian silk merchant who had been ennobled by queen Christina of Sweden and had served as French resident in Hamburg from 1661 to 1682.[3] Through his father's influence Asfeld had begun his career in the Swedish army. He and his brother Alexis had served in Stralsund in 1675 when the town was besieged by the elector of Brandenburg's troops;[4] afterwards Asfeld was made lieutenant-colonel of a Swedish infantry regiment and governor of Buxstehode, a fortress in the duchy of Bremen.[5] He had thus shared Sweden's fortunes in a way denied to all but a few of his French contemporaries. He had also visited many of the European courts. In 1679 he had sought out Frederick William of Brandenburg[6] to secure the restitution of the barony of Wildenbruch to his family after its conquest by the elector's army. Asfeld's knowledge of several languages (he spoke German, Danish, Swedish, Dutch and Latin),[7] his quick intelligence and the connections of his family and himself in the north, fully explain Croissy's choice. At the end of 1689 the Bidal family also had a valid personal reason for sending one of their number to Sweden. Their Harsefeld estate had been a victim of Charles XI's *reduktion* policy,[8] and Swedish opinion would therefore assume that the objective of Asfeld's journey to Sweden was a private audience of the king to ask for the restoration of Harsefeld.

In his instructions of 27 November 1689 Asfeld was commissioned to offer Charles XI a firm alliance on the lines of the treaty concluded between the two countries of 14 April 1672. Croissy thought it likely that the king of Sweden would be reluctant to tie himself closely to France : Louis XIV would therefore be satisfied if the king agreed not to give any military help to the Vienna allies.[9] If Asfeld could not conclude either an 'active' treaty or a simple neutrality treaty speedily, he was at least to ensure that Charles XI did not send troops to the emperor in his capacity as a German prince as he had done in 1688.[10] In 1689 the Swedish councillor, Count Nils Bielke, with whom Asfeld had been in touch for several years, had managed to stop his master from giving military help to Leopold I.[11]

After long months of discussions with Charles XI's principal advisers Asfeld was given assurances that they would 'make such difficulties over everything'[12] that the Swedish contingent would not reach its destination in time for the 1690 campaign. He was unable, however, to conclude an alliance[13] and decided to rejoin his brother, the abbé Etienne Bidal, who had been French resident at Hamburg since 1682, especially as a prolonged stay in Stockholm might betray to the allied ambassadors why Charles XI was not complying with his duty to the emperor.[14] Bidal expected to return to France, but as the court of Versailles had been approached by Ernst August, the duke of Hanover, Croissy judged Asfeld best qualified to discover that prince's real aims.[15] He had learned in Stockholm of negotiations for an alliance between Charles XI and Ernst August,[16] and good relations between these two princes could only further France's plans for a third party.

The interests of the king of Sweden and the duke of Hanover appeared to coincide at the start of 1690. It was true that the dukes of Brunswick-Lüneburg had always had designs on the duchy of Bremen, but at this time Charles XI and Ernst August were pursuing similar policies in the Lower-Saxony circle. In 1689 they had co-operated to uphold the independence of the duke of Holstein-Gottorp. They both wished to protect the town of Hamburg against Denmark. And over the question of the succession to the duchy of Sachsen-Lauenburg[17] Sweden did not rule out the idea of Ernst August's troops invading the duchy : pending the emperor's settling that question, it was far better for Sweden to have this strategically important region occupied by the troops of the House of Brunswick-Lüneberg rather than those of the elector of Brandenburg or, worse still, of the king of Denmark. Charles XI in fact agreed to this eventuality in a secret article of the treaty concluded at Stockholm on 13 October 1690 by Oberg in the name of his master, Ernst August. For the rest, the treaty amounted to a defensive alliance by which the two contracting parties promised to help each other if their German possessions were attacked.[18] Co-operation with the dukes of Brunswick-Lüneberg would help Sweden oppose the intrusion of Denmark into the Lower-Saxony circle.

Charles XI of Sweden and Ernst August of Hanover viewed the general situation in the Empire in roughly the same way. Both wanted peace, the king of Sweden because he hoped that his mediation in the European conflict would be accepted, and the duke of Hanover because the last campaign to help Leopold had cost him dear.[19] They were both tempted to stay out of the war, though remaining under arms, and to form a third party to promote peace. Nothing could be more favourable to Croissy's plans. Neither the king of Sweden nor the duke of Hanover, however, seemed to want to make a preliminary move towards France.

At the beginning of March 1690 Asfeld was told by the Swedish diplomat Mauritz Vellingk, in the name of the chancellor Bengt Oxenstierna (whose attitude towards Louis XIV had often perplexed the French), that the latter was displeased at the scant regard shown by the Vienna allies for Sweden. He believed that Charles XI would only be respected if he had an army in Germany, but, since the stationing of large numbers of troops in Bremen or Pomerania could not fail to disturb the north German princes, Sweden needed one of these princes as a firm ally. That the chancellor had Hanover in mind was clear from Vellingk's revelation that Oxenstierna hoped the House of Hanover could be persuaded to propose that Charles XI should spearhead a neutral bloc, a third party.[20] By 15 March Asfeld hoped that the situation would resolve itself without direct French intervention. 'Fortunately', he reported to Croissy, 'this house seems to wish to take all steps necessary to build a third party, or rather they thought of it at the same time as M. Oxenstierna ordered M. Veling [Vellingk] to propose it to M. Goerst [the Hanoverian envoy accredited to Hamburg]'.[21] That the diplomatically experienced Vellingk played an important role in the affair is shown by a letter which Count von Platen, one of Ernst August's ministers, wrote to him at this time :

> His Highness, my Master, having been informed by M. Goers [Friedrich Wilhelm von Goertz, or Görtz], who is now at The Hague, of M. Oxenstiern's and your sentiments about building a third party in the present circumstances, has ordered me to assure you that he is glad to learn of them . . . and wants . . . H.M. to send you to Germany as soon as possible with full powers to negotiate and conclude an agreement between the King of Sweden and him, and thus to lay the foundation of the said third party.[22]

The rest of the letter explained the kind of third party envisaged by the duke of Hanover. Five points had to be settled : 1. Should France take part in this association? 2. Even if they [the king and the duke] decided not to act in agreement with Louis XIV, should they try to discover on what conditions the king of France would agree to make peace? 3. How could they support the 12,000 troops each ruler was to keep in Germany? 4. Should they ask France for subsidies or the emperor for winter quarters for these troops? 5. Which German princes should they ask to join the association?

The duke of Hanover's desire to discuss a third party *entente* is here evident, but so is his determination not to fall under Louis XIV's domination.[23] But already, on 20 April 1690 Croissy informed Asfeld that Ernst August had made direct approaches to Versailles through an emissary, the abbé Luigi Ballati.[24] The question was : Why did the duke make a move indicating his desire for a French alliance?

Since 1683 Ernst August had spent more than two million crowns for the emperor's benefit.[25] He would certainly welcome a neutrality treaty with Louis XIV which would be accompanied by the payment of subsidies.[26] It would also suit his purposes to make the emperor fear a Hanoverian agreement with Louis XIV : this might bring him the electoral title which he had wanted for so long. The subject had been broached when the Electoral College met to elect Leopold's son Joseph king of the Romans in the winter of 1689–90, but the outbreak of war had prevented further discussion. Louis XIV now promised to help

Ernst August become an elector. Croissy wrote to Asfeld on 24
May 1690:

> His Majesty orders . . . [me] . . . to tell you that, having con-
> sidered how passionately the Duke of Hanover wants to obtain
> the rank of Elector for himself and his House, he will allow
> you not only to engage His Majesty to support strongly, as
> far as he can, the said Duke of Hanover's pretensions, but
> even, in return for the Emperor's according him this rank, to
> promise that he will agree at the peace treaty to raze which-
> ever of the two fortresses of Philippsburg or Freiburg the Em-
> peror and the states of the Empire choose.[27]

This astonishing offer shows that Louis XIV expected a lot from
Ernst August, namely that he should persuade the emperor and
Empire to make peace. Louis XIV, it is true, had already more
than once agreed to help the duke of Hanover achieve the
dignity of an elector. The first time was in the treaty concluded
between France and Hanover by Verjus de Crécy on 10 December 1672.[28] Later Louis XIV's promise of good offices to obtain
the desired title for Ernst August made up the essential part of
the secret articles of the alliance of 1 November 1687. Louis
XIV had, however, attached little importance to these promises.
In 1690 his attitude was very different; the offer to raze either
of two important fortresses shows that he was serious in wishing
to help Ernst August become an elector, if that prince contributed
to bringing the war to an end. This plan was not far-fetched: it
was intended that Ernst August should play a role similar to that
of Duke Maximilian of Bavaria in 1648. Then Maximilian had
promised France he would lead a peace party in the Empire provided France helped him keep the electoral title conferred on
him by the emperor Ferdinand II. Early in 1690 Louis XIV
believed that many would follow an Imperial prince campaigning openly for peace; the creation of a ninth electorate as a
reward could then be made a part of the general peace treaty.
His calculation, however, proved false. The situation in the
Empire had changed a great deal since the Peace of Westphalia,
and Ernst August did not want to become elector with Louis
XIV's help but through the offices of the emperor.

    In June 1690 Asfeld met Ernst August's emissary, the abbé
Luigi Ballati, in Hamburg. The French envoy found it difficult

to pin down the wily abbé, and the duke's initial demands proved high. Not till 1 December 1690 was a neutrality treaty between Hanover and France signed at Hamburg by Ballati and Asfeld.[29] Backdated to 27 November, so that the subsidies could be reckoned from November, it contained twenty-five articles, nine of them secret.[30] The latter are the most interesting : Ernst August promised to join a third party as soon as Sweden or another state had agreed to form such a bloc. In return Louis XIV engaged himself to do his best to press the emperor to confer the rank of elector on Ernst August; if he failed, France would pay the duke 400,000 crowns six months after the ratification of the general peace.

Asfeld was reckoned to have handled a difficult negotiation well. Already on 10 December 1690 Croissy had new instructions sent to him to go in great secrecy to Stockholm.[31] He was to use the title of envoy extraordinary only if he found the well-disposed Swedish councillors in agreement with this step. His task would be to re-establish, if at all possible, 'the ties of interest and friendship' which had 'existed for so long between France and Sweden'.[32] Louis XIV wished Charles XI to promise, by a secret article in a French–Swedish treaty, that he would not require Louis to agree to conditions less favourable to France than those of the Truce of Ratisbon, and also to let him keep the fortress of Philippsburg which had been seized after the signing of the truce. Recent military successes had raised Louis XIV's demands. The 1690 campaign, with the victories of Fleurus and Staffards and the conquest of Savoy, had been more successful than that of 1689. Croissy thought that other princes, especially the bishop of Münster and the dukes of Wolfenbüttel, would join the king of Sweden and the duke of Hanover. Asfeld was ordered, however, not to appear too eager to gain them for the third party lest they ask subsidies as high as those demanded by Ernst August. Croissy left Asfeld quite free to negotiate in Hanover rather than in Stockholm : after consultations with Count Bielke it was for Asfeld himself to choose the best way to build the third party.

Asfeld did not return to Sweden and his attempts to achieve a Franco-Swedish *rapprochement* proved unsuccessful. Let us examine the obstacles which he perceived. In November 1691 he confessed to the marquis de Béthune[33] that he was worried by

H*

differences among the Swedish councillors and by Charles XI's desire to keep out of the war. He explained that king's pacifism by his concentration on efforts to regain the alienated parts of the royal domain. According to Asfeld there were three parties around the king : the well-disposed, favourable to France; the followers of Bengt Oxenstierna, the champion of the allies; and finally, the group round Charles's principal financial advisers, Jacob Gyllenborg and Lars Wallensted, in charge of the *reduktion*, who 'feared a war which would demand all the attention of their master, the King, and cause him to abandon all his prosecutions against his subjects. Because of this they would lose all their credit, and they were therefore trying by all means possible to make all serious proposals for an engagement with either side suspect to the King'.[34]

Charles XI was certainly very preoccupied with financial matters,[35] and this contributed to his desire for neutrality. But Asfeld over-simplified the situation when he blamed the king's reserve solely on the *reduktion*, since his desire for neutrality is perfectly explicable by the political situation in Europe. Sweden had not forgotten the Dutch War when Northern Europe allied against her and seized her German possessions because she was an ally of France. Asfeld was misled by his friends and especially by Bielke who was trying to usurp the principal role in Franco-Swedish negotiations for himself. This was quite natural as he was receiving substantial gratifications from Croissy. In November 1690 the secretary of state went so far as to promise him the enormous sum of 200,000 crowns if he succeeded in building a third party after the conclusion of the alliance between Louis XIV and Charles XI.[36] For a long time Asfeld believed it would be possible to buy the king of Sweden's alliance. He underestimated the political weight of Bengt Oxenstierna and shared the opinion of most of his contemporaries that Oxenstierna was on the payroll of the Vienna allies.[37] But, as A. Stille has shown, this minister always seems to have pursued a Swedish national policy. His sole aim appears to have been to achieve a European balance based on the observation of the treaties of Westphalia.[38] The *entente* between the king of Sweden and the duke of Hanover, which made Asfeld think that the 'well-disposed' party had got the better of Oxenstierna's group, was in fact indispensable to the chancellor's policy. We have already seen that it was useful for Sweden to have an ally in the Empire : Charles XI's advisers followed the interests of their country, not the advice of the French envoy.[39]

Asfeld could not stay long in Hamburg as the Brandenburg general, Rolas du Rosay, had been sent to arrest him.[40] Having concluded that he would be of no use in Stockholm, he went to Hanover for asylum. His arrival at Duke Ernst August's court made Hanover the centre for Louis XIV's negotiations to attract as many of the German princes as possible to the third party through the mediation of Ernst August. It is not necessary to examine Asfeld's activities at the Hanoverian court in detail, as Schnath has already done so in his *Geschichte Hannovers*. Something can, however, be added about the role played by Asfeld in Croissy's first scheme for a third party.

When Asfeld had to leave Hamburg he was in the middle of negotiating an alliance between Louis XIV and the bishop of Münster, Frederick Christian von Plettenberg, an ambitious prelate who wished to rouse the ecclesiastical princes against the annexionist pretensions of their powerful Protestant neighbours.[41] Plans for a third party fitted in well with his general aims. He had managed to stay neutral till March 1689 when he was forced to sign an agreement with the emperor. In 1690 he had, of his own accord, sought co-operation with the duke of Hanover; and on 27 January 1691 Count von Platen had signed an alliance in Ernst August's name with Frederick Christian von Plettenberg.[42] The two princes proclaimed their 'unique aim' to be that of 'mediators of peace between the Empire and France' and decided to take no active part in the war, beyond sending their obligatory contingents to the emperor. This alliance formed a prelude to the treaty which the bishop of Münster proved ready to negotiate with Louis XIV.

Although Jean-Casimir Frischmann de la Ranconnières[43] represented the French king at Münster, Croissy entrusted the negotiation with Plettenberg to Asfeld[44] who met with great difficulty in reducing the demands the prince-bishop made for French financial help. On 1 March 1691 Croissy, on Louis XIV's orders, limited such aid to 250,000 crowns per annum.[45] Thereupon Plettenberg informed Verjus de Crécy and his own agent in Paris, Brosseau, that he wished to negotiate his French treaty with Frischmann instead of Asfeld :[46] the astute prince-bishop may have expected that it would be easier to manage the French envoy at Münster than Asfeld, whose skill was becoming well known in Germany. But on 25 March he signed a neutrality treaty with Louis XIV along the lines laid down by Croissy; for an annual subsidy of 250,000 crowns he agreed to maintain and support an army of 12,000 men in his own territories.

After some delay in ratifying the French treaty,[47] he did try to win over the German princes, and especially the Catholic ones in the Rhineland, to a 'third party'. He proposed French neutrality treaties with the archbishop-electors of Trier and Mainz as well as with the chapter of Cologne;[48] but Louis XIV refused, arguing that princes who could not raise more than 10,000 men would not be of much use.[49] Behind this refusal we glimpse financial calculations : if the Rhenish archbishop-electorates became France's allies, Louis XIV could not continue to draw those contributions from their territories which he had levied since the French occupation took place at the beginning of the war. These contributions were vital for the subsistence of Louis' French soldiers; Croissy told Asfeld to refuse membership of the third party to 'all those whose territories pay contributions to the King'.[50]

Plettenburg had greater success when he suggested a deal between Louis XIV and the duke of Sachsen-Gotha.[51] Asfeld was once more put in charge of negotiations and on 12 April 1691 a neutrality treaty was signed between Louis XIV and Frederick I of Sachsen-Gotha : the duke promised in the future to send the emperor only his obligatory contingent, to recall all other troops to his own territories and to maintain 6000 men in return for a French subsidy of 13,000 crowns a month.[52]

In the spring of 1691 Asfeld might have been forgiven for believing that he had helped lay the first stone of the third party in Germany. Neutrality treaties had been signed with the duke of Hanover, the bishop of Münster and the duke of Sachsen-Gotha. The army of this third party amounted to 31,000 men.[53] Croissy was even more pleased with Asfeld's next important diplomatic success, the signature on 27 March 1691 of an alliance between Louis XIV and Christian V of Denmark.

The French ambassador to Copenhagen, Martangis, had found it difficult to bring Christian V's financial demands down to a level acceptable to France. Christian's asking price had been

300,000 crowns. Louis XIV finally agreed to 200,000 crowns in return for Danish neutrality, but agreed to pay an extraordinary subsidy of 600,000 crowns if Christian V were attacked by the emperor or his allies.[54] It is worth noting that it was not Croissy, but Asfeld, who gave Martangis the final orders to sign the Danish treaty.[55] Croissy had sent the project approved by Versailles to Asfeld as well as to Martangis, and the latter had been told to wait for the former's response. Asfeld checked that none of the articles in the project would embarrass the negotiations still being conducted with the Swedes, and then authorised Martangis' signature.

The importance Croissy attached to Asfeld's advice is thus clear. A skilful and tireless diplomat, he had won the respect of the secretary of state and at the beginning of 1691 French hopes for a powerful third party rested on him.

Meanwhile in Hanover Ernst August's ministers and Count Bielke, Charles XI's emissary, were discussing the best way to achieve European peace. By May 1691 they had formalised a plan. This provided for an army of 30,000 men, Sweden to provide 18,000 and the duke of Hanover 12,000. If another prince were to join them, the army would be increased by 6000 men. The ninth article of the Suedo-Hanoverian project dealt with the role envisaged for this army : 'the aim of the said [troop] movement will be to save the Empire on this side of the Rhine from force, from whatever quarter, and to protect those Imperial states who want to join this peace-seeking party against all violations and exactions contrary to the Imperial constitution'.[56] This third party felt strong enough to take upon itself the defence of the Empire against attack, and contemplated resistance to attacks also from the French side. There seemed a real danger, as Asfeld had predicted the previous year, that a third party might try to 'get better conditions for Germany than those of the truce [of Ratisbon]'.[57] Croissy realised that Louis XIV must make his peace terms known quickly and have the duke of Hanover accept these, otherwise the German princes united in a third-party bloc might well turn their troops against Louis if they should disapprove of his objectives.[58]

French demands were therefore submitted to Ernst August through Asfeld. Louis wishes the Truce of Ratisbon to be converted into a peace treaty. What had been accorded him 'provisionally' should be accorded 'definitively' and 'incontrovertibly'. In addition, he claimed the right to keep Philippsburg.[59] The duke replied that no German prince would agree to these proposals, especially as Louis, by his manifesto of 24 September 1688, had already offered to return either Philippsburg or Freiburg.[60] In June 1691 the Imperial princes let Croissy know through Ballati, then in Paris, the conditions on which they would consent to form a third party: Louis must raze the fortifications of Mont-Royal, pay subsidies to the margraves of Baden-Baden and Baden-Durlach as well as to the duke of Württemberg to ensure their neutrality, and stop levying contributions on the occupied Rhenish states which, for the most part, wanted to become members of third party.[61] These conditions were reported to the French king who particularly resented the demand to free the occupied states from contributions; in his opinion 'the more the neighbouring princes and states on the Rhine [suffered] the discomforts of the war, the more eager they would be to have it finished'.[62]

The negotiations of 1691 – first in Hanover and then in Loccum – between Asfeld and Dean Schmising, the representative of the bishop of Münster, Hardenberg, the envoy of the duke of Sachsen-Gotha, and the Hanoverian ministers, Count von Platen and Otto Grote, eventually failed.[63] In the summer of 1691 Louis XIV did make concessions which Croissy passed on to Asfeld: the French king agreed to the razing of Philippsburg, to the admission of the duke of Württemberg to the third party, and even to the exemption from military contributions of all the princes who, before May 1692, joined the third party and bound themselves 'to procure peace on fair terms.'[64] These concessions are explicable by the change in French foreign policy which followed the death of Louvois on 16 July 1691.

But Louis' conciliatory attitude did not help the third party negotiations. By August the duke of Sachsen-Gotha's behaviour was such that Asfeld suspended his French subsidies.[65] Ernst August remained intransigent, declaring Croissy's concessions insufficient. When Count von Platen suggested that four or five fortresses should be restored by Louis XIV, the king and his secretary of state realised that they could not depend on the duke of Hanover:[66] one of the foundations Croissy needed to build the third party was on the point of collapse. Measures were now taken to prevent Ernst August's joining France's enemies; and in the autumn of 1691 Croissy turned to the elector of Saxony, hoping for an alliance with a prince strong enough to keep Hanover faithful to the third party.

Hitherto Croissy had shown no enthusiasm to have the elector of Saxony in the third party alongside the king of Sweden, the duke of Hanover and the bishop of Münster. With the addition of Saxon forces the third party might become too powerful[67] and Louis risked losing control of his creation. But by August, when Croissy had nearly despaired of an alliance between Louis XIV and Charles XI of Sweden, and the duke of Hanover had become suspect, there was no longer any need to fear a strong third party. John George III's alliance therefore seemed desirable. Asfeld put out feelers to the elector of Saxony's chief adviser, General Schöning,[68] via one of his Swedish officer friends who was sent to Dresden to prepare for Asfeld's own arrival at the elector's court.[69] Before the negotiations could get under way John George III died on 22 September 1691, but, as the Franco-Hanoverian negotiations had meanwhile reached a deadlock, Asfeld still left for Saxony to try his luck. On 8 November he was sent full powers to sign an agreement with the new elector, John George IV :[70] if the elector promised to provide the emperor only with his obligatory contingent, Louis offered to pay him subsidies equal to those enjoyed by the bishop of Münster – 250,000 crowns a year. Asfeld was warned that he would have to proceed with caution. He must not commit France in the business of the Sachsen–Lauenberg succession, the bone of contention between Saxony and Hanover, for to favour John George IV would mean breaking with Ernst August. Although it would be easy to provoke a conflict in north Germany by stirring up the one against the other – and French arms might well profit from such a conflict – Croissy advised Asfeld 'to bring the elector of Saxony and the duke of Hanover together rather than make them quarrel with each other';[71] for if once they had made military preparations to attack one another, they might well join forces against France.

Croisy hoped for great results from Asfeld's negotiations in Dresden. Success 'could produce a great change in the affairs of Europe'.[72] Louis XIV now believed that the conclusion of a neutrality treaty with Saxony was 'the only way to maintain the

interests of his crown in Germany, which the bad faith of the
Court of Hanover had greatly endangered'.[73] But before Asfeld
could achieve anything in Dresden, Ernst August's negotiations in
Vienna had succeeded : on 22 March, 1692 Leopold had agreed
to bestow an electoral cap on the duke of Hanover, who in return
signed a treaty of perpetual union with the House of Austria.[74]

With the desertion of the duke of Hanover French plans for
a third party depended on a speedy alliance with the elector
of Saxony, and Croissy now ordered all French diplomats in the
Empire and the north to maintain close relations with Asfeld,[75]
who was to co-ordinate the negotiations to neutralise Germany.

Hanover's defection led to changes in Croissy's actual conception of the third party. The secretary of state now hoped for an
alliance between Sweden, Denmark-Norway, the elector of
Saxony, the bishop of Münster and the dukes of Wolfenbüttel
to oppose the ninth electorate and to work 'against anything for
the duke of Hanover's satisfaction and advantage'.[76] The third
party was henceforth to unite all princes hostile to the House
of Brunswick, his master Croissy having decided to exploit the
Empire's resentment against the advancement of Ernst August
and his policy in the Sachsen-Lauenburg succession issue.

The dukes of Wolfenbüttel were the first to oppose the creation
of the ninth electorate for Ernst August. Rudolf August of Wolfenbüttel and his brother Anton Ulrich were descended from Heinrich
von Danneberg, the elder son of Ernst of Lüneburg. The Wolfen-
büttels argued that the electoral title should have gone to them
as they represented the senior branch of the house of Brunswick-
Lüneburg. They found an ally in the king of Denmark; on 5
April 1692 they concluded a treaty of friendship with Christian
V,[77] who declared himself prepared to oppose the duke of Hanover's pretensions and even to move troops into north Germany.
This was welcomed by Louis XIV :[78] any diversion in Lower
Saxony would force the dukes of Brunswick-Lüneburg to keep
their troops at home and make it impossible for them to join
France's enemies in Flanders.

While a measure of success was thus gained, Asfeld's efforts
to bring the elector of Saxony into the third party failed. Croissy
no longer hoped for a formal alliance between the French king
and the elector of Saxony and authorised Asfeld to offer John
George IV 25,000 crowns a month in return for a verbal neutrality

convention. The secretary of state preferred such an agreement which would engage the elector personally, to Asfeld's proposals which envisaged bribing the elector of Saxony's ministers, especially Schöning, so that they might dissuade their master from sending troops to help France's enemies.[79] Asfeld's suggestion could not be followed up – even if Croissy had wanted to do so – for on the night of 22/23 June the emperor Leopold had the pro-French Schöning arrested at Teplitz in Bohemia where he was taking the waters.[80] Croissy at first hoped that Asfeld could use the affront the Saxon elector had suffered in the person of his chief adviser to inflame him against the emperor.[81] He was soon undeceived. The elimination of Schöning allowed a *rapprochement* between the elector of Saxony and the duke of Hanover, and on 29 July 1692 the Hanoverian minister, Grote, and John George IV's representative, Ilten, signed a defensive alliance between their masters.[82]

Even before this treaty was signed Asfeld, well aware of the negotiations in progress, had realised that France could achieve nothing at Dresden. Croissy, however, did not wish Asfeld to return to France as 'his retreat at this time . . . would ruin France's affairs there [in the Empire] entirely' and advised him to retire to Danish territory, i.e. to Sleswig.[83]

Croissy appreciated that Louis XIV had not succeeded in forming a German-led third party, which could effect the issue of the coming campaign. Having failed to force the emperor to make peace by raising the German princes against him, Louis XIV and Croissy shifted their attention to the north once more.[84] In the summer of 1692 the cards Croissy still held were the bellicose aspirations of Denmark; the bitter resentment of the dukes of Wolfenbüttel over the recent promotion of the junior branch of the house of Brunswick-Lüneburg; and the quarrel over the Sachsen-Lauenberg succession, which meant that almost all the north German princes were opposed to the dukes of Hanover and Celle. In these circumstances Croissy judged it worthwhile to strengthen the ties of friendship between France and Denmark which had been created by the treaty of 27 March 1691. He hoped to persuade Christian V to attack the duchy of Sachsen-Lauenberg. 'The test', he wrote to Asfeld, 'which would show His Majesty the sincerity of the intentions of those princes who want to ally with him, is the unambiguous determination to drive the troops of Celle and Hanover out of the territory of Sachsen-Lauenburg.'[85]

Martangis, who had expected that negotiations with Denmark would fall to him and not to Asfeld, asked permission to return to France for some months because of the poor state of his health, which had 'deteriorated owing to the Northern fogs'.[86] The secretary of state did not wish to leave the post of ambassador to the king of Denmark vacant at such a vital juncture and on 20 October 1692 appointed in his place François d'Usson, marquis de Bonrepaus, who had a brilliant career as intendant for the navy behind him.[87] Someone had to represent Louis XIV at Copenhagen until he arrived, and Croissy asked Asfeld – who had sought refuge at Rensburg – to fill the gap between the departing and the arriving ambassador.[88]

On 20 November 1692 Crossy let Asfeld know what Louis XIV was prepared to offer Christian V in return for action in north Germany. The Danes, however, dragged out the negotiations; Asfeld's ability and guile were well known and they hoped to persuade Bonrepaus to give better terms. In this they were mistaken, and on 11 March 1693 Bonrepaus and the king of Denmark's ministers, Plessen and Jessen, signed a treaty which had in fact been prepared by Asfeld.[89] In it Christian V pledged himself to attack Ratzeburg and drive the Celle and Hanoverian troops out of the duchy of Sachsen-Lauenburg with all possible speed.

On 13 August 1693 the Danish marshal Wedel ordered the bombardment of Ratzeberg, the most important fortress in the duchy of Sachsen-Lauenburg. Christian V came in person to hold a council of war and declared himself ready to cross the Elbe.[90] Such an extention of the conflict would have pleased Louis XIV. Yet it was not to be. All the belligerents backed down because of strong diplomatic intervention by the emperor, the elector of Brandenburg and the king of Sweden, who all wished to prevent an inter-German conflict. On 29 September 1693 Ernst August and Christian V signed a treaty whereby the Danish ruler withdrew from the duchy of Sachsen-Lauenberg and the duke of Hanover promised to demolish the fortifications of Ratzeburg.[91] Croissy's work lay in ruins: he had hoped to persuade the king of Denmark to offer the duchy of Sachsen-Lauenburg to the elector of Saxony as a reward for joining the third party.[92] He wrote to Asfeld (back in his Rensburg retreat after the signature of the Franco-Danish treaty of March) to explore all avenues which might lead to an alliance between Louis XIV and the elector of Saxony: 'The bad agreement just made by the Danish court with the Dukes of Celle and Hanover means that you can no longer use these means to engage the Elector of Saxony in a negotiation.'[93]

News from Saxony proved disappointing however. General Schöning had been set free, but when Asfeld tried to renew contact with him the Saxon minister refused: the consequences of being accommodating to France were all too fresh in his memory.[94] Asfeld admitted failure and on 23 December 1694 asked Louis XIV's permission to return to France.[95] This was granted and Asfeld, one of the most active representatives of French diplomacy in north Germany and Scandinavia from 1690 to 1694, now rejoined the French army, taking part in the remaining campaigns of the Nine Years War and in those of the War of the Spanish Succession.[96]

The third party thus never materialised and four years of intense diplomatic activity ended in failure. Louis XIV had spent a great deal of money to further the efforts of Croissy and his agents, the most important of them being Asfeld. An 'Account of the warrants payable to bearer drawn by Monseigneur de Croissy from 1 January 1690 till December 1693 last'[97] makes it possible for us to give details of the subsidies paid to the duke of Hanover, the bishop of Münster, the king of Denmark, the duke of Sachsen-Gotha and the dukes of Wolfenbüttel.

Recipients	amount given (in livres)		
	1691	1692	1693
The duke of Hanover	1,526,000	327,000	—
The bishop of Münster	938,000	562,500	722,500
The king of Denmark	555,000	712,500	789,500
The duke of Sachsen-Gotha	42,000	—	—
The dukes of Wolfenbüttel	—	—	80,000
Total	3,061,000	1,602,000	1,592,000

To these sums must be added the gratifications given to the ministers and advisers at these courts. In 1691, the year when the subsidies paid to the German princes and the king of Denmark came to more than three million livres, gratifications for the Hanoverian ministers amounted to 72,900 livres,[98] 45,000 livres were spent on those of the bishop of Münster,[99] and the king of Denmark's entourage received 50,000 livres.[100] These sums were apportioned according to the advice of Asfeld and Martangis. Louis XIV had his reputation as a generous prince to maintain and presents of money were paid to those ministers and advisers who played the most active part in promoting the treaties between their masters and the king of France. In addition Louis XIV paid pensions to foreign ministers who were considered by his envoys to be willing to defend France's interests in general and to watch over the fulfilment of treaties. Nils Bielke, the Swedish councillor, enjoyed a pension of 20,000 livres a year, while the sum of gratifications paid in Sweden amounted to 150,000 livres a year. The duke of Hanover's minister, Count von Platen, and the elector of Saxony's adviser, Schöning, each benefited annually by 18,000 livres from France.

The historian would obviously like to know how large a part of the French budget was made up by subsidies, gratifications and pensions. One way of assessing this is to look at the details of receipts for the year 1693 in Forbonnais' *Recherches et considerations sur les finances de la France depuis l'année 1595 jusqu'à l'année 1721*. The creation of four posts of 'refiners' in Lyons, to control the goldsmiths and the 'manufacture of gold braid' in the town, brought the state 600,000 livres.[101] This sum is almost equivalent to the total paid in subsidies to the bishop of Münster or to the king of Denmark in the same year. Let us take another example. The creation of twenty-six paymasters and as many controllers of the *rentes* on the *hôtel de ville* brought the royal finances the sum of 2,257,500 livres,[102] which amounts to about the same as the subsidies paid to the bishop of Münster over three years. One might therefore conclude that the subsidies paid by France between 1690 and 1693 were not an excessive part of the royal budget, were it not for the fact that the actual creation and sale of these offices were signs of the deterioration in France's financial position. The effects of the economic stagnation caused by the Nine Years War told heavily on all belligerents. France had to resort more than her enemies to such expedients as the sale of offices, recoinage and loans, so as to cope with the ever-growing military expense. Money was worth less: 'The 107 million in coin in the royal treasury in 1693 equalled in weight and precious metal content only 96 million in 1689.'[103]

In 1694 France had difficulty in paying the subsidies she owed to her allies, the king of Denmark and the bishop of Münster. To pay the prince-bishop, Croissy had to resort to substituting *rentes* on the *hôtel de ville* for ready cash, a solution suggested by Plettenberg's treasurer general, Arnold Gérard von Vintgens.[104] The Parisian banker, Christophe Crousseau, who between 1692 and 1695 was generally designated 'resident of various German princes to His Majesty',[105] was instructed to take up some *rentes* on the *hôtel de ville* in Vintgens' name.[106] From this time onwards we find frequent letters between the two men, and Brosseau also corresponded with Frischmann (the French diplomat accredited to Plettenberg) who frequently instructed him to act as his proxy in business dealings in Paris.[107]

The co-operation between Brosseau, Frischmann and Vintgens seems related to attempts to have French subsidies paid to the bishop of Münster for the year 1694, even though by this time all hope of forming a third party in Germany had gone. The prince-bishop had on 11 February 1693 joined the princes at Regensburg hostile to the creation of a ninth electorate. But some months later he declared that he no longer wanted to 'hear anything about a third party',[108] and he showed little enthusiasm for keeping to the letter of his engagements with Louis XIV. In 1694, for example, he sent the emperor a larger body of troops than his obligatory contingent. Despite this Croissy paid the subsidies, since Frischmann always insisted on the prince-bishop's continued goodwill towards France.[109]

Brousseau, Frischmann and Vintgens were undoubtedly interested in the maintenance of good relations between Louis XIV and the prince-bishop of Münster. Frischmann had helped Asfeld's efforts to create a third party and was most anxious to keep France's alliance with Plettenberg in being, an alliance which he had worked to maintain for more than four years and which by 1694 was the only surviving French alliance with a German prince. Brousseau represented the interests of several German princes in Paris and therefore had to try to maintain good relations between them and Louis XIV. As for Vintgens, he knew that he could only balance his master's budget with the help of

French subsidies. Their collusion permitted the prince-bishop
to hide the fact that he was evading the stipulations of the treaty
with Louis XIV, and in 1694 he consequently enjoyed the
250,000 crowns provided for in the alliance of 25 March 1691.
On 18 March 1695, however, the prince-bishop joined the anti-
French side openly, becoming a member of the 'Grand Alliance
of Vienna'.

If the subsidies paid to the bishop of Münster in 1694 had
no influence on his policy, it would seem desirable to check
whether the same is true of subsidies paid to the princes of
northern Europe by Louis XIV between 1690 and 1694. Is the
impression of failure which emerges from Asfeld's and even
Croissy's dispatches justified? The fact that the Vienna allies were
very worried about the negotiations for a third party points to a
different conclusion, and an examination of the correspondence
between William III and the Grand Pensionary Heinsuis has
proved illuminating.

In November 1693, for example, William wrote to Heinsius:
'I am terribly apprehensive about the creation of a third party
and I can hardly see what we can do to stop it.'[110] If we recall
that at this very time Croissy had almost given up hope of creating
a neutral bloc in Europe, this fear (which was often voiced in
William III's letters) is sufficient justification for Croissy's perse-
verance in trying to dissolve the Grand Alliance of Vienna.
Though French diplomacy failed to reach the goals it had set
itself, we can yet conclude that it disturbed its enemies seriously
enough to have been worthwhile.

Why did Louis XIV's attempts to set up a third party fail?
The years after the Peace of Nijmegen of 1678–9 proved a
decisive stage in the development of relations between Louis XIV
and the Empire. From this time onwards the German princes
began to look on the king of France as an enemy rather than as
a powerful neighbour and guarantor of the treaties of Westphalia.
The *Réunions* policy, which began in 1679, loosened the long-
standing ties of friendship between France and the majority of
the German princes. For the first time the French monarch's lust
for conquest affected areas outside the possessions of Spain: the
Empire was now under attack. In 1681 Louis XIV occupied
Strasbourg and, shortly after the Truce of Ratisbon, he fortified
several bridgeheads on Imperial territory, the principal one being

Mont-Royal at Trarbach on the Moselle. His action aroused a movement fiercely hostile to France in Germany; and hostility to Louis XIV was intensified by the grand monarch's persecution of the French Huguenots. Everything conspired to make the Imperial princes aware that they had interests in common totally opposed to those of their over-mighty neighbour.

The failure of attempts to build a neutral party in Germany can not, however, be explained fully by Louis XIV's territorial encroachments on the Empire and by the fear inspired by the power of the *Roi-Soleil*. We must also take account of changes within the Empire itself. Indeed, Louis XIV made the mistake of appearing particularly arrogant towards the Imperial princes and showing a lust for conquest at the very time when he was losing his ability to exert enough pressure on them to force them to follow his policies. The Empire's internal situation was undergoing rapid change. Louis XIV's post-1685 anti-Protestant stance prevented his supporting the Protestant German princes against the Catholic head of the House of Habsburg (as his predecessors had done since the beginning of the Reformation to further their own aims). But even if this had not been the case, by 1690 there was no hostility between Protestant and Catholic princes worth speaking of which he could exploit. The creation of the eighth electorate in 1648 had provoked religious passions since it threatened to destroy the balance between Catholic and Protestant electors. Nothing comparable happened in 1685 when the Catholic House of Neuburg inherited the Palatine electorate, although this succession brought the number of Catholic electors to five out of eight.

Another route along which the court of France had traditionally meddled in the Empire's internal affairs was also denied to Louis XIV. The kings of France had always posed as the defenders of 'German liberties'. It was ostensibly in defence of these liberties that Louis XIV in 1690 tried to raise the princes against the emperor by forming a third party. But this argument met with no response at the courts of these princes. The majority of them no longer acted as members of one body, the Empire, but as independent and absolute monarchs whose sole preoccupation was to extend their own domestic authority and – at times – their territory.

During the Nine Years War therefore Louis was constrained

to attempt the building of a neutral party in the Empire through the payment of subsidies. This is the reason why subsidies became one of the favourite weapons of contemporary French diplomacy. Louis XIV had no hesitation in dispensing large sums of money to keep the states of the north outside the conflict which had broken out in 1688. His plan failed not only because of Sweden's neutralist and Denmark's capricious attitudes; but even more, because of the caution of the German princes, who by then had hardly any political or religious interests impelling them towards an alliance with France. This explains why the major part of Asfeld's negotiations for a third party consisted of interminable discussions about the amount of subsidies to be paid by Louis XIV. The only result from a large expenditure of gold was the temporary immobilisation of part of the military potential at the emperor's disposal in Germany.

Yet, after his failure to end hostilities by the formation of a neutral party in northern Europe, Louis XIV was to succeed – by 'neutralising' Italy in 1696 – in forcing the Vienna allies to conclude peace in 1697–8.

NOTES

1 The Thirty Years War and the first wars of Louis XIV's reign provide many examples of French attempts to neutralise Germany under the aegis of a Scandinavian power; 1675 for example saw the search for a neutral bloc to bring together the elector of Bavaria, the duke of Hanover and the king of Sweden: H. Regelmeier, *Die Politischen Beziehungen der Fürsten Nordwest Deutschlands zu Frankreich und den Nordischen Seemächten in den Jahren 1674 bis 1676* (Hildesheim, 1908) p. 29.

2 'Memorial to serve as instructions for Baron d'Asfeld going on the King's service [to Stockholm]', 27 Nov 1689, Archives des Affaires Etrangères, Correspondance Politique, Suède, suppl. vol. 5, ff. 146–53.

3 On 12 October 1653 Queen Christina of Sweden had settled the Bidal family in north Germany, Pierre Bidal's title of baron being accompanied by the gift of the manors of Harsefeld in the duchy of Bremen and of Wildenbruch in Pomerania: J. Fayard, 'L'ascension sociale d'une famille de bourgeois parisiens au XVIIᵉ siècle: les Bidal d'Asfeld', *Bulletin de la Société de l'Histoire de Paris et de l'Ile-de-France* (1965) 83–109.

4 A.A.E., C.P., Hambourg, vol. 10, 18 Nov 1675, Madame Bidal to Pomponne.

5 Ibid., vol. 15, 16 Aug 1680, P. Bidal to Croissy.

6 Ibid., vol. 13, 11 Sep 1679, P. Bidal to Pomponne.
7 Ibid., vol. 4, 9 Oct 1671, P. Bidal to Pomponne.
8 Ibid., vol. supp. 5, f. 358.
9 Memorial cited above, note 2.
10 First draft of Baron d'Asfeld's instructions of 27 Nov 1689, A.A.E., C.P., Suède, suppl. vol. 5, f. 115.
11 Nils Bielke, governor-general of Swedish Pomerania from April 1687, had made several stops at Hamburg where he had got to know Asfeld's brother, the abbé Etienne Bidal, French resident in the city since 1682.
12 A.A.E., C.P., Suède, vol. 69, 21 Jan 1690, Asfeld to Croissy.
13 A. Stille, *Studier över Bengt Oxenstiernas Politiska System* (Upsala, 1947) p. 117 ff.
14 A.A.E., C.P., Suède, vol. 69, 26 Apr 1690, Asfeld to Croissy.
15 Knowing that his brother, Abbé Bidal, would soon have to leave Hamburg because of the hostilities between Louis XIV and the emperor, Asfeld chose a Swede, Charles Cantersten, former steward of Queen Christina and secretary of Olivekrans, to help Abbé Bidal's own secretary, Leclerc, to keep the French court informed and, above all, to send on to Versailles letters from the 'well-disposed' Swedish ministers. As Leclerc was arrested on the orders of the Imperial resident, Cantersten became the French government's only informant in Hamburg from July 1690 to February 1698, when the abbé Bidal again took up his post in Hamburg.
16 These negotiations were in the main concerned with attempts to force the king of Denmark to restore the duke of Holstein's rights, and followed on a Suedo-Hanoverian treaty of 1687, renewed in 1688 and also in 1689. The alliance achieved its objective when Christian V accepted the proposals of the mediators (the Maritime Powers as well as the dukes of Brunswick Lüneburg) at the Congress of Altona on 20 June 1689. There had, however, also been some discussion in Stockholm of transforming the alliance into one of mutual defence.
17 For the Sachsen-Lauenburg succession question see G. Schnath, *Geschichte Hannovers im Zeitalter der neunten Kur und der englischen Sukzession* (Hildesheim, 1938) p. 449; L. Laursen, *Danmark-Norges Traktater*, x: *1690–1693* (Copenhagen, 1933) pp. 566–609; G. Überhorts, *Der Sachsen-Lauenburgische Erbfolgestreit 1689–1693* (Berlin, 1915).
18 Schnath, *Geschichte Hannovers*, p. 524.
19 Ibid., p. 511.
20 A.A.E., C.P., Suède, vol. 69, 4 Mar 1690, Asfeld to Croissy.
21 Ibid., vol. 69, 15 Mar 1690, Asfeld to Croissy.
22 Copy of the letter from 'Platen, written in Hanover last March, to Veling, in reply to that written by him to M. Goeurs [Goertz] about the third party', enclosed with Asfeld to Croissy, 5 Apr 1690: A.A.E., C.P., Suède, vol. 69, f. 122.
23 Asfeld certainly regarded a close alliance between Charles XI and Ernst August as somewhat dangerous for France: 'I must not hide from you that once these two powers are united they might try to get

better conditions for Germany than those of the truce [of 1684], but it does not seem to me that we should be worried about this yet. . . . From all appearance if we achieve a union between them this will reawaken a desire for peace in the majority of the Imperial princes who are suffering from this war': A.A.E., C.P., Suède, vol. 69, 15 Mar 1690, Asfeld to Croissy.

24 Ibid., 20 Apr 1690, Croissy to Asfeld. From January 1690 Ballati had been telling Louis Verjus de Crécy, French ambassador at the Diet of Ratisbon, of Ernst August's wish to come to an agreement with Louis XIV: ibid., Munster, vol. 8, 31 Mar 1691, Verjus de Crécy to Croissy, f. 237.

25 Schnath, *Geschichte Hannovers*, p. 512.

26 Ernst August wished to put his relations with France on the same footing as before the opening of hostilities. By the terms of his treaty (for eight years) with Louis XIV, of 1 Nov 1687, signed by Gourville, the then French ambassador to the dukes of Brunswick-Lüneburg, the king of France was to pay the duke of Hanover, for the upkeep of 4500 men, 12,000 crowns a month in peacetime and 24,000 in case of war. The war which broke out between Louis XIV and the emperor in 1688 had prevented Ernst August from profiting from the monetary advantages of this alliance: Schnath, *Geschichte Hannovers*, p. 410.

27 A.A.E., C.P., Suède, vol. 69, 24 May 1690, Croissy to Asfeld.

28 Schnath, *Geschichte Hannovers*, p. 472.

29 For the full text of the treaty see ibid., pp. 761–9.

30 The treaty assured the neutrality of Ernst August, who was to keep 13,000 troops in his territories; for these he was to receive subsidies of 400,000 crowns a year as well as 36,000 crowns arrears.

31 'Memorial to serve as instructions for Baron d'Asfeld, colonel of a cavalry regiment, on the King's service', 10 Dec 1690, A.A.E., C.P., Hambourg, vol. 19, ff. 299–305.

32 Ibid., f. 192.

33 When Marquis de Béthune in November 1691 was appointed French ambassador to Sweden, Croissy asked Asfeld to draw up a memorial on the state of Franco-Swedish relations: A.A.E., C.P., Brunswick, vol. 29, memorial enclosed with Asfeld to Croissy, 11 Nov 1691, ff. 185–204.

34 Ibid., f. 192.

35 F. F. Carlson, *Geschichte Schwedens*, v (Gotha, 1875) p. 196.

36 Such a sum allows us to put into perspective gratifications which were normally given to the ministers of foreign rulers after the conclusion of a treaty and which were in fact only presents. It should be stressed that Bielke at this time was also much courted by the emperor: A.A.E., C.P., Hambourg, vol. 19, 9 Nov 1691, Croissy to Asfeld.

37 Bengt Oxenstierna was in fact receiving money from the Vienna allies but only 8000 crowns a year: O. Klopp, *Der Fall des Hauses Stuart und die Succession des Hauses Hannover in Gross-Britannien und Irland im Zusammenhang der europäischen Angelegenheiten von 1660–1714*, v (Vienna, 1877) p. 201. France tried to discover what he was

getting from the allies and Asfeld was ordered to offer Oxenstierna 100,000 crowns as well as a pension of 20,000 crowns a year if he succeeded in forming the 'third party' and in this way re-establishing peace: A.A.E., C.P., Suède, vol. 59, 15 May 1690, Croissy to B. Bidal. For further information on Oxenstierna's receipt of large sums of money from William III see Ragnhild Hatton, 'Gratifications and Foreign Policy: Anglo-French Rivalry in Sweden during the Nine Years War', in Ragnhild Hatton and J. S. Bromley (eds), *William III and Louis XIV. Essays by and for Mark A. Thomson* (Liverpool, Toronto, 1968) pp. 68–94, especially 76–7.

38 Stille, *Oxenstiernas Politiska System*, p. 144.

39 Carlson stressed the importance of Asfeld's negotiations in Stockholm: Carlson, *Geschichte Schwedens*, v, p. 409. Stille demonstrated, with reason, that Asfeld's 'friends' could not create a pro-French party at Charles XI's court, and concluded that Asfeld himself did not control the situation in Stockholm, but as a skilful diplomat remained content to take advantage of events: Stille, *Oxenstiernas Politiska System*, p. 144.

40 Schnath, *Geschichte Hannovers*, p. 528.

41 F. Scharlach, *Fürstbischof Friedrich Christian von Plettenberg und die münsterische Politik im Koalitionskriege* (Münster, 1923) p. 29.

42 Copy of the treaty between the bishop of Münster and the duke of Hanover, A.A.E., C.P., Brunswick, vol. suppl. 2, f. 224.

43 Jean-Casimir Frischmann was the son of Jean Frischmann, French resident at Strasbourg from 1656 to 1675 and a well-known publicist: P. Wentzcke, *Johann Frischmann, ein Publizist des 17 Jahrhunderts* (Strasbourg, 1904). He became secretary to the French ambassador at Ratisbon, Count Verjus de Crécy, in 1681: B. Auerbach, *La France et le Saint Empire Romain Germanique depuis la paix de Westphalie jusqu'à la Révolution Française* (Paris, 1912) p. 234. He bought the estate of Rançonnières near Bourbonne-les-Bains on 18 July 1687: Archives Nationales, Minutier central, étude cvii, liasse 259, 14 June 1692.

44 From October 1689 Plettenberg had shown willingness to negotiate with Louis XIV through Verjus de Crécy, and his brother, Father Antoine Verjus: A.A.E., C.P., Munster, vol. 8, 31 Mar 1691, Verjus de Crécy to Croissy, f. 237. Croissy did not respond immediately to these overtures since Jean-Casimir Frischmann was absent from Münster (on a mission to the elector of Saxony, which incidentally proved unsuccessful). On his return Croissy charged him with testing the bishop's intentions. Full power to negotiate was sent by Croissy on 1 February 1691 and was accompanied by orders to be guided by Asfeld: 'although I have sent you the powers with the said treaty project, as His Majesty has previously fully informed M. de Vaupré [i.e. Asfeld] of his intentions on this subject and as he has complete confidence in him, you should do and promote nothing except what he stipulates verbally or in letters signed in the name of Vaupré': ibid., vol. 8, 15 Feb 1691, Croissy to Frischmann.

45 For details see A.A.E., C.P., Brunswick, vol. 27, 1 Mar 1691, Croissy to Asfeld.

46   Ibid., Munster, vol. 8, 5 Mar 1691, Croissy to Frischmann.

47   Ibid., Brunswick, vol. 27, 1 Apr 1691, Asfeld to Croissy: the reason
      for this delay was unease at French troop movements towards the
      Moselle.

48   The chapter was suggested as Louis XIV had not recognised the new
      archbishop-elector of Cologne, Joseph Clement of Bavaria, whose
      appointment by papal brief had been one of the causes for the opening
      of hostilities between France and the Empire in 1688.

49   A.A.E., C.P., Munster, vol. 8, 3 May 1691, Croissy to Asfeld.

50   Ibid., Brunswick, vol. 27, 26 Apr 1691, Croissy to Asfeld.

51   The duke had on 23 March 1691 concluded a treaty with Ernst August
      by which the two rulers promised to act jointly to persuade Louis XIV
      and the emperor to make peace: Schnath, *Geschichte Hannovers*, p. 533.

52   Copy of the treaty between Louis XIV and the duke of Sachsen-
      Gotha: A.A.E., C.P., Saxe, vol. 14, f. 162; Count Otto Frederick von
      Moltke signed on the duke's behalf.

53   Ibid., Brunswick, vol. 27, 26 Apr 1691, Croissy to Asfeld.

54   Ibid., Danemark, vol. 37, 1 Mar 1691, Croissy to Martangis.

55   'Contents of the separate articles drawn up between the Duke of
      Hanover and M. Bielke', ibid., Brunswick, vol. 27, f. 529.

56   Ibid., Suède, vol. 69, 15 Mar 1690, Asfeld to Croissy.

57   Ibid., Brunswick, vol. 27, 7 June 1691, Croissy to Asfeld.

58   Ibid., 20 Apr 1691, Croissy to Asfeld.

59   Ibid., vol. 28, 8 June 1691, Asfeld to Croissy.

60   Ibid., 21 June 1691, Croissy to Asfeld.

61   Ibid., 5 July 1691, Croissy to Asfeld.

62   Schnath, *Geschichte Hannovers*, p. 542.

63   A.A.E., C.P., Brunswick, vol. 28, 2 Aug 1691, Croissy to Asfeld.

64   Ibid., vol. 31, 10 Aug 1691, Asfeld to Croissy.

65   Ibid., vol. 28, 20 Sep 1691, Croissy to Asfeld.

66   Ibid., 16 April 1691, Asfeld to Croissy.

67   Before becoming adviser to the elector of Saxony, Schöning had been
      in the elector of Brandenburg's service: P. Haake, *Generalfeldmarschall
      Hans Adam von Schöning* (Berlin, 1910) p. 58.

68   'Copy of a letter from M. Jordan, lieutenant-colonel in the service of
      the King of Sweden, Dresden, 18 December 1691', enclosed in letter
      to Asfeld: A.A.E., C.P., Brunswick, vol. 29, f. 395.

69   Ibid., vol. 29, 9 Nov 1691, Croissy to Asfeld.

70   Ibid., 11 Oct 1691, Croissy to Asfeld.

71   Ibid., Saxe, vol. 14A, 24 Jan 1692, Croissy to Asfeld.

72   Ibid., 21 Feb 1692, Croissy to Asfeld.

73   Schnath, *Geschichte Hannovers*, p. 605.

74   A.A.E., C.P., Danemark, vol. 38, 13 Mar 1692, Croissy to Martangis;
      ibid., Suède, vol. 71, 16 Mar 1692, Croissy to Marquis Béthune.

75   Ibid., Saxe, vol. 15, 23 June 1692, Croissy to Asfeld.

76   L. Laursen, *Danmark-Norges Traktater 1523–1750*, IX: *1690–1699*
      (Copenhagen, 1933) p. 260.

77   A.A.E., C.P., Saxe, vol. 15, 17 June 1692, Croissy to Asfeld.

78 Ibid., 26 June 1692, Croissy to Asfeld.
79 Haake, *Hans Adam von Schöning*, p. 103.
80 A.A.E., C.P., Saxe, vol. 15, 21 July 1692, Croissy to Asfeld.
81 Schnath, *Geschichte Hannovers*, p. 627.
82 A.A.E., C.P., Saxe, vol. 15, 21 July 1692, Croissy to Asfeld.
83 Ibid., 30 July 1692, Croissy to Asfeld.
84 Ibid., Brunswick, vol. 32, 25 Sep 1692, Croissy to Asfeld.
85 Ibid., Danemark, vol. 38, 3 Sep 1692, Martangis to Croissy.
86 A. Geffroy (ed.), *Recueil des Instructions données aux Ambassadeurs*, vol. xiii, *Danemark* (Paris, 1895) p. 73.
87 A.A.E., C.P., Danemark, vol. 38, 13 Nov 1692, Croissy to Martangis.
88 Laursen, *Danmark-Norges Traktater*, ix, pp. 439, 441.
89 Ibid., p. 603.
90 Ibid., p. 629. The Sachsen-Lauenburg question agitated north Germany for a long time. The House of Brunswick had taken advantage of the emperor's struggles against the Turks and Louis XIV to put troops into the duchy. This was much resented by the elector of Saxony who, however, on being elected king of Poland in 1697 ceded his rights to the succession in Sachsen-Lauenburg to the duke of Hanover. The affair was finally settled by an Imperial decision in favour of the House of Brunswick in 1716: B. Erdmannsdörffer, *Deutsche Geschichte vom westfälischen Frieden bis zum Regierungsantritt Friedrichs des Grossen 1648–1740*, ii (Berlin, 1893) p. 51.
91 A.A.E., C.P., Brunswick, vol. 32, 18 Dec 1692, Croissy to Asfeld.
92 Ibid., Petites principautés, vol. 30, 5 Nov 1693, Croissy to Asfeld.
93 Ibid., 23 Dec 1694, Asfeld to Croissy.
94 Ibid.
95 Promoted marshal on 3 January 1696, he fought in Italy and in Germany during the War of the Spanish Succession. He was decorated with the croix de Saint-Louis on 20 January 1703 and died in July 1715: Archives de la Seine, DC 6, 213, f. 4.
96 A.A.E., Mémoires et Documents, France, vol. 303, ff. 166–9.
97 The 72,000 livres were divided as follows: 15,000 to Count Platen, 15,000 to his wife, 15,000 each for Grote and Balati, 6000 for Councillor Buch and 6900 for three secretaries: 'State of the gratifications made by the King to the ministers of the courts of Hanover, Münster and Saxe-Gotha on M. d'Asfeldt's advice', A.A.E., C.P., Allemagne, vol. 324, f. 262.
98 Dean Schmising received 21,000 livres: ibid.
99 '2,000 ducats to M. Guldenleu [Gyldenlöve], 2,000 ducats to Count Reventclau [Reventlow], 2,000 ducats to M. Youl [Juel], 2,000 ducats to M. Jessen, 1,759 to the said M. Jessen for the clerks, the total coming to 50,000 livres': ibid. For these Danish statesmen, see List of Persons.
100 [—] Forbonnais, *Recherches et Considérations sur les Finances de la France depuis l'Année 1595 jusqu'à l'Année 1721*, ii (Basle, 1758) p. 72.
101 Ibid., p. 70.
102 Ibid., p. 72.

103 See A.A.E., C.P., Munster, vol. 13, 21 July 1694, Frischmann to Croissy for this suggestion.

104 Archives Nationales, Minutier central, étude CVII, liasses 264, 265 ff. Brosseau had been agent for the dukes of Brunswick since 1673: L. Bittner and L. Gross, *Repertorium der diplomatischen Vertreter aller Länder seit dem westfälischen Frieden* (Berlin, 1936) p. 73. During the Nine Years War he also became agent for the bishop of Münster. On 29 September 1689 Louis XIV also agreed that he should represent the Hanseatic towns at his court: A.A.E., C.P., Hambourg, vol. 18, 29 Sep 1689, Croissy to Abbé Etienne Bidal. Brosseau played a similar role in respect of the dukes of Hanover and the bishop of Münster as the Formont brothers did on behalf of the Great Elector of Brandenburg. He did not conduct important negotiations between Louis XIV and the princes for whom he acted as an agent, but was satisfied with looking after their day-to-day political business and especially their financial interests. In particular he was charged with sending on Louis XIV's money supplies to them: A.A.E., C.P., Brunswick, vol. suppl. 2, ff. 253–61. Brosseau in 1691 lived in the Rue Geoffroy-Lasneir and in 1693 in the Rue du Parc-Royal in the parish of Saint-Gervais.

105 On 20 September 1694 Brosseau took up 186,030 livres of *rentes* for Vintgens at the *hôtel de ville* in four transactions: Archives Nationales, Minutier central, étude CVII, liasse 373.

106 Ibid., liasse 258, 16 Apr 1692 and liasse 222, 8 Mar 1695.

107 H. Weber, 'Frankreich, Münster und Kurtrier, 1692–1693', in K. Repgen and S. Skalweit (eds), *Spiegel der Geschichte, Festgabe für Max Braubach zum 10 April 1964* (Münster, 1964) p. 547.

108 A.A.E., C.P., Munster, vol. 13, 24 June 1694, Croissy to Frischmann.

109 Sirtema de Grovestins, *Guillaume III et Louis XIV. Histoire des luttes et rivalités politiques entre les puissances maritimes et la France dans la dernière moitié du XVIIᵉ siècle* (Saint-Germain-en-Laye, 1868) p. 414.

110 G. Pagès, *Louis XIV et l'Allemagne*, Sorbonne lectures no. 5 (Paris, 1937) p. 183.

10 The End of an Era: Louis XIV and Victor Amadeus II*

RALPH D. HANDEN

Historians have, in recent years, emphasised the importance of the decade which began in 1680 for the creation of a new pattern of the inter-state relations in Europe, a pattern consecrated by the treaties of Ryswick and Utrecht and characterised by the expression 'balance of power'. For it was in the 1680s that the unparalleled victories of the emperor Leopold I in the east, coupled with a succession of ill-advised political and military adventures on the part of Louis XIV, lost for France the hegemony she had exercised over European affairs since the Peace of the Pyrenees. Although neither Louis XIV nor his advisers seem to have been fully aware at the time of the fundamental change which was transpiring in the structure of international relations, the effects of that change were already manifest in the events of the Nine Years War (1688–97) and its aftermath. Perhaps nowhere are these effects more strikingly revealed than in the reversal of traditional French policy in Italy during that war, a reversal nowhere better demonstrated than by the dramatic alteration of France's relationship with the House of Savoy.[1]

The dukes of Savoy were active, if minor, participants in the dynastic struggles which engaged the states of Europe in the sixteenth and seventeenth centuries. As rulers of the principality of Piedmont, the county of Nice, and the duchy of Savoy, the descendants of Humbert the Whitehanded found themselves in control of strategically important valleys and passes and were caught up in the struggles between the Habsburg rulers of Spain and Austria and the Valois and Bourbon kings of France for

* Specially commissioned for this volume.

control of Italy.² Since the late fifteenth century, from the time
of the struggle between Louis XI and Charles the Bold, the dukes
of Savoy had been forced into the role of unwilling allies of the
French crown. From the time of the Italian invasions of Charles
VIII and Louis XII until the accession of Duke Emmanuel-
Philibert (1553–80), the court of Turin was a virtual prisoner
to French interests, its territories annexed one by one to the House
of Valois. By the Treaty of Cateau-Cambrésis in 1559, however,
Emmanuel-Philibert regained his lost territories and devoted himself to the task of rebuilding his state.

His son and successor, Charles Emmanuel I (1580–1630),
espoused the cause of the league during the French civil wars.
Deserted by Spain at the Peace of Vervins, he was obliged to
accept a *détente* with Henri IV at Lyons (1601) and at Brussol
(1610). By the first treaty, each party renounced ambitions on the
other's side of the Alps; by the second, Charles Emmanuel was
to receive the duchy of Milan in exchange for Savoy upon a
successful conclusion of Henri IV's projected war against Spain.³
Turin sought in vain to assert its independence of Paris during
the War of the Mantuan Succession (1627–31) by opposing
the claims of the French candidate, Charles, duke of Nevers.
However, the public and secret treaties signed at Cherasco in
1631 sealed the fate of Savoy until the end of the century:
Victor Amadeus I was forced to cede Pignerol and the valley
of Perosa to France and Savoy became once again the reluctant
ally of the Bourbon monarchy.

The Franco-Savoyard alliance was cemented in the following
years by the marriages of Victor Amadeus I to Christine of
France, sister of Louis XIII, and of his successor, Duke Charles-
Emmanuel II, to Mademoiselle de Valois and, upon her death,
to Jeanne Baptiste de Savoy-Nemours. Upon Charles-Emmanuel's
death in 1675, this imperious lady ruled as regent for her young
son, Victor Amadeus II.

From the Peace of the Pyrenees (1659) France cautiously
pursued a policy of negotiation and attempted alliance with the
minor states of Italy; her cultivation of the court of Turin was
but one aspect of a programme designed ultimately to neutralise
the power of Habsburg Spain in the peninsula. Louis XIV successfully negotiated the purchase of the important town and
fortress of Casale from the dissolute duke of Mantua in 1681,

securing thereby a stronghold at the very gates of the Milanese. However, the king and his ministers failed to reckon with the very real fear of French power on the part of the independent states of Italy. As Jean Meuvret has made clear, Venice, Tuscany, Genoa, Parma and Modena preferred the reality of decaying Spanish Habsburg power to the prospect of French Bourbon hegemony over the peninsula.[4] The French illusion that the Italians desired Louis XIV's intervention in the peninsula was, however, not finally shaken until the events of the War of the Spanish Succession.

The aggressive policies of the French in Italy, symbolised by the purchase of Casale and the bombardment of Genoa (1684), brought a renewal of the Franco-Savoyard alliance in 1682 which included the forced marriage of Victor Amadeus II to Anne-Marie d'Orléans, niece of Louis XIV. Although the young prince successfully deposed his mother and assumed the reins of government in 1685,[5] he was soon obliged by Louis XIV to allow Catinat's army to campaign against the Savoyard Waldensians. Furious at this interference, Victor Amadeus began secret negotiations with representatives of Spain, the emperor and Max Emmanuel of Bavaria. After the outbreak of war between France and the allied powers in 1689, new French demands on the Piedmontese court, including delivery of the citadel of Turin to Catinat, provoked the duke into signing treaties of alliance with Spain and Austria (3 and 4 June 1690).[6]

Much to the dismay of Victor Amadeus, the French had the best of the campaign of 1690. On 18 August, Catinat won a decisive victory at Staffarda; in the following weeks the whole of Savoy, except the fortress of Montmélian, fell to the French. Finally, in November, Catinat captured the important Alpine fortress of Susa in western Piedmont. It was at this juncture that the duke, having reason to doubt the ability of his allies to defend his dominions, began to explore the possibility of a negotiated settlement with Louis. In December, Catinat told Louvois that Victor Amadeus was willing to break with his allies, provided the French would guarantee the integrity of his territories and, further, that a secret three-month truce be signed between Turin and Versailles. Suspecting a ruse, Louis' minister of war, Louvois, replied that Catinat should agree to no more than a four-week suspension of arms. As a test of the duke's sincerity, Louvois

I

demanded that French troops be allowed to occupy the towns of Verrua, Saluzzo, Villefranche and Carmagnola, as well as the fortress of Montmélian, until the signing of a general peace. Louis XIV, for his part, would restore the duchy of Savoy to the duke immediately and would consent to the neutralisation of Italy until the general peace.[7] Victor Amadeus refused the French offer and negotiations were broken off. After the fall of Nice to the French on 6 April 1691, the duke tried to reopen talks with Versailles; but when French occupation of Nice was made a precondition for any agreement, he withdrew.[8]

Given Catinat's victories during the first year of hostilities, the toughness of French demands is understandable. It is surprising, however, that Louis XIV and his ministers should assume that Victor Amadeus would find their proposals sufficiently attractive to break with his allies. Something more serious than the loss of his territories west of the Alps, or something more attractive than the restitution of the *status quo ante*, would be required to tempt the duke into reconciliation with France.

In July 1691 Louvois died. Not only was the king from henceforth to exercise a dominant role in the formation of military policy, but the removal of Louvois from the scene also meant a more moderate direction in the future for French diplomacy.[9] It is perhaps due in part to the pacific influence of the marquis de Pomponne, who at this time was readmitted to the *conseil d'en haut*, that Versailles became progressively more generous in the terms it offered the duke of Savoy. However that may be, it is certain that from this date the correspondence relating to Savoy multiplies considerably in the archives of the *Ministère des Affaires Etrangères*, and that *mémoires* in the crabbed hand of Colbert de Croissy, secretary of state for foreign affairs, begin to appear with increasing frequency.[10]

In September 1691 Louis sent the comte de Rébenac on a secret mission to Italy to attempt a union of the independent states in a league directed against the House of Austria. Rébenac was, in addition, to approach the elector of Bavaria and the duke of Savoy in the hope of detaching them from the Grand Alliance.[11] Although he failed in the wider aspect of his mission, Rébenac did succeed in signing secret alliances with the dukes of Parma, Modena and Mantua and with the grand duke of Tuscany. His work bore fruit in the autumn of 1696, when, after

the defection of Victor Amadeus from the Grand Alliance, Catinat's troops swept virtually unopposed to the gates of the Milanese.

Before that event lay years of frustrating negotiations between
Turin and Versailles. Discussions were reopened early in 1692
when the marquis de Chamlay was sent to Pignerol at the request of the duke of Savoy. Chamlay brought more generous
terms with him than those put forward in the previous year:
the restoration of the duke's territories upon the signing of a
treaty, except for the fortresses of Nice, Villefranche, Montmélian
and Susa; Casale to be occupied by Swiss and Venetian troops
until the general peace; an indemnification of the duke for the
cost of the war; and, finally, in the event of the death of the king
of Spain, Louis XIV's promise to assist Victor Amadeus to gain
possession of the Milanese.[12]

The proposal regarding the duchy of Milan was, of course, a
resurrection of an idea expressed already in the Treaty of Brussol
of 1610. As a promise it cost the French nothing, but it was
meant to serve as a bait to draw the duke out of the Grand
Alliance. Chamlay's terms did not, however, offer the solid advantages – particularly with regard to the future of Casale and
Pignerol – which the duke hoped for and at the end of February
negotiations were suspended.

The failure of Chamlay's mission was particularly disappointing to the French, because Louis XIV had for some time been
pursuing a policy of reconciliation with the papacy, designed both
to heal the religious wounds of the 1680s and to provide France
with a strong base for anti-Habsburg support in Italy.[13] Once
convinced of the sincerity of France's desire for the neutralisation
of Italy, Innocent XII's representatives began to work for the
cause of peace. Unfortunately, the papal emissaries found slight
hearing in the courts to which they were sent; indeed, Victor
Amadeus used the occasion to reaffirm his allegiance to the Grand
Alliance in positive terms. Louis XIV, piqued at the duke's
behaviour, published a full account of the secret negotiations
between Chamlay and the court of Turin. Although disclosure
of the duke's dealings with the enemy confirmed the emperor's
distrust of his erstwhile ally, William III still believed in Victor
Amadeus's good intentions.[14]

In August 1692 the armies of the duke of Savoy made a

dramatic incursion into Dauphiné, capturing Embrun and Gap.
Although these victories proved short-lived, they demonstrated
the state of the war : that of a stalemate in which either side
might win battles but neither was capable of winning the war.
In this respect, the war in Italy was of a piece with the war as a
whole; it was becoming clear that France was unable to pursue
a multiple-front war to a victorious conclusion. It is therefore
not surprising that early in 1693 Louis XIV and his ministers
began seriously to explore ways of breaking up the Grand Alliance that they might end the war on at least one front. As it
happened, the duke of Savoy became the key figure in these
French efforts.

Before Versailles' wooing of Victor Amadeus could begin, an
event occurred which caused great concern in Vienna and Versailles. Victor Amadeus, in the hour of his victories in Dauphiné,
had been stricken with smallpox. His illness lasted into the winter
and spring of 1693. The excitement and alarm occasioned by his
sickness was due to the fact that the duke had no male heirs; in
the event of his death the succession would pass to his cousin, the
prince of Carignano, the leader of the pro-Habsburg party in
Turin. In the event of the death of Carignano and his infant son,
the crown of Savoy would pass to the comte de Soissons, brother
of Eugène of Savoy.[15] Reports reached Versailles that if Victor
Amadeus died the emperor planned to seize the ducal family
and procure the succession for Carignano's son, under the tutel-
age of Eugène. Fortunately for the French, the duke slowly
began to recover for his illness, thus ending the immediate threat
of a pro-Habsburg *coup* in Turin.[16]

Meanwhile, negotiations between Versailles and Turin were
renewed in February 1693 when the comte de Tessé, the military
commander at Pignerol, was visited by an agent of Victor
Amadeus named Gropello. In a *mémoire* of 8 February, Colbert
de Croissy discussed at length the prospect which now opened.
Croissy believed that Victor Amadeus was genuinely interested
in an accommodation with France. It would still have to be discovered, however, just how far he was willing to go to achieve
the neutrality of Italy and what price he would demand for a
change in alliances. For the moment, the minister continued,
France could offer to place the captured fortresses in Nice and
Savoy in neutral hands until the general peace; as an added

boon, the marriage of the duke's elder daughter, Maria-Adélaïde, to the duke of Burgundy might be proposed. The king accepted Croissy's plan and it was agreed that Maria-Adélaïde and the young son of the prince of Carignano were to be invited to France to serve as pledges for the duke's good faith.[17]

Victor Amadeus at first consented to give the hostages demanded but insisted in return on an immediate restitution of his lost fortresses.[18] When this demand was rejected by the French, he proposed that the return of the fortresses take place upon the evacuation of his territories by the Allies, and that hostages be dispensed with.[19] Louis XIV, not yet desperate enough to risk sacrificing the fortresses until peace was clearly in sight, turned a deaf ear to this proposal. Furthermore, since an Austrian *coup* in Turin was feared in France, the king hoped, with the princess and young Carignano in his possession, to ensure the duke's loyalty and at the same time to prevent Imperial control of the House of Savoy. Over these two principal issues – the return of the fortresses and the question of hostages – the two sides had reached a stalemate by the spring of 1693.

During the summer both attempted to break out by force from the *impasse* which they had reached at the negotiating table. Victor Amadeus struck first, moving at the head of an allied army against Pignerol. Although the siege of Pignerol lasted, with interruptions, until September, the allies proved unable to take the town : when threatened by the advance of a reinforced army under Marshal Catinat, they withdrew. Ignoring Prince Eugène's advice that the allied force fall back to a defensive line near Turin, Victor Amadeus chose to risk battle with Catinat at Marsaglia. There on 4 October Catinat won the most striking victory of his career.

Louis XIV's reaction to Marsaglia was unambiguous. He clearly expected that Victor Amadeus would now be ready to treat seriously.[20] In the following weeks, however, it became clear that the French were not in a position to follow up their success. Catinat's inability to capitalise on his victory was due not so much to the marshal's extreme caution, but to a fact already noted : that while Louis XIV was able to sustain a war on each of his frontiers, he was unable to press a momentary advantage (such as Marsaglia) on any front to a favourable conclusion. What made matters worse, the year 1693 was an extremely

difficult one for the people of France. The harvest of 1692 had
been disastrous, that of 1693 promised to be no better. High
prices, shortages, famine, disease and death struck the French with
frightful desolation. It is not surprising that under such circumstances Louis XIV was unable to benefit from his battlefield
successes of the year (Neerwinden, Charleroi, Heidelberg, Marsaglia). It was clearer than ever that France could not hope to
achieve a quick end to the war by military means alone.[21]

With these facts in mind, it is understandable that in Mark
Thomson's phrase 'the year 1693 witnessed what we should now
call a peace offensive on the part of France'.[22] Innocent XII
renewed his efforts at Vienna, Madrid and The Hague to mediate
a peace, although with little success. More promising was the
renewal of talks between Tessé and Gropello shortly after the
battle of Marsaglia. In November Tessé travelled secretly to Turin
for conferences with the duke. Some progress was made in that
Victor Amadeus promised to take the field with the French
if the Allies did not agree to the neutrality of Italy. On the
other hand, while the duke consented to send Marie-Adélaïde to
France as soon as the marriage contract was signed, he stead-
fastly refused to send the young Carignano as a hostage.[23] Victor
Amadeus obviously feared a French *coup* in Turin as much as
Louis XIV did an Austrian seizure of power.

The French response to Victor Amadeus's proposals was embodied in two *projets de traité*. The first provided for the marriage
of Marie-Adélaïde and the duke of Burgundy. Louis XIV also
agreed to treat the duke's ambassadors as those of crowned
heads and promised him an indemnity of two million livres for
loss of revenues from his lands during the war. Since the young
Carignano would not be given in hostage, Versailles promised
restoration of land and fortresses only after the complete evacuation of German troops from Italy. The second *projet* provided
for joint Franco-Savoyard action against the Allies if they refused
a separate peace for Italy. Conquests made in the Milanese in
this event were to be divided though, if the king of Spain died
before the end of the war, Louis XIV promised to support Amadeus's claim to the whole of the Milanese. Once again the prospect of territorial aggrandisement at the expense of Milan was
an important part of the proposed Franco-Savoyard *détente*.[24]

The slender hope of acquiring the Milanese was not in itself sufficient to bring the duke into the French camp. The French demand that the duke's lands be restored to him only upon the withdrawal of the Germans from Italy was justified, given his demonstrable unreliability. Nevertheless, Victor Amadeus found the French proposals entirely unacceptable. He had hoped to secure additional benefits from the French, either Casale or Pignerol. A silence of more than a year's duration was his only response to the French proposals.

Meanwhile, he was active on other diplomatic fronts. During his conversations with Tessé at the end of 1693, he had promised to send his trusted adviser, the abbé Grimani, to Vienna.[25] Grimani, so Tessé had been told, was to inform the emperor of the French offers and request his consent to the neutrality of Italy. True to his word, Victor Amadeus sent the abbé to the Austrian capital – not, however, to plead for peace in Italy. Indeed, Grimani was instructed to request additional men and money for the war in Italy, to press for a marriage between Marie-Adélaïde and the young archduke Joseph, Leopold's elder son. Leopold, aware of the *double jeu* of the duke, informed Louis XIV of the true nature of Grimani's mission to Vienna, hoping to embarrass Victor Amadeus and disrupt his negotiations with France.

Rebuffed by the emperor and unable to extract the gains he desired from Versailles, the duke of Savoy temporised for the remainder of 1694. As a gesture of goodwill to the French, he entered into an unwritten agreement with Catinat and Tessé to maintain the *status quo* that summer between the opposing armies. The campaign of 1694 was, as a result, considerably less intense than that of the previous year. Prince Eugène did lay siege to Casale, but with the first snow the siege was lifted and the Imperial troops retired to winter quarters. A blockade of the town was, however, maintained throughout the winter. Louis XIV, realising that Victor Amadeus's connivance made the blockade possible, ordered Tessé to suspend all communications with the court of Turin.

The defensive posture of the French in Italy was maintained also on the Rhine and in the Low Countries during 1694. The serious financial and economic condition of the country and the diminishing prospects for a decisive military solution to the war had, in the meantime, moved Louis XIV to renew his peace

overtures in other European courts. In Stockholm, Munich,
Vienna, Rome and The Hague, French agents explored means
of breaking up the Grand Alliance and bringing the war to a
conclusion, albeit with little success.[26]

Meanwhile, at Versailles, one voice advocated a final, all-out
assault on the Italian front. The comte de Saint-Maiole, an
adviser to the foreign office on Italian affairs, believed that Italy
was the logical place to end the war. It could be done, he
affirmed in a series of *mémoires* addressed to the king,[27] by landing a large seaborne force on Genoan territory as soon as the
allegiance of the princes of Italy had been secured. With their
support the French army would be able either to isolate the duke
of Savoy and force him to sue for peace or to inflict such losses
upon the Imperial troops that the emperor himself would come
to terms. Saint-Maiole's plan suffered from two serious flaws.
First, it had become obvious to everyone (except perhaps Saint-
Maiole) that Louis XIV was unable to launch a full-scale offensive against the enemy on any front. In Italy as elsewhere, both
sides were exhausted: to the consternation of both sides, a military stalemate had been reached everywhere. Secondly, Saint-
Maiole had misread the situation; there was little enthusiasm in
the Italian states for a French invasion of their territories. For
one thing, the princes had good reason to doubt the ability of
Louis XIV to carry off successfully an offensive of such magnitude. Whatever impression Catinat's victory at Marsaglia may
have made on Italian observers had faded with the passing
months. Furthermore, as we have seen, he was incorrect in stat-
ing that the princes would welcome French troops as the 'liber-
ators of Italy'. Indeed, if a choice had to be made between
Bourbon and Habsburg overlordship, the Habsburgs would win
since the inefficient but benign rule of the latter was clearly to
be preferred to the more demanding rule of the French.[28]

While Saint-Maiole was building his castles in the air, another
commentator was drawing painful lessons from the recent past.
In an unsigned *mémoire* entitled 'Réflexions sur la Rupture de
Savoye' he asserted that France's 'previous ministers' had not
paid sufficient attention to the feelings of foreign courts. France's
alienation of the states of Europe had made possible William of
Orange's seizure of the English throne; France's quarrel with
the papacy – particularly the affair of the franchise – had cost

her the support of Rome; the alliance with the House of Savoy
had been ruined by the treatment the duke had received at the
hands of French ministers, Louvois in particular. Indeed, the
'mauvaise politique de M. de Louvois' was at the heart of
France's difficulties with the court of Turin. What made matters
worse, the author claimed, was that this could have been prevented : an attitude of conciliation and generosity on the part of
France would have kept the duke of Savoy faithful to the French
alliance. The future alone would reveal, the *mémoire* concluded,
the unfortunate consequences of the break with Savoy. Having
already cost France dear in men and money, it might result in the
loss of Casale and Pignerol and even in an invasion of France
itself.[29]

It was not long before the author of this document proved
himself to be a prophet. As allied plans for an all-out siege of
Casale matured in 1695, the duke of Savoy was confronted with
a perplexing problem. Although he desperately desired to see the
French evicted from Casale, the prospect of the fortress in the
hands of the emperor was a sobering one. Not only had the duke
no wish to exchange one master for another, but Imperial control of Casale would also block Savoyard designs on the Milanese. Weighing the alternatives, Victor Amadeus decided to try to
obtain an agreement with Louis XIV which would, if it did not
deliver Casale to the House of Savoy, at least ensure that it
would not fall to the emperor.

To this end, Tessé was contacted at Pignerol by Gropello early
in March, and discussions concerning the fate of Casale were
begun. Although naturally reluctant to surrender the fortress,
Louis XIV had good reason to doubt his own ability to hold it.
The allies, under Prince Eugène, were massing both men and
material in such numbers and quantity that the outlook was
bleak. If France were to extract any comfort from an already
desperate situation, it would be to ensure that Casale did not fall
with its fortifications intact to the emperor Leopold. Tessé therefore received powers and instructions to negotiate with Victor
Amadeus on 27 April. By these Louis XIV agreed to surrender
Casale to the duke of Savoy, for him to return it to the duke of
Mantua, on condition that the fortifications be entirely demolished, that the French garrison remain until the demolition was
completed, and that a truce be observed in Italy for the rest of

K

the campaign season. If the allies did not consent to this plan, Victor Amadeus was to renounce his alliance with them and join his troops to those of Catinat.[30] The duke of Savoy agreed to these terms early in May, and an elaborate plan was drawn up spelling out the formal offers and responses each side would make for the benefit of the duke's erstwhile allies.

The siege of Casale began on 17 June. On 8 July Victor Amadeus called on the marquis de Crenan, the commander of Casale, to surrender. Crenan accepted the offer as privately agreed and the duke of Savoy confronted his allies with a *fait accompli*. The allied generals were, of course, furious, but at the duke's threat to go over to the French side they grudgingly accepted the surrender of the town and its fortress. On 11 July a formal capitulation was signed by Victor Amadeus, the marquis de Leganez (representing the Allies) and Crenan, by which the town was officially restored to the duke of Mantua. Finally, on 18 September the French garrison of 2500 men marched out of Casale and made its way to Pignerol.

Later that year, after solemnly renewing his membership of the Grand Alliance, Victor Amadeus sent word to Tessé that he was prepared to break with his allies on condition that France restored Pignerol to the House of Savoy. Colbert de Croissy, in a *mémoire* written late in November, noted that 'in any other time it [the duke's offer] would not merit the slightest consideration'. However, under present circumstances, Croissy argued, the future of Pignerol was most uncertain. The allies stood a good chance of capturing the place the following spring. 'Perhaps', he continued, 'it would be wise for France to gain some advantage from the loss of Pigerol, by using it as a means of detaching Monsieur de Savoy from the League.' As an outright cession was not thought desirable, Croissy expressed the hope that France would receive some ducal territory in exchange, preferably the county of Nice.[31]

Discussions between Tessé and Gropello, begun at Pignerol early in February 1696,[32] showed that Victor Amadeus was unwilling to sacrifice Nice for Pignerol. By March Louis XIV reluctantly granted Tessé powers to treat on the return of Pignerol even if no equivalent was forthcoming. The king's anxiety for the success of the negotiation is indicated by the closing words of Tessé's new instructions: 'Finally, whatever difficulty may be encountered in the negotiation, it is His Majesty's desire that he [Tessé] should not break them off for any reason, that he merely inform His Majesty of the difficulties raised by the other side, however unreasonable they may be.'[33]

Three months of difficult and even exasperating bargaining lay ahead before Victor Amadeus would commit himself, but as early as 10 April Tessé and Gropello had agreed upon two *projets de traité*. By the first, Victor Amadeus withdrew from the Grand Alliance and promised to persuade its members to accept the neutrality of Italy. Failing this, he would join with Louis XIV 'to make war in Italy'. In return he would receive the fortress and town of Pignerol, together with all other territories held by France in Italy once the German and foreign troops had 'left Italy and arrived at the banks of the Rhine and the Danube'. The second *projet* regulated the joint conduct of the two rulers in the war against the Allies in Italy. Upon his declaration of war, Victor Amadeus was to be put in possession of his territories occupied by the French with the exception of the fortresses of Nice, Montalban and Villefranche, which would be held (as Pignerol) until the Imperial troops had moved out of Italy.[34] To the surprise of the French, Victor Amadeus objected vigorously to the terms of the draft treaties, especially to the delay in the return of his own fortresses. He demanded two French princes of the blood as hostages, and also a suspension of arms for a specified period during which he would try to bring the Allies to accept the treaty of neutrality for Italy. These new conditions, and others of lesser importance, threatened to disrupt the negotiations completely. But, after both negotiators had made concessions, two treaties and a convention providing for a ninety-day truce were signed on 29 May. By agreeing to the truce, Tessé had secured Gropello's consent to French garrisons in the fortresses at Montmélian, Susa and Pignerol until the Germans withdrew from Italy.[35] Louis XIV, though not pleased, duly ratified the treaties and signed the convention on 4 June.

Much to the consternation of the French, and of Gropello himself, Victor Amadeus disowned the work of his negotiator, returning to his old demand of the cession of Pignerol upon the ratification of the treaties. Tessé, in a personal audience with the duke, tried in vain to bring about a compromise in respect of Pignerol. To put pressure on Victor Amadeus, Tessé and

Gropello now agreed – in a signed convention – to have Catinat send an official emissary to Turin with a public proposal for the neutrality of Italy. Word of this proposal reached Milan and Venice in a matter of days and helped to soften Victor Amadeus. On a second visit to Turin, Tessé was at last able on 29 June to obtain the duke's signature to two compromise treaties. These provided for the return of the duke's territories upon his declaration of war; while the French would hold the fortresses of Montmélian and Susa till the end of the war, they would garrison the citadel only of Pignerol. As a security for the eventual return of the three places Louis XIV promise to send to Turin two hostages 'of highest rank'. The marriage of the duke of Burgundy and Marie-Adélaïde was also agreed on.[36]

On the day of the duke's ratification of the treaties, Catinat made a public offer of neutrality for Italy. Victor Amadeus responded – as arranged – with a proposal for a suspension of arms. The allied commanders in Turin, faced with the duke's threat to go over to the French immediately, reluctantly agreed to open negotiations for a truce. Tessé, sent to Turin as a hostage by Louis XIV, was in a good position to control both Victor Amadeus and the negotiations.

During July and August the duke of Savoy was subjected to strong pressure from the emperor and William III to return to the anti-French alliance. But he, with the French treaties in his pocket, remained firm and by 5 August the allied commanders reluctantly withdrew from Turin to positions near the Milanese. It was now obvious that Victor Amadeus held the balance of power in Italy and had, by virtue of his alliance with Louis XIV, tipped that balance in favour of the French. In a final attempt to persuade him to reconsider his decision, Leopold in the middle of August sent Count Mansfield to Turin.[37]

Mansfield's proposal that neutrality be declared for Piedmont alone was sharply rejected by Louis XIV and, after some hesitation, by Victor Amadeus. On 29 August, Tessé formally signed the 'public' Treaty of Turin, identical with the first of the treaties which he had signed with Louis on 29 June.[38]

On 1 September, in expectation of the coming campaign against the Allies, Catinat entered Turin and presented the duke with a patent as commander-in-chief of the joint Franco-Savoyard army. Catinat then rejoined the main body of the

French army and advanced towards Casale, which he occupied on 8 September. The allied representatives in Turin were thrown into confusion by this course of events. The marquis de Leganez, representing Spain, pressed for the acceptance of the French offer of neutrality for Italy; Mansfeld, however, remained firmly opposed. On 16 September Victor Amadeus and Tessé left Turin to join Catinat who had now laid siege to Valenza. In view of the certain fall of the fortress and their untenable overall position in the Milanese, the Allies agreed on 7 October to the Treaty of Vigevano. This provided for the mutual withdrawal of troops from Italy and for the neutrality of the peninsula until the signing of a general peace.[39]

Although Victor Amadeus had been unable to realise his dream of conquests in the Milanese, he had attained what he most desired, the removal of the French from Casale (which was handed over to the duke of Mantua as stipulated) and his own repossession of Pignerol. The marriage of his daughter to the grandson of Louis XIV was seen as a gain in prestige. For France, the loss of her remaining outposts in Italy was the price of her release from a debilitating and costly stalemate. The treaties of Turin and Vigevano, by cracking the Grand Alliance, paved the way for the negotiations which led to the Peace of Ryswick in 1697. The loss of Casale and Pignerol meant the end of all that France had worked for in Italy since the time of Richelieu. It was, in fact, symptomatic of an important shift in emphasis in French foreign policy, from the traditional Italian orientation of the cardinal-ministers to that of Louis XIV which was directed almost exclusively towards the northern and northeastern borders of France.[40]

In the years immediately following the Peace of Ryswick, the alliance between France and Savoy seemed solid enough. The marriage of Marie-Adélaïde to the duke of Burgundy in 1697 was hailed as a token of the new relationship between the two crowns. Beneath the surface, however, new strains were developing which led to a reversal of alliances in 1703. The basic issue was the problem of the Spanish succession. In 1698 Louis XIV concluded the First Partition Treaty with England and the Dutch Republic. By its terms the dauphin was to receive upon the death of Carlos II the Spanish territories in Italy, except for Milan and Sardinia. Two years later the Second Partition Treaty

assigned to the dauphin the duchy of Milan as well, though it
was to be exchanged for Lorriane, or, according to a secret
article, for Savoy and Nice if the duke of Lorraine refused the
offer.[41]

Although the prospect of French rule in Italy after 1700 was
greeted with dismay on the part of the Italian princes, we know
from Meuvret and others that Louis' intentions were not directed
towards a permanent French control over Italy. Although the
king was under considerable pressure from French commercial
interests in the Mediterranean, he looked upon the promised
Italian territories essentially as pawns to be traded for (from his
point of view) more desirable territories elsewhere, such as Lorraine, Luxembourg or Savoy, Nice and Piedmont. Indeed, Tessé
was sent to Turin in October 1700 to try to get Victor Amadeus's
assent to an exchange of Naples and Sicily for all the duke's territories or (and this was more to the duke's liking) of the Milanese for Savoy and Nice.[42]

The negotiations, if successful, would have resulted in the
almost entire abandonment by France of her claims on Italy.
Such an action might have persuaded the Italian princes, and
the duke of Savoy in particular, of the disinterestedness of
French policy in regard to the peninsula. Unfortunately Victor
Amadeus, greatly as he desired to assume the title of duke of
Milan, refused to give up Nice, his sole outlet to the sea, and
Tessé's negotiations languished.[43]

As it happened, the will of Carlos II overthrew all the prior
calculations and arrangements of the European powers. By
accepting the will Louis XIV gave up the advantages stipulated
for France in the Second Partition Treaty, since he was now
committed to preserving the territorial integrity of his grandson's dominions.[44] Although several Italian states recognised
Philip V without much hesitation, Versailles' growing influence
in Madrid soon became a cause for Italian concern. The close
relationship between the two Bourbon courts was symbolised by
the movement of French troops into Spanish territories, in Italy
as elsewhere, to counter the growing threat of Austrian intervention. In an attempt to shore up his relationship with Victor
Amadeus, Louis XIV concluded the Treaty of Turin on 6 April
1701. By its terms the duke would contribute 10,500 troops to
a joint Franco-Spanish force, of which he would serve as nominal

commander-in-chief. In return he was to receive a subsidy of 150,000 livres per month and his second daughter was to be married to Philip V.[45] Unfortunately for the French, no provision could be made for the territorial aggrandisement of Victor Amadeus.

Given the cupidity of that prince it is not surprising that he began, even as fighting broke out in northern Italy in June, to explore the possibility of a new arrangement with the emperor. Alarmed by the danger to his lands posed by Bourbon control of Milan and angry at increasingly peremptory treatment by the French, Victor Amadeus finally went over to the Allies on 8 November 1703. With the promise of territorial gains which included Sicily and parts of the Milanese the duke of Savoy withdrew from the French alliance, an action which determined the frustration of Louis' army in Italy as surely as it opened the way to the future progress of the House of Savoy in the peninsula.

The shift of French interest in Europe from Italy to the north and east, accomplished during the reign of Louis XIV, continued under his successors. It is not possible to assess with certainty – nor is it necessary – the degree to which this reorientation of policy was due to the exigencies of war and alliance rather than to the deliberate and conscious choice of Louis XIV. In a world in which even the grand monarch had to settle for only partial realisation of his goals the question of priorities had to be faced. In this case, because of the king's primary concern for the security of France's eastern frontiers, the sacrifice of two centuries of French policy in Italy was a regrettable but unavoidable necessity, the ambitions of the duke of Savoy an opportunity to be used and a burden to be borne.

NOTES

1 The best recent discussion of French policy in Italy is that of Jean Meuvret, 'Louis XIV et l'Italie', *XVIIe Siècle* (1960) 84–102. For a summary of Franco-Savoyard relations from their beginnings, see vol. xiv of *Recueil des Instructions données aux Ambassadeurs et Ministres de France*, ed. Horric de Beaucaire, *Savoie-Sardaigne et Mantoue*, i (Paris, 1898) pp. v–lxi.

2 See for the period after 1490 Domenico Carutti, *Storia della diplomazia della corte di Savoia*, 4 vols (Turin, 1875–80).

3 Ibid., I, 493–8.

4 Meuvret, 'Louis XIV et l'Italie', pp. 84, 92.

5 The standard account of the reign of Victor Amadeus II is Domenico Carutti, *Storia di Vittorio Amadeo II*, 3rd ed. (Turin, 1897).

6 Ibid., pp. 145–53. For the break between Versailles and Turin see Camille Rousset, *Histoire de Louvois et de son administration militaire*, 3rd ed., 4 vols (Paris, 1879) IV, pp. 291–347.

7 Archives de la Guerre, Al-l 69, Louvois to Catinat, Jan 1691.

8 Rousset, *Histoire de Louvois*, IV, p. 457, n. 3.

9 John B. Wolf, *Louis XIV* (New York, 1968) pp. 464–5. Jean Meuvret dates the more moderate stance of French policy in Italy in the 1690s from the death of Seignelay in 1690: 'Louis XIV et l'Italie', p. 93 ff.

10 Although the most influential Frenchman in Italy was the comte de Tessé, a soldier and protégé of Louvois, his reports to the king were increasingly directed through Croissy's office: from 1693 the documents in the *archives de la guerre* relating to diplomatic matters are mostly copies of originals in the foreign office. In the later stages of the Franco-Savoyard negotiations, even Catinat reported almost as often to Croissy (and, later, to Torcy) as he did to Barbezieux.

11 Archives des Affaires Etrangères, Correspondance Politique, Venise. vol. 116, ff. 230–54; printed in Beaucaire, *Savoie-Sardaigne*, I, pp. 145–62,

12 For Chamlay's mission, see Arsène Legrelle, *La diplomatie française et la succession d'Espagne*, 2nd ed., 6 vols (Braine-le-Comte, 1895–9) I, pp. 439–40.

13 Jean Meuvret, 'Les aspects politiques de conflit gallican', *Revue d'Histoire de l'Eglise de France* (1947) 257–70.

14 Carutti, *Storia della diplomazia*, III, p. 213, n. 1.

15 A.A.E., C.P., Turin, vol. 94, 'Relation de la Cour de Savoye', 15 July 1692.

16 Ibid., Tessé to Croissy, Pignerol 6 and 8 Mar 1693.

17 Ibid., *Mémoire* of Croissy, 8 Feb 1693.

18 Ibid., *Mémoire* of Croissy, 20 Apr 1693.

19 Ibid., 'Articles Proposés par M. le duc de Savoie, Réponses de le comte de Tessé', 31 May 1693.

20 Bibliothèque Nationale, Fonds-français, 1888, f. 158, Louis XIV to Catinat, Versailles, 10 Oct 1693. My references are to the documents in the A.A.E. since Tessé's *Mémoires et lettres du maréchal de Tessé*, ed. Grimoard, 2 vols (Paris, 1806), is unreliable and should be used with care; the same holds good for the *Mémoires et Correspondance du maréchal de Catinat*, ed. Bernard le Bouyer de Saint-Gervais, 3 vols (Paris, 1819).

21 Wolf, *Louis XIV*, pp. 472–5; Pierre Goubert, *Louis XIV et Vingt Millions des Français* (Paris, 1966) pp. 166–70.

22 Mark A. Thomson, 'Louis XIV and William III, 1689–1697', *English Historical Review* (1961) 37–58; reprinted in *William III and Louis XIV, Essays by and for Mark A. Thomson*, ed. Ragnhild Hatton and J. S. Bromley (Liverpool, Toronto, 1968).

23 A.A.E., C.P., Turin, vol. 94, *Mémoire* of Croissy, 18 Dec 1693.

24 Ibid.

25 For Grimani's mission see G. P. O. de Cleron, Comte d'Haussonville, *La duchesse de Bourgogne et l'alliance savoyarde sous Louis XIV*, 4th ed., 3 vols (Paris, 1906) I, pp. 57–66.

26 Legrelle, *La Diplomatie française*, I, pp. 383–94.

27 There are more than a dozen *mémoires* for the period 1691 to 1695 by Saint-Maiole in A.A.E., C.P., Turin, vol. 94.

28 Meuvret, 'Louis XIV et l'Italie', *passim*.

29 A.A.E., C.P., Turin, vol. 94, 'Réflexions sur la rupture de Savoye', 1694.

30 Ibid., 'Pouvoir pour M. le Comte de Tessé', 17 Apr 1695.

31 Ibid., *Mémoire* of Croissy, Nov 1695.

32 A somewhat impressionistic account of Tessé's negotiations is given by Paul Canestrier, 'Comment M. de Tessé a préparé en 1696 le traité de paix entre Louis XIV et Victor-Amédée de Savoie', *Revue d'histoire diplomatique* (1934) 370–92.

33 A.A.E., C.P., Turin, vol. 95, f. 17, 'Plein pouvoir à M. le Comte de Tessé pour convenir d'un traité avec M. le duc de Savoye', Versailles, 18 Mar 1696.

34 Ibid., vol. 96, ff. 168–75, 176–82. The two undated draft treaties are bound (incorrectly) after Tessé's account of the treaties of 19 May 1696.

35 Ibid., vol. 95, f. 23, 'Ratification d'articles convenus pour la neutralité d'Italie', 4 June 1696.

36 Ibid., vol. 97, ff. 3–14, Tessé to Louis XIV, Rivalta, 1 July 1696; ibid., vol. 95, ff. 85–91, 'Articles convenus pour la paix et neutralité d'Italie', 29 June 1696; ibid., ff. 33–42, 'Traité d'action', 29 June 1696. Although the prospect of Franco-Savoyard conquests in the Milanese by this time were dim, Article 14 of the second (secret) treaty signed on that day reaffirmed the principle of an exchange of territory in Savoy for lands conquered in the duchy of Milan.

37 Mansfeld's mission, along with the other major events of the summer and autumn of 1696, is described in Max Braubach, *Prinz Eugen von Savoyen: Eine Biographie* (Munich, 1963) I, pp. 239–71.

38 29 August 1696 was thus the official date of the Treaty of Turin or Peace of Savoy; for Louis XIV's ratification of the treaty on 7 September see A.A.E., C.P., Turin, vol. 95, f. 104.

39 Ibid., ff. 208–13: Tessé's annotated copy of the treaty, sent to Versailles on 10 October 1696.

40 The importance of this shift in French policy is noted by John C. Rule in his essay, 'Roi-Bureaucrate', in *Louis XIV and the Craft of Kingship*, ed. John C. Rule (Columbus, Ohio, 1969) pp. 7–8. In the same volume, Ragnhild Hatton argues persuasively that a dominant concern of Louis' foreign policy was with 'the interpretation of 1648' in respect of the eastern frontiers of France: see her 'Louis XIV and his Fellow Monarchs', ibid., especially pp. 168–73, and above pp. 30–4.

41 For the text of the partition treaties and related documents, see Pierre Grimblot (ed.), *Letters of William III and of Louis XIV and their Ministers, 1697–1700*, 2 vols (London, 1848) II, p. 482 ff. The issues raised by the

K*

treaties are explored by R. Hatton, 'Louis XIV and his Fellow Monarchs', pp. 171–9, and above pp. 32–40.

42 Meuvret, 'Louis XIV et l'Italie', pp. 100–1. For a fairly complete account of Franco-Savoyard relations in this period see Legrelle, *La Diplomatie française*, IV, 29–79. For Tessé's mission, see Beaucaire (ed.), *Savoie-Sardaigne*, I, pp. 232–46.

43 Meuvret, 'Louis XIV et l'Italie', p. 101.

44 Andrew Lossky discusses the alternatives open to Louis by the will of Carlos II in 'Some Problems in Tracing the Intellectual Development of Louis XIV from 1661 to 1715', in Rule (ed.), *Louis XIV and the Craft of Kingship*, pp. 336–7, reprinted in *Louis XIV and Absolutism* (1976) pp. 101–29.

45 L. André, *Louis XIV et l'Europe* (Paris, 1950) p. 301.

11 Colbert de Torcy, an Emergent Bureaucracy, and the Formulation of French Foreign Policy, 1698-1715[*]

JOHN C. RULE

In this essay I will discuss three interrelated problems of French diplomacy in the later years of Louis XIV's reign : first, the emergence of a bureaucratic hierarchy in the French foreign ministry; secondly, the manner in which the foreign minister collaborated with his *commis*, or secretaries, in collecting, sorting, evaluating and disseminating information; thirdly, the influence the foreign minister and his associates had on decisions arrived at in Louis XIV's most important administrative council, the *conseil d'en haut*.

The era of French diplomacy studied, the years 1698 to 1715, coincides with the tenure in office of Jean-Baptiste Colbert de Torcy as minister-secretary of state and was selected not only because Torcy and his associates left well-documented accounts of the administration of diplomacy, but also because the seventeenth-century *fin de siècle* and the early eighteenth-century years of the War of the Spanish Succession mark a crucial stage in the emergence of a French bureaucracy.

I

Turning first to a discussion of the bureaucratic establishment, we find that Max Weber and his later interpreters have in the

[*] Specially commissioned for this volume.

twentieth century provided the historian with criteria for testing the maturity of bureaucratic governments in the Age of Absolutism : among these are the emergence of a hierarchy of offices and a chain of command within a bureaucracy; the appearance of jurisdictional boundaries, of specialised bureaux, and of a general code of ethics by which officials are guided; recognition given by the head of the bureaucracy to tenure of office and to periodic payment of salaries and pensions; reliance on 'experts' to advise the prince and his ministers; the preservation of documents in a central archive or depot,[1] establishing an administration based upon written records. The bureaucratic hierarchy of the French foreign ministry had by Weberian tenets reached early maturity during the War of the Spanish Succession. Colbert de Torcy, following the lead of his predecessors in office, Colbert de Croissy and Arnauld de Pomponne, helped establish within the civil *Maison du Roi* a *maison du secrétaire d'état des affaires étrangères*.[2] This ministerial household was made up of a dozen or so bureaux (in the sense of civil servants rather than of royal commissions); in wartime a dozen embassies and in peacetime several dozen embassies abroad; also pensioners of the *maison* and a host of lesser functionaries and servants. In order better to understand the composition of the official hierarchy of the foreign office, it might be of some value to delineate some eight categories or groupings of diplomats and civil servants who served in Torcy's *maison*.

At the upper fringe of the bureaucratic hierarchy were those who in the seventeenth century were called *les grands* or *les importants*.[3] Most often *les importants* were members – lay or cleric – of the older nobility, the *noblesse d'épée*, or were men of the highest military distinction, generals or marshals of France. *Les importants* were so called not for their profound insight into foreign affairs, but because they wielded political influence independent of the secretary of state for foreign affairs. These men of importance – who boasted ties with the great noble court families or with the newly arrived, wealthy, urban nobility – contributed to the foreign ministry's service such distinguished ambassadors and plenipotentiaries as the duc de Gramont, the duc de Noailles, the duc d'Aumont, the comte de Luc (of the renowned Vintimille family), the marquis d'Alègre; the cardinals d'Estrées, Trémoille, Forbin-Janson and Polignac; and the marshals Tallard, d'Harcourt, d'Huxelles and Villars. During the Succession War it was from among these noblemen that Torcy often recruited his ministers-plenipotentiary to peace congresses and his ambassadors on special missions to the Low Countries, to Spain or to the pope. Abbé (from 1713 a cardinal) Melchior de Polignac, for example, served as plenipotentiary to the Gertruydenberg and Utrecht conferences of 1710 and 1711–13; the marquis d'Alègre was named companion of honour to visiting diplomats from 1711 to 1715 and was afterwards nominated as ambassador to England; marshals d'Harcourt and d'Huxelles, returning from missions abroad, became advisers to the foreign office, as did the cardinals d'Estrées and Forbin-Janson. Torcy, admittedly, had his favourites among *les importants*: the duc d'Aumont, named ambassador to England in 1713, was a frequent visitor in the minister's Paris *hôtel*; the comte de Luc, a close friend of Torcy, became, after 1707, ambassador to the Swiss cantons; and Melchior de Polignac, a boyhood companion of the minister, was recalled from Rome in 1709 to counsel Torcy on the peace negotiations under way in the Low Countries. But not all of *les importants* who served the foreign office were the minister's confidants. Torcy mistrusted and even disliked many of them; for example, Marshal d'Harcourt, who early in the Succession War had insistently sought a place on the *conseil d'en haut*; and the marshals d'Huxelles, Tallard and Villars, whom Torcy feared because of their close ties with the rival Le Tellier clan and with Mme de Maintenon, who was no friend to the Colberts.[4] Yet despite the minister's likes and dislikes *les importants* rendered the state valuable service: Villars, d'Harcourt and Tallard displayed superior talents as negotiators, and the eighteenth century boasted few more consummate diplomats than Polignac, the comte de Luc or Forbin-Janson.

A second category in the secretary's *maison* was comprised of men whose origin could be traced to the lesser *noblesse d'épée*, to the nobility of the robe, and even to the *haute bourgeoisie*. They can be designated envoys and advisers *de la plume*,[5] representatives of an emerging bureaucratic nobility that often purchased offices as *secrétaires du roi* or as *conseillers du roi*. Though these nobles of the pen held less exalted positions in the court hierarchy than did *les importants*, they were with increasing frequency named by Torcy to the posts of ambassador or envoy extraordinary or as special advisers to the minister. Among those thus favoured was Baron Pierre Rouillé, a president of the Parlement of Paris, ambassador to Portugal and plenipotentiary to the Dutch in 1708–9; François de Callières, chief negotiator at the Congress of Ryswick, envoy to Lorraine (1702–3), and subsequently *secrétaire du roi*; Nicolas Mesnager, a plenipotentiary to the Congress of Utrecht and adviser on economic matters to the minister; Michel Amelot, a councillor of the Parlement of Paris, and ambassador to Spain, 1705–9; and the d'Ussons, uncle and nephew, both of an old robe family. The uncle, François d'Usson, marquis de Bonrepaus, had been sent on several missions to England in the 1680s, then as envoy in the 1690s to the Danes and the Dutch; his nephew, Jean-Louis, marquis de Bonnac, represented French interests with the northern German princes (1700–4), in Prussia (1705) and, on Torcy's express nomination, in Spain (1711). Yet another dynasty *de la plume* were the de Mesmes, comtes d'Avaux, four generations of them, all scions of a great robe family. Claude de Mesmes (d. 1650) had been one of the chief negotiators of the Peace of Westphalia (1646–8); Jean-Antoine (d. 1709) served as ambassador to Savoy (1672), to the Congress of Nijmegen, to Ireland (with the Jacobites, 1689–93), and subsequently to Sweden (1693–9) and to the United Provinces (1701). Jean-Antoine was a favourite of Colbert de Croissy; and Torcy, like his father, sought Jean-Antoine's advice on affairs in the Low Countries, Sweden and England. Jean-Jacques de Mesmes (d. 1688), a president of the Parlement of Paris, was sent on several minor missions abroad, and his son, Jean-Jacques, became an ambassador in 1715. These men of the pen were handsomely compensated by the treasurers of the foreign office; many of them, for example Rouillé, Mesnager, Amelot, Callières and the marquis de Bonnac, continued as pensioners of the *maison du secrétaire d'état* after their return from embassies abroad; on the other hand only the most impecunious of *les importants*, like the abbé de Polignac and Marshal d'Huxelles, remained on the list of pensioners after their return to France.

A third category of the secretary's *maison* was comprised of members of Torcy's family, the Colberts,[6] and of their in-laws, the Arnauld de Pomponnes and the Spinolas. Chevalier de

Croissy, Torcy's brother, served during the Succession War on secret missions to Lorraine and to the Low Countries; in 1715 he was accredited to Charles XII of Sweden. Torcy's brother-in-law, the abbé de Pomponne, was posted as ambassador to Venice from 1705 to 1710, and François-Marie Spinola, the duc de Saint-Pierre, another brother-in-law, was employed as the minister's personal observer at the congresses of Utrecht and Baden. These men were valuable informants and close confidantes, tied to Torcy by bonds of family, fortune and loyalty.

Separated by rank, family and fortune from the above three categories were the *premiers commis*,[7] the first secretaries of the ministry, who sprang in large part from the lesser *noblesse de robe* or *plume* or the *haute bourgeoisie*; however, unlike the nobles of the pen, they seldom held ambassadorial or even ministerial rank. The *premiers commis* constitute excellent examples of Weber's ideal bureaucrats, men upon whom the minister relied for the routine business of drafting letters and summarising reports, men who exerted great influence within the bureaucratic hierarchy and usually served in the ministry all their lives and trained their sons 'in the service'. Nine *premiers commis* served under Torcy: Clair Adam, Antoine Pecquet *père*, Charles Mignon, Michel Fournier, François Blondel, Pierre Aubert, Jean-Yves Saint-Prest, Jean de Prévost and Jean-Gabriel de la Porte du Theil. Closely associated with the *premiers commis*, often as chiefs of their own bureaux, with salaries comparable to the *premiers commis*, were: Léon Pajot d'Ons-en-Bray, *directeur* of the posts and head of the secret service; and Abbé Joachim Le Grand, one of the chief advisers to the *Académie politique*.

Torcy's closest associate among the *premiers commis* was Clair Adam,[8] who on returning from missions to Denmark and the Germanies in the early 1690s had been named *premier commis* in 1694. Soon thereafter Adam had become Torcy's personal intendant and *tuteur onéraire* to Torcy's sister, Mlle Thérèse de Croissy; in 1706 he was named one of the three (only two were appointed during Torcy's tenure) *trésoriers des ambassadeurs*. Adam also handled such diverse and delicate tasks for the minister as the acquisition of Cardinal Richelieu's papers and the opening and reading of the minister's letters when Torcy was away from Versailles.

Another influential *premier commis* was Antoine Pecquet *père*,[9] who had broad administrative experience, having served as a *commis* to the controller-general Claude Le Peletier from 1683 to 1689 and having supervised the transfer of the bulk of foreign archives from Versailles to Paris in the years 1711 to 1713. Pecquet trained his able son for a post in the foreign office and under Louis XV Antoine *fils* became a major political force in the secretariat; both men had 'les sages et prudentes traditions' of Torcy.[10]

A *premier commis* who wielded great influence among his colleagues at the foreign office was François Blondel, who early in Torcy's administration was named the minister's personal secretary and also *chef du secrétariat du Ministre*; it was Blondel's task to write 'sous la dictée du ministre, expédier les ordonnances et les passeports, garder les doubles des chiffres, expédier les lettres des correspondance secrètes, reservées à la connaissance personnelle du ministre'.[11] Blondel's nephew, Jean-Gabriel de la Porte du Theil, who had served as secretary to Marshal Tessé and later as principal secretary to the plenipotentiaries at the congresses of Utrecht and Rastadt, became a premier commis in the last year of Torcy's term of office. Blondel's associate in the office of *secrétariat du Ministre* was Victor Goullet, Sieur de Ligny. Jean de Prévost,[12] a treasurer to the ambassadors, was often entrusted with secret missions to bankers in Paris, Lyons and abroad; his close associate, Nicolas Mesnager, a merchant of Rouen, was sent on special assignments to Spain and later to the Low Countries and to London. Charles Mignon[13] played an important role in the earliest years of Torcy's ministry. Along with his sons, and his nephew, Michel Fournier, Mignon was responsible for transcribing many of the minister's most secret letters. In the early years of the War of the Spanish Succession he was succeeded as *premier commis* by his nephew, Michel Fournier, a *trésorier* of the bureau of finances at Rouen; Fournier proved to be one of Torcy's ablest administrators. Another influential *premier commis* was Jean-Yves Saint-Prest, who became head of the depot of the Archives des Affaires Etrangères in 1711 and supervisor of the *Académie politique* in 1713; a shrewd administrator and a literary editor he was responsible for the compilation of the 'Instructions' to the ambassadors and the editing of the important series of documents entitled *Rétablissement de la France*

dans son ancien éclat par les Traités de Münster, des Pyrénées,
etc. Saint-Prest also headed 'une sorte de bureau de la presse' : to
quote Piccioni 'en effet et pour la première fois on s'occupe de son
temps d'influencer les nouvelistes, et l'infatigable Torcy collabora
dans ce but avec Saint-Prest et rédigea même quelquefois de sa
main des nottes destinées aux gazetiers.'[14]

Associated with Saint-Prest in this so-called *bureau de la presse*,
which I would prefer to label the *bureau des rédacteurs*, were
the abbés Jean-Baptiste DuBos and Joachim Le Grand. Jean
de la Chapelle,[15] son of a *financier*, a playwright and member of
the French Academy, was the author of *Lettres d'un Suisse*, a
series of tracts published in Paris, bearing a Basle imprint, which,
translated into German, Italian and English, were widely cir-
culated between 1702 and 1710 in the Low Countries, the Rhine
valley, Switzerland, northern Italy, and even the British Isles.
The *Lettres d'un Suisse* – nearly fifty in all – so accurately represent Torcy's thoughts on war and peace that they echo the
same Torcian rhetoric that we find in Torcy's *Journal* and
Mémoires : the evocation of *patrie*, the *gloire* of the state, reference to greedy allies, and pleas for a 'balance of Europe'. Abbé
Jean-Baptiste DuBos also aided Torcy's wartime propaganda
efforts. DuBos, a celebrated historian, wrote early in the war
years *Les Intérêts de l'Angleterre malentendus dans la guerre
présente*. It is a clearly argued, well-devised attack on England's
entry into the Grand Alliance of The Hague. Torcy, obviously
pleased with its closely reasoned arguments, had it reprinted
several times during the war. Abbé Joachim Le Grand,[17] an
oratorian and diplomat, entered Torcy's *maison* in 1706 as a
commis and served the minister as a propagandist and as adviser
to the *Académie politique* until 1715. While editing *mémoires*
for the minister, Le Grand found documentary materials to serve
as a base for his well-known attack on the Dutch entitled *Lettre
d'un Conseilleur du Grand Conseil de Genève à un Bourgemaistre
d'Amsterdam* (which appeared in July 1709 just after the abortive
Hague conference). Le Grand followed this work in 1710 with
a *Lettre à Mylord, traduit de l'Anglois*, in which he attacked
Marlborough and his associates for their seeming lack of concern
for the balance of Europe and at the failure of the Gertruydenberg conference. Others also served Torcy as propagandists,
among them Rousseau de Chamoy, François de Callières and

Saint-Prest; the minister thus boasted a stable of talented writers, in many ways comparable to the brilliant gaggle of English pamphleteers of the day on the other side of the Channel.

A fifth category of advisers and servants of the foreign office were the *commis*, or more exactly *simples commis*, and their assistants, the *garçons de bureau*, the office boys. They fulfilled the quotidian duties of copyists, decipherers, clerks-in-ordinary, translators, issuers of passports, editors of diplomatic reports. Often a *simple commis* was the son or nephew of a *premier commis* : two of Torcy's *commis* were sons of Charles Mignon; one was a nephew of Mignon and another a son of Clair Adam; Jean de Prévost was a son-in-law of Clair Adam; Jean-Gabriel de la Porte du Theil, a *commis* until 1715, was François Blondel's nephew. Like most of the French bureaucratic hierarchy, the emerging *noblesse de la plume* of the foreign office was infected with nepotism born of venality of office. Yet this very system of venality assured the minister of continuity of viewpoint and of tradition.

The sixth category in the foreign office was the secret agents, those invaluable gleaners of intelligence from foreign courts or purveyors of news from Paris and the provinces. Their names, as given in the Archives des Affaires Etrangères, are often disguised; but we can identify, *inter alia*, Groffey in Leipzig and Danzig, de Vaux in Berlin, Gaultier in London, Pasteur in Vienna, Hooke in Scotland, Bourke in Spain. A seventh class was the *courriers du cabinet* – usually a dozen in number – who at times also served as agents abroad. An instance of this latter function was dourly reported from The Hague by the first secretary of the English embassy in February 1710 when he noted that 'the [French] Courrier du Cabinett [is] . . . still . . . active, finding out how matters are disposed.'[18] An eighth and final group was made up of the foreigners in the service of the king of France : examples are Chevalier Rossi,[19] whom Torcy sent on missions to The Hague and to Rome, and Cardinal Gualterio,[20] a pensioner of the *Maison du Roi*, who, as a personal friend of the minister, sent him reports of the political activities of the Roman curia. In all the foreign ministry's resident bureaucrats, along with the ambassadors and ministers abroad, numbered fifty or sixty and were paid from a budget of more than 1,000,000 livres a year. When gratuities, gifts, bribes and subsidies are added to the personnel budget, the foreign office dispensed on an average more than 5,000,000 livres a year.[21]

How did the minister channel the efforts of these men who served the foreign office? Largely through some ten specialised bureaux. I would define a bureau more strictly than do Picavet and Piccioni by underscoring its functional aspect : the personnel of a bureau must display clearly differentiated duties and boast a budget for at least two *commis*; in addition, a bureau must maintain files of correspondence upon which to base a retrospective view of foreign policy. By using these criteria I can identify some ten to eleven bureaux that either existed or were emerging in the period 1698 to 1715.They were the bureau of the posts, the *archives politiques* (or *modernes*), the *archives anciennes* (or *historiques*), the bureau *de la presse*, the *Académie politique*, the bureau of the *trésoriers des ambassadeurs*, the bureau of economic affairs, a bureau for *chiffre*, the bureau for passports and special documents, and some three or four bureaux (merged into two in 1714)[22] charged with the correspondence with ambassadors abroad.

The bureau of the posts was directed by Léon Pajot d'Ons-en-Bray, who, in addition to his duties as deputy-chief postmaster of the realm, supervised the secret service, both domestic and foreign, and the *courriers du cabinet*.[23] It was in Pajot's Paris bureau that clerks opened letters to or from 'suspected persons'. At the beginning of his administration Torcy submitted to the Post Office a list of such 'suspected persons', which at one time or another included the names of Mme des Ursins, the duchesses of Burgundy and Orléans, the duke of Chartres (later Orléans) and, as we know from her own testimony, Mme de Maintenon. In a special secret or darkened room of the Post Office known as the *cabinet noir* the letters of persons on this list were opened by clerks, read, copied, resealed and sent on their way, often on the same day they were received. Torcy maintained his own *cabinet noir* at Versailles, but the clerks there were largely engaged in deciphering messages from secret agents rather than in copying illicitly seized mail.

Another important bureau was that of the *archives*, which in 1711 was divided into two bureaux : the *archives politiques* (or *modernes*) for the most recent papers (usually those from the last twelve years) were retained in the handsomely appointed library of the ministers' wing of the palace of Versailles, while the *archives anciennes* were removed to the Louvre. The *archives politiques* were headed by the *premier commis* Jean-Yves Saint-Prest and the *archives anicennes* by Nicolas-Louis Le Dran,[24] who himself became a *premier commis* in 1725. Closely associated with the staff of the archives were a group of editors – *rédacteurs* – led by Saint-Prest, Le Dran, Lullier, Du Theil and Dupuisse; these editors helped frame the 'instructions' to ambassadors and ministers going abroad and were later responsible for rewriting the ambassadors' and envoys' reports in the form of *mémoires* for the *archives politiques*. Torcy built a small workshop for these *rédacteurs* in the gardens of the *hôtel* de Torcy-Croissy on land rented from a nearby monastery.[25] This same *bureau des rédacteurs* supervised matters pertaining to the gazettes and, ultimately, to propaganda.

Jean-Yves Saint-Prest also headed the *Académie politique*,[26] where he was assisted by Abbé Joachim Le Grand and by a permanent secretary to the academy, Depuisse. The idea of an academy had in part been suggested to Torcy in the early war years by the reforms that the Pontchartrains, father and son, had instituted in the French Academy and the *Académie des Sciences*.[27] The Ponchartrains had between 1699 and 1701 added twenty students – *élèves* – to the staff of the science academy, and in 1710 Torcy suggested to the king that an *Académie politique* be founded where some six students could be trained for the posts of secretaries in embassies abroad. As an aid to the programme Torcy wrote in his own hand a guide for the *élèves,* much as he had done for his *commis* in matters pertaining to protocol. In 1710–12, as Torcy worked out his plan for an *Académie politique* (largely with the advice of the abbé Le Grand), he also found inspiration for his work from the plans for reorganisation of the ministry of marine's *dépôt* of maps and plans (begun in 1696–7)[28] and in his own pilot project for France's Rome embassy, where the minister had already established a special local bureau for archives. By 1712 six students and a staff of four moved the newly-formed *Académie politique* into rooms adjacent to the *archives anciennes* in the Louvre.

In 1706 Torcy established a special bureau for financial affairs. Three *trésoriers des ambassadeurs*[29] were to be appointed to head this bureau, but only two were actually named in Torcy's day:

Clair Adam and Jean de Prévost. These men were charged with the disbursement of foreign ministry funds and kept detailed records of their transactions. More loosely organised than the aforementioned bureaux was one that concerned itself with economic affairs : Nicholas Mesnager and several other merchants and bankers who advised Torcy headed this establishment. These economic advisers were responsible, among other things, for drafting the *asiento* with Spain early in the Succession War and in counselling the ministry on the economic treaty with England in 1712–13. There was also a special bureau for *chiffre*,[30] for ciphers, with headquarters at Versailles. Unlike the clerks of the Paris *cabinet noir*, the clerks at Versailles did not open and/or decipher intercepted mail but rather rendered readable the coded messages from French secret or official agents abroad. They often worked around the clock in order to keep the king, minister and *conseil d'en haut* informed of the latest dispatches to reach the administrative capital. Torcy himself arose at an early hour when he was at Versailles or Marly in order to read the dispatches that might have reached his *commis* in the late evening or early morning hours. In case urgent dispatches marked *garder le secret au sujet* arrived while he was yet asleep he left orders to have his secretary-on-duty, often Blondel, awaken him in order that he could carry the latest news to the king at his first *levée*. If an outgoing letter was marked 'secret' Torcy would insist that he himself render the letter in code. Among the commis working in the bureau for *chiffre* were Du Theil, J-B. Fournier, Bergeret (before 1700), and Le Dran (before his appointment to *chef* of the *archives anciennes*). Two *premiers commis* supervised their activities; Clair Adam, when he was at court, and François Blondel.

Torcy's *bureau de passeports* was supervised by François Blondel and directed by the *commis* Lullier who bore the title *chargé de l'expédition des passeports*. Lullier played an important role in guiding the routine business of this bureau : every month he reviewed the reports from the lieutenant-general of police in Paris, Marc-René d'Argenson,[31] and other lieutenants-general from across the whole of France. These reports listed the names of aliens, newly arrived or departed from the capital or from provincial centres, and included a description of each foreigner, a note as to his nationality and the intention of his visit. If Blondel

or Lullier had reason to believe that a foreigner or a group of
foreigners might become, or were, enemies of the state they laid
their evidence before the minister who could then, by invoking
his powers as secretary of state, keep the alien under surveillance,
have him interrogated by his own agents or by the local police,
imprison him by a *lettre de cachet*, or have him expelled from
the country. In wartime, particularly, the passport bureau wielded
formidable power.

Correspondence with French envoys abroad was largely supervised by three *premiers commis*: Clair Adam, Antoine Pecquet
père and Michael Fournier, aided by the *commis* Jean-B. Adam
(until 1706), Le Dran – who could read and translate from and
into English – Jean-G. de la Porte du Theil and by Charles
Mignon's two sons. Before 1714 the *premiers commis* would ap-
point one or two *commis* to copy out the letters and maintain
letterbooks to important embassies, such as Spain, England or
the Empire, or to a block of lesser powers, such as the Northern
Crowns, or the Polish-Lithuanian Commonwealth, or the Italian
states. After 1714 the routine task of drafting replies to French
embassies abroad and to foreign powers was co-ordinated by
two bureaux, one headed by Pequet *père*, the other by Michel
Fournier, with Clair Adam[32] serving as the co-ordinator of affairs,
Adam thus becoming a *premier premier commis*.

Were the *premier commis* and the *commis* well compensated
for their services to the state? The answer is: exceedingly well.
The average salary for an ambassador on service abroad during
the Succession War was about 36,000 livres a year; it could range
up to 72,000 livres for one on duty in Madrid or Rome. Though
these are munificent sums on paper, the difficulty lay first of all
in collecting the money from one of the many funds administered
either by the *trésoriers des ambassadeurs* or by the controller-
general, and, secondly, the ambassador had to defray from them
not only his own expenses but also those of his staff. By comparison a *premier commis* earned in real personal wages nearly
as much as did an ambassador: he drew a salary (or *emplois*) of
between 7000 and 18,000 livres a year, out of which he paid
his normal living expenses but did not have to support a large
staff of secretaries and servants. The *simples commis* were less
well paid, drawing some 2000 to 5000 livres a year, on which
salary they could live not sumptuously but well. Apart from

salary, pensions and *acquits patents*, the minister often rewarded his *commis* with personal gifts, with inspectorships in the postal service, with rights to land or to seigneurial privilege gained at the king's grace and favour, or by supporting favourable marriage alliances between his *commis* and the older nobility of the robe or sword.[33]

II

How did the minister instruct his *commis* as to his wishes? When possible by personal consultations. Unfortunately, such conferences were often interrupted for the minister by a summons from the king to attend him at his *lever*, or after mass, or to meet him in his chambers *aprés-diner*. Louis XIV was an exacting master. Moreover, there could be no regular schedule as to time or place of meeting because Torcy, who was certainly the most itinerant of his colleagues, travelled most weeks from Versailles or Marly to Meudon for a meeting with the grand dauphin (before 1711), to Saint-Cloud to read recent dispatches to the duke of Orléans, then on to Saint-Germain-en-Laye to visit the exiled court of England, and finally to his *hôtel* in Paris on the rue de Vivienne where he received foreign ambassadors in audience.[34]

Because of his disordered schedule and because many of the *commis* were themselves on mission, Torcy conveyed his instructions largely in writing, spelling out his wishes by means of a simple set of symbols set down in the margins of the incoming letters or by cryptic notes written into the text of these letters or on drafts of outgoing letters, treaties or agreements. Let us observe for a moment the written evidence of Torcy's industry. On incoming letters he pencilled in the margin with large numerals (1, 2, 3) the main points made by the envoy; these numerals were used in part to guide him when reading excerpts in the *conseil d'en haut*. When an envoy repeated his arguments – as Marshal Villars often did – Torcy repeated the numerals, indicating that the writer was returning to a previous point. In one instance Torcy, annoyed at the repetitiveness of Villars' argument, made a marginal comment upbraiding the marshal; but whether Torcy remarked on Villars' discursiveness in council is not known.[35]

Once Torcy had indicated the writer's argument, he proceeded to annotate the letter, or the draft memoir, or treaty. At first reading he did this in pencil because it was easier to use a pencil while riding in a coach, or while waiting in the king's anteroom, or while noting down his own comments or those of the king and his colleagues. Once Torcy began his second reading of the document, he either erased his pencil jottings or crossed them out in ink; the used of ink would indicate that most of the second readings took place in his own cabinet; it was then that he often thoroughly re-edited the work before letting his secretaries copy it out *en clair*. Sometimes while rewriting a dispatch Torcy would dictate a section which was later amended by the striking out of a single word, or phrases, or sentences, or even whole paragraphs. When he deleted a paragraph, the minister often scratched in the margin the word *'inutile'*. He left his secretaries to add the ritual forms of address, which he had outlined for them in a protocol manual (which has been preserved),[36] and to copy out enclosures of various kinds. Once the letter or document was completed, Torcy signed it and often, if he knew the recipient well, added a postscript that retailed the latest court gossip, the state of peace negotiations, or recent news from the battlefield. The letters and/or documents were then sent to foreign embassies either by one of the dozen or so *courriers du cabinet* (if the packet was express), by an envoy returning home, by an officer on his way to the front, or by the ordinary post.

What sources of information did the minister and his *commis* depend upon in order to advise the king and his council? First there were the written reports from French ambassadors abroad. During wartime, though the number of embassies had declined, there were still French missions scattered from Stockholm to Constantinople and from Muscovy to Morocco. With that fine precision that is his hallmark Torcy early in his ministry urged his envoys to send him in addition to the weekly or semi-weekly reports three other types of information : what he termed *pièces publiques* : proclamations, laws, reports of parliaments, *cortes*, states-general; *pièces jointes* : economic reports, shipping records, business news; and *ecrits fugitifs* : pamphlets, broadsides, newspapers and occasional journals. The letters of envoys abroad along with supporting materials today fill hundreds of volumes of the Archives des Affaires Etrangères under the (modern) title of 'Correspondance Politique'.[87]

Another source of information tapped by the foreign minister was the personal audiences with French envoys recently returned home from their tour of duty abroad. Torcy closely questioned them as to their impression of the ruling prince or oligarchy, as to possible shifts in the power structure and as to general prognostication of the state of relations. At the same time he asked them to draw up a written *mémoire* of their mission, an account which may strike the casual observer as a conscious emulation of the Venetian *relazione* or ambassador's report to the Venetian senate. Torcy, however, cautioned his envoys that *mémoires* should resemble the *relazioni* in form only, because, as he noted, the Venetian style of writing contained 'beaucoup de paroles, nulle conclusion'.[38] These summary reports were later turned over to his *commis* to be incorporated in their histories of French negotiations and today many of them may be found in the Archives des Affaires Etrangères under the title, 'Mémoires et Documents'.[39]

A third source of ministerial intelligence was garnered from the reports of the secret and not-so-secret agents at home and abroad.[40] The ministry, which spent substantial sums on intelligence, decoded agents' letters in the central Post Office in Paris or in the special room in the ministers' wing of the palace of Versailles mentioned above. From time to time, agents of foreign powers, for example M. Shum from Denmark, Comte Tarlo from Poland,[41] Chevalier Rossi from Rome,[42] or Herr Herman Petkum from The Hague,[43] brought letters in person to the Hôtel de Torcy-Croissy in Paris, where the foreign minister would often grant them a private interview. Such meetings were recorded by Torcy in his 'Journal' for the day.[44]

A source of intelligence jealously guarded by Torcy was that gleaned from the 'suspected persons' whose letters were opened in the Paris Post Office or in the minister's own *cabinet noir* at Versailles. Often before Louis XIV himself had received news from abroad the minister's staff had sent Torcy a copy of, say, Princess des Ursins' letter to Mme de Maintenon,[45] the elector of Bavaria's instructions to his minister in Paris, or the duke of Berwick's note to one of his Jacobite agents. From this invaluable *coffre* of information Torcy often drew bits of information with which to titillate Louis XIV's insatiable curiosity.[46]

The Post Office, however, especially in wartime, proved to

be a cause of concern to the minister; the very secrecy that
veiled the activities of the Paris office of the *cabinet noir*[47] shielded
a nest of spies. In 1706, alone, some twenty employees of the
central Post Office were arrested on charges of having sold information to newsmongers.[48] Such leaks were difficult to plug,
as Harley, when British secretary of state, learnt to his
cost.

Torcy also gathered news from envoys of foreign powers resi-
rent in Paris. Weekly, or every other week, on Tuesday or Thurs-
day mornings, Torcy was at home to foreign envoys; even in
wartime a dozen to twenty heads of missions, and often their
secretaries, attended the minister's *lever*. Torcy met often during
the Succession War with the papal nuncios (there were two, one
ordinaire, and one *extraordinaire*), with Spain's ambassador, the
duke of Alba, with the various ambassadors from Venice and
the other Italian states, with the envoys from Sweden, with
Count Monasterol, the elector of Bavaria's minister, and with
Count Bergeyck, Philip V's roving ambassador. Upon occasion
special envoys were received; an agent of Prince Rákóczi, representatives of Poland, Tuscany or Denmark.[49] Following the
minister's *lever* envoys who had requested the honour in writing
were granted private audience at which time they could submit
memoranda or a request for an audience with the king. Once
the envoys had withdrawn, Torcy dictated his impression of the
interviews, public and private, to an amanuensis, usually Blondel;
later the minister noted down his thoughts on the ambassadors'
lever in his *Journal.*[50]

Torcy and his *commis* found an occasional source of enlightenment in the pages of papers purchased or confiscated by the
government. Throughout his years in office Torcy nursed both
a collector's mania to purchase manuscripts and a minister's
desire to read his associates' unedited notes and dispatches. In
order to ascertain what private collections might become available
to the crown, either through seizure at the time of death or
purchase, Torcy urged the lieutenant-general of the Paris police,
d'Argenson, and other lieutenants-general across France, to keep
him informed of the illnesses and/or financial distress of the
members of the great ministerial and noble families. In addition
the minister solicited news of collectors and of book publishers
through Saint-Prest, Abbé Joachim Le Grand, Pajot and the

antiquarian-scholar Sieur de Clairambault. As a result of his gleanings Torcy was able in 1705 to acquire for the foreign ministry archives Cardinal Richelieu's papers; in late 1710, after conferring with d'Argenson and the cardinal-archbishop of Paris, Noailles, the minister ordered the police to seize the archives of Port-Royal des Champs; and in 1715, after years of negotiations, Torcy purchased the magnificent historical collection of François Roger de Gaignières, which contained registers of peace negotiations, letters of many important noble families and important genealogical charts. These were but the more important of Torcy's acquisitions.[51]

Possession of official *mémoires* and correspondence and of unofficial family papers and *autres curiosités,* placed a powerful weapon in Torcy's grasp. Ready to hand were the records of a century or so of diplomacy from which the minister could reconstruct a history of past policy as he interpreted it. Torcy indeed made abundant use of this written memory. From the political correspondence and the fugitive materials he forged his own record of diplomacy which he presented in synoptic form to the king and, when it was called for, to the *conseil d'en haut.* Torcy thus served as the link between the bureaucrats and the king – the middleman, the honest broker. In the crucial years of 1706 to 1713 Torcy did more than serve as a go-between : he became the advocate of bureaucratic power and of bureaucratic immunity.

III

Torcy conveyed his advice and that of his bureaucrats to Louis XIV and to his fellow ministers through frequent audiences with the king, by debate in the *conseil d'en haut,* and more covertly through a *secret du ministre.*

Torcy's audiences with Louis XIV were brief but frequent.[52] When the king was at Versailles or Marly, the foreign minister appeared at the king's first *lever,* that is at about 8.15 in the morning; if Louis had instructions to give to Torcy or if the minister wished to retail the latest news it was done then (about 8.30) or immediately after mass, that is at about 9.15. If additional meetings between king and minister proved desirable – usually on the days when the council did not meet – Torcy arrived at Louis' cabinet early in the evening. Three or four times a week the *conseil d'en haut* assembled in the king's cabinet at about 9.30 or 9.45 a.m., the meetings lasting until 11.45 or 12 noon. If the foreign minister had not had the opportunity to speak to the king at his first *lever* or after mass, he would sometimes hurry to the council in advance of the other ministers in order to say a word to the king about the agenda he intended to follow. If important negotiations were on foot, Torcy remained for a few minutes after the council meeting either to listen to Louis' instructions or to elaborate on or to amend the draft dispatches. Exigencies of wartime on occasion demanded that Louis recall his council *après-dîner*, at about 2.30 p.m.; the ministers then continued work until 4 p.m. and even at times – but rather rarely – met for a third session in Mme de Maintenon's rooms at about 8 o'clock in the evenings.

How was the *conseil d'en haut* conducted[53] in the later years of the reign? The king sat at the head of the table in his cabinet with Torcy to the king's immediate right; the foreign minister read excerpts from the correspondence recently arrived from abroad and outlined the policy the French government had adopted. When the king solicited opinions as to the course of action he should follow, he would usually call first on Torcy to defend or to elaborate his policies; next he asked for suggestions from the members of the council in order of their appointment, the most recent speaking first: thus in 1710, after Torcy had spoken, Louis would call on Voysin, then Desmarets, Beauvillier, and finally Chancellor Pontchartrain. After his ministers had spoken, the king turned to his son, the grand dauphin, and then to his grandson the duke of Burgundy. After listening to his councillors and heirs debate the issues of the moment, the king would either espouse a course of action at once, or postpone his decision until that evening or the next council meeting. Louis was usually swayed by majority opinion, but did not invariably follow it. As Louis de Pontchartrain once observed, nineteen out of twenty times the king would go along with the majority, on the twentieth he would, in order to assert his authority, countermand an order or overrule the advice of a minister. This arbitrary display of regal authority was typical of Louis XIV, but at times Louis' façade of outward assurance seemed to mask deeper feelings of anxiety and inadequacy. As Torcy often noted in his

Journal, the king would make up his mind and then later change it: he would vacillate, postpone, procrastinate, even prevaricate. Especially as he grew older Louis, in order to hide his feelings of disquiet or frustration would bluster and bully, blaming his ministers for being slow or negligent. An example of the king's ill-temper is recorded in Torcy's *Journal* for the day 27 January 1710:

> [As was often the case] Louis became irate with those who pressed him on matters of state. His Majesty felt that his councillors' excessive desire [for peace] had revealed to the enemy the fact that France would conclude a treaty at any price. His reproaches fell principally on M. de Beauvilliers, whom His Majesty singled out, but I too got my share of the blame for having urged upon His Majesty the necessity of reaching a decision [in the matter of the ambassadors who were to be sent to the Low Countries]. . . . The King added [ironically] that he much admired my newfound zeal – I who was the slowest of all men in carrying out negotiations. I confess that I did not grasp the reason for His Majesty's reproach, nor why I deserved it, for I had never delayed the execution of his orders: in fact I anticipated them. But since masters believe themselves never to be wrong, I held my tongue and tried to profit from this mortification. . . . [54]

Yet, despite Louis' growing petulance, king and minister usually got on well. Torcy was an ideal foil for Louis. The minister was unobtrusive yet tenacious of his opinions. During his long apprenticeship Torcy played the confidential clerk to perfection: he usually presented the monarch with two or three courses of action; then submitted these schemes, with supporting evidence, for his colleagues on the *conseil d'en haut* to debate; if the judgement of the conseil went against Torcy, he abided by it – at least for the time being – awaiting a chance to represent his ideas. Tenacity and temperance, as Torcy's career proved, were important traits in a successful minister.

Torcy's apprenticeship, however, was not an easy one. In the years from 1690 to 1699 he had to submit to a triple tutorial imposed by his father Croissy, by his father-in-law Pomponne, and by the king. Only in 1699, after the death of his father in 1696 and of his father-in-law in 1699, did he

reach his political majority at the age of thirty-four. There
then followed years of ministerial apprenticeship in which the
greatest threat to his authority appeared in the guise of the war
minister, Michel Chamillart, a creature of Mme de Maintenon,
and a man who continually and ineptly meddled in the making
of foreign policy. Only with Chamillart's disgrace and the decline
of Mme de Maintenon's influence – both coming in the year
1709 – did Torcy emerge as the king's most important arbiter
of foreign affairs.[55] Yet in the *conseil d'en haut* he still had to
depend upon the support of his colleague and cousin Nicolas
Desmarets. Together they formed a centre party in the council
which, searching for a *via media*, threaded its way cautiously in
the years 1709–11 between the dauphin's and Chancellor Pontchartrain's war party on the one hand and the duke of Burgundy's and Beauvillier's peace party on the other. Tragically,
the internecine conflict sparked by these three factions in part
caused the failure of the Gertruydenberg peace negotiations in
1710. For months the king and his ministers quarrelled over
what course of action to take in Spain, the grand dauphin
advocating a more active participation of France in the Peninsular
War; his son, Burgundy, supporting a policy of peace at any
price; and Torcy and his cousin urging the king to accept either
territorial indemnification for Philip or, in the last instance, to
authorise complete withdrawal of French troops from Spain.
Only in the year 1711, with the death of the dauphin, and in
early 1712, with the death of the duke of Burgundy and the
ultimate decline of Beauvillier's power, was Torcy's ascendancy in
foreign affairs clearly acknowledged at court. It was then that the
abbé Gaultier from London addressed a letter to Torcy as '*premier ministre*', while Matthew Prior referred to him as 'first minister after Madame de Maintenon'.[56]

Paradoxically by late 1710 the chief challenge to the foreign
minister's authority appeared to be the king himself. Historians
of the nineteenth and the early twentieth centuries – Emile Bourgeois, the duc de Broglie, Arsène Legrelle, Albert Sorel and A.
Baudrillart[57] – speak of the *secret du roi*: the king's secret correspondence with his ambassadors abroad or with fellow monarchs, a correspondence that was conducted outside the
bureaucratic hierarchy of command, and without consultation
and even at times without the knowledge of the foreign minister.

Such a correspondence between the French king and another crowned head and his ministers did exist in Louis XIV's last years as we can read in Louis' letters to Philip V of Spain and to Philip's advisers. This challenge to Torcy's position, although not as yet carefully studied, can be clearly documented. What is not discussed – indeed seldom acknowledged by historians – is the existence of a *secret du ministre* that emerged at the same time parallel to the development of the *secret du roi*. In early 1710 when the English coalition government showed signs of impending collapse, Torcy encouraged one of his agents, the abbé Gaultier, to put him in touch with the leaders of the new coalition, particularly with the Duke of Shrewsbury and with Robert Harley. Only scant references to this secret correspondence seem to have been made to the king and none to the *conseil d'en haut* until early in 1711, and then only because Gaultier arrived in Paris following the Franco-Spanish victory over the Allies at Brihuega. Torcy, who initiated this *détente* in 1710–11 in order to break up the so-called 'old system' (that is the alliance of Great Britain, the United Provinces and the emperor), ran a calculated risk. If his policy had failed it might well have spelt his disgrace; but since it did not, Torcy basked in the glow of royal favour. The success of the *secret du ministre* was again demonstrated in the Anglo-French negotiations of late 1711, and in the suspension of arms of the summer of 1712.[58] Following the duke of Burgundy's death in 1712 and the duke of Beauvillier's subsequent illness, Torcy took a firm grip on foreign policy that he relinquished only with the king's death in September 1715.

A second variation of the *secret du ministre* at this time relates to Torcy's several attempts to arrive at a ministerial consensus on an issue before a meeting of the *conseil d'en haut*. Louis XIV never countenanced – in fact expressly forbade – a meeting of ministers at which the king was not present. Several times Torcy disobeyed the spirit of the king's injunction by consulting with his colleagues singly or in pairs before a session of the high council. Torcy appears to have been striving, albeit often vainly, for ministerial agreement before meetings. Examples of his tactics were inadvertently recorded in his *Journal* and were also noted in Saint-Simon's *Mémoires*. On 20 November 1709,[59] after a long conversation with the agent Herman Petkum, Torcy

approached his cousin Desmarets to enlist his vote in a forthcoming council meeting for renewed peace negotiations; on the
evening of 7 December 1709[60] Chancellor Pontchartrain, the duc
de Beauvillier, Voysin, Desmarets and Torcy met at the chancellor's *hôtel* in the town of Versailles to discuss a matter of noble
privilege; on 27 July 1710[61] Torcy spoke to his cousin Desmarets
of 'l'utilité de l'alliance du Nord'; on 10 September 1710,[62] at
the king's behest, Torcy approached Chancellor Pontchartrain
on matters pertaining to the court of Rome (and even though
this interview was sanctioned by the king, it was not monitored
by him); on 5 January 1711 Torcy impressed upon Voysin in a
private interview '*les précautions à prendre dans le traité de neutralité*'[63] in the Spanish Low Countries; on 24 January 1711,
Torcy made an effort to consult 'les autres ministres' regarding
peace negotiations before the meeting of the *conseil d'en haut*; he
did this, he says, because he thought it his duty to consult them
('je crus devoir consulter')...[64]

Despite mutual suspicions aroused by the *secrets du roi et du
ministre*, Louis and Torcy, as king and councillor, increasingly
shared secret confidences of their own after January 1712. The
duc de Saint-Simon reported that on 21 June 1712 'Torcy took
the dispatches to the King. Voysin and Desmarets [who were
already with Louis] left and waited with the courtiers until Torcy
left . . . the courtiers waiting in the drawing-room witnessed this
lack of formality.'[65] Not only did Torcy's sudden appearance in
Louis' chambers create a mood of informality, it also underscored the foreign minister's premier position among the king's
ministers. Repeatedly in the years 1712 to 1715 Torcy interrupted the king's daily routine of meetings by bringing him dispatches that needed an immediate reply; often, it would appear
that Torcy dictated the king's reply to his own secretaries rather
than to a *secrétaire du roi*. Even the letters in the king's own hand
we cannot be certain were written by Louis because – as Torcy
himself reveals in his *Journal* – he could copy not only the King's
signature by his handwriting as well.[66] After the winter of 1713,
with Beauvillier gravely ill and the chancellor Pontchartrain
impatient to retire, Torcy increasingly circumvented the council
when making his recommendations to the king, usually informing his cousin Desmarets of his recommendations, but no other
minister. Torcy's policy of ministerial consensus and of direct

consultation with the king foreshadowed the decline of the *conseil d'en haut's* influence in the eighteenth century and presaged the rise to prominence of the individual minister and his *commis*.

NOTES

1 Max Weber's most important essays on the theory of bureaucracy have been reprinted in *The Theory of Social and Economic Organization*, trans. A. M. Henderson and Talcott Parsons, and edited by the latter (New York, 1947); see also Michael T. Dalby and Michael S. Werthman (eds), *Bureaucracy in Historical Perspective* (Glenview, Ill., London, 1971) especially Max Weber's 'The Ideal Type of Bureaucracy', pp. 3–15, and 'The Durability of Bureaucracy', pp. 140–2; and Peter M. Blau, 'The Implications of Weber's Construct', pp. 16–21.

2 No adequate study exists of the development of French bureaucratic government in the early eighteenth century. The works of Georges Pagès still serve as a brief introduction to the field, especially the last two courses he gave at the Sorbonne in 1937–8: *Les institutions monarchiques sous Louis XIII et Louis XIV*, repr. (Paris, 1961) and *Les origines du XVIIIe siècle au temps de Louis XIV, 1689 à 1715*, repr. (Paris, 1961). Roland Mousnier has recently edited a useful work on *Le Conseil du Roi de Louis XII à la Révolution* (Paris, 1970): see especially the essay by Jean Bérenger on 'Charles Colbert, Marquis de Croissy', pp. 153–74; and William Roth's 'Jean-Baptiste Colbert, Marquis de Torcy', pp. 175–203, the latter a sociologically oriented examination of Torcy's family and fortune. Torcy's career as minister is reviewed in John C. Rule, 'King and Minister: Louis XIV and Colbert de Torcy', in Ragnhild Hatton and J. S. Bromley (eds) *William III and Louis XIV: Essays by and for Mark A. Thomson* (Liverpool, Toronto, 1968) pp. 213–36, hereafter cited as Rule, 'Louis XIV and Colbert de Torcy'. The institutions of diplomacy are surveyed by C. G. Picavet, *La diplomatie française au temps de Louis XIV* (Paris, 1930) especially pp. 27–50. A recent study by J. F. Bosher, *French Finances 1770–1795: from Business to Bureaucracy* (Cambridge, 1970), cautions the reader against assuming that the words 'bureau' and 'bureaucratic' were used with the same precision before the French Revolution as they were during and after that watershed (p. 272 ff). As Bosher suggests (p. 277): 'Bureaucratic organization – collective, unified, regular, mechanical – necessarily depends upon the systematic application of general laws and regulations. The aristocratic society of the ancien régime inevitably undermined all general laws and regulations because privileges, *graces*, favours and marks of distinction consisted in personal exemptions and exceptions.' Bosher's caveats are well taken; but as regards the foreign office, *mutatis mutandis*, I find that marks of favour and privileges did not so much hinder but in some cases, as I hope to show, hastened the growth of the bureaucratic establishment. It should be noted, more-

over, that, unlike the controller-general's office, the ministry of foreign affairs was less encumbered by venal offices.

The references in the first section of my paper are drawn particularly from the Archives des Affaires Etrangères, Paris (A.A.E.), Correspondance Politique (C.P.) and Mémoires et Documents; especially useful for the emergent bureaucracy are A.A.E., Mémoires et Documents, Hollande, 59; A.A.E., Mémoires et Documents, France, 308, 309, 310, 458, 1186 and 1427; helpful throughout are Colbert de Torcy's records of the years 1709, 1710, 1711 as published in Frédéric Masson (ed.), *Journal inédit de Jean-Baptiste Colbert, Marquis de Torcy* (Paris, 1884) hereafter cited as Torcy, *Journal*.

3   Corporately *les importants* have not been studied as a part of the emergent bureaucracy; but individual biographies are illuminating, e.g. Pierre Paul, *Le cardinal Melchior de Polignac* (Paris, 1922) and Henry Mercier, *Une vie d'ambassadeur du Roi Soleil. Les missions de Ch.-F. de Vintimille, comte de Luc, auprès des ligues suisses 1708–1715 et du Saint-Empire 1715–1717* (Paris, 1939).

4   See for Mme de Maintenon's faction at court A. Baudrillart, 'Madame de Maintenon: son rôle politique', *Revue des questions historiques* (1890) p. 111 and *passim* and Rule, 'Louis XIV and Colbert de Torcy', p. 221.

5   The rise of the *noblesse de la plume* is discussed in Georges Pagès, *Les origines du XVIIIᵉ siècle*, pp. 5–11. Typical of careers among the *noblesse de la plume* are those of Michel-Jean Amelot, Nicolas Mesnager and François de Callières. For Michel-Jean Amelot's mission to Spain see Torcy, *Journal*, p. 251, which comments on Amelot as a diplomat; see also Henry Kamen, *The War of Succession in Spain, 1700–15* (London, Bloomington, Ind., 1969) pp. 45, 47 ff. Of Amelot Kamen notes (p. 48) that 'the years of his ambassadorship were not simply the high point of French influence in the period: they were the most favourably remembered'. See also A.A.E., Mémoires et Documents, France, 309, f. 13r. For Nicolas Mesnager see the duc de Saint-Simon, *Mémoires*, ed. A. de Boislisle, 43 vols (Paris, 1879–1930) xviii, 18; and Torcy, *Journal*, p. 229. For Callières' career see Stephen D. Kertesz's Introduction to Callières' *On the Manner of Negotiating with Princes*, trans. A. F. Whyte (New York, 1963) v–xiv.

6   For the Colbert clan see Rule, 'Louis XIV and Colbert de Torcy', pp. 213–14, 218.

7   For a discussion of the *premiers commis* in French diplomacy see Camille Piccioni, *Les premiers commis des affaires étrangères au XVIIᵉ et au XVIIIᵉ siècles* (Paris, 1928) especially pp. 29 ff and 160 ff. On the basic question of finances Piccioni's work seems to rest on rather thin research.

8   Clair Adam's financial accounts are in A.A.E., Mémoires et Documents, France, 309, f. 13r and ff.

9   For the careers of Antoine Pecquet *père* and *fils* see Piccioni, *Les premiers commis*, p. 179. It would appear that the Pecquets drew up their *Discours sur l'art de négocier* (published in Paris, 1737) for study in Torcy's *Académie politique*; the original draft is in A.A.E., Mémoires et

Documents, France, 458, ff. 14–21, under the title 'Sur l'Art de Negotier'.

10 Picavet, *La diplomatie française*, p. 31.

11 Piccioni, *Les premiers commis*, p. 28.

12 Jean de Prévost had been a close associate of Marshal de Boufflers before entering the service of the foreign ministry; he was also *capitoul* of the city of Toulouse; see A.A.E., Mémoires et Documents, France, 309, ff. 13–14.

13 Piccioni, *Les premiers commis*, p. 20.

14 Ibid., p. 23.

15 For Jean de la Chapelle and his intellectual milieu see the detailed article by René Roux, 'Les missions politiques de Jean de la Chapelle, de l'Académie française (1655–1723)', *Revue d'histoire diplomatique* (1926) 239–81.

16 For DuBos' life see A. Lomabard, *L'abbé Du Bos* (Paris, 1913). The Sunderland Papers (D.I. 18) show DuBos as Marshal d'Huxelles' personal secretary at the Gertruydenberg conference of 1710. I am indebted to Dr E. G. Gregg for this reference.

17 Le Grand's papers are in the Bibliothèque Nationale, collection Clairambault, vols 515, 518–21, and scattered through a number of subsequent volumes of the same collection. On at least one of his drafts (B.N., Clairambault, 518) for the 'Constitution' of the *Académie politique* may be found Torcy's own notes: Armand Baschet, *Le duc de Saint-Simon: son cabinet et l'historique de ses manuscrits* (Paris, 1874) p. 227 ff.

18 John C. Rule, 'France and the Preliminaries to the Gertruydenberg Conference, September 1709 to March 1710', in R. Hatton and M. S. Anderson (eds), *Studies in Diplomatic History: Essays in Memory of David Bayne Horn* (London, 1970) p. 112.

19 See Torcy, *Journal*, pp. 315–17.

20 Ibid., p. 200, n. 1; for the Gualterio correspondence with Torcy see *British Museum*, Add. MSS. 20319, vol. II: Papers of Cardinal F. A. Gualterio to Marquis de Torcy, 1709–27. In 1715 Gualterio received a pension of 20,000 livres from the French government: A.A.E., Mémoires et Documents, France, 310, f. 239v.

21 A.A.E., Mémoires et Documents, France, 308, 309, 310, *passim*, contain detailed financial accounting of the foreign ministry.

22 Frédéric Masson, *Le département des affaires étrangères pendant la Révolution, 1787–1804* (Paris, 1877) p. 11.

23 See E. Vaillé, *Histoire générale des postes françaises* (Paris, 1951) v, pp. 312–25. Pajot accompanied Torcy to The Hague during May and June 1709; there he and Torcy talked with several of their Dutch agents. For examples of summary reports from French secret agents to Torcy and Pajot see A.A.E., Mémoires et Documents, France, 308, ff. 1–6v, 'Mémoires Secrets'.

24 For Le Dran's career see Baschet, *Le duc de Saint-Simon*, p. 228; and Leopold Delisle, 'L'origine des Archives du Ministère des Affaires Etrangères', *Bibliothèque de l'Ecole des Chartes* (1874) p. 16.

25 See R. Mousnier, 'Le Conseil du Roi de la mort de Henri IV au gouvernement personnel de Louis XIV', *Etudes d'histoire moderne et contemporaine*, I (1947) 187.

26 See Le Grand's 'Projet de l'estude', B.N., Clairambault, 519, f. 321; also J. J. Jusserand, *The School for Ambassadors and other Studies* (New York, 1925) pp. 3–61, and H. M. A. Keens-Soper, 'The French Political Academy, 1712: 'A School for Ambassadors', *European Studies Review* (1972) 329–55.

27 See the 'Règlement ordonné par le Roi pour l'Académie royale des Sciences', in Bernard le Bovier de Fontenelle, *Eloges des académiciens avec l'histoire de l'Académie royale des Sciences*, I (The Hague, 1740) p. 9.

28 See John C. Rule, 'Jérome Phélypeaux, Comte de Pontchartrain and the Establishment of Louisiana, 1696–1715', in John F. McDermott (ed.), *Frenchmen and French Ways in the Mississippi Valley* (Urbana, 1969) pp. 181–5, in which I discuss the reorganisation of the ministry of marine.

29 The edict creating the *trésoriers des ambassadeurs* was promulgated in December 1706: A.A.E., Mémoires et Documents, France, 307, ff. 82–5. In this edict the *trésoriers* are referred to as 'principaux Commis'; see also A.A.E., Mémoires et Documents, France, 309, f. 12v–13r, in which Jean de Prévost is given the title 'Trésorier general alternatif des ambassadeurs'.

30 The bureau for *chiffre* had been reorganised in the 1660s by Hugues de Lionne; at that time the bureau came under the direction of *commis* Pachau and 'deux garçons'; by 1710 the bureau employed at least five full-time *commis*.

31 See Paul Cottin (ed.), *Rapports inédits du Lieutenant de Police, René d'Argenson 1697–1715* (Paris, 1891) where pp. 9, 63, 90 and 195 have letters from d'Argenson to Torcy.

32 Both Clair Adam and Pecquet *père* could sign Torcy's name in his absence: see Piccioni, *Les premiers commis*, p. 22.

33 A.A.E., Mémoires et Documents, France, 309, f. 13 ff, reveal that Jean de Prévost and Clair Adam received 7500 livres per annum for services rendered to the ministry; this was, however, only one of their sources of income; others included pensions, *acquits-patents*, special assignments to the *conseil d'en haut* and to the Post Office. Ibid., ff. 60–70r, gives for the year 1711 the salary (*emplois*) schedule for most of the *commis* in the ministry: for example, Abbé Le Grand received 500 livres every two months; Du Theil, before he became a *premier commis*, was paid at the same rate; Lullier, as a *commis*, was paid 1500 livres per annum, plus supplements, which perhaps doubled his salary; Aubert, as a *premier commis*, received between 7000 and 10,000 livres per annum; St Prest was paid at the same rate; La Chapelle received between 2000 and 4000 livres per annum; in 1715 Lullier had a pension or 'gratification ordinaire' of 2000 livres: A.A.E., Mémoires et Documents, France, 310, f. 238.

34 Ibid., 309, f. 141 ff.

35 Ibid., 449, ff. 47r–70r, 100r ff, contain the letters of Torcy to Marshal

de Villars over several years (1710–13) and give us a good example of the use of the 'postscript'. A.A.E., C.P., Autriche, 94 supplies a splendid example of Torcy's work, especially in 'Observations sur le projet du Traitté de paix', ff. 121r–138r. This is the draft treaty of Rastadt, dated January 1714, largely dictated by Torcy and containing corrections, additions and a running commentary in Torcy's own hand.

36 The revised protocol manual, entitled 'Protocole pour les lettres du Roy . . .' is dated 31 December 1712: A.A.E., Mémoires et Documents, France, 309, ff. 258–66. Another manual, undated, is titled 'Formulaire du Cabinet du Roy pour les lettres de la main de Sa Mt^e': ibid., 310, ff. 161–2.

37 See A. Baschet, *Histoire du dépôt des Archives des Affaires Etrangères* (Paris, 1875) p. 93 ff.

38 Torcy, *Journal*, p. 77.

39 Baschet, *Histoire du dépôt*, p. 109 ff.

40 Usually Torcy kept very exact accounts of his meetings with envoys under the title 'Mémorandum du audiences accordé par le Ministre de Torcy aux . . . diplomatiques étrangers': A.A.E., Mémoires et Documents, France, 308, ff. 3r–4r; ibid., 310, f. 23 ff. See also Torcy, *Journal*, pp. 9–10, 103, 229–30 and *passim* for the use Torcy made of these memoranda.

41 Torcy, *Journal*, p. 145.

42 Ibid., p. 316 ff.

43 See Rule, 'France and the Preliminaries to Gertruydenberg', in Hatton and Anderson (eds), *Studies in Diplomatic History*, p. 99 ff.

44 For the 'memorandum' see above, note 40.

45 *The Secret Correspondence of Madame de Maintenon with the Princess des Ursins*, I (London, 1827) p. 83 and *passim*.

46 Torcy, *Journal*, p. 47.

47 E. Vaillé, *Le cabinet noir* (Paris, 1950) pp. 110–26.

48 A.A.E., Mémoires et Documents, France, 1145, ff. 233–46 and 261–4r, contain correspondence of d'Argenson concerning the interrogation of members of the Post Office in Paris.

49 Ibid., 310, f. 23 ff; and Torcy, *Journal*, pp. 95–7, 126, 190–1, for descriptions of the foreign minister's audiences with foreign envoys.

50 A.A.E., Mémoires et Documents, France, 308, f. 3r ff; ibid., 310, f. 23 ff; these volumes contain examples of the *carnets* Torcy kept of his audiences; other examples may be found scattered through A.A.E., Mémoires et Documents, France, vols 308–11.

51 Baschet, *Histoire du dépôt*, p. 101 ff.

52 Torcy, *Journal*, *passim*; in this confidential chronicle Torcy records, among other things, his impressions of meetings of the *conseil d'en haut* and his private working sessions with the king.

53 A synoptic view of Louis XIV's later councils appears in a letter of Abbé Charles Irénée St Pierre, dated 1702, printed by Merle L. Perkins under the title 'The Councils of Louis XIV', in *French Review* (1957) 395–7. This paragraph is drawn largely from the accounts of Abbé St Pierre and from Torcy's *Journal*.

54 Torcy, *Journal*, p. 125.

55 For the letter in which the princess des Ursins welcomes Chamillart's successor see M. A. Geffroy (ed.) *Lettres inédites de la Princesse des Ursins* (Paris, 1887) pp. 368–9.

56 This paragraph is drawn largely from my articles: 'Louis XIV and Colbert de Torcy', and 'Jérome Phélypeaux, Comte de Pontchartrain'.

57 For a detailed description of the king's *secret* see A. Baudrillart, *Philippe V et la cour de France*, I (Paris, 1890) p. 8 ff.

58 The record of the secret English negotiations is in A.A.E., C.P., Angleterre, 231, f. 31 ff; see also G. M. Trevelyan, 'The Jersey Period of the Negotiations Leading to the Peace of Utrecht', *English Historical Review* (1934) 100–5.

59 Torcy, *Journal*, p. 33.

60 Ibid., p. 57.

61 Ibid., p. 231.

62 Ibid., p. 265.

63 Ibid., p. 337.

64 Ibid., p. 356.

65 Saint-Simon, *Mémoires*, trans. and ed. Lucy Norton, II (London, 1968) p. 259.

66 Torcy, *Journal*, p. 323, for 26 December 1710: 'Elle [Sa Majesté, Louis] voulut lui écrire une lettre de Sa Main. Lorsque je Lui en montrai la minute que je devais transcrire en imitant Son écriture . . .'

Glossary

Aulic Council: a court of the Holy Roman Empire (established in 1495) more under the emperor's control than the Imperial Chamber.

Burgundian Circle: one of the ten circles of the Holy Roman Empire, ceded to the line of the Spanish Habsburgs on the abdication of Charles V in 1556.

Bureau de chiffre: cipher office.

Chambres des Réunions: courts established at Metz, Besançon and Brisach (Breisach) charged with investigating claims acquired by Louis XIV at the peace-makings of Münster, Aix-la-Chapelle and Nijmegen in respect of alienated territorial dependencies and sovereign rights of new conquests..

Commis: clerk.

Conseil d'en haut: 'the high council', Louis XIV's small inner council which advised him on policy.

Décapole: the ten cities of Alsace which at the 1648 Peace were ceded to France only in respect of their 'provincial overlordship', but which were later occupied and eventually ceded to France with full sovereignty: Colmar, Haguenau, Kaysersberg, Landau, Munster, Obernai, Rosheim, Sélestat, Turkheim, Wissembourg. The German names of the members of the Zehnstädebund of 1354 are Kolmar, Hagenau, Kaysersberg, Münster, Oberehnheim, Rosheim, Schlettstadt, Türkheim, Weissenburg and Landau (which replaced Mülhausen when in 1510 it joined the Swiss cantons).

Devolution: law of *Jus Devolutionis*, a local Brabant law which specified that a child of a first marriage was entitled to demand his inheritance, on the death of his father, ahead of children of a later marriage.

Electors of the Holy Roman Empire in this period: the ecclesiastical archbishop-electors of Cologne, Mainz, Trier; the secular electors of Bavaria, Bohemia, Brandenburg, Brunswick-Lüneburg (Hanover), the Palatinate, Saxony.

Exekutionstag: assembly at Nuremburg in 1649, to put into effect the terms of the treaties of Westphalia.

Frontière de fer: literally 'iron-frontier', referring to French fortresses in the north and east of France to protect the heart of the country from invasion.

The Germanies: indicating both the Holy Roman Empire of the German Nation and the Austrian Habsburg dominions.

Grand Dauphin: Louis XIV's son, the dauphin, was frequently given this title after the birth of his own son.

King of the Romans: a title bestowed on the eldest son (or other relative) of the Holy Roman Emperor of the German Nation as a promise that he would be elected the next emperor.

Landeshoheit: literally 'majesty over the land', the near-sovereignty granted to individual German princes by the emperor at the Peace of Westphalia 1648.

Pfaffenstrasse: literally 'the pope's street', term used to indicate the three Catholic archbishopric-electorates of Cologne, Mainz, Trier (*see also* Electors).

Reduction: (from Swedish *reduktion*) resumption, usually of alienated crown land and/or revenues, used particularly of that effected by Charles XI of Sweden from the 1680s onwards.

Réunions: the 'reunited territories', the absorption into France of one-time dependencies of areas gained at the peace-makings of 1648, 1668 and 1678/9, used particularly in respect of the reunions affected by Louis XIV after the Peace of Nijmegen in 1678/9 and largely abandoned at the Peace of Ryswick (1697).

Rhenish archbishopric-electorates: see Electors.

Wildfang: a privilege granted to the elector palatine by the emperor in early times and confirmed by Maximilian I and Charles V under the title *Bastardorum et aescriptitiorum wildfangorium haereditates.* This caused trouble after 1632 when the elector interpreted the privilege to cover not only his own subjects but also 'foreigners', Germans and non-Germans, who came into his territories. He also attempted to extend the privilege to enclaves of other princes inside the Palatinate territories. This later interpretation was forbidden by imperial authority on 17 February 1667.

Chronology

1635   France at war with Philip IV of Spain (till 1659).

1636   France at war with the Austrian Habsburgs.

1638   5 September. Birth of Louis, dauphin of France, son of Louis XIII and Queen Anne (Ana of Austria).

1642–9   Civil war in England, Ireland and Scotland; Stuart cause lost to Cromwell.

1643   14 May. Death of Louis XIII, accession of Louis XIV; regent (after setting aside Louis XIII's will) the queen-mother Anne with Mazarin, Louis XIV's godfather and governor, as *premier ministre*.

1645–69   Candian war between Venice and Ottoman empire; France helps Venice; Candia (Crete), besieged 1658–69, is obliged to give in and Venice cedes the island (bar some fortified places) in 1670.

1648   *January*. Separate peace between Spain and the Dutch Republic whereby Dutch independence is recognised with some cession of land from the Spanish Netherlands (in Limburg, Brabant and Flanders) known henceforth as the Generality Lands; the river Scheldt closed to European maritime traffic. Peace of Westphalia (negotiated at Osnabrück, Sweden presiding, and at Münster, France presiding, between 1644 and 1648): France, as *satisfactio* for helping the anti-Austrian side and preventing the Habsburg attempt at achieving a *Monarchie*, obtains the sovereignty of Metz, Toul and Verdun, occupied by France since 1552, the Habsburg Landgravate of Upper and Lower Alsace though without seat and vote in the diet, and the city of Breisach.

1648–52   Civil war in France, the Fronde (or the Frondes if distinction is made between the revolt of the *parlements*, the 'revolt of the judges', and the revolt of the high nobility).

1651   Louis XIV declared of age.

L*

1652–4	First Anglo-Dutch war (Denmark-Norway ally of Dutch Republic).
1654	Mazarin gains entry to and a measure of control over the neutral (anti-Habsburg) League of the Rhine.
	Louis XIV consecrated and crowned king at Rheims; takes part in campaigns against Spain on north and north-eastern frontier of France.
1656	Cromwell becomes France's ally in war against Spain.
1657–61	War between Dutch Republic and Portugal over Brazil; Dutch acknowledge Portuguese sovereignty over Brazil.
1659	Peace of Pyrenees. Spain cedes to France frontier fortresses in Flanders and Artois and gives back Roussillon and Cerdagne (ceded to Spain in 1492 in an attempt to buy Ferdinand of Aragon's neutrality in the Italian wars); Spain's ally, the duke of Lorraine, is restored to most of his duchy though the French keep the duchy of Bar, Clermont and some other places and are permitted a 'military route' of communication with the Three Bishoprics (of Metz, Toul, Verdun) and Alsace.
1660	*9 June.* Marriage of Louis XIV and Maria Teresa, infanta of Spain, daughter of Philip IV; she renounces her right of inheritance to the Spanish crown in return for a promised dowry of 50,000 *écus*.
	French mediation ensures Peace of Oliva between Sweden, Brandenburg and Poland.
	Restoration of the Stuarts in England, Ireland and Scotland.
1661	*28 February.* Duke Charles IV of Lorraine accepts the strategic routes but recovers the duchy of Bar.
	9 March. Death of Mazarin; Louis XIV decides to govern without a first minister; beginning of cabinet and *conseil* government and of bureaucratisation.
	Clash of Spanish and French ambassadors in London; Philip IV of Spain apologises, 1662.
1661–4	War between the Austrian Habsburgs and the Ottoman empire; France sends a contingent which participates in the battle of St Gotthard in Hungary.
1662	*6 February.* Treaty of Montmartre whereby Charles IV of Lorraine promises to pursue a pro-French policy and to leave Lorraine and Bar to Louis XIV in his will. The agreement is upset (*a*) because the duke's heir (his nephew) does not agree, and (*b*) because the

French princes of the blood are unwilling to accept Louis' counter-promise : that all members of the House of Lorraine shall enter their ranks.

Defensive alliance of France and the Dutch Republic to secure English recognition of their fishing rights in the Channel and North Sea.

Charles II offers to sell Dunkirk (won from Spain in war of 1656–9) to Louis XIV; accepts 5,000,000 francs for the place.

1662–4   Quarrel in Rome between French ambassador and the pope over diplomatic privileges (Corsican guard incident) : Louis XIV occupies Avignon and the county of Venaissin until apologies are offered and France's allies, the dukes of Parma and Modena, have had territories occupied by the pope restored.

1663   Louis XIV adopts device *Nec Pluribus Impar* (not unequal to many).

Fruitless negotiations between Philip IV and Louis XIV on Maria Teresa's right of inheritance in the Spanish Netherlands (the Law of Devolution) since dowry has remained unpaid. Louis indirectly (via subsidies to England) supports Portugal's struggle for independence (begun 1640, completed 1668) from Spain; in 1667 direct subsidies by France to Portugal.

Renewal of the League of the Rhine to which Denmark, Saxony and Brandenburg accede.

Louis XIV occupies Marsal in Lorraine as Duke Charles IV has taken the emperor's side, thus breaking the Treaty of Montmartre.

1664   Louis XIV's negotiations with the Dutch Republic on the future of the Spanish Netherlands break down.

1664–71   Hungarian struggle for independence from Austria, with Turkish help.

1665–7   Second Anglo-Dutch War, in which France is the ally of the Dutch Republic, is ended by Treaty of Breda, by which the Dutch cede the New Netherlands in North America to England and receive in return Surinam and concessions in the Navigation Act, while France cedes to England Antigua, Montserrat and St Kitts and receives in return Acadia.

1667   Renewal (last) of League of the Rhine.

1667–8   War of Devolution (War of the Queen's Rights). Philip IV had died in 1665, and Louis argues that by a local law of inheritance in the Spanish Netherlands Maria

1667–8 *cont.* Teresa, the only surviving child of Philip IV's first
marriage, could demand that the son of the second
marriage, Carlos II, should cede parts of the Low
Countries to her; he lays claims also to part of
Franche-Comté and Luxembourg: at the Peace of
Aix-la-Chapelle Spain cedes twelve fortified places in
the Spanish Netherlands.

1668   Secret partition treaty (first proposed by Louis in
1665) between Louis XIV and Leopold I as to the
Spanish inheritance on the death of Carlos II: Louis
to receive the Spanish Netherlands, Franche-Comté,
Naples and Sicily with the Tuscan ports (the *Presidios*),
Navarre, the Phillippines and the African har-
bours of Spain; Leopold to have Spain with its overseas empire, the duchy of Milan, Minorca and the
Balearic islands.

1670   Occupation of the whole of Lorraine by Louis XIV,
occasioned by the duke's continued anti-French policy.

1670–2   French attempts to isolate Dutch Republic diplomatically as countermoves to Dutch diplomatic activities
(from 1668) to stop French encroachments in the
Spanish Netherlands, now conceived as a buffer, or
barrier, between the Republic and France. French
tariffs aimed against the Dutch; Dutch boycott of
French goods.

1672–   The so-called Dutch War, a general war occasioned
1678/9   by an Anglo-French attack on the Republic. Charles
II was forced by public opinion as expressed in parliament to make peace with the Dutch in 1674. Louis'
other ally, the bishop of Münster, also makes peace;
and Sweden, which reluctantly comes into the war on
the French side in 1675, does so only in respect of
Brandenburg and is in its turn attacked by Denmark-
Norway which hoped to recover provinces lost in 1658
and 1660. The Republic's allies, from 1673 onwards,
embraced Spain, the emperor and the Empire. At the
Peace of Nijmegen the Republic (as the attacked
party) receives *satisfactio* in the form of commercial
concessions (a lowering of the French tariffs) and William of Orange, now *stadholder* of the Republic, has
his principality of Orange restored; Lorraine is also
restored with the exception of Nancy and Longwy and
the four military routes, but its duke preferred to live
in exile and French occupation continued till 1697.

Spain, having declared war on France, cedes Franche-Comté, many towns in the Spanish Netherlands and Haiti in the West Indies. The emperor accepts the French interpretation of sovereignty over the *Décapole* in Alsace and cedes Freiburg (Fribourg).

1674–8   Messina revolt against Spain, supported by France until peace negotiations in the Dutch war started in earnest in 1677.

1680   City of Paris bestows title of Le Grand on Louis XIV.

1680 onwards   Construction of Vauban's *frontière de fer*, first in respect of the Spanish Netherlands frontier, then also in the east.

1680–4   Reunion policy carried out by the courts of reunion (*Chambres des réunions*) at Metz, Besançon and Brisach to ascertain and claim for France former dependencies of areas ceded to France between 1648 and 1697 : annexations of Montbéliard, county of Chiny, towns in the Saar and in Lower Alsace; sovereignty claimed also over Baden and Zweibrücken, and attempts to obtain the duchy of Luxembourg as equivalent for claims in the Spanish Netherlands.

1681   Louis obtains the 'voluntary' union with France of Strassburg (henceforth Strasbourg) which in 1674 and 1677 had permitted its bridge over the Rhine to be used for the invasion of France; local autonomy and religious freedom granted.

Louis XIV buys Casale, the key to northern Italy, from the duke of Mantua.

1682–99   War between Ottoman empire and the Austrian Habsburgs (with contingents from the Empire and in alliance with Poland from 1683). Siege of Vienna 1683. From 1684 War of the Holy League, inspired and partially financed by the pope, in which Venice as well as Poland participates and which Muscovy (Russia) joins in 1686. Greater Hungary (under Turkish rule since 1541) reconquered by Imperial generals. Louis refuses to take part in war, claiming that France is doing its share by fighting the infidel in North Africa. Growing French fear of Austrian gains in land in Eastern Europe and in prestige.

1683   France tries to isolate the town of Luxembourg as part of the reunion policy. Spain declares war on France to safeguard the Spanish Netherlands and Luxembourg.

1684   *May*. Genoa, the active ally of Spain, is bombarded.
        June. The fortress of Luxembourg is taken by France.
        August. Truce of Ratisbon (Regensburg) for twenty
        years. Louis XIV obtains recognition from the em-
        peror Leopold I, the Empire and Spain of the exten-
        sion of his frontiers achieved by the reunion policy,
        his control of Strasbourg, his occupation of Lorraine,
        and Luxembourg. In return he promises to present
        no further claims. The Dutch Republic accepts the
        terms of this truce, which Louis hopes will become per-
        manent.

1685   Doge of Genoa ordered to visit Louis XIV.
        Siamese embassy visits Versailles.
        Palatine succession issue to the fore on the extinction
        of the direct line; the new ruler, the duke of Neuburg,
        is a close ally of the emperor and therefore feared by
        Louis, who raises the issue of his sister-in-law's claims
        (for her *immeubles* and for some allodial land) from
        her late brother's estate.
        Revocation of the Edict of Nantes; revulsion against
        Louis in the Protestant states.

1686   League of Augsburg by Spain, the emperor and some
        German princes to guard against expansionist policy
        of Louis XIV.

1687   Tension between Pope Innocent XI and Louis XIV
        over the franchise (*quartier*) issue. French ambassador
        excommunicated, and, secretly, also Louis XIV.
        French occupation of Avignon.

1688   The Cologne issue : Louis hopes that Wilhelm-Egon
        von Fürstenberg, the pro-French coadjutor of the late
        archbishop-elector, will achieve papal dispensation
        for his election by less than the stipulated majority of
        the chapter; the pope refuses this as well as Louis'
        compromise solution that Joseph Clement of Bavaria,
        the emperor's candidate, should become Fürstenberg's
        coadjutor, and gives his dispensation to the Bavarian
        prince (who needed it because he was under age).
        Birth of a son to James II and Mary of Modena;
        political and religious crisis in England leads to in-
        vasion by William III of Orange. James flees to
        France and establishes a court in exile at Saint-
        Germain-en-Laye.
        French occupation (and in 1689 devastation) of the
        Palatinate (*a*) to prevent Imperial occupation and (*b*)

to create a diversion that might persuade the Turks to carry on the war against Austria.

1689   James II having been deemed to have abdicated, William III and Mary are made joint monarchs of England, Scotland and Ireland.

James II's attempt, with French help, to keep Ireland fails; a rebellion in his favour in Scotland is defeated. Louis melts down royal gold and silverware to help finance the war.

1689–97   Nine Years War, also called the War of the First Grand Alliance, the Palatinate War, the War of Orléans (after Elisabeth d'Orléans) or, more misleadingly, the War of the League of Augusburg (since not all the signatories took part in the war). The anti-French allies include Austria, the Maritime Powers, many German princes (Bavaria, Brandenburg and, in time, all the Brunswick-Lüneburg dukes), Spain and Savoy.

1692   Ninth Electorate (Brunswick-Lüneburg, usually called Hanover) to gain Ernst August for the war against France.

Louis XIV's plan to help James II invade England fails.

1693   Louis XIV reconciles himself with the pope, Avignon occupation comes to an end.

1696   Louis XIV buys peace with Savoy at the cost of sacrificing Pignerol and Casale; this peace leads to neutralisation of Italy and, eventually, to end of the European war.

1697   Peace of Ryswick. Louis XIV restores most of the re-unions (though eighty-two Spanish places are retained). He also restores Lorraine with the exception of Saar-Louis and Longwy. In return he receives confirmation of his possession of Strasbourg and of the French interpretation of sovereignty over the *Décapole*. The fourth article, now known to have been inspired mainly by Leopold I, stipulates that the Catholic religion must not be changed in the territories returned. Navigation on the Rhine is declared free and the contested issues in the Palatinate and Cologne are submitted to the arbitration which Louis had in vain sought in 1688; in both cases the decision goes against him. William III recognised as king of England, Ireland, and Scotland by Louis XIV.

1698   First Barrier Convention between the Dutch Republic and Spain (foreshadowed during the Ryswick negotiations when Louis XIV had consented to it) whereby
Dutch troops were to garrison certain towns in the
Spanish Netherlands to provide a 'barrier' against
French invasions. The arrangement had certain economic advantages for the Dutch, and the money spent
on the garrisons was to be repaid in the future. The
king of Spain had the right to give three months'
notice to cancel the agreement and ask the Dutch
garrisons to leave.

October. First partition-treaty to solve the Spanish
succession issue between France and the Maritime
Powers. Joseph Ferdinand, electoral prince of Bavaria,
to inherit Spain, the Spanish Netherlands, and its
empire overseas; Spain's non-Iberian territories in
Europe to be given in compensation for the claims of
Louis XIV and Leopold : the archduke Charles of
Austria (Leopold's second son) to receive the duchy
of Milan; the dauphin to have Naples, Sicily, the
Tuscan ports and the province of Guipúzcoa in
Spain.

November. Carlos II, to counteract the partition plan,
makes Joseph Ferdinand his sole heir.

1699   *6 February*. Death of Joseph Ferdinand.

1700   *3, 25 March*. Second partition treaty made necessary by
the death of Joseph Ferdinand. The archduke Charles
to receive the whole of Spain, the Spanish Netherlands
and Spain's overseas possessions; the dauphin's share
to be augmented with the duchy of Milan though a
secret clause stipulates its exchange with either Lorraine or Savoy and Nice; Naples, Sicily, the Tuscan
ports and the Guispúzcoa as before; invitations to
others to accede, and especially to Leopold I who,
however, proves unwilling to tolerate encroachment
of other powers in Italy.

Lorraine accepts exchange Lorraine–Milan in principle; Louis negotiates with the duke of Savoy for
an exchange which would give the duke Naples and
Sicily against all, or the larger part of his north
Italian territories; William III, who had at first been
much against this idea, comes round to it when he
realises parliamentary opinion is against French possession of Naples and Sicily.

August. Portugal accedes to the Second Partition Treaty on being promised Alcantara and Badajoz.

October. Carlos II, after consultation with the pope, leaves Spain and all its possessions undivided to Louis' grandson Philip, duke of Anjou or, failing him, his younger brother Berri; if Louis does not accept on behalf of either grandson, the same offer of undivided possession to go to Archduke Charles and, if Leopold refuses, to Victor Amadeus of Savoy on account of his Spanish blood (his great-grandmother had been a sister of Philip II).

1 November. Death of Carlos II.

16 November. Louis XIV accepts Carlos' will though he takes care not to let Philip cross the Spanish frontier until the time limit (already prolonged) for Leopold to accede to the Second Partition Treaty has expired.

1700–21   Great Northern War; attack on Sweden by Denmark-Norway, Saxony-Poland and Russia, joined in 1715 by Prussia and Hanover.

1701   *February.* Dutch garrison troops recalled from the Barrier after Louis XIV, at the request of the Spanish council, has moved in French troops to forestall a feared take-over of the country by its governor, Max Emmanuel, and the Dutch Republic.

Frederick III, elector of Brandenburg, given permission by the emperor Leopold to assume the title König in Preussen.

France buys the unexpired portion of the asiento held by a Portuguese company.

April. Franco-Savoyard treaty, French subsidies in return for Victor Amadeus' help to defend northern Italy against Leopold I.

July. Austrian troops enter the duchy of Milan.

7 September. Grand Alliance against Louis XIV is formed by Austria and the Maritime Powers after fruitless negotiations to achieve a new partition treaty at The Hague. Gains stipulated for the Allies. Invitations to others to adhere to alliance; Brandenburg joins early.

17 September. Louis XIV recognises James Edward Stuart as king of England.

1702   *March.* Death of William III, Queen Anne succeeds him. The Dutch Republic enters its second stadholderless period (till 1747).

1702–
1713/14   War of the Spanish Succession. Louis XIV's allies are
           Philip V of Spain, Maximilian of Bavaria and his
           brother Joseph Clement, archbishop-elector of
           Cologne, and the archbishop-elector of Trier. The war
           aims widen during negotiations in 1703 for the alliance
           of Portugal and Savoy, and the slogan 'Spain entire'
           is adopted. Main English war aim : safeguarding the
           Protestant succession, share in Spanish overseas trade,
           conquests in the Caribbean, on the Spanish Main and
           in the Mediterranean; chief Dutch war aim : an en-
           larged Barrier, preferably forcing France back to her
           1659 frontier with the Spanish Netherlands, share in
           Spanish overseas trade and conquests in the Caribbean
           and on the Spanish Main; Austrian war aim : over-
           turning the 1648 and 1678 settlements and a German
           barrier against France, control of Italy by possession
           of Milan, Naples and Sicily and recovery of ancient
           fiefs.

1703–11   Hungarian and Transylvanian independence move-
           ment intertwined with the War of the Spanish Suc-
           cession. 1711, Peace of Szatmar brings compromise
           settlement : Habsburg government is made hereditary
           against an undertaking to respect the Hungarian con-
           stitution.

1704   Devastation by the allies of Bavaria.
           March. Archduke Charles lands at Lisbon.
           August. An Anglo-Dutch force captures Gibraltar in
           in the name of 'Charles III'.

1706   *May*. Anglo-Dutch condominium over the Spanish
           Netherlands (till 1715).

1706–10   Various and separate peace negotiations between
           Louis XIV and members of the Grand Alliance; all
           unfruitful.

1710   Change of government from Whig to Tory in England
           and peace preliminaries signed in October 1711 with
           France.

1712   *July*. Suspension of arms by England as against
           France.

1713   General peace settlement at Utrecht, negotiated be-
           tween England and France. The Protestant succession
           is confirmed, James Edward Stuart has to leave
           France; the permanent separation of France and
           Spain is stipulated; the fortifications of Dunkirk are to
           be demolished; France restores or cedes to Britain

Newfoundland, the Hudson Bay territory, Acadia and St Kitts, and abolishes tariffs imposed since 1664; in return France is permitted to incorporate the principality of Orange into France and has Lille restored to her. The partition of Spain is effected in so far as the Spanish Netherlands, the duchy of Milan, Naples and Sardinia is given to the emperor Charles VI, while Sicily goes to Victor Amadeus of Savoy (with the title king of Sicily). Spain cedes to Britain Gibraltar and Minorca and grants her the slave-trade *asiento* for the record period of thirty years. The Republic receives a Barrier, but much smaller than expected, and France keeps all territory gained between 1659 and 1702; Portugal achieves minor frontier rectifications at Spain's expense in South America.

1714   Peace of Rastadt (with emperor) and Baden in Argau (Empire) in so far as Louis XIV is concerned : the Peace of Utrecht is confirmed, so is the Peace of Ryswick, thus upholding the French interpretation of sovereignty over the bishoprics and Alsace. Landau is ceded to France as the campaign of 1713–14 had gone in Louis' favour, and the electors of Bavaria and Cologne are restored.

12 August. Death of Queen Anne, succession of Georg Ludwig, elector of Hanover, as George I.

1714–18   War between Turkey and Venice in which Austria intervenes in 1716.

1715   Louis XIV proposes a 'diplomatic revolution' to Charles VI, a Habsburg–Bourbon alliance. There is some interest in Vienna; but suspicion, this time unfounded, that France has been egging on the party in Turkey which wants to attempt a reversal of the Peace of Karlowitz (1699) brings failure of negotiations and the *renversement des alliances* is not achieved till 1756.

Barrier treaty between Austria, the Dutch Republic and Britain : the Dutch Barrier is fixed and payment for the Dutch garrisons arranged. A further Barrier convention, for the security of payment, is made in December 1718.

1715–16   Stuart rebellion in Britain in favour of James III is crushed; no help given by Louis XIV.

1717–20   Aftermath of the War of the Spanish Succession : efforts to make peace between Charles VI and Philip V. By

1717–20
cont.

1720 Philip V accepts the loss of Sardinia, Sicily, Naples and the duchy of Milan against Charles VI's accepting him as king of Spain; Philip also receives a promise of succession to Parma, Piacenza and Tuscany for the elder son of his marriage with Elisabeth Farnese. As part of the Quadruple Alliance settlement of this European problem Victor Amadeus agrees to exchange Sicily for Sardinia.

1719–21

A series of peace settlements (the last at Nystad with Russia) ends the Great Northern War; thanks mainly to French efforts (by Louis XIV in 1714–15 and after that by the Regent for Louis XV) Sweden keeps a foothold in the Empire (until 1815), but she loses most of Pomerania to Prussia, Bremen and Verden to Hanover, and all her east Baltic provinces to Russia. She sacrifices the Holstein-Gottorp alliance and her freedom from Sound dues to Denmark's benefit.

List of Persons

Abraham of Sancta Clara (Johann Ulrich Megerlin or Megerlee) 1644–1710, Catholic preacher and writer.

Adam, Clair (*c.* 1640–50–1725), French official.

Alègre, Yves, marquis d' (1653–1733), French officer and diplomat.

Alfonso VI (Affonso o Bravo), king of Portugal 1325–57 (b. 1290).

Amelot (de Gournay), Michel Jean (1655–1724), French diplomat.

Anne (1600–66), infanta of Spain and therefore styled Ana (Anne) of Austria, queen of France after her marriage to Louis XIII, regent for Louis XIV after 1643.

Anne, queen of Great Britain 1702–14 (b. 1665).

Anne-Marie d'Orléans, niece of Louis XIV, *see* Montpensier.

Argenson, Marc-René de Voyer, marquis d' (1652–1721), lieutenant-general of police in Paris from 1697.

Asfeld, Benôit Bidal, baron d' (1658–1715), French officer and diplomat.

Auersberg (also Auersperg), Joh. Weichard, *Graf* von (1615–77), statesman in Austrian service.

Augustus of Saxony and Poland, (1670–1733), Frederick Augustus I as elector of Saxony 1670–1733; Augustus II as elected king of Poland from 1697.

Aumont, Louis, marquis de Villequier, later duc d' (1666–1723), French officer and courtier, used on diplomatic mission.

Avaux, Claude de Mesmes, comte d' (1595–1650), French diplomat.

Avaux, Jean-Antoine Mesmes, comte d' (1640–1709), French diplomat, nephew of the above.

Barbezieux, Louis-François-Marie Le Tellier, marquis de (1668–1701), French war minister, son of Louvois.

Bart, Jean (1650–1702), French privateering captain and naval officer.

Bayle, Pierre (1647–1706), French philosopher who in 1681 settled in the Dutch Republic.

Beauvillier (also Beauvilliers), Paul, comte de Saint-Aignan and duc de (1684–1714), member of the *conseil d'en haut* 1691–1712.

Bernard, Samuel (1651–1739), French financier.

Berwick, James Fitz-James (1670–1734), 1st duke of, natural son of Charles II, marshal of France.

Béthune, François-Gaston, marquis de (1638–1693), French officer and diplomat.

Bidal, Benôit, *see* **Asfeld.**

Bielke, Nils, count (1644–1716), Swedish field-marshal and statesman.

Bodin, Jean (1530–96), French political theorist.

Bolingbroke, Henry St John, 1st viscount from 1713 (1678–1751), English statesman.

Bonnac, Jean Louis d'Usson, marquis de (1672–1738), French diplomat.

Bonrepaus, François d'Usson (*c.* 1650–1719), French diplomat.

Boufflers, Louis François, duc de (1644–1711), marshal of France.

Bourgogne, *see* **Burgundy.**

Bretel de Grémonville, *see* **Grémonville.**

Burgundy, Louis de France, duc de (1682–1712), grandson of Louis XIV, dauphin from 14 April 1711 to his death 18 February 1712.

Byng, Sir George, Viscount Torrington from 1721 (1663–1733), British admiral.

Callières, François de (1645–1717), French writer and diplomat.

Callot, Jacques (1584–1635), French engraver.

Carlos II, king of Spain 1665–1700 (b. 1661).

Catinat, Nicolas (1637–1712), marshal of France from 1693.

Chamillart, Michel de (1652–1712), French controller-general 1699, secretary of state for war 1701.

Chamlay, Jules-Louis Bolé, marquis de (1650-1719), French officer who prepared reports of Louis' campaigns in the Dutch War.

Charles V, Holy Roman emperor 1519–56 (b. 1500), ruler of the Burgundian state 1506–56, of Spain (as Carlos I) 1516–56, of the Austrian Habsburg dominions 1519–56; abdicated 1556, died 1558.

Charles VI, Holy Roman emperor and ruler of the Austrian Habsburg dominions 1711–40 (b. 1685); recognised as 'Carlos III' of Spain by the anti-Louis coalition 1704–13.

Charles the Bold, duke of Burgundy 1467–77.

Charles II, king of England, Scotland and Ireland 1660–85 (b. 1630), called Charles Stuart when in exile 1642–60.

Charles IV, duke of Lorraine 1634–75 (in exile 1642–59).

Charles V, duke of Lorraine 1675–90 (lived in voluntary exile for most of the period).

Charles X, king of Sweden 1654–60.

Charles XI, king of Sweden 1660–97.

Charles XII, king of Sweden 1697–1718.

Charles-Emmanuel (Carlo-Emanuele) II, duke of Savoy 1638–75 (regency of his mother till 1663).

Chartres, duc de, *see* **Orléans, Philippe II.**

Chevreuse, Charles Honoré d'Albert de Luynes (1646–1712), adviser to Louis XIV.

Christian V, king of Denmark 1670–99.

Christine of France (1606–63), daughter of Henri IV, duchess of Savoy by marriage (1619) to Victor Amadeus I.

Clairambault, Pierre de (1651–1740), French genealogist.

Colbert, Jean-Baptiste (1619–83), member of *conseil royale des finances* 1661, of *conseil d'en haut* 1669–83; important minister of Louis XIV.

Colbert de Croissy, *see* **Croissy.**

Condé, Louis II de Bourbon, prince de (1621–86), during the lifetime of his father (Henri II, 1588–1646) known as duc d'Enghien.

Courtin, Honoré (1626–1703), French diplomat and writer.

Crécy, Louis Verjus, comte de (1629–1709), French diplomat.

Crequi (or Créquay), François de Blanchefort de (1629–87), marshal of France 1668.

Croissy, Charles Colbert, marquis de (*c.* 1626–96), French secretary of state for foreign affairs from 1679.

Crozat, Antoine (1655–1738), French official and financier.

Dangeau, Philippe de Courcillon, marquis de (1628–1720), Louis XIV's *aide de camp* 1672, author of a journal for 1684–1720 published in 1854 in 19 volumes.

De Witt, Jan, Grand Pensionary (*Raadpensionaris*) of the province of Holland in the Dutch Republic 1653–72.

Desmarets (also Desmaretz), Nicholas, marquis de Maillebos (1648–1712), French controller-general of finance, member of *conseil d'en haut* 1709–15.

Dijkvelt, Everard von Weede, heer van (1626–1702), Dutch diplomat and statesman.

DuBos (or Du Bos), Jean-Baptiste (1670–1742), French diplomat and historian.

Erasmus, Desiderius (1466–1536), Netherlands philosopher.

Ernst August, duke of Hanover 1679–98, elector from 1692.

Estrées, César d' (1628–1714), French cleric, cardinal from 1674, also used on diplomatic mission.

Fouquet, Nicolas, marquis de Belle-Ile, comte de Melun et Vaux (1615–80), French superintendent of finances 1653–61.

Francis (François) I, king of France 1515–47 (b. 1494).

Frederick (Friedrich Willhelm) III, elector of Brandenburg 1688–1701, from 1713 king Frederick I (title, king in Prussia).

Frederick William (Friedrich Wilhelm), elector of Brandenburg (the Great Elector) 1640–88.

Frederick William (Friedrich Wilhelm) I, king in Prussia 1713–40.

Frederick (Friedrich) II, king in Prussia 1740–86.

Fürstenberg, Franz-Egon (François-Egon), prince of the Empire (1626–83), bishop of Strasbourg 1663–82.

Fürstenberg, Wilhelm Egon (Guillaume–Egon), prince of the Empire (1629–1704), bishop of Strasbourg 1682, cardinal from 1686.

Galen, Christoph Bernard, *Freiherr* von, bishop of Münster 1650–78.

George I, king of Great Britain 1714–27 (b. 1660), elector (Georg Ludwig) of Hanover 1698–1727.

Godolphin, Sidney, 1st earl of (1645–1712), British statesman.

Gramont, Antoine, III, duc de (1604–78), marshal of France, also used on diplomatic mission.

Gramont, Philibert, comte de (1621–1707), friend of Louis XIV, married to Elizabeth Hamilton.

Grémonville, Jacques Bretel, chevalier de (1625–86), French diplomat.

Grimmelhausen, Hans Jacob Christoph (Christoffel) von (1620–1–1676), German soldier and author.

Gropello, Giambattista, count of Borgone, Savoyard statesman.

Gyldenlöve, Ulrik Frederik, count (1638–1704), Danish statesman.

Hamilton, James Douglas, 4th duke of (1658–1712), premier peer of Scotland.

Harcourt, Henri, marquis de Beuvron, duc de (1654–1718), marshal of France, used also on diplomatic missions.

Harley, Robert, 1st earl of Oxford (1661–1724), English statesman.

Heinsius, Antonie (Anthonie) (1641–1720), Grand Pensionary (*Raadpensionaris*) of the province of Holland in the Dutch Republic.

Henri II, king of France 1547–59 (b. 1519).

Henry VIII, king of England 1509–47.

Humières, Louis de Crevant, duc d' (?–1694), marshal of France.

Huxelles, Nicolas de Laye du Blé (or Bled), marquis d' (1652–1730), marshal of France 1703, used also on diplomatic missions.

Innocent XI, pope 1676–89.

Innocent XII, pope 1691–1700.

James I, king of England and Ireland 1603–25, king of Scotland (as James VI) 1567–1625 (b. 1566).

James II, king of England, Scotland and Ireland 1685–8 (1633–1701).

James II's queen, *see* **Mary of Modena.**

James III, James Francis Edward Stuart (1688–1766), son of James

II and Mary of Modena, known as James III to Jacobites and recognised as such by some countries, e.g. France until 1713, thereafter known as Chevalier de Saint George; in England often called The Pretender (later, to distinguish him from the Young Pretender, the 'Old Pretender').

Jessen, Thomas (1648–1731), Danish statesman.

John of Austria, Don, Philip IV's illegitimate son (1629–79), Spanish soldier and administrator 1677–9.

John George III, elector of Saxony 1680–91.

John George IV, elector of Saxony 1691–4.

John III Sobieski, king of the Polish-Lithuanian Commonwealth 1674–96.

Joseph, archduke, *see* **Joseph I.**

Joseph I, Holy Roman emperor and ruler of the Austrian Habsburg dominions 1705–11 (b. 1678).

Joseph Clement of Bavaria, archbishop-elector of Cologne 1688–1723.

Juel, Jens (1631–1700), Danish statesman, *friherre* 1672.

La Chappelle, Jean de (1655–1723), author of *Lettres d'un Suisse,* French official and propagandist.

La Vallière, Louise de la Baune Le Blanc, duchesse de (1644–1716), mistress of Louis XIV.

Le Grand, Joachim (1653–1733) abbé, French official and historian.

Leopold I, Holy Roman emperor and ruler of the Austrian-Habsburg dominions 1658–1705 (b. 1640).

Leopold Joseph, duke of Lorraine 1690–1729 (restored to duchy 1697).

Le Peletier, Claude (1630–1707), controller-general of finances and chancellor of France 1683–97.

Le Tellier, Charles Maurice (1642–1710), archbishop of Rheims.

Le Tellier, Michel (1603–85), in charge of the French war office, member of *conseil d'en haut* from 1661.

Le Tellier, Père Michel (1643–1719), Jesuit confessor of Louis XIV 1714–15.

Leibniz, Gottfried Wilhelm (1646–1716), German philosopher, mathematician and historian.

Leyen, Karl-Kaspar von der, archbishop-elector of Trier 1652–76.

Lillieroot, Nils (1636–1705), count 1704, Swedish diplomat, *Friherre* 1697.

Lionne, Hugues de (1611–71), member of *conseil d'en haut* from 1663.

Lisola, Franz Paul von, *Freiherr* (1613–75), diplomat and publicist in Austrian service.

Lobkowitz Wenzel, prince (1609–77), Austrian statesman.

Louis XI, king of France 1461–83.

Louis XIII, king of France 1610–43.

Louis, dauphin of France (1662–1711), the grand dauphin, son of Louis XIV.

Louvois, François Le Tellier, marquis de (1641–91), member of *conseil d'en haut* from 1672.

Louvois' son, *see* **Barbezieux.**

Luxembourg, François Henri de Montmorency-Bouteville, duc de (1628–95), marshal of France.

Maintenon, François d'Aubigné, marquise de (1635–1719), second (morganatic) wife of Louis XIV.

Margareta Teresa (1651–73), Spanish infanta, daughter of Philip IV, married in 1666 to Emperor Leopold I.

Maria Teresa (Marie-Thérèse) (1638–83), queen of France after her marriage to Louis XIV in 1660, daughter of Philip IV of Spain.

Marie-Adelaïde of Savoy (1685–1712), daughter of Victor Amadeus II, married in 1697 to duc de Bourgogne, Louis XIV's eldest grandson (dauphin from 1701).

Marlborough, John Churchill, 1st duke of (1650–1722), English soldier and diplomat.

Mary, queen of England, Scotland and Ireland 1689–94 (b. 1667), daughter of James II, wife of William III.

Mary Beatrice of Modena (1658–1718), second wife of James II of England from 1673.

Matthias, Holy Roman emperor and ruler of Austrian Habsburg dominions 1612–19 (b. 1537).

Maximilian (Max) Emmanuel, elector of Bavaria 1679–1726 (b. 1662); governor of the Spanish Netherlands 1691–1706.

Maximilian-Henry of Wittelsbach, archbishop-elector of Cologne 1672–88.

Mazarin, Jules (Guilio Mazarini) (1601–61), Italian-born French statesman, cardinal from 1641.

Mesnager, Nicolas Le Bailiff, comte de Saint-Jean (1658–1714), adviser on economic matters to the French government, used also on diplomatic missions.

Middleton, Charles (1640?–1719), Jacobite with James II in exile.

Molière, Jean-Baptiste Poquelin, known as (1622–73), French actor and playwright.

Montecuccoli, Raimondo, count, duke of Melfi 1679, 1609–80, general, field-marshal from 1658 in Austrian service.

Montespan, Françoise (Athénais) de Rochechouart Montemart, marquise de (1641–1707), mistress of Louis XIV.

Montpensier, Anne-Marie-Louise d'Orléans, duchesse de (1672–93), daughter of Gaston d'Orléans.

Moscherosch, Hans Michael (1601–69), German poet and writer.

Navailles, Philippe de Montault de Bénac, duc de (1619–84), French marshal.

Navailles, duchesse de (b. Mlle de Neuillant), wife of the above, lady of honour to queen of France; lost favour because of her intrigues at court.

Neuburg, *see* **Philip Wilhelm.**

Noailles, Louis-Antoine de (1651–1729), archbishop of Paris from 1695, cardinal from 1700.

Noailles, Anne-Jules, duc de (1650–1729), marshal of France, used also on diplomatic missions.

Norris, Sir John (1660–1749), British admiral.

Obrecht, Ulrich (1646–1701), historian and jurist, professor of law at Strasbourg 1684.

Orange, William, prince of (1650–1702), *stadholder* of the Dutch Republic 1672–1702, king of England, Scotland and Ireland 1689–1702.

Orléans, Philippe (I), duc de (1640–1701), brother of Louis XIV.

Orléans, Philippe (II), duc de 1701–23 (b. 1674), son of above and duc de Chartres until his death, nephew of Louis XIV, regent for Louis XV.

Orléans, Elisabeth-Charlotte, Princess Palatine, Liselotte von der Pfalz (1652–1722), second wife of Philippe d'Orléans from 1671.

Ormonde, James Butler, 2nd duke of (1665–1745), English army officer, Jacobite supporter.

Oxenstierna, Bengt Gabrielsson, count (1623–1702), Swedish statesman.

Philip IV, king of Spain 1621–65 (b. 1605).

Philip V, king of Spain 1700–46 (b. 1681), earlier title duc d'Anjou 1683–1700, grandson of Louis XIV.

Philip Wilhelm of Neuberg, *Pfalzgraf* am Rhein 1685–90 (b. 1615).

Platen, Franz Ernst, *Freiherr,* later *Graf* von (1632–1709), in Hanoverian service from 1659.

Pointis, Jean-Bernard-Louis Desjean, baron de (1645–1707), French naval officer.

Polignac, Melchoir de, abbé, from 1713 cardinal (1661–1742), French diplomat.

Pomponne, Simon Arnauld, marquis de (1618–99), secretary of state for foreign affairs, disgraced 1679, restored to *conseil d'en haut* 1691.

Pontchartrain, Jérôme Phélypeaux, comte de (1674–1747), secretary of state for the navy 1699–1715.

Pontchartrain, Louis Phélypeaux, comte de (1643–1727), French controller general of finances 1689, later chancellor.

Portia (or Porzia), Johann Ferdinand, *Graf,* later prince of (1605–65), tutor, later adviser, to Leopold I (q.v.).

Portland, Hans Willem Bentinck, 1st earl of (1649?–1709) Dutch soldier and statesman in the service of William III.

Prior, Matthew (1664–1721), English poet and diplomat.

Pufendorf, Samuel, *Freiherr* von (1632–94), German jurist, historian and philosopher.

Reventlow, Conrad, count (1644–1708), Danish statesman.

Richelieu, Armand Jean du Plessis, duc de (1585–1642), French statesman, cardinal from 1622.

Rochefort, Henri-Louis d'Aloigny, marquis de (d. 1676), French lieutenant-general, marshal from 1675.

Russell, Edward, earl of Orford (1653–1727), British naval officer.

St John, *see* **Bolingbroke.**

St Pierre (Saint-Pierre), Charles-Irénée, abbé de (1658–1743), French diplomat and writer on international relations.

Schomberg (Schönberg), Frédéric-Armand, comte de (1615–90), Palatinate-born army officer, left French service in 1686.

Schönborn, Johann Philip von (1605–73), archbishop-elector of Mainz 1647.

Schöning, Hans Adam von (1641–96), Brandenburg and Saxon field-marshal.

Schröder (Schroeder) Wilhelm, *Freiherr* von (?–1689), Austrian cameralist.

Seignelay, Jean Baptiste Colbert, marquis de (1651–90), son of the great Colbert, member of *conseil d'en haut* from 1685.

Sévigné, Marie de Rabutin-Chantal, marquise de (1626–96), French letter writer.

Sillery, Fabio Brulart de, bishop of Soisson (1655–1714).

Sobieski, *see* **John III Sobieski.**

Soissons, Eugène Maurice de Savoy-Carignon, comte de (1633–73), brother of Eugène of Savoy.

Sophia, née Sophia von der Pfalz (1630–1714), wife of Ernst August, duke of Hanover, electress from 1692, heir apparent to the English crown from 1701.

Stanhope, James, 1st earl (1673–1721), British officer and statesman.

Suleiman I (the Magnificent), Turkish Sultan, 1520–66.

Sully, Maximilian de Béthune, duc de (1559–1641), French statesman.

Tallard, Camille d'Houston de la Baune (1652–1728), marshal of France, used also on diplomatic missions.

Temple, Sir William (1628–99), English diplomat and writer.

Tessé, Marc-Jean-Baptiste-René de Froullay, comte de (1651–1725), marshal of France 1703, also used on diplomatic missions.

Torcy, Jean-Baptiste Colbert, marquis de (1665–1746), secretary of foreign affairs 1696, member of *conseil d'en haut* 1699–1715.

Tourville, Anne Hilarion de Cotentin, comte de (1642–1701), French admiral.

Townshend, Charles, 2nd viscount (1674–1738), English statesman and diplomat.

Turenne, Henri de la Tour d'Auvergne, vicomte de (1611–75), marshal of France.

Ursins, Anne Marie de la Trémoille-Noirmoutier, princesse des (*c.* 1641–1722) Italian-born *camarera mayor* to Philip V's first wife Maria-Luisa (Marie-Louise of Savoy).

Vauban, Sebastian Le Prestre, marquis de (1633–1707), marshal of France.

Verjus, *see* **Crécy.**

Victor Amadeus (Vittorio Amadeo) I, duke of Savoy 1630–7.

Victor Amadeus (Vittorio Amadeo) II, duke of Savoy 1675–1730 (took over government 1680).

Villars, Claude Louis Hector, duc de (1653–1734), marshal of France 1702.

Volmar, Isaak, *Freiherr* von Rieda (1582–1662), Austrian statesman.

Voysin (also Voisin), Daniel-François (1654–1717), member of *conseil d'en haut* 1709–15.

William III, king of England, Scotland, Ireland 1689–1702; *see also* **Orange, William.**